ten

statement

fortran

plus

fortran iv

PRENTICE-HALL INTERNATIONAL, INC., *London*
PRENTICE-HALL OF AUSTRALIA, PTY. LTD., *Sydney*
PRENTICE-HALL OF CANADA, LTD., *Toronto*
PRENTICE-HALL OF INDIA PRIVATE LTD., *New Delhi*
PRENTICE-HALL OF JAPAN, INC., *Tokyo*

second edition

ten statement fortran plus fortran iv

sensible, modular, and structured programming with WATFOR and WATFIV

michael kennedy/ martin b. solomon

university of kentucky

prentice-hall, inc., *englewood cliffs, n.j.*

Library of Congress Cataloging in Publication Data

KENNEDY, MICHAEL
Ten Statement Fortran Plus Fortran IV

1st ed. published in 1970 under title:
Ten Statement Fortran Plus Fortran IV for the IBM 360
1. FORTRAN (Computer program language) I. Solomon, Martin B., joint author II. Title
QA76.73.F25K45 1975 001.6'424 74-18468
ISBN 0-13-903385-8

Current printing (last digit):
10 9 8 7

Printed in the United States of America

Dedicated to the memory of

Silvio O. Navarro

Director of the Computing Center and Chairman of the Computer Science Department at the University of Kentucky, who not only permitted but encouraged the teaching experiment which led to the development of this text.

TABLE OF CONTENTS

PART II

PART III

PART IV

PART V

PREFACE TO THE SECOND EDITION[1]

Sometimes older things are nice, such as antiques, large trees, and grandmothers. But old computer languages don't qualify, particularly ones like Fortran which have been revised and patched so much that the original article is hardly apparent. If we could just say "Hail and Farewell, Fortran," many of us would be much happier. But the world doesn't seem to work that way. If a person in the mathematical, scientific, or engineering area wants to learn <u>a</u> computer language which will be of maximum value to him/her and a garden-variety employer, it probably ought to be Fortran. Hence this expanded and revised version of TEN STATEMENT FORTRAN PLUS FORTRAN IV.

Having put Fortran down -- and you aren't anybody until you've done that -- we must admit that it is more suited to teaching some new ideas emerging in computer programming -- structured, modular, and sensible programming, we call them -- than we had dared imagine.

The first edition of TEN STATEMENT FORTRAN (TSF for short) was written to aid the student in learning an algorithmic approach to problem solving using a subset of the Fortran language as a vehicle. While retaining this goal, we set our sights more ambitiously in the present edition. We want the student to adopt a more scientific approach, as opposed to a craft-like one, to the matter of problem solving with a computer.

If you are not familiar with the previous edition, you might want to read its Preface, which is included next. The major additions and changes in this edition are:

1. The reorganization of the book into five parts instead of three. The organization is parallel to that of the authors' text, <u>Eight Statement PL/C (PL/ZERO) plus PL/ONE</u>. The parts are:

    Part I - Ten Statement Fortran

----

[1] This material is for the instructor. Textual material for students starts with Part I.

Part II - Essential Fortran IV

Part III - Selected Fortran Topic Modules

Part IV - Laboratory Problems

Part V - Appendices

2. An overhaul of Parts I and II. Most noticeable is the inclusion of a number of shaded boxes, which deal with such matters as good programming practice, testing, program structure, debugging, documentation and other non-language-specific topics. By setting off the material which is not syntax-related while at the same time including it at appropriate points, we feel we continue the character of the first edition: an effective teaching tool which is also quite flexible.

   Comments and INTEGER division have been included as part of the TSF language and thus moved from Part II to Part I. The section on subscripted variables in Part I has been considerably expanded. Also, PRINT now precedes computation.

   In Part II the order of topics remains the same. More introductory material has been provided for FORMAT, alphanumeric data handling, and subprograms.

3. In Part III new material has been added to previous topics and two new Modules have been added. The new Modules are Fortran Data Forms in the IBM 360/370 and Non-Numeric Data: Storing, Sorting, and Searching.

4. Several interesting new laboratory problems have been added. All the problems are now grouped according to General, Math and Science, and Business.

5. Part V, Appendices covering general computer science topics and reference material, has several new additions. Two in particular expose the student to ideas regarding the philosophy of program development: Structured, Modular, and Sensible Programming, and Problem Solving with a Computer --Reprise. These sections further emphasize the book's overall theme that considerably more is involved in making use of a computer than just writing language code.

Other new Appendices are Compilers and Compiling; Debugging: In General and in WATFOR/FIV; and Conversational Computing.

Developing a Course

It is still our view that the way to learn program development is to develop programs -- many times. An instructor who is convinced that students can work only four problems in a semester and understand what programming is about will be unhappy with this text and the results it produces.

Assuming you are still interested, we offer two forms of assistance in tailoring a course to various needs such as school term length, student background, student interest, etc. The first is contained within the text. Appendix N, A Key to Course Organization, serves the same purpose as in the preceding edition.

Secondly, we are happy to announce the availability of a separate Instructor's Guide written by Dr. Edward K. Bowdon, Sr., Professor of Electrical Engineering, University of Arkansas, Fayetteville, Arkansas and formerly of the University of Illinois. A copy of the Guide is available from Prentice-Hall, Inc.

One of the concepts of systematic programming is that both program and design are blended into a process that goes from the most general to the most specific. A strong parallel exists between that concept and the one used by this text. By working within a small language we blend instruction in the design of programs together with instruction in coding. We take a quite general view first and follow it by filling in the specifics.

As a precautionary note regarding the teaching of structured programming, we add that one still does need to know how to write Fortran statements to program in Fortran -- it's not a sufficient ability but it is a necessary one. "Structured" is the adjective and "programming" is the noun. We try to teach programming in such a way that once the student understands what it is about, we can teach him/her to "structure" what he/she does (walking before running, that sort of thing). To illustrate, consider that most of us who teach program development emphasize the use of flowcharts prior to coding. WHY DO WE DO THIS? Because flowcharts reduce the amount of structure that a problem solver has to cope with. They allow him/her another dimension to operate in. They permit another degree of freedom from the system imposed by the computer language and its necessarily linear structure.

We can understand the excitement that some of our fellow authors feel about structured programming, but our view is that the concept is meaningless to someone who doesn't even know what a GOTO or subscripted variable is. We have kept carefully in mind the students to whom this text is addressed; thus the ideas of structured programming come on slowly -- from the beginning, but slowly. As with the majority of the material in the text after Parts I and II, there is a good bit of flexibility about when to bring in the newer concepts; the decision is the instructor's.

TSF Compilers

At least two compilers written specifically for the Ten Statement Fortran Language are now available:

A fast, in-core TSF compiler has been written by Donna Bergmark and Jack Foster. It has been documented in a publication of the Ithaca College Computer Center called Guide to Ten Statement Fortran: A Fast Fortran Compiler. One version of the compiler runs on the RCA SPECTRA 70 and another version is for the IBM 360/370. For further information on availability contact Donna or Dom Bordonaro (a really nice guy who can guide a super tour of New Orleans) at the Ithaca College Computer Center, Ithaca, New York.

Also to be available concurrently with the publication of this edition is a fast, in-core, table-driven TSF compiler for the Control Data Corporation 6000 series machines. This compiler, written in PASCAL, is under development by Dr. J. W. Atwood, Department of Computer Science at Sir George Williams University at the University of Montreal, Quebec, Canada.

Acknowledgements

The list of acknowledgements in the previous Preface still stands. For some reason the production of the second edition seemed to be as arduous a task as the first. As we draw the project to a close we find ourselves deeply grateful to:

Ms. Elizabeth Churchill Nichols, our text editor (human), who used TEXT/360, our text editor (machine), to produce the camera-ready text. It isn't just the Pentagon that has 125% cost overruns and 300% time overruns; authors do, too. Through it all Ms. Nichols smiled -- sometimes cheerfully, sometimes grimly -- but she always smiled.

Dr. Jane Ellen Phillips, University of Kentucky Department of Classics, who read the entire text. She provided a fresh, overall look at the book at just the right time.

The programming consultants at the University of Kentucky Computing Center, who provided some of the ideas incorporated in Appendix M, Problem Solving with a Computer -- Reprise,

Dr. Thaddeus Curtz, Chairman of the Department of Computer Science of the University of Kentucky, who also contributed to that section.

Ms. Lavine Thrailkill, of the University of Kentucky Computing Center who detected many errors,

Dr. J. W. Atwood, who contributed several interesting laboratory problems and provided us with advice at some critical points.

John Drake, University of Kentucky College of Architecture, who worked the problems and exercises and contributed to the Index, Table of Contents, and other portions.

Ben Rice, Ernie Mains, Phil Planck, and the entire operations crew for their good work and support.

And special thanks go to Deans Charles P. Graves and Anthony Eardley of the University of Kentucky College of Architecture who gave their encouragement and support.

A PREFACE FOR THE INSTRUCTOR[1]
(almost unchanged and unexpurgated)

To those who would teach:

> Consternation and frustration will come to him who attempts to instruct from this book without first reading the Prefaces and Appendix N.
>
> Ancient Chinese Proverb

This text has been designed to aid the student in learning an algorithmic approach to problem solving. The text itself does not teach this subject; indeed, there is some question as to whether the subject can really be taught. What this text does is teach a vehicle by which algorithmic problem solving can be learned. The vehicle is the Fortran language.

The design of TEN STATEMENT FORTRAN plus FORTRAN IV is based on several premises. The authors believe:

1. That students should write their first program(s) as early in the course as possible.

2. That too much language detail at the beginning can interfere with the student's developing problem solving ability. Thus he is given only ten statements with which to work. The authors strongly suggest that as soon as he learns those ten statements (PART I of the book) he be given many problems to solve but not be exposed to further language details until he has demonstrated his problem solving ability.

---

[1]This material is for the instructor. Textual material for students starts with Part I.

3. That drill exercises and complete laboratory problems are especially important to developing algorithmic problem solving ability. The text contains numerous questions and exercises, the answers to which are found in Appendix P. The text also contains 55 laboratory problems. The first 11 of these are in PART I of the text and it is suggested that each student be required to work all of these problems. The remaining 44 problems are in Part IV and the instructor may assign these on the basis of the direction and content of his course. Each problem tells what knowledge of Fortran is required by the student to solve the problem.

4. That different instructors have different methods of teaching, place different importance on different topics, and will wish to take up topics in different orders. More than half the book is composed of Appendices and Modules which enable the instructor to use the book in a modular fashion. Fortran is taught under many conditions, at many rates of speed, to people of varied backgrounds, for varying lengths of time. The text, with its modular construction, is suitable for use in short courses, such as are taught to graduate students, as well as full semester courses. Appendix N, A Key to Course Organization, should be examined carefully before this book is used for instructional purposes.

5. That the use of a subset of Fortran, which has a name of its own (TSF), is important to introducing Fortran. By means of this separate language, teachers can honestly make definite and precise statements about the subset which would either be lies or qualified truths about Fortran itself. For example, one cannot say that there are two types of variables in Fortran; but this is a true statement about TSF. Experience has shown the authors that extensions of TSF to full Fortran come quite easily after the basics are learned.

6. That variable declaration and typing is an important idea to be advanced initially. Thus the REAL and INTEGER statements are in the subset. This simplifies the move from scalar to subscripted variables.

7. That FORMAT clutters up understanding of both problem solving and Fortran in the initial stages.

Thus the book features Waterloo Fortran (WATFOR and WATFIV) with its format-free input-output capabilities. If the text is used in an environment where WATFOR is not available, Appendix O describes a procedure by which the advantages of format-free I/O can still be used with some modification. In either case FORMAT is not studied initially.

8. That trying to explain program compilation and execution before the student has done any programming is a mistake. With this text initially, as far as the student is concerned, the program and data go in and answers come out. With WATFOR/FIV this, of course, is the way it really looks. Questions about executable versus non-executable statements are avoided by having only one numbered statement in TSF: CONTINUE. After the student has learned a bit about programming the executable statement concept is strongly stressed -- at a time when it can be backed up by examples.

9. That Fortran is no longer a simple language. (Remember the cartoon in the computer-coloring book of a few years ago with the un-prepossessing stick man: "This is a FORTRANner--color him naive.") Fortran is a language to be reckoned with. It has power and complication to match. Complete Fortran can no longer be blissfully taught in three or four weeks. It also cannot be efficiently taught by plowing straight through the language as it is logically arranged: "A constant is a fixed, unvarying quantity. There are six types of constants in Fortran. They are INTEGER, REAL, DOUBLE PRECISION, LOGICAL..." An alternative approach is used by this text.

10. That Fortran, as it exists today, was not designed--it evolved. As with most products of evolution Fortran contains some unnecessary appendages. The authors give them passing mention so the student will recognize fossils when he finds them.

In various forms this text was used to teach the basic Computer Science course at the University of Kentucky for three years before it was commercially available.

A set of eight video tapes (one-half hour each) has been developed which covers the material in PART I of this text plus DO loops. These video tapes are available. A ninth videotape covering conversational computing is also available. For further information contact University of Kentucky Department of Media Services, Taylor Education Building, Lexington, Kentucky 40506.

THE WATFOR COMPILER

The university community is deeply indebted to the University of Waterloo in Ontario, Canada for its excellent Fortran compiler: Waterloo Fortran or Watfor. Watfor is an extremely fast one-pass compiler which can translate Fortran at extremely high rates of speed. The typical beginning student problem requires about one-half second per run. Standard Fortran compilers require about 100 times as much computer time. Therefore without the Watfor compiler, many universities would not be able to process the large (and growing) numbers of student problems and the entire field of undergraduate education would suffer.

The Watfor compiler produces clear, concise diagnostic messages which enable the beginning student to locate and correct errors more quickly. This book is tailored for use with the Watfor compiler on the IBM System/360 and as such should be more useful to the student in universities using Watfor than standard texts.

ACKNOWLEDGMENTS

The authors received the invaluable assistance and support of many people over the period of time during which this text was developed. We sincerely express our gratitude. The persons are:

Kathy Allen, who keypunched the text in TEXT/360 format, and greatly aided in the development of new sections and revisions of old ones;

William Allen, who taught the basic Computer Science course at the University of Kentucky using the first edition and encouraged development of the present text;

Elizabeth Churchill Crossen, who read the entire manuscript several times and made untold suggestions for improvement;

Lynda McC. Kennedy, who proofed the final manuscript;

Dr. A.C.R. Newbery, whose straightforward presentation of numerical pitfalls in computing inspired Appendix H;

James Painter, who helped create the second edition at the University of Kentucky;

Linda Quim Nagami and Barbara Buchholz, who typed early versions of the text;

Mary Ellen Solomon, who read the manuscript from the point of view of a student and pointed out difficulties which the authors experienced years ago and had forgotten;

Jim Watts, who directed the teaching of the basic Computer Science course at the University of Kentucky for four semesters never knowing if books would be available from which to teach;

Selwyn Zerof, who earlier inspired many ideas which are now incorporated into the text;

And the staff of the University of Kentucky Computing Center.

part i

ten statement fortran

INTRODUCTION

Many centuries ago we of the human race learned that we could put together natural substances and materials to increase our physical strength and power; we became tool-making animals. And many years ago we learned that we could devise tools that were quite complex, at least in concept. These tools we called machines. By combining these machines we made other machines which operated automatically; we merely supervised their performance. Now we have learned to construct devices which increase our mental ability -- which do many of the chores we commonly associate with thinking or, at least, "figuring."

These latest machines are called computers because they were originally developed to do arithmetic computation.

Probably the first real use of computing equipment was, as is true with many inventions, to serve as an aid to our ability to make war. The close of World War II saw modern computer development well on its way. Since that time the amount of information a computer can remember and the speed with which it can process that information increased roughly 10,000-fold. This tremendous increase in power was accompanied by an associated increase in complexity. As with other automatic machines, however, much of this complexity went toward making the machine itself easier to use.

One of the outgrowths of this tendency toward complexity is the development of artificial languages used to communicate with computers. Each type or brand of computer has what is called a machine language -- a (usually) complicated set of instructions which instructs the machine to do simple things such as add two numbers together.

Instructing or programming a computer to do things -- even easy things -- in its machine or "natural" language was pretty tedious. Soon it was realized that artificial languages could be used with computing equipment and that the computer itself could translate the artificial language into its own language and obey those instructions to solve problems.

Many artificial languages exist for computers today. One of these languages is called Fortran, which stands for formula translation.

Fortran itself is a fairly complex language. It is not necessary, however, to learn all of Fortran to be able to instruct a computer to solve problems. In fact, it is possible to learn a few statements of Fortran and still be able to use a computer to solve most numeric problems. Part I of this text describes, in detail, ten statements of the Fortran language; we call this part, or subset, of the Fortran language by the name Ten Statement Fortran or TSF.

With every artificial computer language such as Fortran, one or more programs, called compilers, must be developed to translate the artificial language into the computer's own language.

Two of the programs which do this for TSF and Fortran are called WATFOR and WATFIV. WAT stands for the University of Waterloo, Ontario, Canada, which developed both programs; FOR implies FORtran; WATFIV is the second version of WATFOR. We usually lump both programs together, since they are quite similar, and call the result WATFOR/FIV.

To summarize the jargon, then:

Fortran is the general language which you are about to learn,

TSF is a small subset of Fortran which you can begin using immediately to learn the fundamentals of problem-solving by computer, and

WATFOR/FIV is a computer program which translates TSF or Fortran into the machine language of the IBM System/360 (and IBM System/370) computer.

A major reason one learns about computers and their languages is so that he/she can use them to solve problems.[1] In the beginning we will solve problems which deal with numbers, but later we will deal with problems whose only restrictions are that they must be couched in terms of symbols. To solve any problem on a computer, one must

---

[1] The English language, in this day of women's liberation, is in need of a <u>good</u> set of neuter singular pronouns. In the absence of such we use he/she, her/him or vice versa, and hers/his or vice versa. We aren't happy with the procedure, though it has some precedent in "and/or." Should an occasional he, him or his appear, it is meant in the eunuchoid sense.

approach the task in a systematic way. The next section indicates how this might be done.

There is nothing magical about computers. Any answer that a computer can arrive at could also be arrived at by a human if he/she lived long enough, had enough pencils, etc. (That isn't to say that a person (or persons) can solve any problem a computer can. Sometimes temporal considerations are a part of the problem. The numbers which tell the rockets on a space ship what to do after the first stage lets go can't take six months for a human to compute. If more than a second or so is required, a satellite may be falling down somebody's chimney.) What's important to remember is that, regardless of the speed at which a computation is done, the process is a straightforward, one step at a time, matter.

PROBLEM SOLVING WITH A COMPUTER

A person who wants to use a computer must learn to be precise. One does not communicate with a computer by hand waving and mumbling. A computer can be of service only if it is instructed carefully and according to preset rules. The following steps outline the procedure for using a computer to solve a problem. In each step precision is the watchword.

1. Formulate the problem. It is not enough to have only a fuzzy idea of what sorts of answers are desired for a final solution. A major advantage of using a computer to solve a problem is that one is forced to define the problem exactly.

   In this context you must determine if the problem is computer-solvable. A question such as "Should I ask him/her to marry me?" is not one which yields easily to computer solution. On the other hand, "What is 2 times 3?" is computable but is decidedly more trouble to do on a machine than by other means. In between there are all sorts of problems which are efficiently computable. Knowing which problems are and which are not makes the difference between the creative computer user and the technician.

2. Decide on a method for solving the problem. This is where the human skill comes in. Most problems can be solved in more than one way. It is up to the person instructing the computer, called a <u>programmer</u>, to choose a particular method. Such a method -- a step-by-step procedure for solving a problem -- is called an <u>algorithm</u>.

3. Draw a flowchart depicting the algorithm decided upon. Basically a flowchart is a two-dimensional diagram which describes the algorithm in detail. There are several reasons why a flowchart should be drawn <u>before</u> an attempt is made to have a computer solve a problem, but these reasons will not be apparent initially. With simple problems it is possible to "carry the flowchart around in one's head," but since flowcharting is a good habit to get into, this step will be employed from the beginning. Flowcharting techniques are discussed in Appendix D.

4. Using the flowchart as a guide, write the computer instructions. These instructions are usually written on a special coding form. Writing these instructions is one of the easier parts of the process but it must be done with care. A major part of this book describes instructions which may be used to tell the computer how to proceed in order to follow an algorithm. These instructions govern the computer's three main activities: input of data, manipulation of numbers and symbols according to the algorithm, and output of the answers desired. A set of instructions which governs a computer's activities in this way is called a program.

5. Assemble the information the computer is to use in solving the problem. Such information is called data. A single item of information such as a number is called a datum. The program that was previously written in Step 4 determines the order in which the computer will use the data. The programmer must be certain, then, that he/she has precisely the correct number of data and that they are in exactly the proper order.

6. Prepare the written program and the assembled data so that they are in machine-readable form. Usually, this means preparing a data processing card for each line or statement of the program and cards for the data. Appendix B discusses card preparation by means of a device called a keypunch.

7. Submit the machine-readable form of the program and a set of test data to the computer. When the program is executed by the computer a listing will be generated on paper which will consist of the program statements and the answers or results. Analyze the results to verify the correctness of the program.

8. If no answers are produced, or if the answers are incorrect, an error has been made in one of the steps. The action which must be taken depends, of course, on the nature of the error. The process of finding and correcting errors is called debugging.

   It is vastly superior to do steps 1 through 7 carefully enough so that debugging isn't necessary. It is also much more satisfying to the soul to do something right the first time. But since all programmers make errors, we have included a section on program debugging for later on in the course. It is Appendix J.

9. Prepare the documentation. The documentation describes what the program does, how to use it, what its limitations are, who wrote it, and many other informational items. This step actually should be part of almost all of the preceding steps. It should not wait until last to be begun, though it cannot be completed until the others are finished.

10. Use the program. If you are satisfied that the program is correct, your actual data are accurate, and the documentation is complete, run <u>production</u> with your program.

The following illustration is presented to increase your insight into the process described in steps 3 through 6 above.

First a flowchart is shown. This flowchart depicts an algorithm for reading two numbers into a computer, dividing the first by the second, adding 1.5 to the quotient, and printing the result.

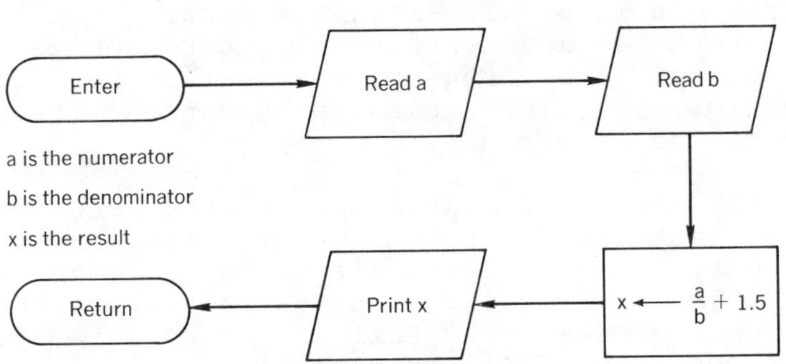

From this flowchart a TSF program is written on a Fortran coding form. The program tells the computer to use A, B, and X as three names to stand for the numerator, the denominator, and the answer; to READ in two numbers; to divide the first (A) by the second (B); to add 1.5 to the quotient and call that sum by the name X; to print out the number associated with the name X. The student is not expected to understand this program completely at the outset. Rather it is presented to emphasize that a computer program can be quite brief and to eliminate some of the mystery that sometimes surrounds programming.

STATEMENT NUMBER		STATEMENT
$JØB		JØHNDØE
		REAL A
		REAL B
		REAL X
		READ, A
		READ, B
		X=A/B+1.5
		PRINT, X
		RETURN
		END
$ENTRY		
55.0		
11.0		

After the program, the data (the two numbers used for A and B in this case are 55.0 and 11.0), and the control statements (those that begin with a $) have been written on a coding form, they are punched onto data processing cards using a keypunch. Each line of the coding form becomes one punched card. The resulting card deck would appear as shown below:

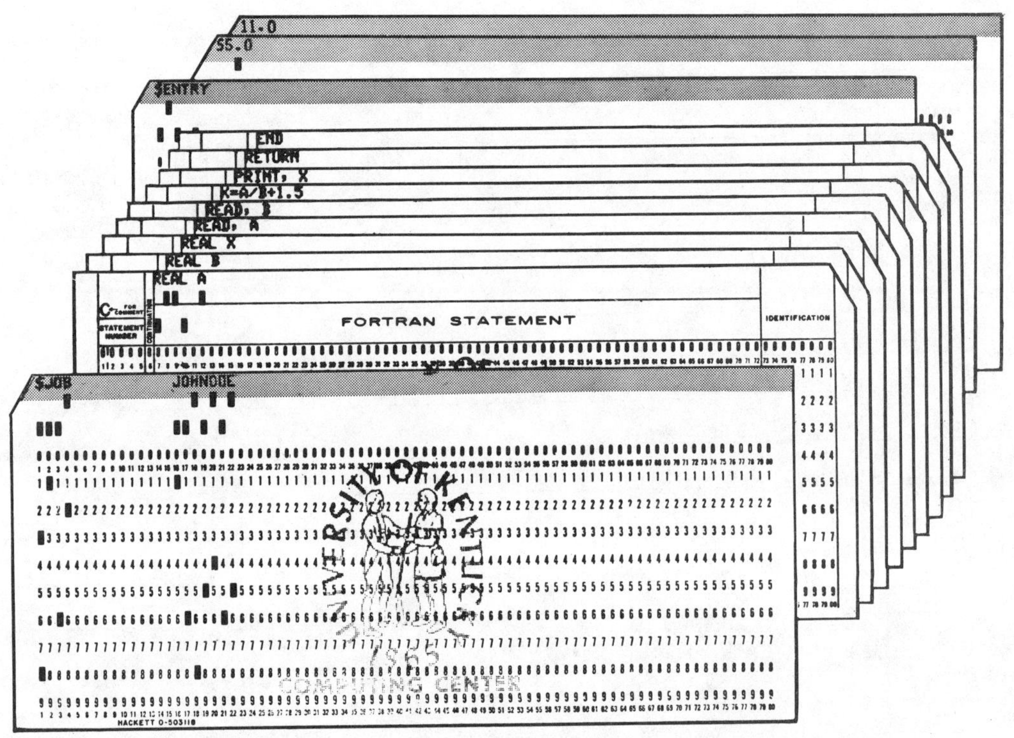

This deck would be submitted to the computer. The computer would produce a listing of all the instructions. This listing, sometimes called hard copy, is shown below:

```
$JOB          JOHNDOE
        REAL A
        REAL B
        REAL X
        READ, A
        READ, B
        X=A/B+1.5
        PRINT, X
        RETURN
        END
```

After the program statements have been listed, the value of X would be printed. Did everybody get 6.5?

LABORATORY PROBLEM 00

To practice the mechanics of submitting jobs to be run on a computer, keypunch and submit this job, calling it Lab Problem 00. Your instructor will provide you with details regarding the particular information you should put on the $JOB card.

Without looking back, try to draw the flowchart for the problem in the space below:

Throughout this book we will use shaded boxes such as this one to give you additional information. Much of this extra information is advice on how to become really good at instructing the computer. We include in the boxes ideas relating to good programming practice, ways to keep things from going wrong, testing programs, and other things we feel are important but which don't relate immediately to learning the grammar and syntax of TSF.

Thus you can read the various sections of the text and just skip the shaded boxes initially if you want to, since you can't use the material in the boxes until you really understand the basic idea. To use a parallel from another field -- learning a new language such as French -- the unshaded parts of the text give you the specifics and the shaded material helps you to learn to use the language idiomatically.

ELEMENTS OF TEN STATEMENT FORTRAN

Characters

The most basic element of the TSF language is the character. There are 46 permissible characters. They are:

Capital Letters	A B C D E F G H I J K L M N O P Q R S T U V W X Y Z
Arabic Digits	0 1 2 3 4 5 6 7 8 9
Special Symbols	* / + - , . = ( ) blank

Note that only the capital letters can be used -- these are the only ones that can be keypunched on a standard keypunch machine.

Statements

The major elements of the TSF language, called statements, are used to make up a program which tells the computer how to solve a certain problem. Each of these statements is made up of characters (capital letters, digits, symbols, and blank spaces) arranged to "make sense" to the computer. Each statement in TSF consists of at least 3 but not more than 66 characters. The first non-blank character of each statement (with one exception) is to be punched in column 7 of an 80-column card. The last character of the statement must not fall in a column numbered higher than 72.

When a new statement is being introduced in this text, its general form will be given. This general form will consist of three different types of elements: capital letters, special symbols, and small letters. There are some characters common to all statements of any particular type. These will always be shown as capital letters and special symbols in the general form of the statement. For example, the general form of one of the more complicated statements is:

```
IF (expression reop expression) GO TO stno
```

Every statement of this type, called the IF statement, must contain

IF (   ) GO TO

Where small letters exist in the general form the programmer will substitute groups of the 46 characters to make the statement complete. Here the programmer would substitute characters for

expression reop expression   stno

These words mean nothing to the student now and are only introduced to illustrate the general form. An example of a complete IF statement might be

STATEMENT NUMBER		STATEMENT
1 2 3 4 5	6	7 8 9 10 11 12 13 14 15 16 17 18 19 20 21 22 23 24 25 26 27 28 29 30 31 32 33 34 35 36 37 38 39 40 41 42 43
		IF (AGE.LT.YEARS-TØIL) GØ TØ 555

where AGE and YEARS-TOIL have been substituted for the two "expressions," .LT. has been substituted for "reop," and 555 has been substituted for "stno," thus producing a complete statement that might appear in a TSF program.

In the above statement blank characters are used in several places to improve readability of the statement. The presence or absence of blanks in no way affects the computer's interpretation of the TSF statement. That is, the example statement above might have been written as

```
IF(AGE.LT.YEARS-TOIL)GOTO555
```

or as

```
I F ( A GE.LT.YEA RS-TO IL)G OT O5 55
```

and still would have had the same meaning.

Comments

Statements are comprised of characters which are arranged in such a way as to "make sense" to the computer -- to tell the computer how to solve a problem. Comments are also comprised of characters but are intended, instead, to "make sense" to the humans who look at the program listing.

Comments do not instruct the computer to do anything. They are simply a device by which information for human understanding can be placed before, within, and after the instructions to the machine. The comments, along with the actual computer statements, are printed out on the program listing.

To place a comment in a program the programmer places a "C" in card column 1. As an example we look again at Lab Problem 00 -- this time embellished with comments.

```
STATEMENT NUMBER | STATEMENT
C PROGRAM: SIMPLE DEMONSTRATION
C PROGRAMMER: KATHRYN HEATHER
C DATE: NOVEMBER 23, 1978
C
C VARIABLE DECLARATION
      REAL A
C A IS THE NUMERATOR
      REAL B
C B IS THE DENOMINATOR
      REAL X
C X IS TO BE CALCULATED AS THE QUOTIENT
C A OVER B PLUS 1.5
C
C VARIABLE INPUT
C
      READ, A
      READ, B
C
C     COMPUTE THE ANSWER
C
      X=A/B+1.5
C ANSWER OUTPUT
C
      PRINT, X
      RETURN
      END
```

Obviously this use of comments is a bit overdone, but a point to consider is that rarely has a program been made less understandable because too many comments were used.

To repeat: if the programmer places a "C" in card column one of a TSF statement card, the contents of the other 79 columns are not used as instructions to the computer. The entire contents of the card will, however, be printed out at the appropriate place on the program listing.

> The computer, of course, is not concerned with the Comments in a program. The machine simply prints them out dutifully to adorn the program listing. You could make an analogy between Comments and the printing that a keypunch does at the top of a card. After all, computers don't need that printing either -- they "read" the holes in the card.
>
> Try punching a program sometime with the keypunch print switch turned off. You'll get an immediate dose of what it is like to try to figure out an unfamiliar or stale program which doesn't have any Comments.

Numbers

Because of the internal structure of most computers, benefits accrue from using two different types of numbers: those which are restricted to whole numbers or integer values and those which might have a fractional part. These two types of numbers may be represented in the computer using TSF. They are called INTEGER numbers and REAL numbers.

INTEGER numbers are numbers which may take on only whole number values which may be less than, equal to, or greater than zero. Whenever an INTEGER number is written down (either by the programmer or by the computer) it consists solely of digits, possibly preceded by an algebraic sign. An INTEGER number may consist of as many as nine digits with a preceding + or - sign. If no sign is present the number is assumed to be positive. Some examples of INTEGER numbers are:

28	3	-999999999
-21	0	999999999
3333	-222	+999999999

The last two numbers in the rightmost column are the same.

REAL numbers are numbers which may contain a fractional part and/or a whole number part. Whenever a REAL number is written it consists of as many as seven digits, and exactly one decimal point. It, too, may have a preceding algebraic sign. Some examples of REAL numbers are:

258.333	-.00005	10.	-999999.
18.5	8888.	.1	999999.
-22.22	0.	10000.01	+999999.

Notice that a REAL number and an INTEGER number might represent the same value. For example:

15 and 15.

Both represent the quantity fifteen. In TSF, however, they are representatives of the two types, INTEGER and REAL, and are not the same to the computer.

Constants and Variables

Each of these two types of numbers, REAL and INTEGER, can be represented in a program in two ways. The number can be represented as a constant in which case the number itself is simply written down, such as 38.2, 86, or -55. Or a name can be written which will stand for the number. This name is called either an INTEGER scalar variable or a REAL scalar variable depending on whether it stands for an INTEGER or a REAL number. A scalar variable in TSF is somewhat similar to a variable in algebra, in that it is a name which stands for a number.

Scalar variable names in TSF consist of from one to six capital letters. Some examples of scalar variable names in TSF are:

LMCK AMK DOGS QQ

H KRK CLEO ZZZZZZ

SUM MEAN SQUARE AVERAG

EVAN JANE GRASS VW

Since there are two types of numbers, the computer must be told which type a particular scalar variable is to stand for. If, for instance, the variable AVG is to stand for a REAL number, there must be a statement at the beginning of the program which says

STATEMENT NUMBER		STATEMENT
		REAL AVG

If the names I, JF, and KP are to stand for INTEGER numbers, statements such as the the following must be included among the first statements of the program:

STATEMENT NUMBER		STATEMENT
		INTEGER I
		INTEGER JF
		INTEGER KP

By means of statements of this form, called Type Declaration Statements, the type of each scalar variable used in the program is declared. Thus, the name of each variable which appears in the program must appear in one and only one Type Declaration Statement. The beginning statements in each TSF program must be statements of this variety, whose general form is:

INTEGER variable

REAL variable

The order in which the variables are declared is unimportant.

> The choice of a variable name is completely that of the programmer. However, it is advisable to use names which are meaningful, such as AVG for average, NETPAY for net pay, and SUM for sum.

No flowchart symbol or box is associated with the Type Declaration Statement. However, it is good practice to list each variable name used in the flowchart together with an indication of its meaning. Of course, in complicated programs one must be careful to provide adequate information about the meaning of all variables, how they are used, the method employed by the algorithm, etc. Such information we have previously called _documentation_ and may take many forms. The development of good documentation is probably the part of the job that olden time programmers did the most poorly. However, most of those programmers now supervise program writing and yell at (or don't employ) newer programmers who don't provide adequate documentation. The moral of this story is . . . obvious?

GETTING IT TOGETHER

Now you have been exposed to the basic elements of TSF. You know that characters go together to make up variables and constants; that these elements, together with more characters, are used to make up statements; and, finally, that the statements go together to make up a TSF program. The art of programming involves arranging these elements so that the finished program instructs a computer to do your bidding. You must have a very clear idea of what you want to do -- so clear that you could explain it, step by step, to a very literal-minded person -- before you can make use of a computer. And even with that understanding of your problem, you must know a language that the computer can take instructions in. We would be less than honest if we didn't admit that, even with these prerequisites, there is sometimes a lot of head scratching, fist banging and muttering before the final product emerges.

Basically, a computer solves a problem by performing three main functions:

1. It calls for and accepts data (in TSF these data are always in the form of numbers),

2. It manipulates data according to preset rules (such as addition, multiplication, etc.),

3. It writes out information produced from the data.

When dealing with numbers, we refer to these three processes as input, computation, and output. Numbering them 1, 2, and 3 does not imply, for example, that all the input must be done before all the computation, but simply that, in general, input precedes computation, which precedes output.

In the event an incorrect instruction or incorrect data are given, the computer itself _may_ detect the error. If so, an _error message code_ will be issued. A list of WATFOR and WATFIV error codes and their meanings appear in Appendix Q.

We now turn our attention to the specific statements in TSF that make it possible to do virtually any numerical problem amenable to computer solution.

Once the variables in the program have been declared as either INTEGER or REAL, a number can be assigned to each variable. One of the ways in which this can be done is by the use of the READ statement. This statement causes one data card to be "read" by a device attached to the computer, which is called a card reader. The number punched on that card is then transmitted to the computer where it is associated with a variable name. The number on the data card must not have any blanks within it but may be punched anywhere on the card.

The general form of the READ statement is

```
READ, variable
```

where variable is a scalar variable name which may be either INTEGER or REAL.

> Notice that the word REAL has no comma after it; the word READ does. If that seems inconsistent, that's because it is.

Suppose a program begins in this fashion:

```
      REAL HEIGHT
      REAL WIDTH
      REAL DEPTH
      READ, HEIGHT
      READ, WIDTH
      READ, DEPTH
```

[1] If a WATFOR/FIV compiler is not available see Appendix O.

This would be a way of instructing the computer to do the following:

1. Declare HEIGHT, WIDTH, and DEPTH as names of REAL numbers.

2. Read three data cards from the card reader and define the variable HEIGHT to have the value punched on the first data card, the variable WIDTH to have the value punched on the second data card, and the variable DEPTH to have the value punched on the third data card.

Suppose that there were three data cards waiting, one behind the other, to be read by the card reader. On the first the REAL number 38.3 is punched, on the second 100. is punched, and on the third 21.5 is punched. The statement

```
READ, HEIGHT
```

will cause the first of these three data cards to be processed by the card reader and the number 38.3 to be transmitted to the computer where it will be associated with the REAL scalar variable HEIGHT. We say, now, that HEIGHT is defined to be 38.3, that HEIGHT is set equal to 38.3, that HEIGHT becomes 38.3, or even that HEIGHT <u>is</u> 38.3.

Having executed the statement

```
READ, HEIGHT
```

the computer begins execution of the next statement

```
READ, WIDTH
```

which causes the variable WIDTH to be given the value 100. Following that, the statement

```
READ, DEPTH
```

is executed, making DEPTH equal to 21.5.

Statements are executed one after another starting at the top of the page and going down. The programmer must be careful to synchronize the order of the data he puts after the program with the order in which the READ statements in the program will be executed.

If this program were used later with a different set of data cards containing different data, new numbers could be assigned to the variables HEIGHT, WIDTH, and DEPTH, without changing the program. This is the first indication of one of the principal advantages of using computers: by using variable names to stand for numbers we can write a program to solve a problem of a particular type and then reuse the program many times, changing only the data.

One other point should be made: a variable can have many different values at different times during one execution of the program. Thus if a fourth data card were present punched with 55.55 and the computer again encountered the instruction

```
READ, HEIGHT
```

the value of HEIGHT would be changed to 55.55 and the original value of 38.3 would be erased.

Finally it should be stressed that it would be an error to attempt to read a card which contained a REAL number (one punched with a decimal point) by use of a statement such as

```
READ, IN
```

where IN had been declared to be an INTEGER variable in a Type Declaration Statement. This is because when reading an INTEGER number the computer expects only the arabic digits with, perhaps, an algebraic sign preceding the number. Therefore, the discovery by the computer of a decimal point would be considered an error. Thus INTEGER data may not contain decimal points. REAL data usually contain decimal points; they are not, however, necessary.

The flowchart symbol associated with input (and also output) operations is a parallelogram:

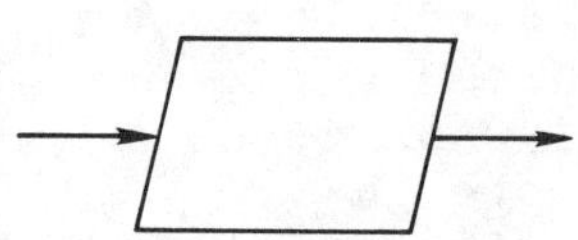

This symbol implies that information is being moved into (or out of) the machine. Different words may be used within the box to indicate an input or output operation (sometimes referred to as an I/O operation). For input we have chosen to use the word "Read" in our flowchart language. Thus a flowchart box which related to an instruction to read a variable "a" would appear as:

Exercise

Note: Appendix P contains the answers to most exercises and questions in this book.

Assume four numbers were punched into data cards which were ready to be read by the computer, and the computer encountered the TSF instructions

```
READ, CAT
READ, CAT
READ, CAT
READ, DOG
```

If the data cards contained

```
5.4
6.0
-777.2
.00098
```

what number would be associated with CAT after the execution of all the READ statements? With DOG?

Once variables have been defined using a READ statement, they may be used in various ways in the program. One action the programmer can instruct the computer to take is to print out on its printing device the values of any previously defined variables. He/she does this by writing a statement whose standard form is

PRINT, variable

where "variable" is a REAL or INTEGER variable name which stands for the number the programmer wants printed out.

The PRINT statement operates very much like the READ statement except that it is used to transfer information out of the machine rather than into it. And while the READ statement gives a certain numerical value to a variable, the PRINT statement lets the outside world know what that value is. The value of the variable is not disturbed in computer memory by this writing-out process. Thus, the following set of statements:

STATEMENT NUMBER (1–5)	6	STATEMENT (7–43)
		INTEGER A
		INTEGER B
		INTEGER C
		READ, A
		READ, B
		READ, C
		PRINT, A
		PRINT, B
		PRINT, C

would write out the values

```
144
 -9
 12
```

if data cards with the values 144, -9, and 12 were present as the first three data cards. After the PRINT statements were executed, the values of A, B, and C would remain intact.

In TSF, when the computer writes a REAL number it does not appear in the form shown above. Instead, each number is represented as the product of two other numbers. One of these numbers lies between .1 and 1.0 (or -.1 and -1.0) and is called a mantissa. The other is the value ten (10) raised to some integer power called an exponent. Writing these two numbers down next to each other constitutes what is known as the exponential form or <u>E form</u> of the intended number.

For example, the computer would write out the number 1234.567 as 0.1234567E 04 on its output device. The E 04 means that the number which has been written out is to be interpreted as if the decimal were moved four places to the right.

If the computer wrote out the number 0.552E-02 this would be its representation of 0.00552 because the minus sign before the 02 indicates that the decimal point should be moved to the left.

Formally,

0.1234567E 04 means .1234567 times 10^4 and
0.552E-02 means .552 times 10^{-2}.

Suppose A, B, and C above had each been declared as REAL instead of INTEGER. Then the values would have been written out as the <u>E form</u> numbers:

```
 0.1440000E 03
-0.9000000E 01
 0.1200000E 02
```

Again, a parallelogram is used in flowchart language to indicate an Input/Output (I/O) operation. For the time being, all output will be on the computer's printing device, so to write out "x", we will use

Exercises

1. What numbers are equivalent to the following?

   a. 0.33E-03
   b. -0.128E00
   c. 0.8338E06

2. Put the following numbers into E form.

   a. 13.381
   b. -7.888
   c. .00313
   d. 9.1×10^{-4}

3. Write the TSF statements necessary to PRINT AXE, RAKE, and HOE.

4. If P, Q, and R are REAL, with values -5, 125.6, and 32000 respectively, what numbers are actually printed if the programmer writes:

   a. PRINT, P
   b. PRINT, Q
   c. PRINT, R

TERMINATING EXECUTION: RETURN

When you have written the instructions to the computer to perform your input, computations, and output, you must write a statement to terminate execution of the program. This statement corresponds to the "return" or "exit" terminal block in the flowchart. The statement that you should write is called the RETURN statement and has the following form:

STATEMENT NUMBER		STATEMENT
1 2 3 4 5	6	7 8 9 10 11 12 13 14 15 16 17 18 19 20 21 22 23 24 25 26 27 28 29 30 31 32 33 34 35 36 37 38 39 40 41 42 43
		RETURN

The RETURN statement indicates to the computer that it has finished with the particular program it was working on and that it should proceed to other work.

Specifically, the RETURN statement <u>returns control</u> of the computer to a master program. Such a master program is called an <u>operating system</u>, and it controls the machine in such a way as to keep account of computer time used, programs executed, etc.

The RETURN statement, then, signifies the end of execution of the program.

Each program written should have at least one and, preferably, only one RETURN statement; likewise each flowchart drawn or algorithm depicted should have only one point of entrance and one point of exit. These comments don't make much sense now because the only programs the student knows about are those which begin with the uppermost statement and proceed "southward" one step at a time. Thus it is obvious that exactly one RETURN is the only possible number. But even when we add the capability of having more than one RETURN statement, remember that exactly one is appropriate in what some call a <u>proper</u> program.

The symbol used to begin or terminate flowcharts is called a terminal block. When used for the RETURN function, it is used with one or more in arrows and no out arrows as shown below.

When used to begin a flowchart, the terminal block has only one out arrow and the word "Enter" is written inside. This symbol used this manner does not correspond to any TSF statement.

A REQUIRED STATEMENT: END

The END statement marks the end of the program. Every program must have one and only one END statement and it must be the last statement in the program. It has the following form:

STATEMENT NUMBER		STATEMENT
1 2 3 4 5	6	7 8 9 10 11 12 13 14 15 16 17 18 19 20 21 22 23 24 25 26 27 28 29 30 31 32 33 34 35 36 37 38 39 40 41 42 43
		END

The END statement does not correspond to any flowchart symbol or box. It has nothing to do with the algorithm being depicted. It is simply a part of the TSF language -- a convention which must be observed if things are to operate properly.

For the present, since the computer considers the statements one at a time, from top to bottom, it is clear that the last two statements in the program must be RETURN and END, in that order.

THE DECK: PROGRAM, DATA, CONTROL CARDS

Solving a problem with TSF requires a TSF program, some control cards, and (usually) some data. Lab Problem 00, which contained all three of these elements, is again shown below with the TSF program unshaded, the data lightly shaded, and the control cards darkly shaded.

```
STATEMENT
NUMBER                      STATEMENT
1 2 3 4 5 6 7 8 9 10 ...
$JØB                 JØHNDØE
            REAL A
            REAL B
            REAL X
            READ, A
            READ, B
            X=A/B+1.5
            PRINT, X
            RETURN
            END
$ENTRY
55.0
11.0
```

Program

In TSF a program is defined to be a sequence of statements of the types discussed previously -- REAL, INTEGER, READ, PRINT, RETURN, END -- and some others which will be presented later. Each statement is punched on a separate card and the set of these cards is called a <u>program deck</u>. A TSF program deck begins with a Type Declaration Statement (either REAL or INTEGER) and ends with the END statement. The program deck may contain only TSF statements and comments.

Data

In TSF the word "data" refers to the numbers which will be brought into the computer by the use of the READ statement. Once the data are written on paper in proper order they are punched into cards. Each card contains one number which may be punched anywhere on the card. No blanks may appear within the number itself. The set of these data cards is called a data deck. Data can be either INTEGER or REAL and the rules for constructing data are the same as those for constants.

The program dictates the order in which the data must be arranged. The first READ statement which the computer executes brings into the computer the first datum. This datum defines the value of the variable following the word READ in the READ statement. The second READ statement executed by the computer brings into the computer the second datum and in so doing defines the value of the variable in that READ statement. This process continues until the last READ statement executed in the program "reads" the last datum. Thus there must be an exact one-for-one relationship between the number of variables defined in the program by READ statements and the number of data.

When a READ statement contains a variable which has been declared as INTEGER, the datum read by that READ statement must be INTEGER: the datum must appear without a decimal point. When a READ statement contains a variable which has been declared as REAL the datum read into the computer by that statement should be punched with a decimal point.

To use a computer to solve a problem, you first give it all the instructions telling it how to proceed and then provide it with the numbers it is to use. This means, then, that the entire program deck precedes the entire data deck.

Control Cards

In addition to the program deck and the data deck some other cards are necessary to run a TSF computer program. These cards are called control cards and may be identified by the $ in card column 1. Control cards may vary from one computing installation to another. It will be necessary to determine the precise form used at any specific computing center. A typical example is pictured below; two control cards, $JOB and $ENTRY, are used.

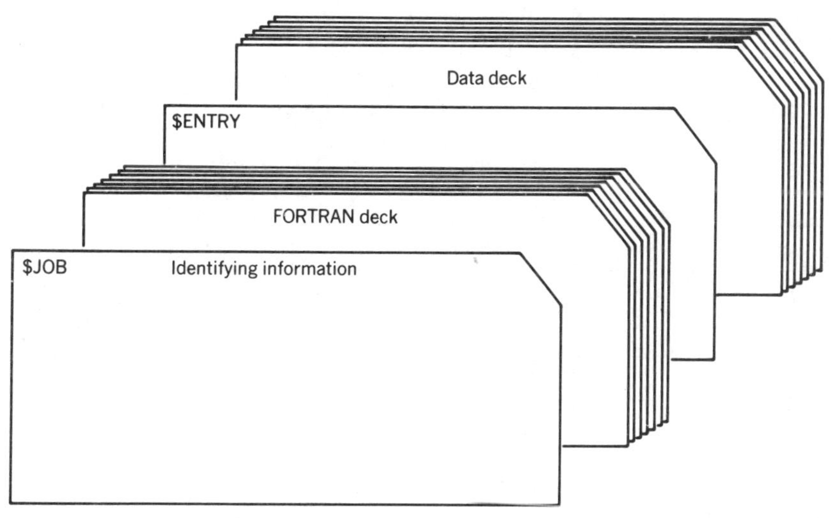

The $JOB card is the first card of a computer run. It usually tells the operating system of the computer the name of the programmer, what course he/she is enrolled in, her/his student number, the problem number, and other information. Appendix C has more complete information on the form of the $JOB card.

The $ENTRY card is placed immediately after the END statement card of the TSF deck and immediately before the first data card. It indicates the end of the program and the beginning of the data. The $ENTRY card is required even if no data cards exist.

Different computing installations may use different sets of control cards. Your instructor will give you the particular form to be used at your installation.

Use the blanks below to write the format of control cards at your particular installation. Extra lines have been left before the program, before the data, and at the end of the deck, though certainly not all of these will be used.

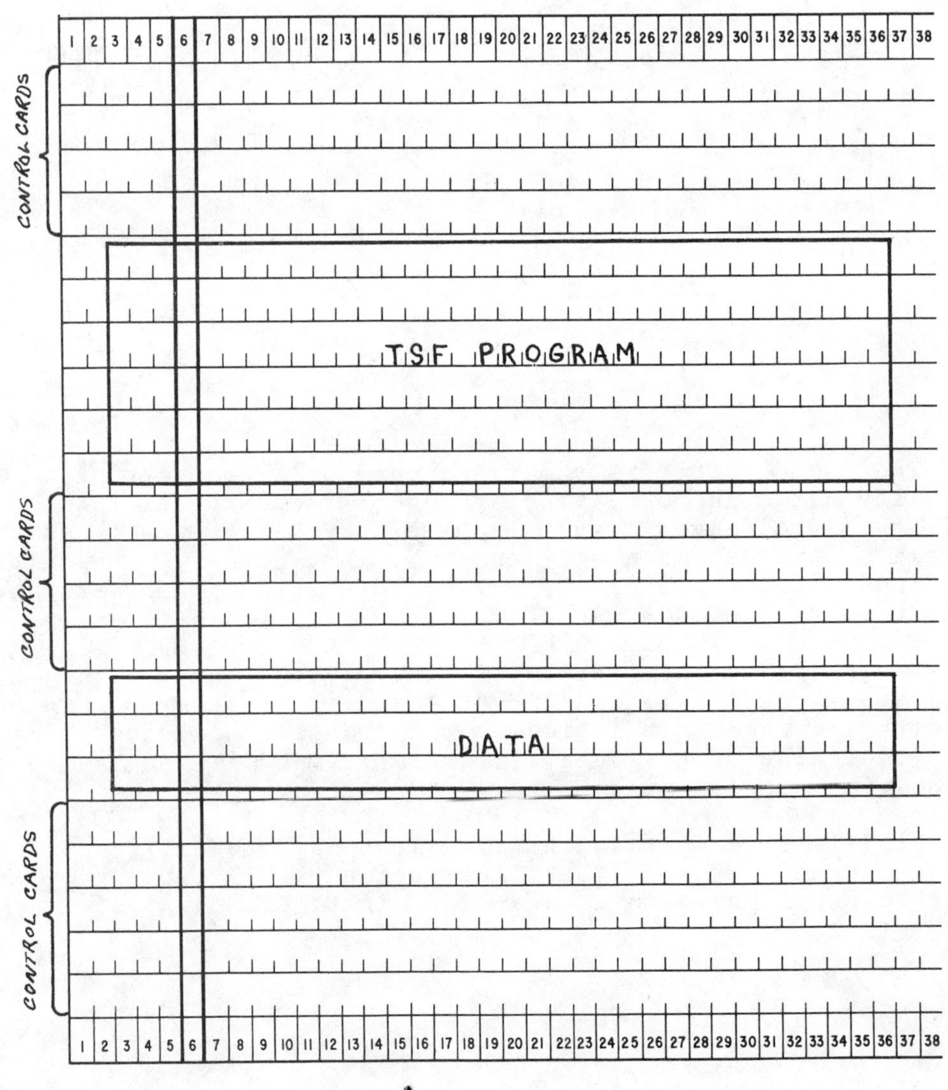

LABORATORY PROBLEM 01

Write and run a TSF program to read in four numbers and write them out in reverse order.

Appendix D discusses flowcharting in detail. Examine the following flowchart and verify that, if obeyed, it would solve the problem.

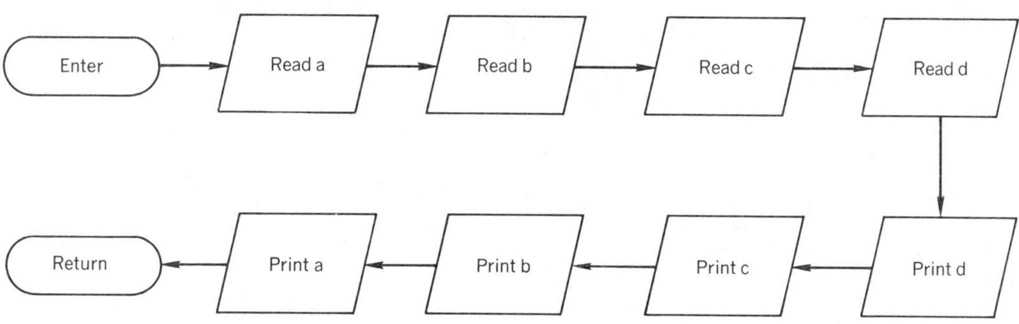

COMPUTATION

In TSF there is one other way, besides input, to define a variable (i.e., to associate a value with a variable). It is the arithmetic assignment statement. Some examples are:

```
X=2.*3.+4.
SUM=10.*GGG-HHH/III
TEST=UGH
```

In each case, the numbers represented as the variable names or constants on the right of the equal symbol are combined according to mathematical rules to produce a number. This number is then associated with the variable name to the left of the equal sign, thus defining its value.

The sequence of symbols to the right of the = symbol is called an arithmetic expression. Before the arithmetic assignment statement can be fully understood the general nature of an arithmetic expression must be examined in detail.

Arithmetic Expressions

An arithmetic expression in TSF combines numbers (either constants or variables) in such a way as to produce a single numerical value. An expression consists of a sequence of constants and/or variables joined by operators which indicate exponentiation, multiplication, division, addition, or subtraction.

As an example consider the expression

```
WIDTH+DEPTH-13.
```

If WIDTH and DEPTH have the values 100. and 21. respectively, the expression has the value 108. The elements present in the expression are: a constant (13.), variables (WIDTH, DEPTH), and operators (+, -). Expressions may also include parentheses to indicate the order in which the calculations are to be done. The five operators which are used in TSF are:

** means exponentiate
a raised to the b power is written A**B

*   means multiply
     ab or a•b or a x b is written A*B

/   means divide
     a/b is written A/B

+   means add
     a + b is written A + B

-   means subtract
     a - b is written A - B

> Multiplication is a faster operation than division for most computers. (And, of course, addition and subtraction are much faster than either.) If you have a chance to substitute a multiplication for a division it is usually wise to do so. For example, a multiplication by 5 would usually be a better deal than using .2 as a denominator.

Arithmetic expressions in TSF are quite similar to those in algebra. There are some differences, however:

1. The multiplication operator must always be present when multiplication is intended. Thus you cannot say AB when you mean A*B. The computer would interpret AB as simply another variable name.

2. Two consecutive asterisks are used to indicate exponentiation.

3. Since TSF statements are simple strings of characters, one after another, you may not make use of the algebraic technique of placing operands (constants and variables) on different levels of the line. Expressions such as A^2 and B^3 are legal in algebra but not in TSF, where they are written A**2 and B**3

The order of computation in TSF expressions is much the same as in algebra; computations are performed in a priority sequence and may be viewed in the following way:

First: Quantities within parentheses are computed. If there are parentheses within parentheses the innermost pair contains the computation done first.

Second: Exponentiation operations are performed.

Third: Multiplication and division operations are done; neither takes precedence over the other.

Fourth: Addition and subtraction take place; neither operation takes precedence over the other.

Fifth: When several operations of the same precedence occur, the leftmost is computed first. (An exception to this rule is when two exponentiations take place consecutively, e.g., A**B**C. In this case, operations are performed from right to left.)

Some Rules of Expression Writing

1. No two numbers (constants or variables) may occur in an expression without at least one of the operators (** * / + -) somewhere between them.

2. No two operators may occur in an expression without at least one number (constant or variable) between them, or, alternatively, without an intervening parenthesis. If, for example, you wished to multiply the quantity A times minus B, you would write A*(-B) or -B*A. A*-B is an illegal TSF expression.

3. Since expressions represent numbers (just as constants and variables do) they are either INTEGER or REAL. An expression is considered to be in the INTEGER mode if it consists entirely of INTEGER numbers and the symbols ** / * + - ( ). Thus, an expression in the INTEGER mode is equivalent to an INTEGER number itself. The result of dividing one INTEGER quantity by another is an INTEGER quantity which is simply the "whole number" part of the quotient. Any fractional part of the quotient in an INTEGER division is ignored.

4. An expression in the REAL mode consists of at least one REAL constant and/or REAL variable and some or all of the symbols ** * / + - ( ). The expression itself represents a REAL number.

5. If an operator joins a REAL and an INTEGER number, TSF converts the INTEGER to a REAL value and then performs the computation. Thus an expression with both kinds of numbers represents a REAL number.

As an example of this rule consider the expression

3*5+7.0/2.0

Here the INTEGER constant 3 would first be multiplied by the INTEGER constant 5 producing the INTEGER value 15; then the REAL constant 7.0 would be divided by the REAL constant 2.0 yielding 3.5 as the REAL result; finally the INTEGER value 15 would be added to the REAL value 3.5 producing the expression value 18.5 as a REAL quantity.

6. An expression can consist of a single constant or variable.

7. If a number is to be raised to a power which is a whole number, it is usually better to express the exponent as an INTEGER constant or variable rather than a REAL one. That is, A**3 is preferred to A**3.0.

> A**3 is computed as A*A*A, whereas A**3.0 is computed as the antilog of the product of 3.0 and the logarithm of A. The latter computation takes longer and cannot be done if A is negative.

Some Frequent Difficulties with Expressions

Some sample expressions are now presented which illustrate difficulties which beginning programmers frequently encounter. It is extremely important that the student understand these difficulties because errors in writing expressions usually are not detected by the computer as are some other types of errors; most errors involving expressions just result in wrong answers.

> In one sense a programmer can make two kinds of errors in writing computer language programs: errors in syntax and errors in semantics. As an example, let's look at an analog with another language, English, and assume that a child doesn't want to eat the kale on his plate. If he says, "I don't want no kale," he has made a syntactic error -- an error in form. On the other hand, if he

says "I don't want any spinach," he has made a semantic error -- an error in meaning.

Computers frequently catch syntactic errors that programmers make. Usually the machine issues some sort of cryptic (or even rude) message, such as those found in Appendix Q. But computers don't catch semantic errors. Errors in meaning are as easy to make, harder to find, and vastly more devastating if allowed to go undetected.

Problem #1: The programmer fails to use parentheses when he wants something other than the natural hierarchy of operations. For example, suppose a programmer wants to write a TSF expression for a-b divided by c-d. What he should write is (A-B)/(C-D) but he fails to include parentheses and writes A-B/C-D, which is interpreted as "a minus b/c minus d."

For another example, A/B*C is sometimes written to mean

$$\frac{a}{b \bullet c}$$

when it really means

$$\frac{a \bullet c}{b}$$

To write the TSF equivalent of "a divided by the product of b times c" one should write A/(B*C).

When asked to evaluate a root of a quadratic equation, a novice programmer will almost certainly leave out a necessary set of parentheses. One correct Fortran representation of

$$x = \frac{-b+\sqrt{b^2-4ac}}{2a}$$

is, (-B+(B*B-4.*A*C)**.5)/(2.*A) from which no set of parentheses can be omitted without producing an incorrect result.

Problem #2: The programmer writes a TSF expression XY when he/she means X*Y. The computer attempts to view XY as just another variable name.

Problem #3: The programmer places two operators in sequence without an intervening set of parentheses such as A/-B when what is meant is A/(-B).

A Unary Operator

There is no exception to the hierarchy of operators when a minus sign is used in a unary rather than a binary sense. Normally, a minus sign denotes subtraction of one variable from another, for example, A-B. Here the minus sign is used in the normal binary sense as it joins two numbers by specifying an operation involving both of them. But consider the expression

```
-B+A
```

Here the minus sign is used in the unary sense because it is involved with only one variable: B. The expression is treated as zero-B+A. One must be careful when using the unary minus. For example, the two expressions below represent the same number:

```
-2.**2
```

and

```
0.-2.**2
```

They both say "square the quantity 'two' and subtract the result from zero" -- which produces the result _minus_ four.

The only other operator which can be used in the unary sense is the plus sign; it provides no trouble because a unary plus sign is assumed in front of every non-signed number.

Exercises

1. Compute the value of each expression.

   a. 10./5.*3.
   b. 10.*3./5.
   c. 5.+3.*4.-2.**3./4.

d. -8.+9./2.-18.
e. 88.2-44.1-44.1
f. 88.2-22.*4.
g. -3+4*3**3
h. 4**3*5+12
i. 12.5+(25./(6.2/3.1))
j. 3*(5*7**3-2)

Computers are fast, but there is no point in wasting their power. For a simple example, if you need to calculate the value of

$$ax^2+bx+c$$

rewrite it as

$$(ax+b)x+c$$

The first case requires three multiplications and two additions. In the second case you save a multiplication. And, for most machines, multiplications and divisions take about 10 to 200 times as long as additions.

Could you extend the above example to any polynomial of arbitrarily high order? How many multiplications would you save?

2. Assume that A, B, C, D, E, and F have been declared REAL variables and I, J, K, L, M, and N have been declared as INTEGER variables. Verify that the Fortran expressions below are equivalent to their algebraic counterparts.

a. A/B*C $\frac{ac}{b}$

b. A*B/C $\frac{ab}{c}$

c. A+B*C-D**3/F $a+bc-\frac{d^3}{f}$

d. -A+B/C-D $-a+\frac{b}{c}-d$

e. 88.2-A-B $88.2-a-b$

f. 88.2-A*B $88.2-ab$

g. -I+J*K**2 $-i+jk^2$

h. K**7*M+N k^7m+n

i. A+B/(C+(D/E)) $a+\frac{b}{c+\frac{d}{e}}$

j. 3*(5*K**3-2) $3(5K^3-2)$

3. Which of the following TSF expressions are invalid? Why?

   a. ABCDEFG*4.+ACE
   b. A + - B
   c. DOG/CAT/RAT/MOUSE
   d. 3.0 * 5 * 0.1 + 1000
   e. - B + A
   f. WATER x WHEEL
   g. A + (B * C) / (D + E) - (F + G)

4. What is the value of each INTEGER expression below?

   a. 6/3
   b. 7/3
   c. 99/100
   d. -15/2
   e. -8/(-3)
   f. 3*4/2
   g. 3/2*4
   h. 3/2
   i. 1+2/4*5

The somewhat strange behavior of the "/" operator can be useful on occasion. Suppose, for example, a programmer wishes to know if the INTEGER variable QUESTN is an even or odd number. He/she can make use of the fact that the fractional part of the number is lost in INTEGER division. He/she can, for example, say

```
      IF (QUESTN/2*2.EQ.QUESTN) GO TO 15
```

If QUESTN is an even number then statement 15 will be executed next. Otherwise the transfer will not take place. Why? Would

```
      IF (QUESTN*2/2.EQ.QUESTN) GO TO 15
```

do the same job?

Arithmetic Assignment Statements

You will recall that the first method studied for defining the value of a variable was the READ statement. Now that you understand arithmetic expressions, we will explain the second method. It is the TSF statement of the form

variable=expression

where "variable" stands for either a REAL or INTEGER variable and "expression" means an arithmetic expression in either the REAL or INTEGER mode.

For example, let a program begin:

STATEMENT NUMBER (1–5)	6	STATEMENT (7–43)
		REAL A
		REAL B
		REAL C
		A=5.0
		B=7.0
		C=A+B

In the last three statements the characters to the right of the = symbol form a REAL expression while a REAL variable lies to the left of the = symbol. The first two of these statements define A as 5.0 and B as 7.0. The last statement in the program segment defines C to have the value 12.0. But it does not affect the values already assigned to A and B. However, if later in the program the statement

```
A = C**2.
```

were encountered the variable A would be redefined as 144.0 and the original value of A (namely, 5.0) would be erased.

An arithmetic assignment statement always assigns the value just computed on the right side of the = symbol to the variable named on the left, erasing the previous value, if any. An arithmetic assignment statement never assigns new values to variables only on the right side of the = symbol.

The meaning of the symbol = will now be carefully explained. First, the value of the expression to the right of the symbol is computed as discussed in the section on expressions. (It is mandatory that every variable appearing on the right hand side of the equal sign has been previously defined, i.e., given a numerical value by either a READ statement or another arithmetic assignment statement). Second, the variable to the left of the symbol = is defined (or redefined) to have the value of the expression just computed. The symbol = therefore means "is replaced by." It does not mean "equals." Therefore it is possible to write

```
B = B+2.0
```

without incurring more than token sarcasm from mathematicians. The statement

```
B = B+2.0
```

merely instructs the computer to:

1. Add 2.0 to the current value of B (which is 7.0 in our example).

2. Redefine B as the value of the expression (namely, 9.0).

Thus the effect is that of increasing the previous value of B by 2.

What value would AZ have after the two following statements were executed?

```
AZ=2.0
AZ=(AZ+AZ)*AZ
```

When checking a program over prior to submitting it to a computer, a good procedure is to examine every variable in each arithmetic expression to be certain that it has been previously defined.

One other question remains to be answered about arithmetic assignment statements: what is the effect if the expression to the right of the = symbol is of a different type than the variable to its left? Specifically, what is the result in each of the two cases below?

```
iv = rexp

rv = iexp
```

where iv means INTEGER variable, rv means REAL variable, iexp means INTEGER expression, and rexp means REAL expression.

Both combinations are valid. The first case implies a situation where the expression can have a fractional part but the variable cannot. In this case iv takes on the value of the integer part of rexp. For instance,

```
if rexp is 15.875 then iv becomes 15
if rexp is -28.3 then iv becomes -28
if rexp is .00215 then iv becomes 0
```

Notice that in this case (iv=rexp), the value of the expression is truncated, not rounded (i.e., the fractional part is discarded). Thus only the whole number is retained and stored in the INTEGER variable on the left.

In the second case (rv=iexp), rv simply becomes the REAL number whose value is equal to the expression. For example, if iexp is -32 then rv becomes -32.0.

In a long or involved calulation, make it a point to insert output statements at points along the way so that you can check intermediate results. There is very little to be saved by using one very long arithmetic expression over using two or three shorter ones. And there is much to be lost. Compute intermediate results and print them out.

LABORATORY PROBLEM 02

Find the area of the geometric figure shown below.

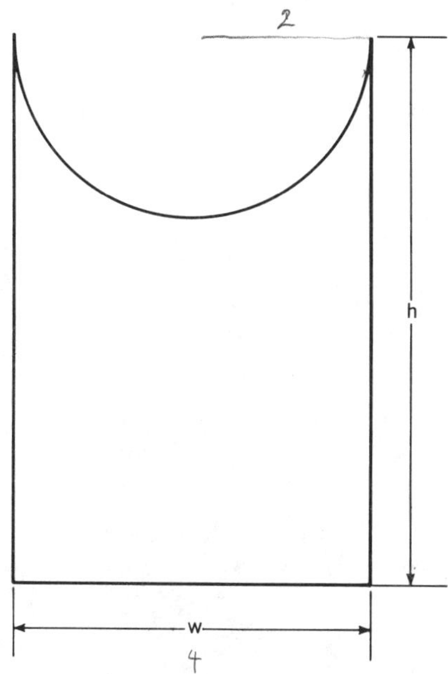

Refer to the steps outlined in the "Problem Solving with a Computer" section.

Examine the following flowchart and verify that it does indeed indicate a solution to the problem. Appendix D discusses flowcharting in detail.

Flowchart for Lab Problem 02

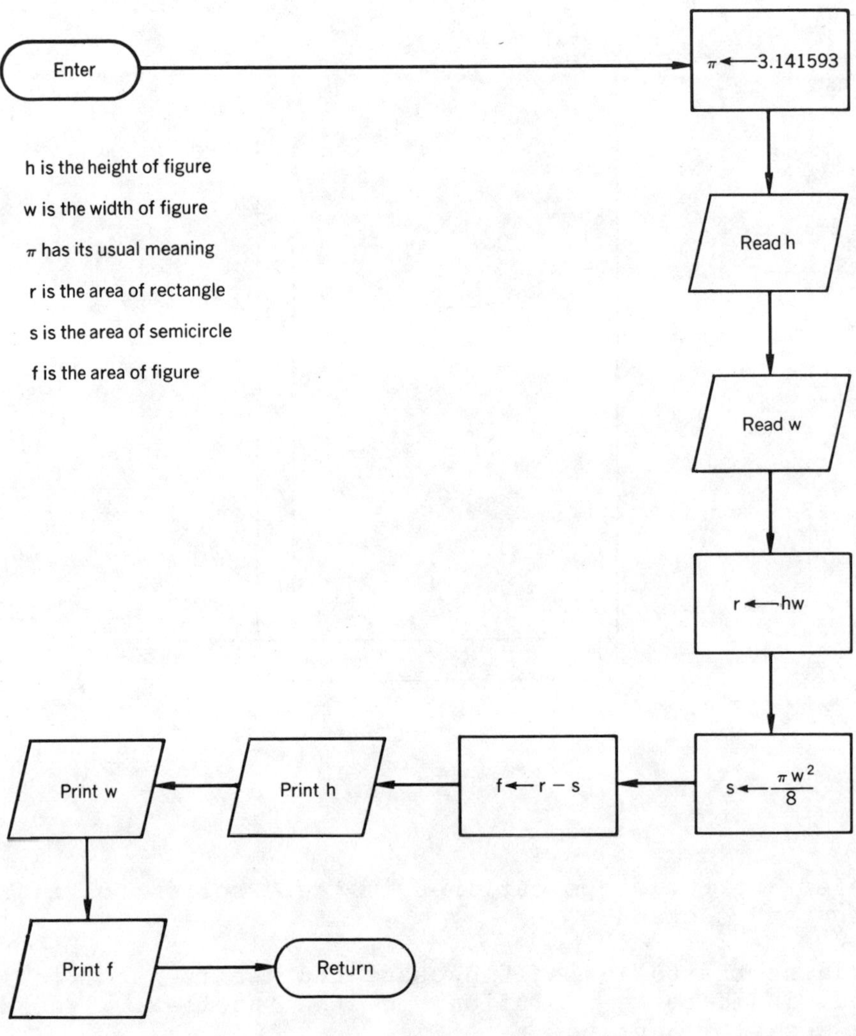

A TSF program which corresponds to the flowchart could be written as follows. Notice that <u>every</u> variable is declared <u>and</u> defined.

```
$JØB          NAME
      REAL HEIGHT
      REAL WIDTH
      REAL PI
      REAL RAREA
      REAL SAREA
      REAL AREA
      PI=3.141593
      READ, HEIGHT
      READ, WIDTH
      RAREA=HEIGHT*WIDTH
      SAREA=PI*WIDTH**2 /8.
      AREA=RAREA-SAREA
      PRINT, HEIGHT
      PRINT, WIDTH
      PRINT, AREA
      RETURN
      END
$ENTRY
```

While the flowchart and the program have some similarities, there are also some differences.

1. The flowchart employs single character names which are described under the enter box. The program, on the other hand, uses multiple character names which tend to be self-explanatory.

2. Algebraic notation is used in the boxes containing computation in the flowchart.

3. The flowchart makes no distinction between REAL and INTEGER numbers.

4. The "is replaced by" or "becomes" symbol is a short arrow pointing to the left whereas in the program the = symbol is used.

5. The flowchart makes no attempt to observe the rules of grammar of TSF.

One reason for these differences is that a flowchart is a description of an algorithm which could be implemented on different computers and by the use of different languages or even on a desk calculator or slide rule. Thus, the flowchart should make sense to any person familiar with flowcharting conventions and should not exclude those who do not know the particular idiosyncrasies of TSF. A person writing a flowchart should resist the temptation to write the statements in any language, including TSF, in the flowchart boxes.

Now you should take the responsibility for the execution of the remaining steps of the process; your instructor will give you data for the problem.

A very good practice is to write a program which prints out the input data as well as the answer(s). Thus, in this example, the height and width of the figure are made to be part of the output. There are two excellent reasons for this. First, it enables a person examining the output to determine which problem has been solved. You can imagine that a piece of paper with only a single answer on it might leave some question as to what numbers went together to produce the solution. Secondly, if the numbers are printed out, and they are in the correct order, you have reasonable assurance that they went in properly. Thus printing out the input data will serve as an aid to confirming program correctness, which is believed by many to be the major difficulty confronting programmers and others who must rely on computers.

DECISION-MAKING ELEMENTS

A re-examination of the laboratory problem concerning the area of the geometric figure (Laboratory Problem 02), reveals a danger which might not be apparent at first. It would be a bit embarrassing if the program produced a negative (or otherwise incorrect) value for the area. From geometric consideration one can see that if the height of the figure is less than one-half the width, the program (and hence the programmer) is in some trouble. That is, the figure might have the degenerate form:

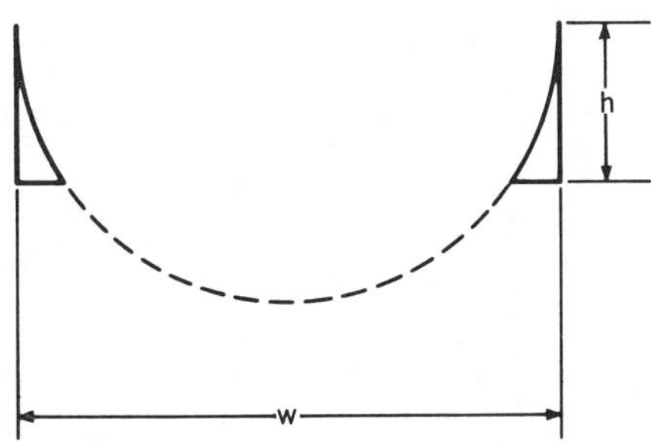

Of course, the programmer could examine the data and decide whether this was the case. But that brings up an interesting question: could the computer examine the data and decide whether the result would be meaningful? The answer is yes. In fact, the real power of a modern computer lies in its ability to make decisions and take appropriate action. The terms of the decision and the computer's subsequent action must be spelled out by the programmer. The flowchart on the next page will illustrate the exact nature of the decision to be made and the action taken subsequent to the decision. The terms used are the same as in the original flowchart of the problem.

Revised Flowchart for Lab Problem 02

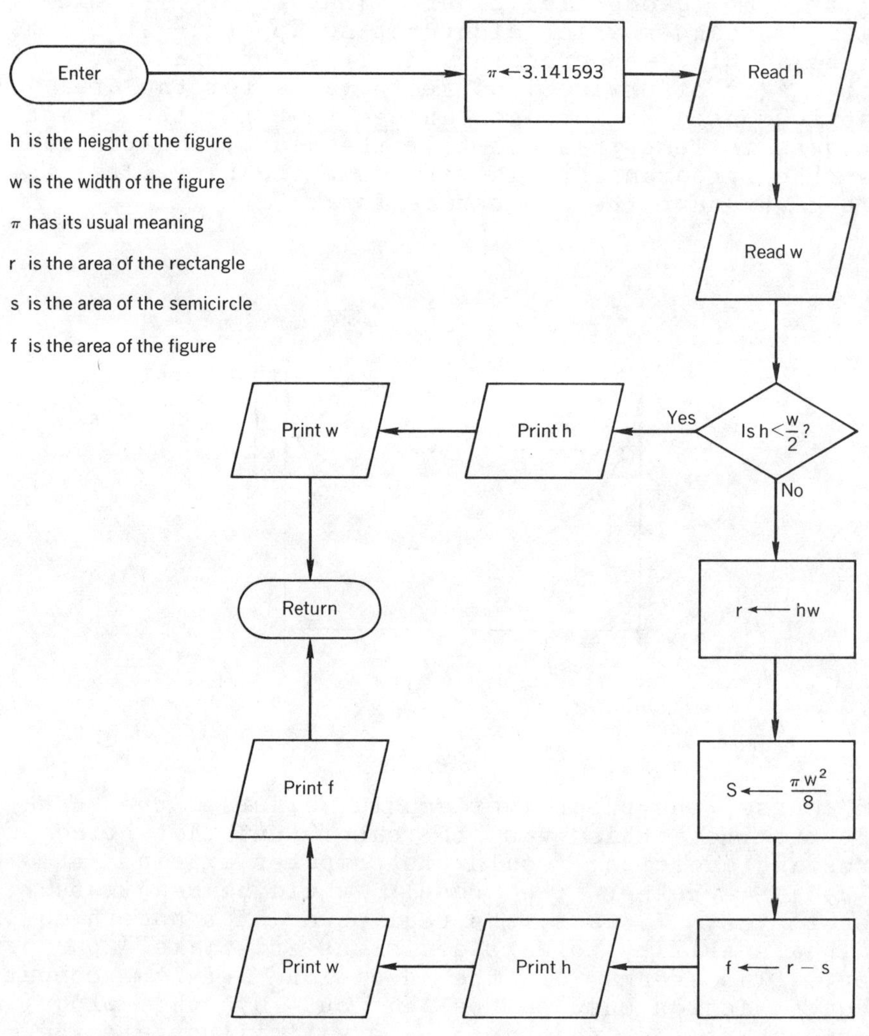

Some statements not yet introduced are necessary before the computer can be told to execute a program which follows the above flowchart. Clearly a statement will be needed which corresponds to the diamond shaped _decision box_. Also required will be a method by which the natural sequence of execution can be interrupted. Normally statements are executed in their _physical_ order, that is, the order in which they appear in the program. However, as the flowchart implies, when the computer makes a decision it must be able to go to one of two different statements, thereby interrupting the normal sequence. The order in which a computer actually executes statements is called the _logical_ order.

To permit this interruption of the normal sequence a _statement number_ is used. For the present, the statement number will be combined with a statement called the CONTINUE statement. The general form is

stno CONTINUE

where "stno" stands for an INTEGER number, written without a sign, which is punched in columns 1 through 5 of a Fortran statement card. The number must be between 1 and 99999 inclusive. Its choice is completely up to the programmer with one other restriction: no two statement numbers may be the same in any one program.

There is no flowchart box for the CONTINUE statement. But the joining of one arrow with another

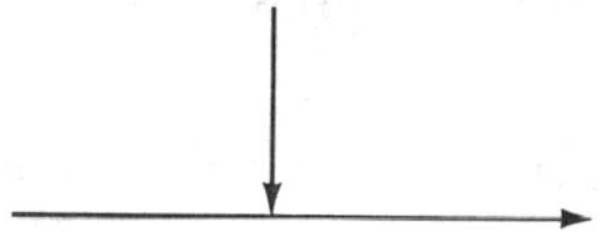

or the entrance of more than one arrow into a flowchart box

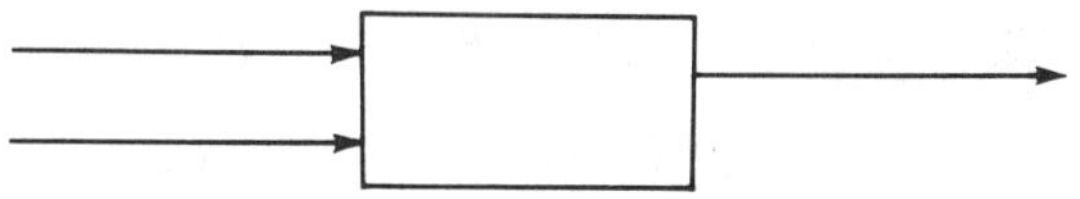

implies the need of a CONTINUE statement in TSF.

The CONTINUE statement works in conjunction with the decision making statement of TSF which is called the logical IF statement. The general form of the IF statement is

IF(expression reop expression) GO TO stno

where

<u>stno</u> is the statement number of a CONTINUE statement outlined above;

<u>expression</u> is an arithmetic expression such as that appearing to the right of the = symbol in an arithmetic assignment statement;

<u>reop</u> is a relational operator. It is composed of exactly four characters. The first and last of these are periods (decimal points). There are six relational operators:

.EQ. which means "equal to" (=)
.NE. which means "not equal to" (≠)
.LE. which means "less than or equal to" (≤)
.LT. which means "less than" (<)
.GE. which means "greater than or equal to" (≥)
.GT. which means "greater than" (>)

A logical IF statement works in the following way. The two expressions within the parentheses are evaluated separately. The expressions, each of which has a single numeric value, are then compared using the relational operator between them. If the relationship is true the computer takes its next instructions starting with the

stno CONTINUE

statement and executes the subsequent instructions. If the relationship is false the next statement following the IF statement is executed. This is illustrated by an example. The preceding flowchart included a decision which depicts an IF statement:

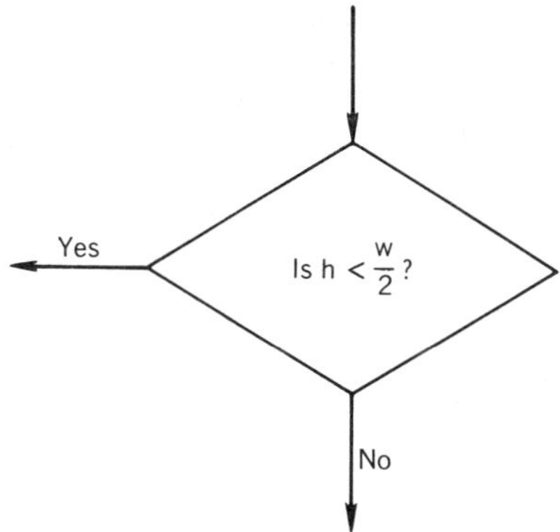

The following IF statement might be used to represent the diamond-shaped box in the Revised Flowchart:

STATEMENT NUMBER		STATEMENT
1 2 3 4 5	6	7 8 9 10 11 12 13 14 15 16 17 18 19 20 21 22 23 24 25 26 27 28 29 30 31 32 33 34 35 36 37 38 39 40 41 42 43
		IF(HEIGHT.LT.WIDTH/2.) GØ TØ 23

The statement means: if the height is less than half the width, *transfer control* to CONTINUE statement number 23 and begin executing the program steps following that statement. *Otherwise* (that is, if the height is *not* less than half the width) proceed normally with the next statement in the program.

If the program does go to statement 23 we say the program *transfers* or *branches* to statement number 23. In general, if the relationship inside the parentheses is true, the program GOes TO the specified CONTINUE statement. If the relationship is false, the statement immediately following the IF statement is executed next.

A complete program based upon the previous flowchart is presented below:

```
$JØB              MYNAME
      REAL HEIGHT
      REAL WIDTH
      REAL PI
      REAL RAREA
      REAL SAREA
      REAL AREA
      PI=3.141593
      READ, HEIGHT
      READ, WIDTH
      IF (HEIGHT.LT.WIDTH/2.) GØ TØ 23
      RAREA=HEIGHT*WIDTH
      SAREA=PI*WIDTH**2/8
      AREA=RAREA-SAREA
      PRINT, HEIGHT
      PRINT, WIDTH
      PRINT, AREA
      RETURN
   23 CØNTINUE
      PRINT, HEIGHT
      PRINT, WIDTH
      RETURN
      END
$ENTRY
```

The above program prints out the height, width, and area if the area printed involves the valid geometric figure. In the event that the area does not mean anything in terms of our problem, the program just prints out the height and width.

The Revised Flowchart for Lab Problem 02 depicts a proper algorithm: one with a single entrance and a single exit. The program, however, uses two RETURN statements. Part of the reason is that the flowchart is a two-dimensional representation of the solution to the problem. Thus a flowchart allows a great deal of flexibility in connecting its elements -- i.e., it's easy to draw lines between the boxes. The program, on the other hand, is a one-dimensional affair, and to connect its elements -- to be able to direct the order in which the statements are executed -- is a slightly more difficult matter. Sometimes one needs to be able to skip a set of statements even when no decision is involved. The IF statement

```
IF (2.LT.3) GO TO __
```

could be used as a way to always transfer control to another statement, but it is not a very good way to do that task. The solution to this difficulty, and the point of introduction of several others, is the tenth statement in TSF: the unconditional transfer statement, which will be discussed shortly.

Exercises

1. Given that A=5, B=3, C=1, determine whether each of the following is true:

   a. A**2.LE.A*B
   b. A**2.NE.A*B+10*C
   c. A.LE.B
   d. A*B*2.GE.B*10

2. Which of the following IF statements are invalid?

   a. IF ABLE IS GREATER THAN B GO TO 5
   b. IF (Q=P) GO TO 6
   c. IF R.GE.S GO TO 7

3. Is there anything wrong with the following statements?

```
      IF (A**2.LE.B) GO TO 75
   75 CONTINUE
      B=B+1
```

4. What values would be printed below?

```
      A=3
      B=5
      C=10
      IF(C.LE.A) GO TO 2
      A=A+5
    2 CONTINUE
      IF (A.EQ.C) GO TO 3
      B=B+3
    3 CONTINUE
      PRINT, A,B,C
```

5. What values would be printed below?

```
      A=1
      B=10
    5 CONTINUE
      IF (B.GE.A) GO TO 6
      IF (B.GT.3) GO TO 7
    6 CONTINUE
      A=A+5
      IF (2.LT.3) GO TO 5
    7 CONTINUE
      PRINT, A,B
```

UNCONDITIONAL TRANSFER

There is one last statement to be added to the repertoire of TSF: the unconditional transfer statement. The general form of this statement is

GO TO stno

where stno stands for a statement number.

Thus, if the statement

STATEMENT NUMBER (1–5)	6	STATEMENT (7–43)
		GØ TØ 888

were encountered during the execution of a program, control would transfer to the statement in the program

STATEMENT NUMBER (1–5)	6	STATEMENT (7–43)
888		CØNTINUE

The GO TO statement is used when a transfer is desired and no decisions by the machine are involved. This is called an unconditional transfer.

SUMMARY OF TSF STATEMENTS

You should now be familiar with the statements used in Ten Statement Fortran. They are listed here for reference.

```
          REAL variable

          INTEGER variable

          READ, variable

          variable=expression

          IF (expression reop expression) GO TO stno

          GO TO stno

     stno CONTINUE

          PRINT, variable

          RETURN

          END
```

LABORATORY PROBLEM 03

Write a TSF program which corresponds to the Revised Flowchart for Laboratory Problem 02. Your program should have only one RETURN statement. Run the program twice: once with data in which HEIGHT is greater than one-half WIDTH and once with HEIGHT less than one-half WIDTH. What other condition might you supply test data for?

> A frequent difficulty with computer programs is that they will work with one set of data but not with another -- because different data direct the execution of the program through different paths. When testing a program it is imperative to keep in mind the ways in which different data will affect the action of the program; attempt to check out all possibilities. Appendix J of the text discusses various features for testing and debugging programs.

LABORATORY PROBLEM 04

Use the computer to find the average of m numbers where m is a quantity which may vary from problem to problem. To do this problem supply m+1 data cards. The first card should contain the INTEGER number m. The remaining cards each contain one of the REAL numbers to be averaged. One possible flowchart for the problem appears below:

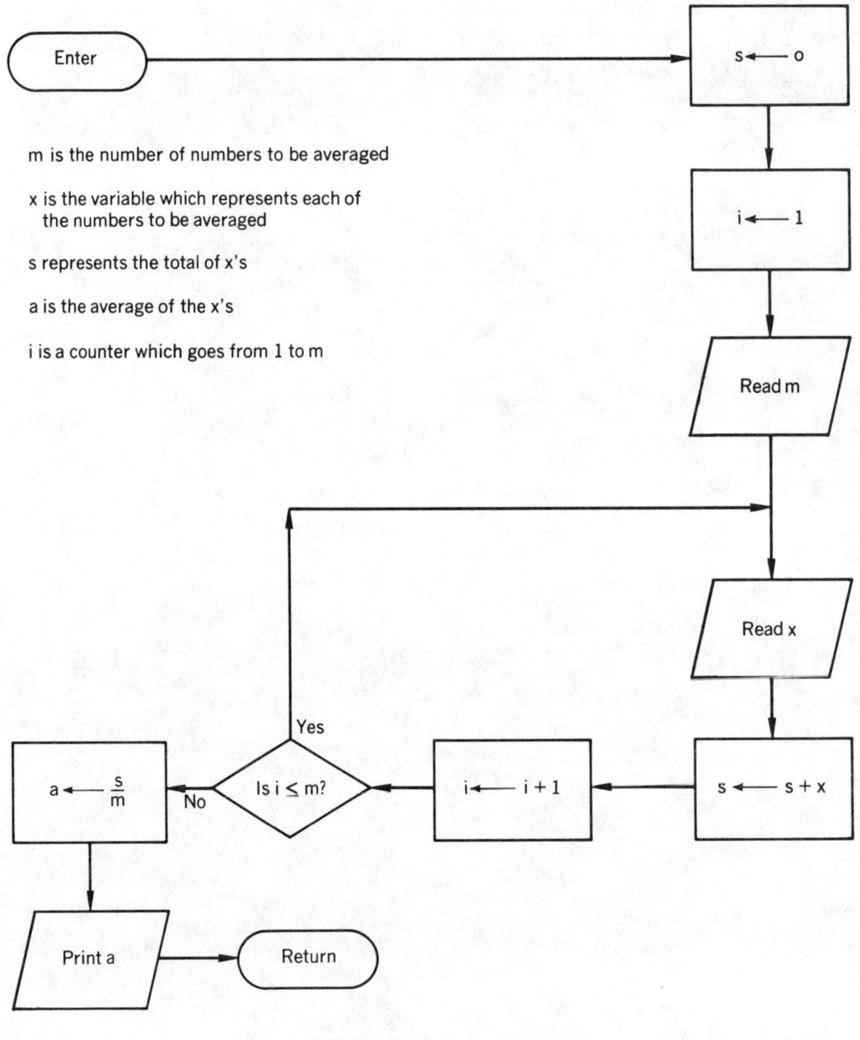

If you do not understand why this flowchart will result in S becoming the sum of the values on the data cards, you might pretend that you are the computer and follow the flowchart through a simple example. You could use the data

```
 4
 3.2
 4.8
 5.1
10.9
```

to see if you could get the answer: 6.0.

A DIALOGUE

BOOK: The purpose of Part I of this book is to acquaint you with a language, Ten Statement Fortran, in which problem-solving algorithms can be expressed.

STUDENT: Why do we learn this language? What is the point of the exercise?

BOOK: Well, knowing this language will enable us to use computers to solve problems whose algorithms we express in Fortran.

STUDENT: Oh, I see. Computers "speak" Fortran. We give them problems in the Fortran language; they understand it, follow the procedure we've defined, and give us an answer.

BOOK: In effect, yes.

STUDENT: "In effect?" What do you mean, "in effect?" Do computers know Fortran or don't they?

BOOK: Errr...Um. Well, not really. But I don't want to confuse you.

STUDENT: Confuse me. Confuse me! That's what this whole bit is about, isn't it? Understanding how computers solve problems?

BOOK: Yes, but at this early stage you can just pretend that the computer understands Fortran. You give it the program and the data and you get back the answers.

STUDENT: Look, I don't want to pretend a darn thing. I'm here to find out what's going on. Either you come through or I'll ask the Prof to get another text for this course.

BOOK: OK! OK! You know how to hurt a guy, don't you? Well, where to begin? . . . Computers do have languages. Each computer has its own "natural" language which is based on the way its transistors and such were wired together. If you give the computer a task to do, describing how to do the task in the computer's natural language, then the job will get done.

STUDENT: What does this natural language look like? Could I read it?

BOOK: Oh, it's a mess, usually. For most computers the natural language amounts to a bunch of 1's and 0's. The beginning of a program might look like 10010010011 101010001011010 . . . For other computers there might be 2's, 3's, etc. thrown in but the whole thing is pretty dismal.

STUDENT: Then how can a computer use Fortran to solve problems?

BOOK: Almost every computer comes with a program, in its natural language, which tells it how to do a very particular kind of task. That task is translating any valid Fortran program _into_ an equivalent program in the natural language. Once that translation is done, of course, the computer can use the product of the translating process to solve the original problem which was expressed in Fortran.

STUDENT: Heavy! I'm not sure I see that.

BOOK: Let's look at an analogy. Suppose you don't read French (but obviously you read English if you've gotten this far). Someone gives you a recipe for a pie, written in French. And he/she also gives you a book of French grammar, written in English, and a French-English dictionary. How do you proceed? One way would be to use the grammar, dictionary, and your mental ability to translate the recipe from French to English. After that, you simply follow the instructions of the English recipe, and combining the ingredients, voila! You've baked something great.

STUDENT: You have a hard time staying on the track, don't you? If I wanted to learn to cook I'd be taking a different course.

BOOK: Now wait. In this analogy, you are the computer; English is the natural language; French is the Fortran language (not the program, the language); the grammar and dictionary are the natural language program which describes how to translate _from_ Fortran _to_ the natural language. The original French recipe is the Fortran program; the recipe in English is the product of the translation -- sometimes called an _object_ program; the ingredients used in the cooking process are the data for the Fortran program; and the pie is the solution. Dig?

STUDENT: OK, I guess that's together. I see what you're saying but it's a pretty rough analogy.

BOOK: You forced me into this, remember. How well do _you_ do on the spur of the moment?

STUDENT: One more question. How does that translating program -- the one that is in the natural language -- what do you call it?...

BOOK: Usually it's called a _compiler_, a Fortran compiler.

STUDENT: OK. . . . How does the compiler get written? Does someone really sit down and do all those 1's and 0's?

BOOK: Oh, no, you don't! That's definitely in the next course, and blackmail won't get you anywhere either. I think you ought to say nice things about me for going through all this now. But I will say this: the compiler is just another computer program.

STUDENT: Hmmmmmm.

A SCHEMATIC COMPUTER

To aid in understanding the process which takes place when a computer executes a program, we now introduce a computer in schematic form. In the most essential ways this computer bears a strong resemblance to present, actual computers. We show this computer as being composed of four major parts:

1. Storage, where the program and the numbers to be operated upon are remembered or held;

2. A device for reading cards and transferring the numbers on those cards into computer storage;

3. A printing device upon which the computer can write numbers from its storage;

4. An arithmetic and comparison unit which performs calculation and compares quantities.

The storage is composed of locations which can store either instructions or numbers. Actually when a program is stored it consists of the machine's own language instructions which the machine itself has translated from the TSF program which the programmer has given it. For simplicity, TSF instructions will be shown in computer storage instead of the actual machine language. To demonstrate what takes place inside a computer, a schematic of the execution of a program which would follow the flowchart of Lab Problem 04 will be presented.

Suppose the following program is used:

```
$JOB         NAME
      REAL S
      REAL X
      REAL A
      INTEGER I
      INTEGER M
      S=0.0
      I=1
      READ, M
    3 CONTINUE
      READ, X
      S=S+X
      I=I+1
      IF(I.LE.M) GO TO 3
      A=S/M
      PRINT, A
      RETURN
      END
$ENTRY
2
15.3
4.7
```

Here S, X, and A have been selected by the programmer to represent REAL numbers because these variables must be able to take on numbers with fractional parts; I and M have been declared as INTEGER because computation can be done faster with INTEGER quantities and only whole numbers will be stored in I and M.

After the TSF program has been compiled (translated) and loaded into (placed in) storage and before the data have been read, a representation of the computer storage might look like this:

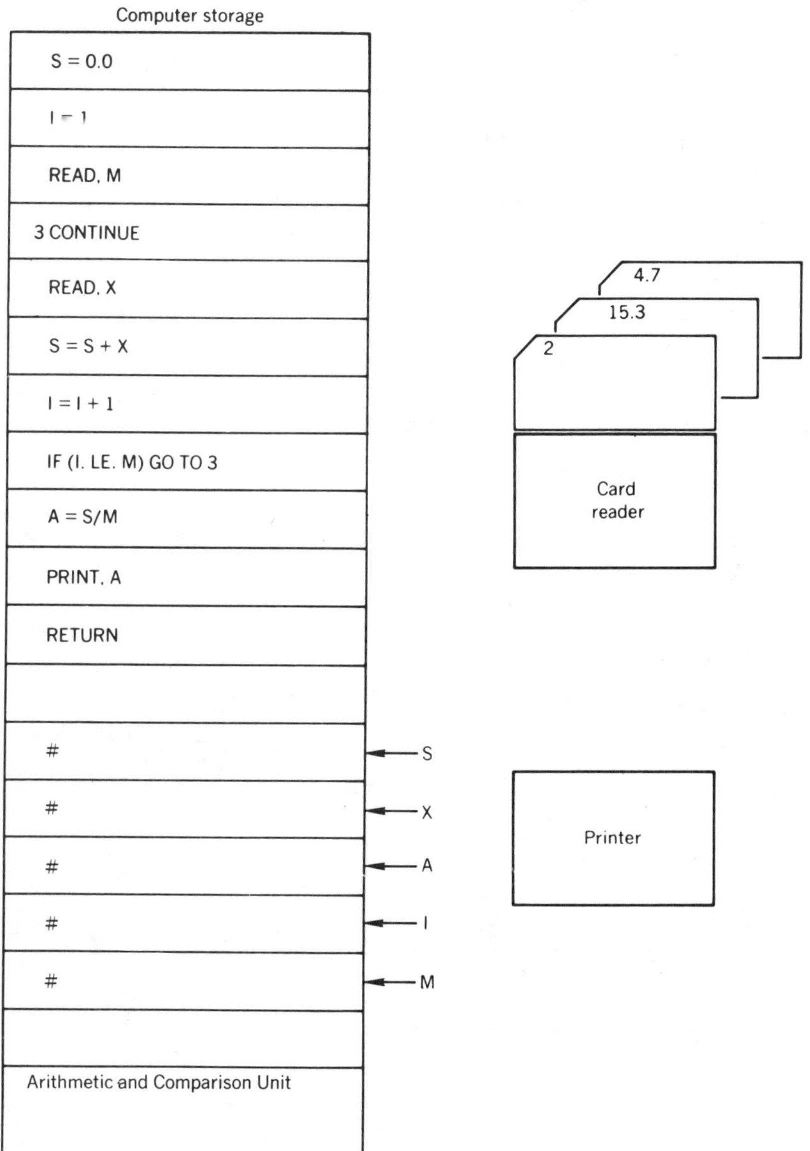
Computer storage
S = 0.0
I = 1
READ, M
3 CONTINUE
READ, X
S = S + X
I = I + 1
IF (I. LE. M) GO TO 3
A = S/M
PRINT, A
RETURN
#
#
#
#
#
S
X
A
I
M
Arithmetic and Comparison Unit
4.7
15.3
2
Card reader
Printer

Here only the statements which are actually used during the execution of the program are shown; these are called _executable statements_. The other statements--REAL, INTEGER, END--are used during the translation or compilation phase of the JOB and are called _non-executable_.

Notice that while the REAL and INTEGER statements have reserved certain locations in the machine to be used for S, X, A, I, and M, nothing has been stored in those locations so that, as far as the programmer is concerned, they contain unusable quantities or _garbage_, indicated by #.

The program will now be schematically "run" with an arrow

showing the particular statement being executed and the rest of the schematic showing the effect. Carefully examine each of the 16 steps in the execution of this program. A thorough understanding of this example will add much to your further progress.

1. Garbage is erased from S and replaced by 0.

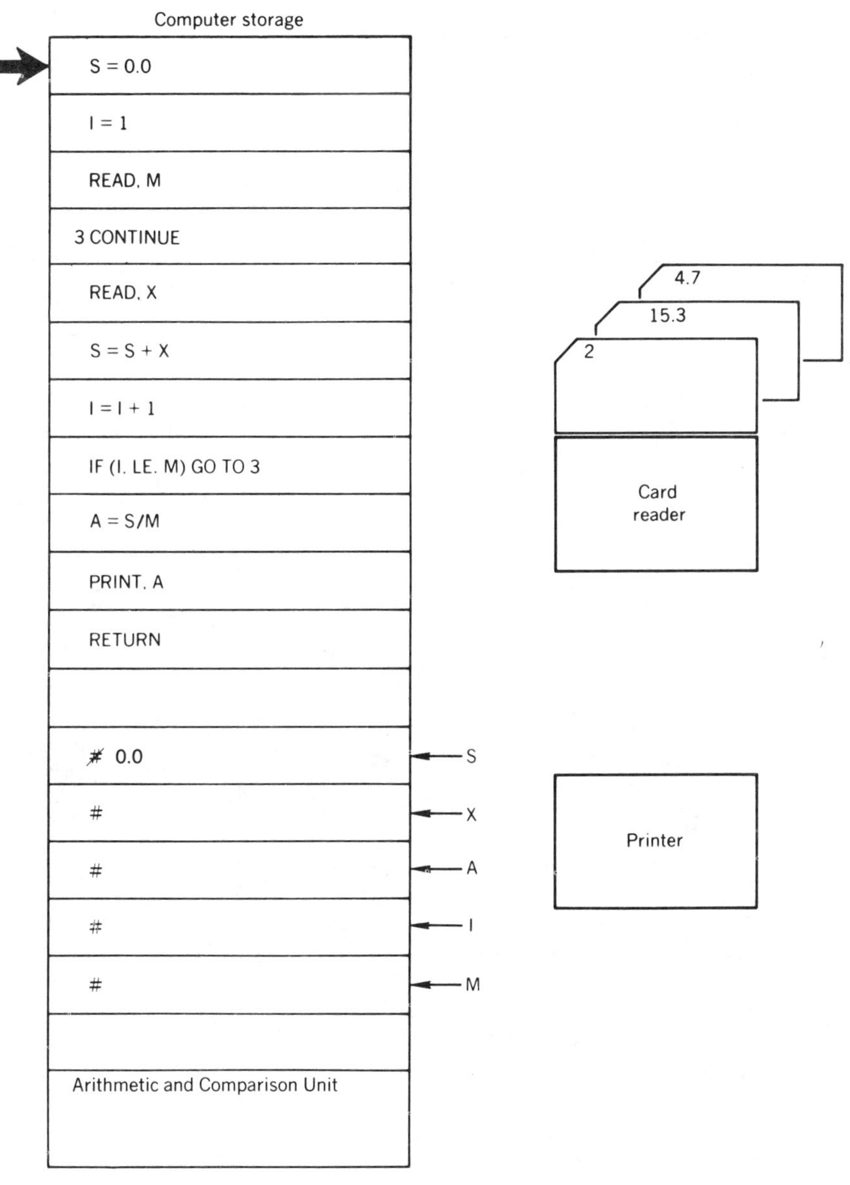

2. Garbage is erased from I and replaced by 1.

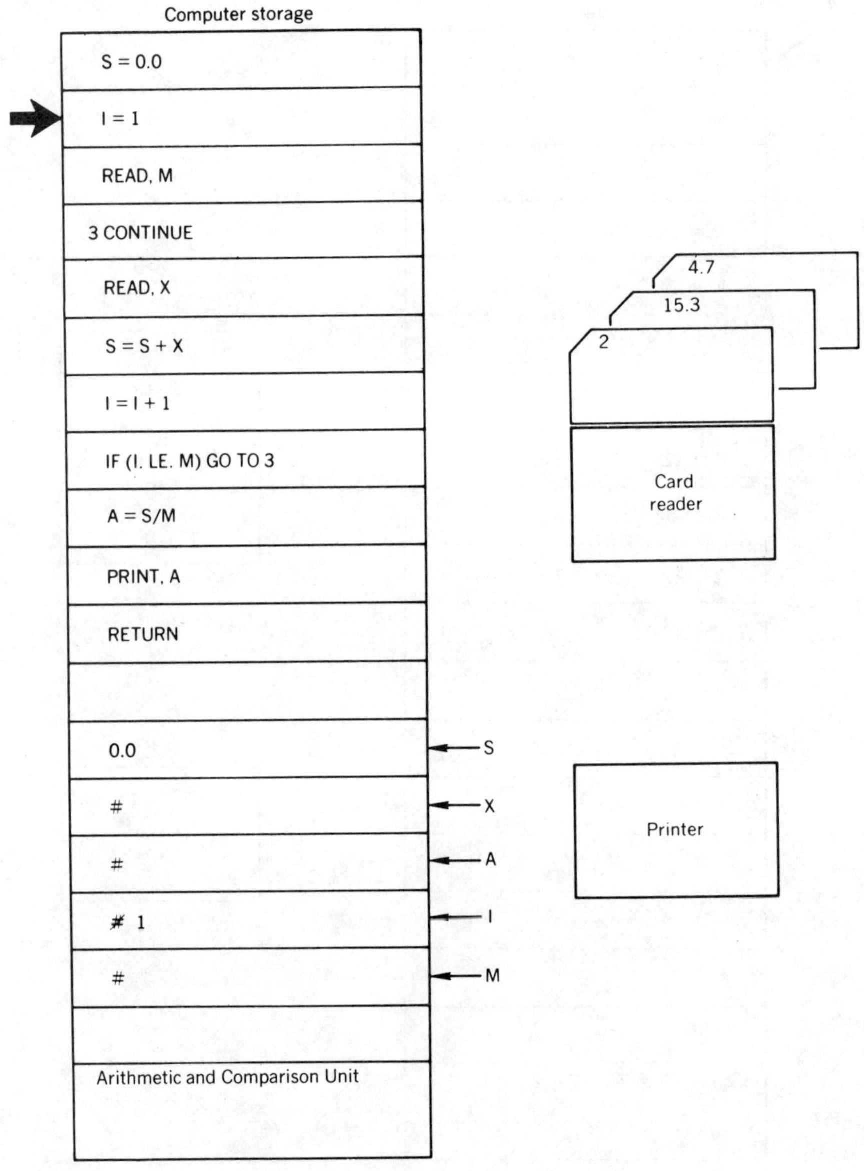

3. A card is read through the card reader and the value 2 on that card is transferred to the location M, erasing the garbage in that location.

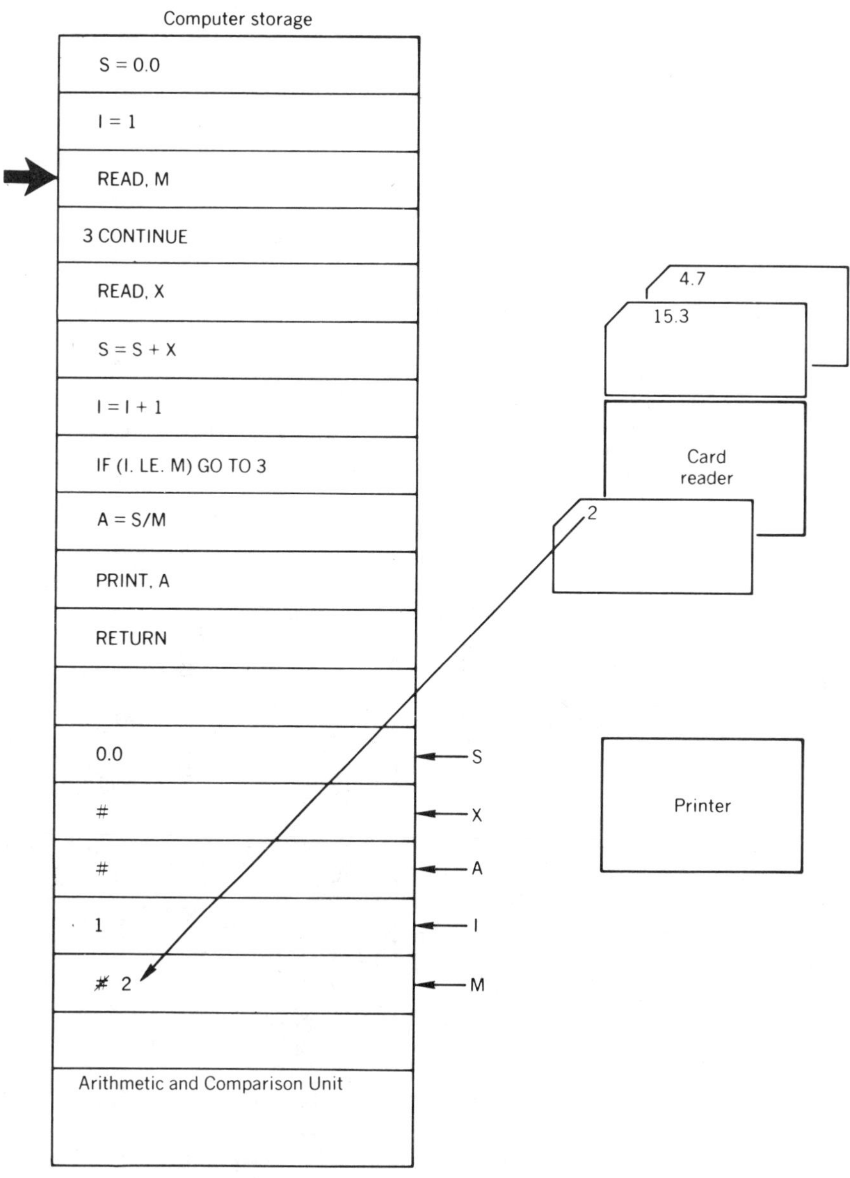

4. No change; this statement will be transferred to later.

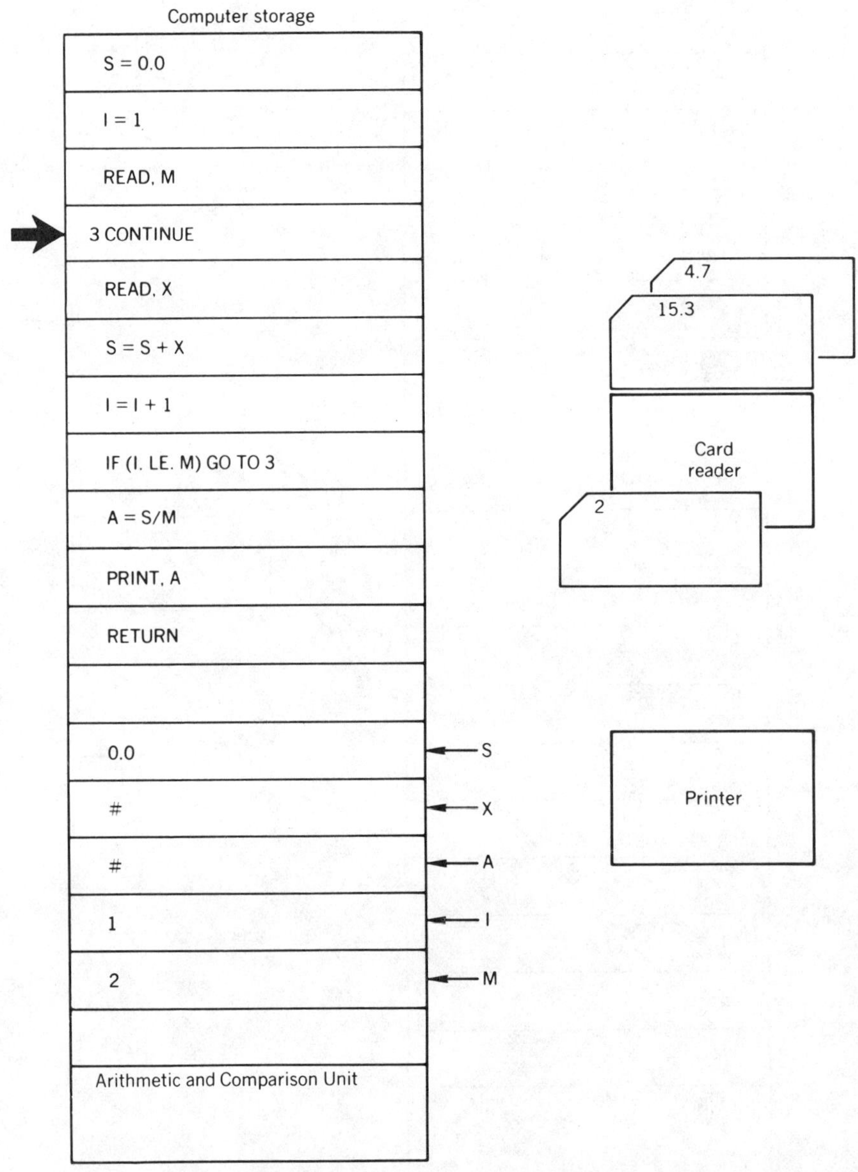

5. A card is read through the card reader and the value 15.3 is transferred to the location X, replacing the garbage.

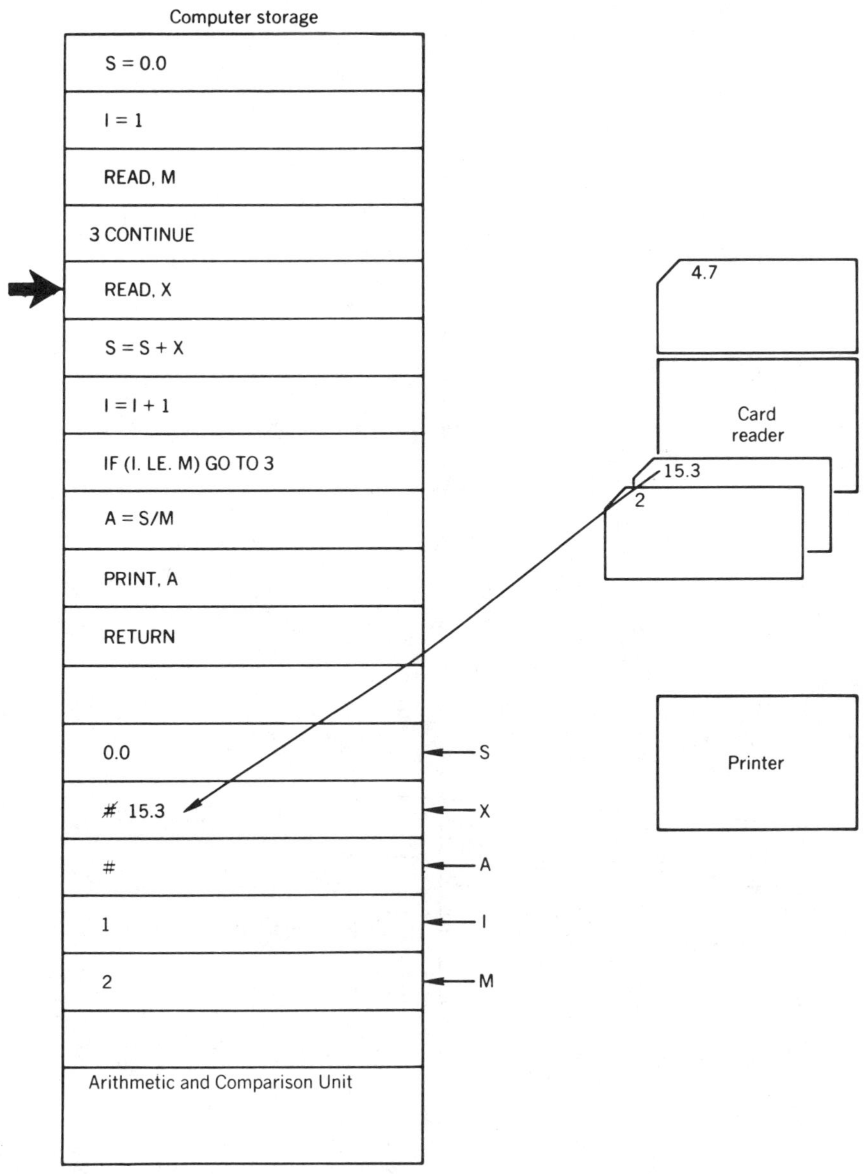

6. The numbers in S and X are added together and the result replaces the 0.0 in location S.

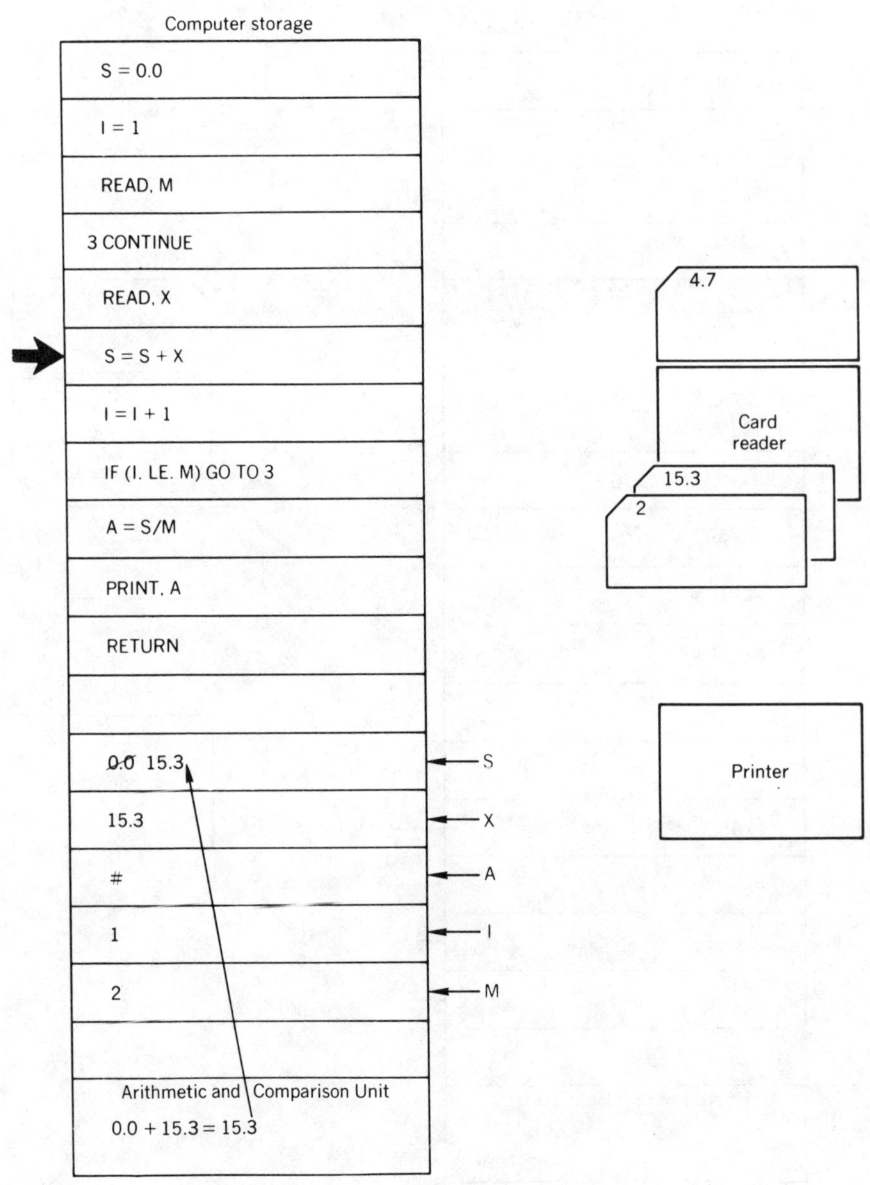

7. The value 1 is added to the 1 which already exists in location I and the result (2) is stored back in location I.

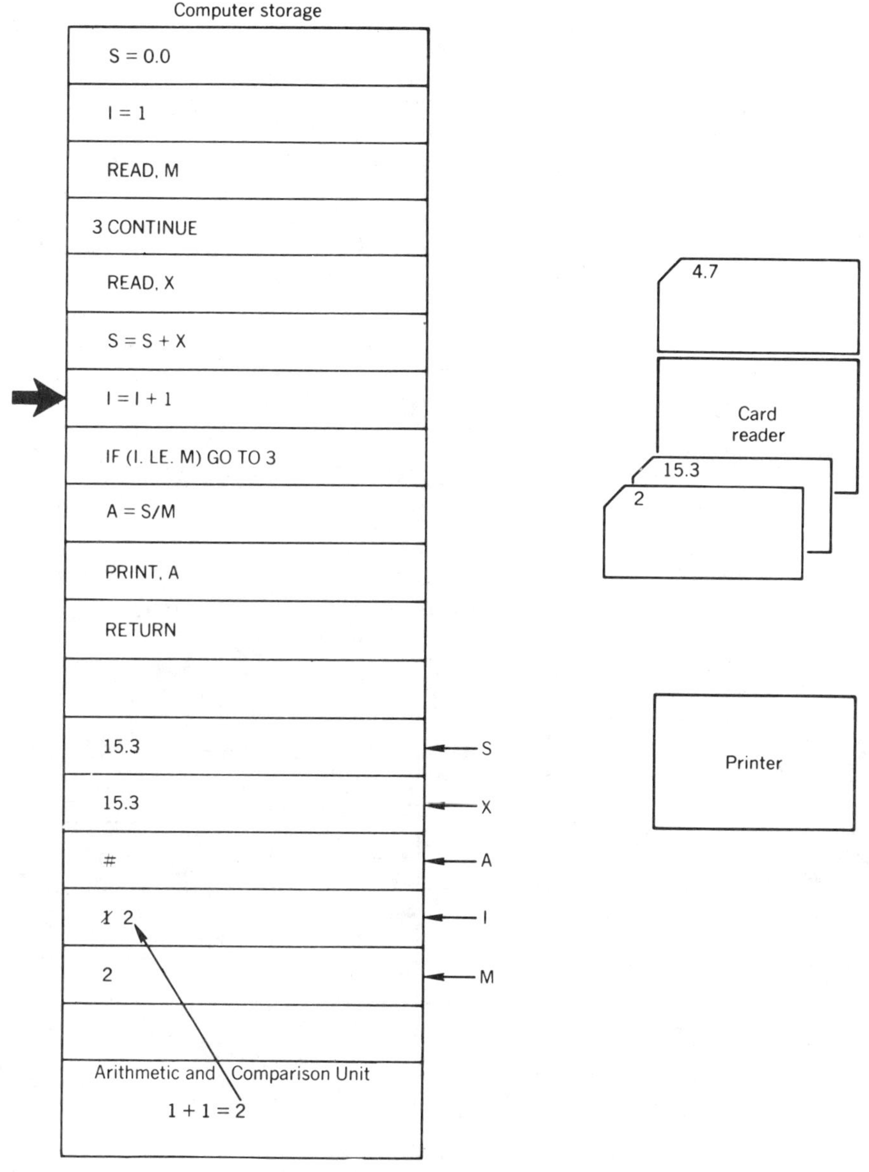

8. I is compared with M; since I is equal to M, control passes back to statement 3 CONTINUE.

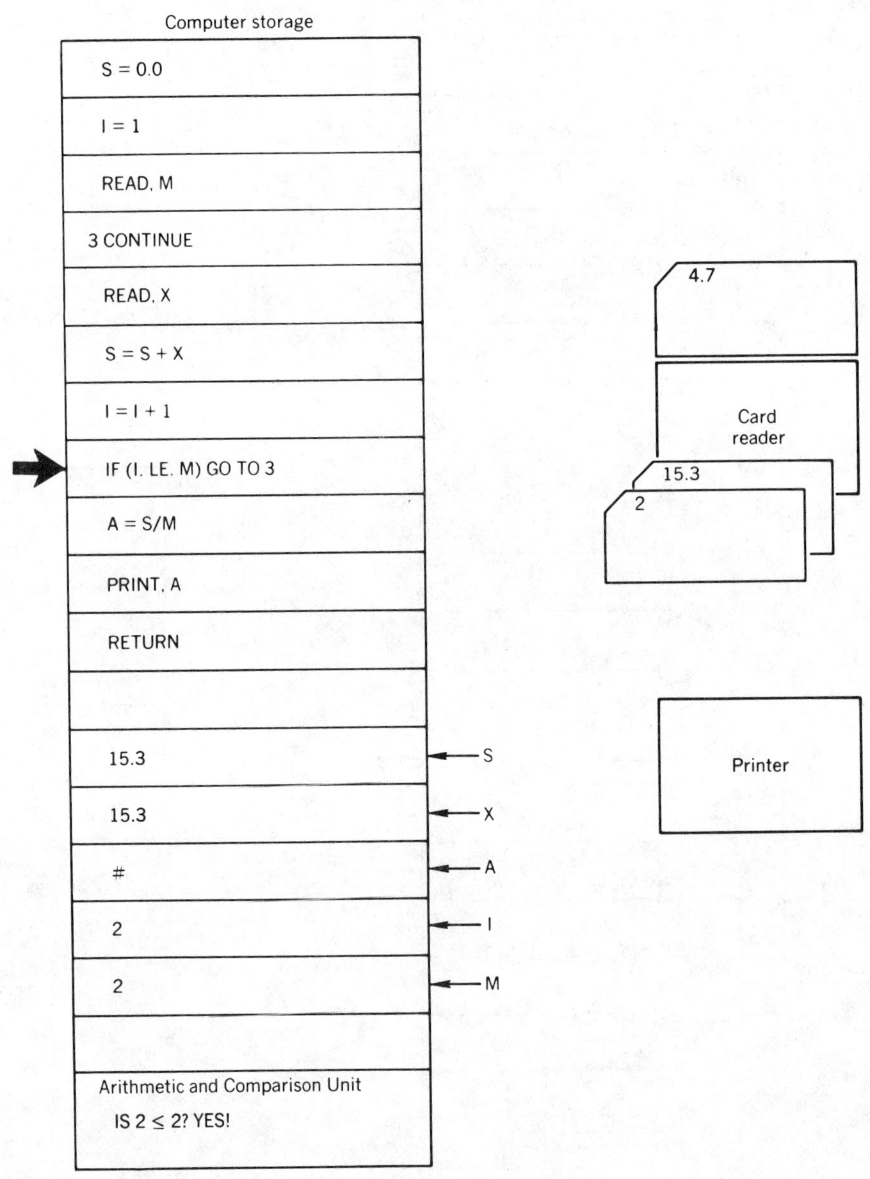

9. No change in computer storage.

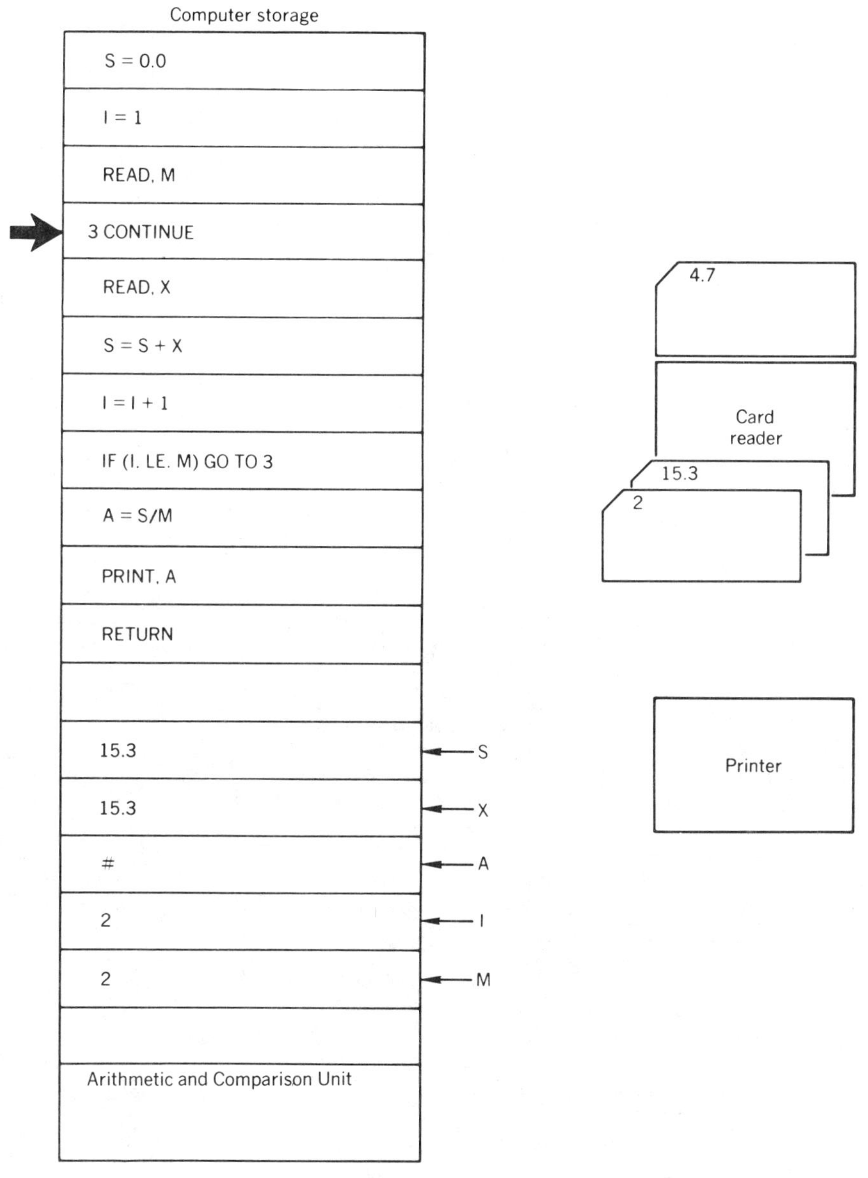

10. A card is read through the card reader and the value 4.7 is transferred to the location X, replacing the value 15.3.

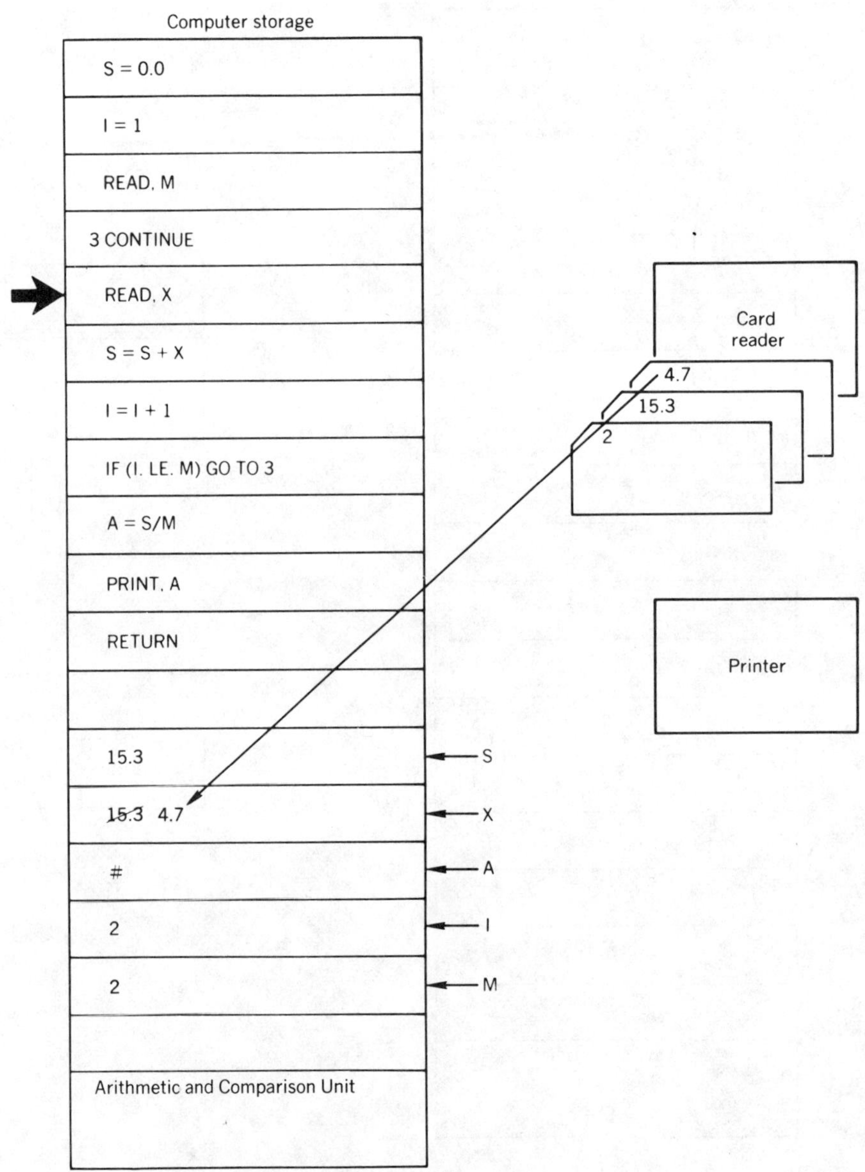

11. The numbers in S and X are added together and the result replaces the 15.3 in location S.

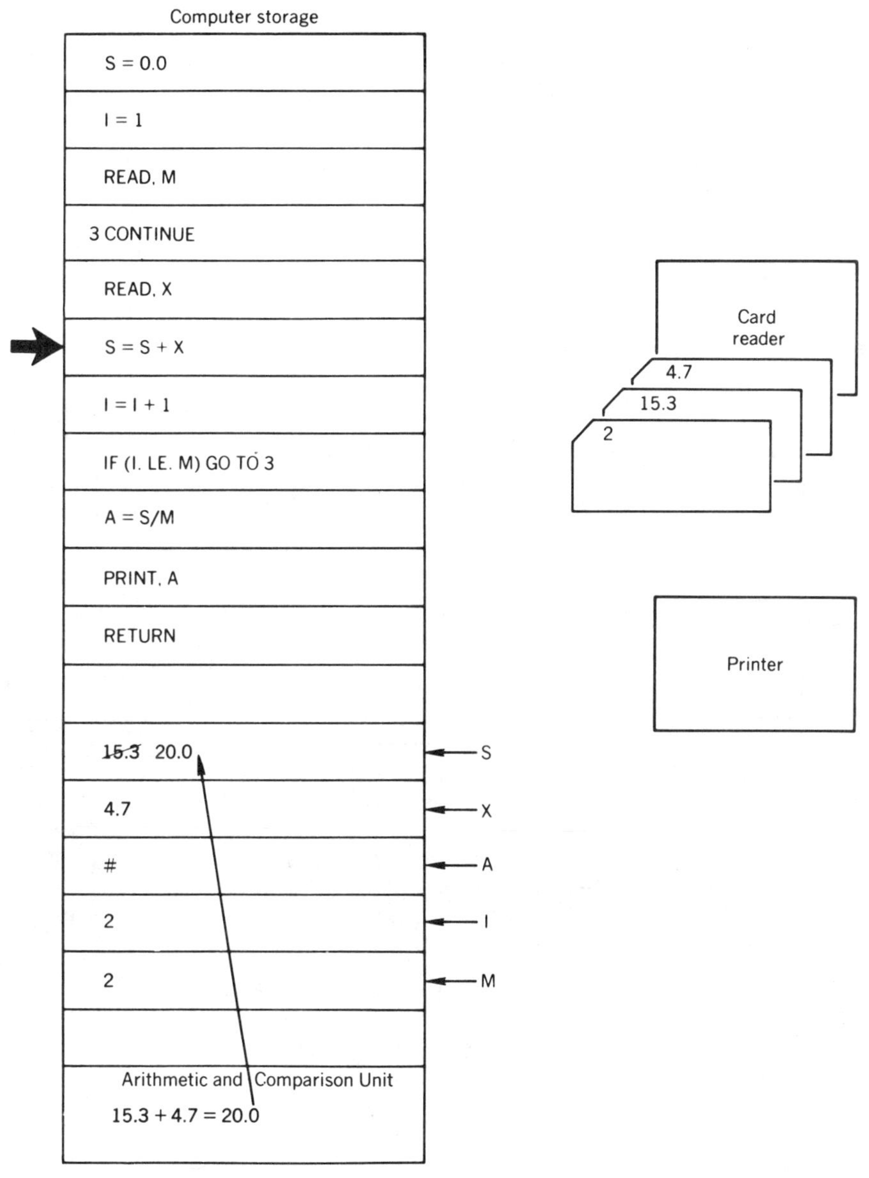

12. The value 1 is added to the 2 in location I and the result (3) is stored back in location I.

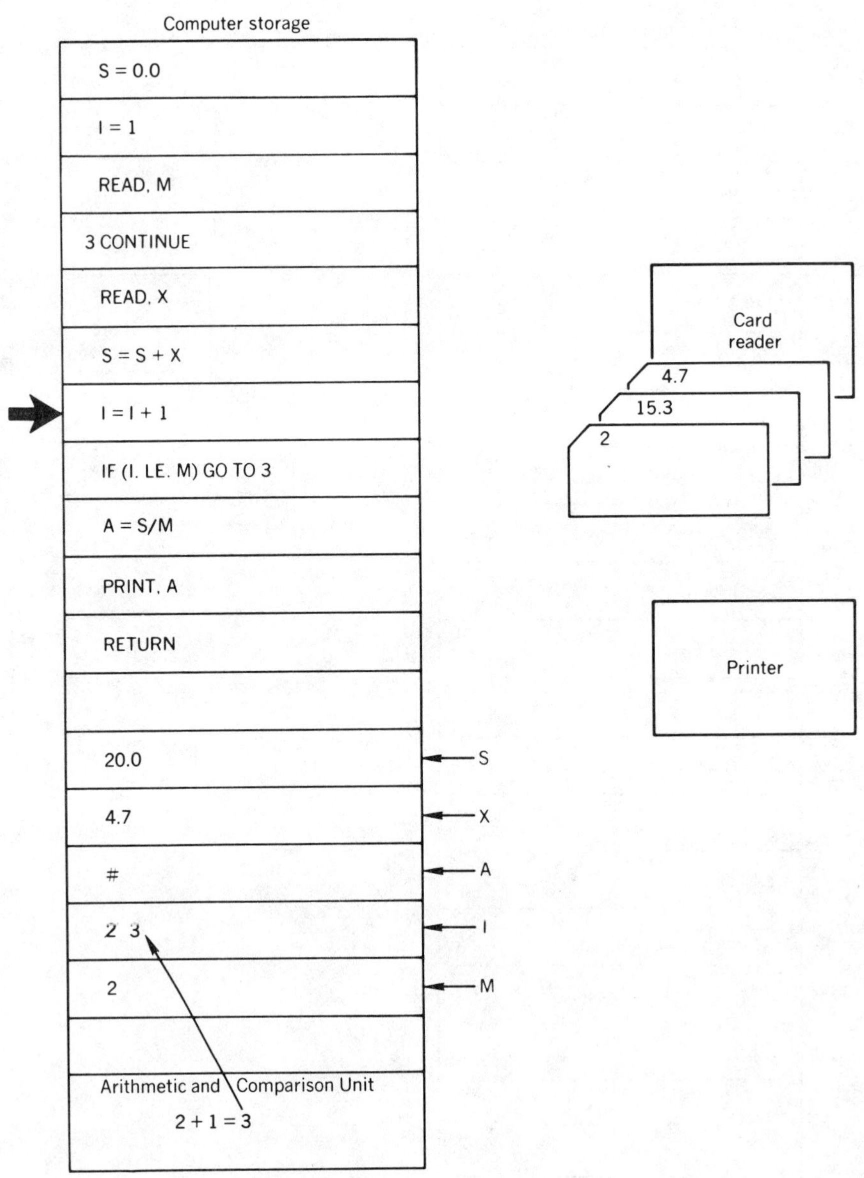

13. Since I is not less than or equal to M, control passes to the next sequential statement.

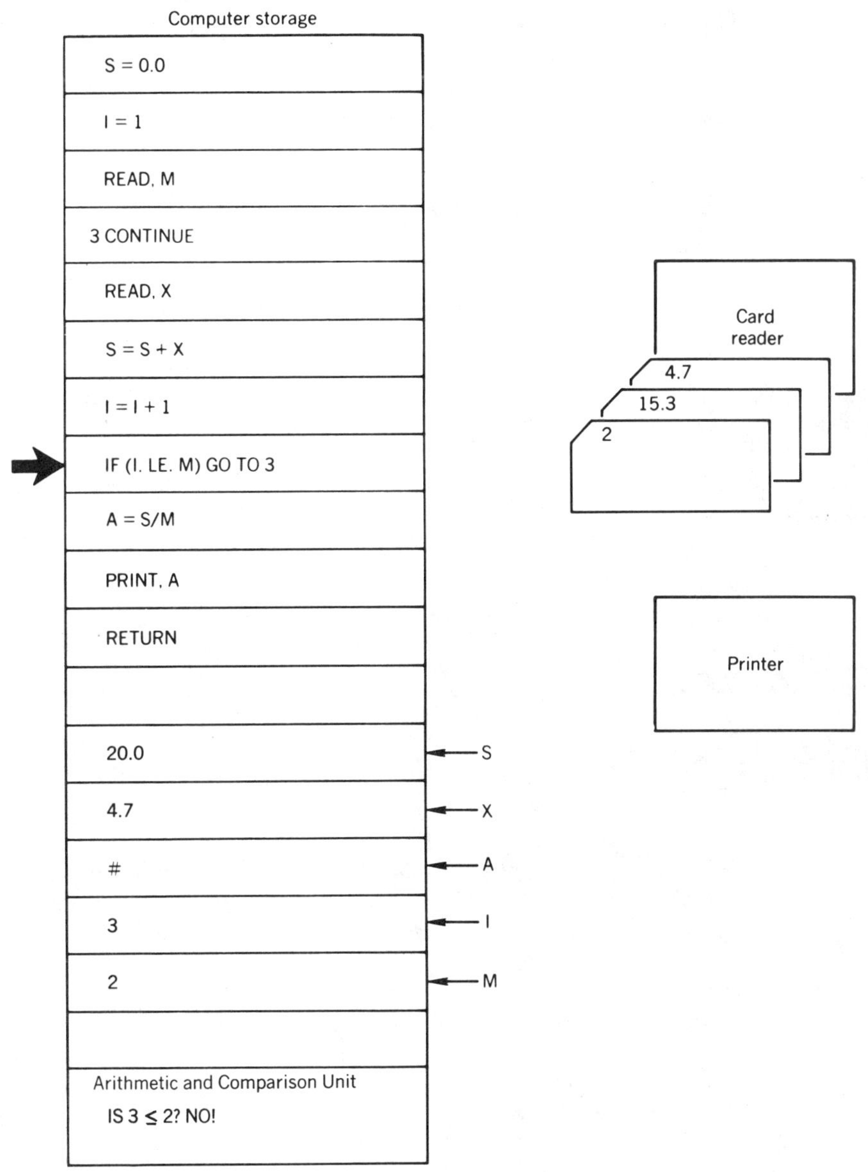

14. The number in S is divided by the number in M and the result is stored in A, replacing the garbage there.

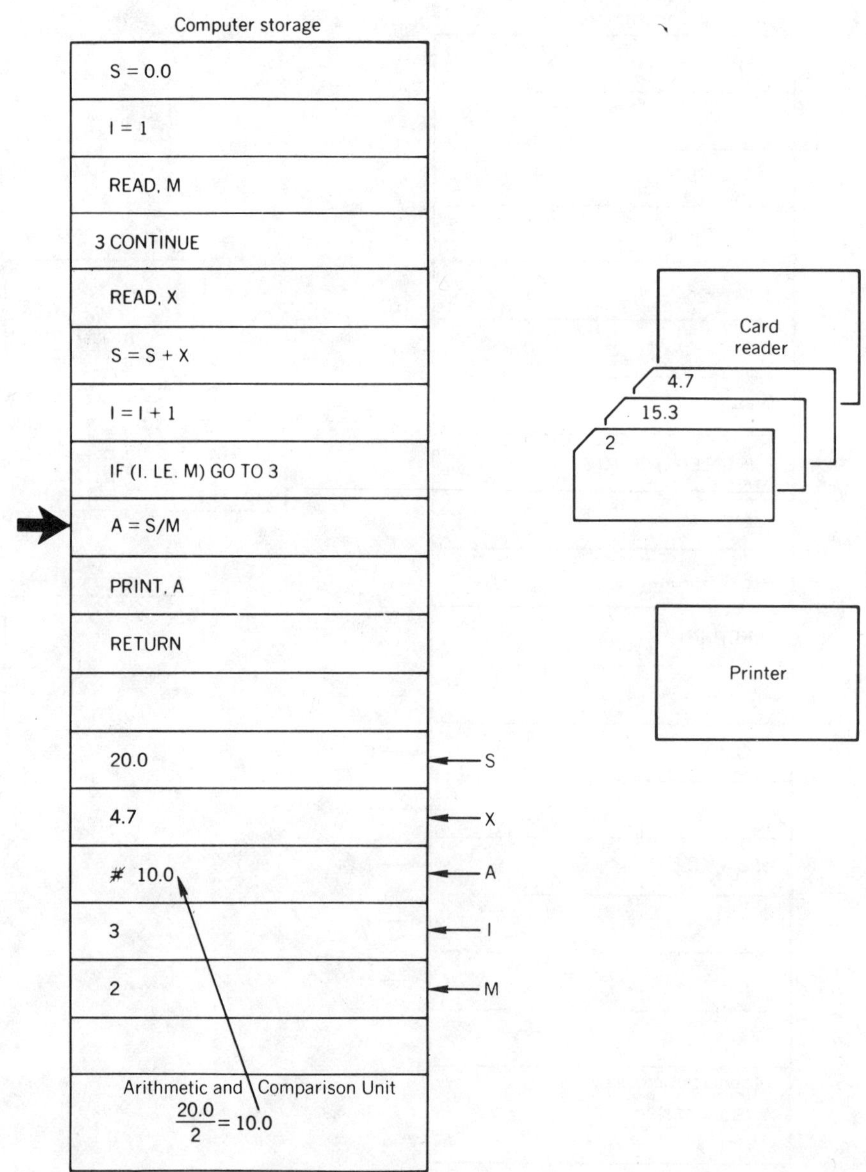

15. The number in A is transferred to the printer and is reproduced on a piece of paper; the number in A remains unchanged.

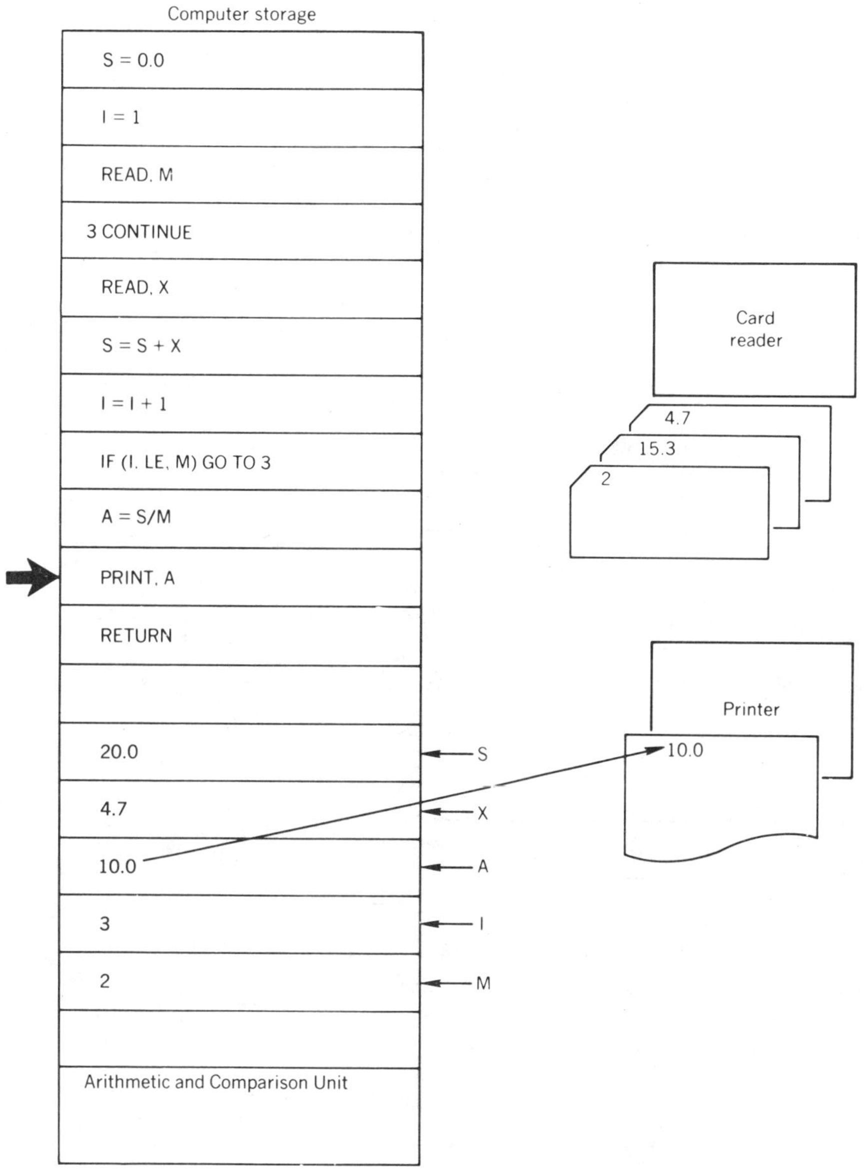

16. Control returns to the operating system of the computer since the job is now complete.

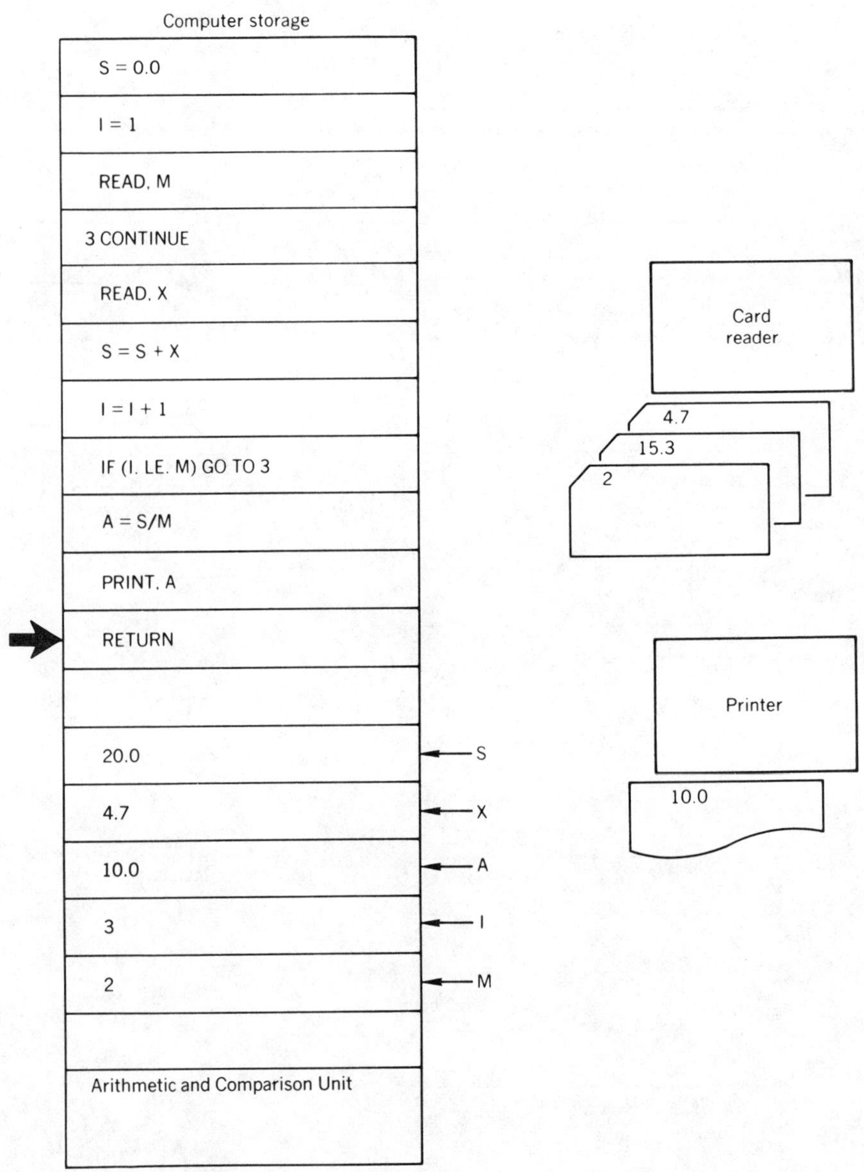

Physical vs. Logical Order

As we mentioned before, statements in a program can be thought of as occurring in two orders or sequences. The first is called the physical order; it is simply the order in which the statements appear on the coding form or in the card deck.

The second order is the logical order. This is the order in which the statements are executed by the computer. This order may well be determined by the data that the program itself reads. Further, there will usually be many more statements executed, in logical order, than there are actual physical statements in the program, because many of the same statements are reused.

The distinction between these two orders is important because rules for writing programs frequently specify that something must happen before something else. And the would-be programmer must know whether "before" means "physically before" or "logically before." For example, if a variable name is used in a program, the Type Declaration Statement which declares that variable should appear physically before any other mention of that variable in the program.

On the other hand, if the value of a variable is printed by the program, the statement defining the value of that variable must logically precede the PRINT statement which writes out the value. As an example of this situation, here is a program segment in which a PRINT statement physically appears before, but logically after, the statement defining the value of the variable to be written:

```
        •
        •
    GO TO 55
66  CONTINUE
    PRINT, X
        •
        •
55  CONTINUE
    X=56.789
    GO TO 66
        •
        •
```

LOOPING

As illustrated by Lab Problem 04 and the Schematic Computer, it is sometimes desirable to execute a group of statements several times. In many cases the number of times the group is to be executed is determined by the data taken in by the program. We want to call particular attention to one method of doing this -- looping. Suppose we wanted to execute a set of statements five times. We might write a program which would follow this flowchart:

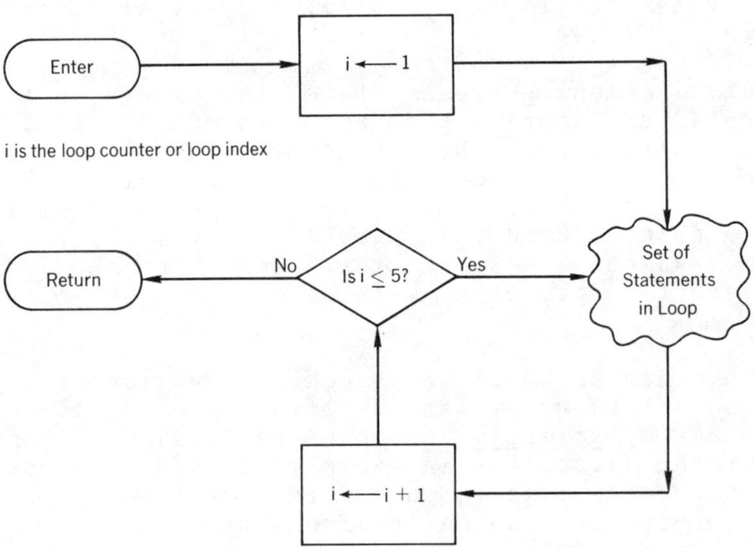

This flowchart provides for the execution of the "set of statements" five times. The first time, the variable "i" will have the value 1 during the execution of the "set," the second time "i" will have the value 2, etc. When the set of statements has been executed five times, "i" will take on the value 6 and the decision box will allow control to pass to the return box. A variable such as "i," used in this manner, is sometimes called an index or control variable.

A program segment which would basically follow this flowchart is now shown. We have made one change, however: instead of limiting ourselves to five passes through the set of statements, we let the computer read a number, M, which dictates the number of loops.

```
      INTEGER I
      INTEGER M
      READ, M
          .
          .
      I=1
  101 CONTINUE
          .  )
          .  )
          .  }  SET OF STATEMENTS IN LOOP
          .  )
          .  )
      I=I+1
      IF (I.LE.M) GO TO 101
          .  )
          .  }  SET OF STATEMENTS
          .  }  AFTER LOOP
          .  )
```

Notice that to employ a loop, four distinct tasks must be performed:

1. Give a beginning value to (initialize) the index,
2. Increment (or decrement) the index,
3. Test the value of the index,
4. Return (branch) to the top of the loop.

These four tasks can be seen in the loop below which reads and sums exactly 36 data values:

```
      INTEGER E
      INTEGER I
      REAL X
      REAL TOTAL
      E=36
      TOTAL=0
      I=1                          (initialize)
  999 CONTINUE
      READ, X
      TOTAL=TOTAL+X
      I=I+1                        (increment)
      IF(I.LE.E) GO TO 999         (test and branch)
            •
            •
            •
```

Notice that this loop could be used to read and sum any number of values by simply changing the first statement which establishes the value of E.

Exercises

1. What value is printed below?

```
      INTEGER I
      INTEGER V
      V=0
      I=1
    2 CONTINUE
      V=V+I
      I=I+1
      IF (I.LE.5) GO TO 2
      PRINT, V
```

2. What value is printed below?

```
      INTEGER Q
      Q=1
    7 CONTINUE
      Q=Q+1
      IF (Q.GE.12) GO TO 7
      PRINT, Q
```

3. What values are printed below?

```
      MV=10
      CV=1
      S=0
    8 CONTINUE
      IF (CV.GT.MV) GO TO 9
      S=S+1
      CV=CV+1
      GO TO 8
    9 CONTINUE
      PRINT, S
```

4. What value would have been printed in Exercise 3 above if the first statement had read MV=3000?

5. What is wrong with the following loop?

```
      Q=20
      T=0
      I=1
    2 CONTINUE
      IF (I.GT.Q) GO TO 3
      T=T+2
      GO TO 2
    3 CONTINUE
      PRINT, T
```

6. What value would be printed below?

```
      MV=0
      S=0
      CV=10
    1 CONTINUE
      IF (CV.GT.MV) GO TO 2
      S=S+1
      CV=CV-2
      GO TO 1
    2 CONTINUE
      PRINT, S
```

LABORATORY PROBLEM 05

The two roots of $ax^2 + bx + c = 0$ can be computed by means of the formula:

$$x = \frac{-b \pm \sqrt{b^2-4ac}}{2a}$$

Use the computer to find the roots where a, b, and c are read in as data. If the roots are not complex (i.e., if $b^2 \geq 4ac$) and if a does not equal zero, write out a, b, c and each of the roots. If the roots are complex or if a equals zero, simply print a, b, and c. The instructor will give you several equations to be solved. The first data card should tell how many equations are to be solved. The remaining data cards are to contain the values of a, b, and c for the given equations. Even if you've peeked ahead to the section on Function Reference, compute the expression under the radical as a power, not as a square root. Draw a flowchart for the solution to the problem in the space below before you write the TSF program.

FUNCTION REFERENCE

Because certain mathematical functions are frequently needed in problem solving, the designers of the language have provided them for use in TSF expressions.

The general form for function usage is:

fname(argument)

where fname is a TSF function name and argument is a REAL TSF expression. Below are shown nine different functions which are available to programmers in TSF and the TSF names for them.

mathematical name	TSF name
sine	SIN
cosine	COS
tangent	TAN
arctangent	ATAN
square root	SQRT
absolute value	ABS
log base 10	ALOG10
log base e	ALOG
e to the x	EXP

As an example, suppose a programmer wanted to add 1.666666 to the absolute value of the product of two previously defined variables, X and Y, and wanted to call the result Z. He might write

STATEMENT NUMBER		STATEMENT
1 2 3 4 5	6	7 8 9 10 11 12 13 14 15 16 17 18 19 20 21 22 23 24 25 26 27 28 29 30 31 32 33 34 35 36 37 38 39 40 41 42 43
		Z=1.666666+ABS(X*Y)

to obtain the proper value of Z.

A discussion of each of the functions follows. In each case the argument or expression is REAL.

SIN(argument) computes the sine of the expression. <u>The expression must represent an angle expressed in radians</u>. (For reference, 180 degrees = pi radians.) Thus

STATEMENT NUMBER (1–5)	6	STATEMENT (7–38)
		PI=3.141593
		X=30.
		Y=SIN(X/180.*PI)

would define Y as the sine of 30 degrees. The COS(argument) function is similar in an obvious way.

ATAN(argument), the inverse tangent or arctangent, produces the angle (again in radians) whose tangent is the expression in parentheses.

SQRT(argument) produces the square root of the argument in parentheses. The argument must be greater than zero or equal to zero.

ABS(argument) produces the absolute value of a REAL argument.

ALOG(argument) produces the natural logarithm (base e) of the argument, which must, of course, be greater than zero.

ALOG10(argument) produces the common logarithm (base 10) of the argument, which must be greater than zero.

Thus the TSF statements

```
X = 23.5
Y = ALOG(X)
```

would define Y as the <u>natural</u> (base e) logarithm of 23.5 while

```
X = 23.5
Y = ALOG10(X)
```

would define Y as the <u>common</u> (base 10) logarithm of 23.5

EXP(argument) produces "e" raised to the power of the argument.

Functions may be freely used in expressions and even as arguments of each other. Thus the Fortran statement

```
Y=SIN(COS(ATAN(SQRT(ALOG(EXP(X)-ABS(Z))*11.5)))/8.8)-22.222
```

is completely legal (although it may not be very useful). Determining what the statement means is left as an exercise for the reader.

There are many other functions available which are not listed here. They may be found in Module 14.

> It is a good idea, when using a constant such as pi in a program, to define it explicitly as a variable to begin with; then use that variable when the constant is needed. The risk of error incurred in writing (or rewriting) the constant is thus minimized.

> For every variable you use in a program you must make the choice between REAL or INTEGER. As time goes on you will learn more about this choice. For the present you might keep the following in mind:
>
> 1. INTEGER and REAL variables take the same amount of space in the machine.
>
> 2. INTEGER variables and constants are usually handled much more quickly by the computer. In the absence of any reason to the contrary, then, INTEGER is preferable.
>
> 3. Most FUNCTIONs which can produce results with fractional parts require REAL arguments.
>
> 4. In deciding whether a variable should be Typed INTEGER or REAL, the major issue is whether the number which the variable is to stand for could ever need to possess a fractional part. If so, REAL must be used.

LISTS

Four of the ten statements previously discussed may now be extended by introducing the concept of a list.

Rather than writing a separate Type Declaration Statement for each variable in a program, it is possible to list several variable names in one Type Declaration Statement, separating them by commas. For example, in the program of Lab Problem 02 it would have been correct to write

STATEMENT NUMBER		STATEMENT
		REAL HEIGHT,WIDTH,PI,RAREA,SAREA,AREA

or

STATEMENT NUMBER		STATEMENT
		REAL HEIGHT,WIDTH,PI,SAREA
		REAL AREA, RAREA

instead of

```
REAL HEIGHT
REAL WIDTH
REAL PI
REAL RAREA
REAL SAREA
REAL AREA
```

The only limitation on the number of variable names used in a list in a Type Declaration Statement is that, in TSF, the last character of the last name used must not be punched beyond column 72 of the Fortran statement card. All of the remarks above also apply to the INTEGER type statement. Using a list rather than a single variable name has the advantage of reducing the number of REAL and INTEGER statements required in a program. Notice that there is no comma between the word REAL (or INTEGER) and the first variable in the list, but commas separate the items in the list from each other.

The other two statements which can be extended by the use of a list are the READ and PRINT statements. Again, the list consists of a sequence of variable names separated by commas. One READ statement still results in the reading of one card; however, if there are two variables in the list of the READ statement the data card should contain two numbers. These numbers which are keypunched into the data card must be separated by at least one blank column. The number of variables in the list should correspond to the number of numbers on the card being read.

For example, one can write

STATEMENT NUMBER		STATEMENT
1 2 3 4 5	6	7 8 9 10 11 12 13 14 15 16 17 18 19 20 21 22 23 24 25 26 27 28 29 30 31 32 33 34 35 36 37 38 39 40 41 42 43
		READ, HEIGHT, WIDTH

instead of

```
READ, HEIGHT
READ, WIDTH
```

If the first method is used, the computer expects to read one card with two numbers punched in it. The number to be used for width is punched in columns which lie to the right of the columns occupied by the number to be used for height. The second set of statements above provides for the reading of two cards, each of which is punched with a single number.

The PRINT statement is extended in much the same way. The statement

```
PRINT, HEIGHT, WIDTH, AREA
```

will result in the printing of one line of output containing three numbers, whereas

```
PRINT, HEIGHT
PRINT, WIDTH
PRINT, AREA
```

will produce three lines of output, each consisting of a single number.

LABORATORY PROBLEM 06

The manager of an airport has asked you to prepare a table to determine the cloud height above the airport. The airport is equipped with a powerful light mounted so as to shine vertically on the bottom of the cloud layer.

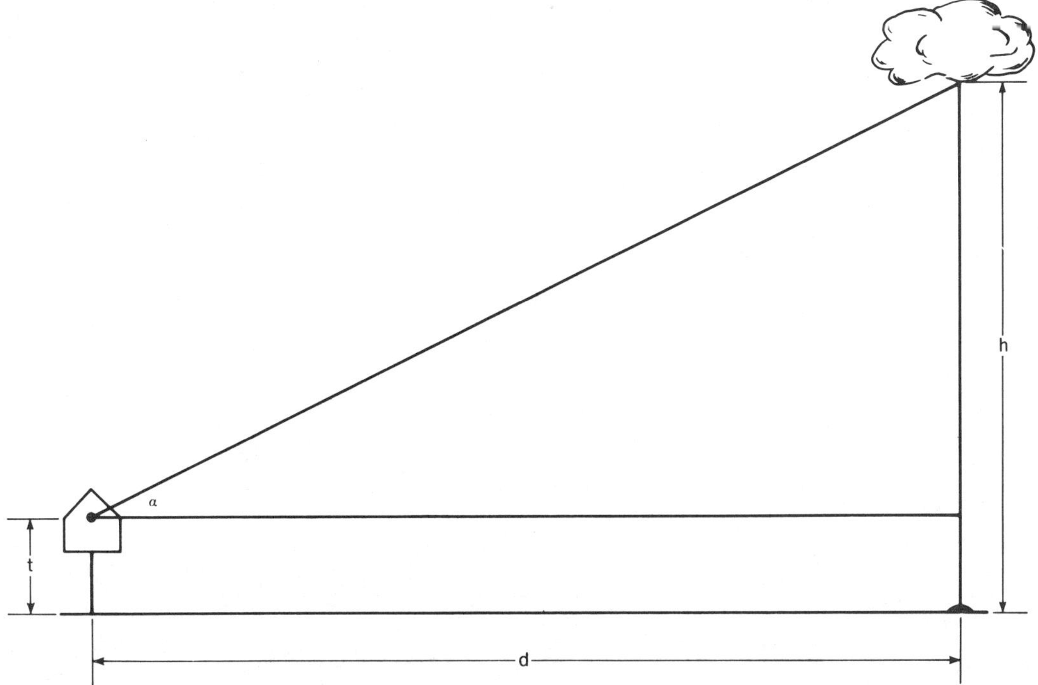

In the diagram above, the tower height above the ground, t, is 61.2 feet and the distance from the tower to the light, d, is 4107.6 feet. Print out a two column table where the first column refers to the angle in degrees and the second column refers to the cloud height, h. Start at 0 degrees and increase by 1/2 degree increments until a maximum of 75 degrees is reached <u>or</u> until a maximum cloud height of 40,000 feet is attained. Your program should check for both maximum conditions and should terminate the table when either occurs. Use no constants in this program. Read all numbers required from punched cards.

> A good programmer usually tries to write a program which is general. It is much better to change the data cards than the program.

LABORATORY PROBLEM 07

Write a TSF program to instruct the computer to READ any three numbers which might be in any order and to print them in ascending order. Draw a flowchart in the space below before you attempt to write the program:

If this problem appears too trivial, try it with thirty numbers instead of only three.

> Sometime in your grammar school years you were probably taught that "Now you are big boys and girls, so you can use pen or ball point instead of pencil." Well, there aren't any big boys and girls when it comes to taking the first shot at a flowchart or program. Use a pencil with an eraser so that you don't end up with a product that has more scratched out than written in. And, above all else, avoid those frazzlable felt tips!

SUBSCRIPTED VARIABLES

If you tried to do the sorting problem (number 07) with thirty numbers, you probably gave up. Another example of a problem for which our present knowledge does not seem sufficient is the following:

> Write a general program to READ several numbers -- the exact number specified by the data -- and simply print these numbers in reverse order. In other words, do Lab Problem 01 again using a varying number of numbers instead of exactly four.

These examples illustrate that there is a class of problems which cannot be easily handled with scalar variables.

The Variable Concept Expanded

The capability which allows solution of such problems is based on an expansion of the concept of a variable. Heretofore, a variable name has represented only a single number at any one time during the execution of a program. We now introduce a variation which makes the variable name vastly more powerful: we allow a single variable name to stand for an entire set of numbers. We initially call such a variable name a _singly subscripted variable_, a _vector variable_, or a _one-dimensional array_.

We have used a variable name to stand for a single location in memory. For example:

```
   GOAT
┌────────┐
│-354.8│
└────────┘
```

Now we have the ability to use the name GOAT to stand for several locations in memory and, hence, for several numbers.

```
   GOAT
┌───────┐
│-808.8│
├───────┤
│  55. │
├───────┤
│   0. │
├───────┤
│  11. │
└───────┘
```

A question immediately arises: if one variable name stands for several numbers, how does the programmer instruct the computer regarding the particular number to be used, say, in a calculation? The solution lies in "attaching" an integer number, called a <u>subscript</u>, to the variable name. The subscript, which appears in parentheses after the variable name, uniquely identifies each number in the set or array. In this case the programmer instructs the computer to identify each number in the array as follows:

```
   GOAT
┌───────┐
│-808.8│   GOAT(1)
├───────┤
│  55. │   GOAT(2)
├───────┤
│   0. │   GOAT(3)
├───────┤
│  11. │   GOAT(4)
└───────┘
```

Then, if the programmer wanted to construct an expression to instruct the computer to divide the second number in the array by the fourth and add 1.5 to the result, he/she could write:

```
X=GOAT(2)/GOAT(4)+1.5
```

This would result in a value for the expression of 55/11+1.5 or 6.5. (Note the similarities and differences between this arithmetic assignment statement and that in Lab Problem 00.)

The name "subscripted variable" comes from the fact that these variables are used to represent quantities that, in mathematics, are written as

$$X_i$$

where X is the variable name and i is called a subscript.

In general, we have expanded the variable concept to allow a variable name to take on the form:

variable(subscript)

where "variable" is a name obeying the rules set up for scalar variable names and "subscript" is a number.

Exercise

To illustrate subscript meaning, suppose that the following values are stored in memory:

X(1)	0.0
X(2)	0.0
X(3)	3.0
X(4)	45.0
X(5)	0.0
LAMB	2
NAT	4

If the assignment statement X(LAMB)=234. were executed, what changes in memory would result? Since LAMB contains the value two, X(LAMB) refers to the second location in the set of locations called X, that is X(2), and therefore the value in X(2) would be changed from 0.0 to 234.0. What happens if the assignment statement X(NAT)=X(NAT)+LAMB were executed? Since NAT contains the value four, this statement says: Add the contents of LAMB to the contents of X(4). The value 45.0 in X(4) would be changed to 47. What value is stored in X(3) by the statement X(3)=X(LAMB)+X(NAT)+LAMB +NAT?

Declaration of Subscripted Variables

Declaration of subscripted variables involves reserving necessary space in computer memory and specifying whether the variables are to be INTEGER or REAL. Subscripted variables can be declared as either INTEGER or REAL just as with scalar variables. To declare a variable as subscripted, the concept is simply extended by appending to the variable name an INTEGER constant, enclosed in parentheses, which denotes the number of locations to be reserved for that subscripted variable. For example:

STATEMENT NUMBER		STATEMENT
1 2 3 4 5	6	7 8 9 10 11 12 13 14 15 16 17 18 19 20 21 22 23 24 25 26 27 28 29 30 31 32 33 34 35 36 37 38 39 40 41 42 43
		REAL WATER(7)

would declare that WATER is a set of seven REAL locations. Memory would appear as follows:

WATER(1)	#
WATER(2)	#
WATER(3)	#
WATER(4)	#
WATER(5)	#
WATER(6)	#
WATER(7)	#

Notice that declaring WATER as a REAL subscripted array of seven locations does not define any of the locations. All locations are still undefined because no numbers have been stored in them. The statement

STATEMENT NUMBER		STATEMENT
		INTEGER BREAD(4), SALT, PEPPER(5)

would reserve the following locations in memory:

BREAD (1)	#
BREAD (2)	#
BREAD (3)	#
BREAD (4)	#
SALT	#
PEPPER (1)	#
PEPPER (2)	#
PEPPER (3)	#
PEPPER (4)	#
PEPPER (5)	#

When a subscripted variable is declared to be of a certain type, all the locations of that variable are automatically of that type. Again, no values are stored in these locations; they are undefined, but declared as INTEGERs.

The number which appears in parentheses after the variable name in the Type Declaration Statement is the number of locations reserved for that variable. This means that, while all the locations reserved need not be actually used, a programmer must not attempt to utilize more locations than have been reserved. For example, we can declare CS as a real subscripted variable with three locations by using the statement

```
                    REAL CS(3)
```

This means that exactly three locations for CS are reserved and an attempt to use CS(4), for example, would be invalid.

Using Subscripted Variables

How does the use of subscripted variables allow us to deal with problems which were not easily solvable with scalar variables? If we declare an array EX of eight locations as follows:

```
                    REAL EX(8)
```

we set up in the machine's memory

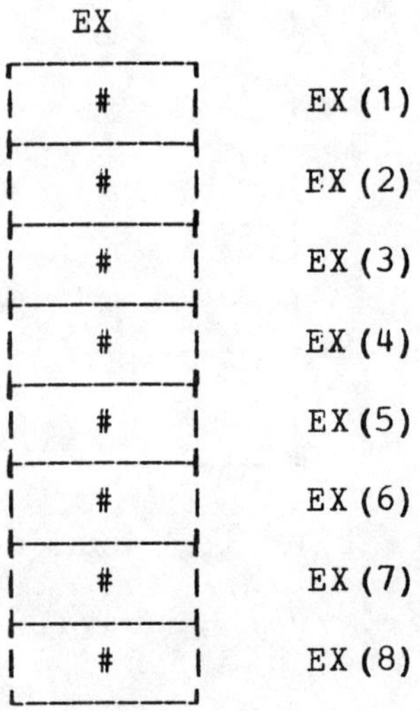

```
           EX
      ┌─────────┐
      │    #    │     EX(1)
      ├─────────┤
      │    #    │     EX(2)
      ├─────────┤
      │    #    │     EX(3)
      ├─────────┤
      │    #    │     EX(4)
      ├─────────┤
      │    #    │     EX(5)
      ├─────────┤
      │    #    │     EX(6)
      ├─────────┤
      │    #    │     EX(7)
      ├─────────┤
      │    #    │     EX(8)
      └─────────┘
```

If the program executes the statement

```
                    READ, EX(2)
```

this results in the reading of a number, say -31.3, which replaces the garbage in EX(2) thusly:

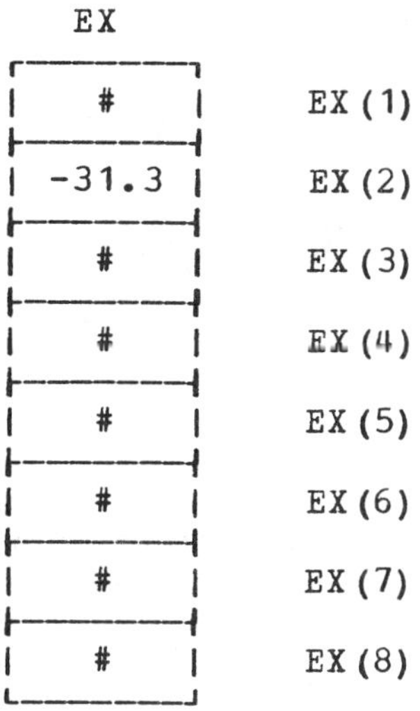

```
              EX
         ┌──────────┐
         │    #     │     EX(1)
         ├──────────┤
         │  -31.3   │     EX(2)
         ├──────────┤
         │    #     │     EX(3)
         ├──────────┤
         │    #     │     EX(4)
         ├──────────┤
         │    #     │     EX(5)
         ├──────────┤
         │    #     │     EX(6)
         ├──────────┤
         │    #     │     EX(7)
         ├──────────┤
         │    #     │     EX(8)
         └──────────┘
```

This, in itself, offers no advantage over the use of scalar variables. However, we specified only that a subscript needed to be a <u>number</u>; we did not say that the subscript had to be a <u>constant</u>. In fact, the power of using subscripted variables lies in using subscripts which are not constants but are themselves variables, or, even, arithmetic expressions.

As an example of the use of a variable as a subscript, observe that we could perform precisely the same operation as

```
READ, EX(2)
```

by writing a pair of statements

```
SUBK=2
READ, EX(SUBK)
```

Even this only hints at the power which we now have. The fact that we can use one variable name as a subscript allows us, in effect, to calculate a portion of another variable name. Suppose, for example, we wished to place the squares of the numbers 11 through 18 in the eight locations of the array. We could write:

```
      INTEGER SSS
      REAL EX(8)
      SSS=1
  101 CONTINUE
      IF (SSS.GT.8) GO TO 102
      EX(SSS)=(SSS+10)**2
      SSS=SSS+1
      GO TO 101
  102 CONTINUE
         •
         •
         •
```

Here, the storage location referenced in the statement

```
EX(SSS)=(SSS+10)**2
```

would be EX(1) the first time through the loop, EX(2) the second time through, EX(3) the third time through, etc. So numbers would be placed in all eight locations. The resulting array would now contain:

EX	
121.	EX(1)
144.	EX(2)
169.	EX(3)
196.	EX(4)
225.	EX(5)
256.	EX(6)
289.	EX(7)
324.	EX(8)

Study this example carefully until you thoroughly understand it.

Now we turn back to the problem of writing a program which will read in several numbers -- the exact number of which will be determined by the data -- and print the list of these numbers in reverse order. We will stipulate that there will be no more than 10 numbers, though there may be fewer. The number of numbers to be read is to be the first number in the data deck and will be called M in the program.

A complete program which would perform this feat is shown here:

```
      INTEGER M,K,N
      REAL VALS(10)
      READ, M
      K=1
  101 CONTINUE
      IF (K.GT.M) GO TO 102
      READ, VALS(K)
      K=K+1
      GO TO 101
  102 CONTINUE
      N=M
  103 CONTINUE
      IF (N.LT.1) GO TO 104
      PRINT, VALS(N)
      N=N-1
      GO TO 103
  104 CONTINUE
      RETURN
      END
```

To show the technique used when writing flowcharts containing subscripted variables we present a flowchart depicting the algorithm followed by the above program. The character V is used to stand for the variable VALS.

> The first loop in this program illustrates a different way of setting up a loop than was used in Lab Problem 04. How is it different? What disadvantage does it have? What advantage?

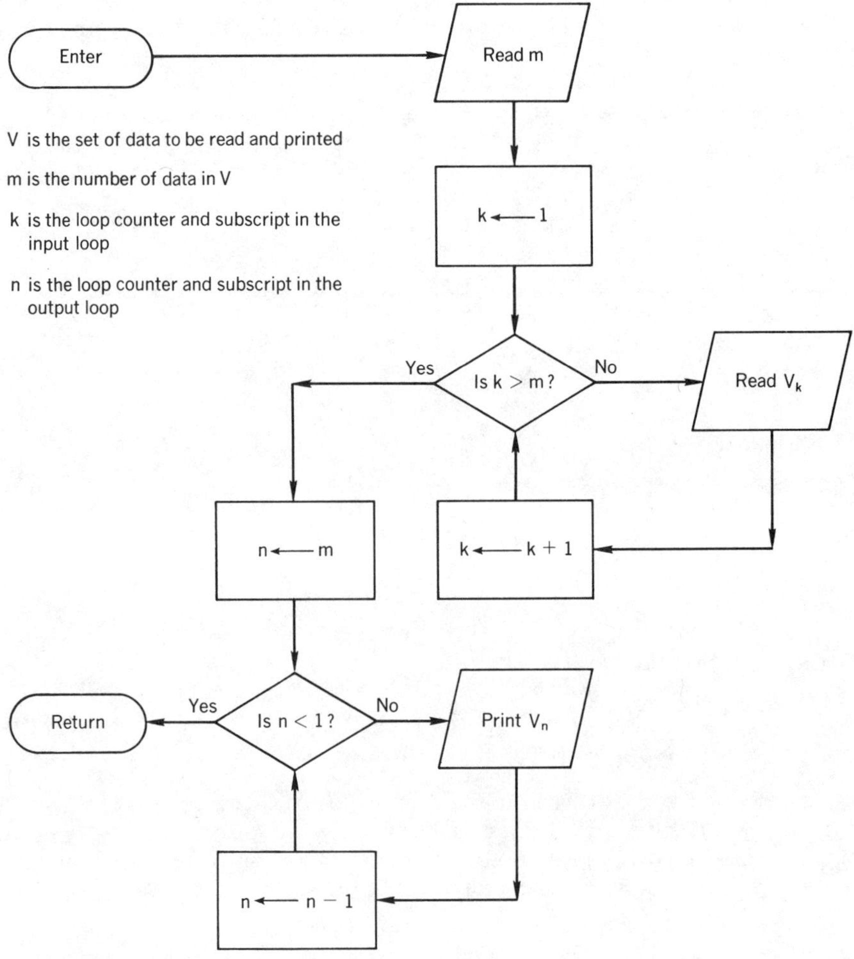

If the previous example is not clear, construct a schematic computer on a sheet of paper. Draw a box for M, K, N and 10 boxes for VALS. Run through the program with the following data:

```
  6
 18.5
  7.3
 -1.2
  5.5
100.
  0.
```

A programmer using subscripted variables must remember that he is subscripting with a <u>number</u> each time he uses a subscripted variable name. He <u>may</u> use a previously defined variable to stand for the subscripting number, but it is the number which is important, not the subscripting name. To illustrate, assume that L=4, KK=3, MMM=2; then all of the following refer to the same location in computer memory:

```
TEST(L)       TEST(L+KK-3)
TEST(4)       TEST(KK*MMM-L/MMM)
```

What location is being referred to?

In the program which reversed the order of numbers on output, we used the variable name K as the subscript during the input part of the program. On output, we used the variable name N as the subscript. We could have used K again in the output phase of the program but we were not obligated to. If K is 4, then VALS(K) refers to location VALS(4); if N is 4 then VALS(N) refers to VALS(4). To re-emphasize, perhaps to the point of nausea: whenever a programmer refers to an element of a subscripted array, the quantity in parentheses must either be a constant, a variable which has previously been defined to have a value, or an expression which has a value.

<u>Exercises</u>

1. If X(1)=2, X(2)=4, and X(3)=6.5, then what value is printed below?

```
K=1
L=3
S=0
S=S+X(K)+X(L)
K=K+1
S=S+X(K)
L=L-2
S=S+X(L)
PRINT, S
```

2. If Y(1)=10, Y(2)=4, Y(3)=3.5, and Y(4)=0.5, then what value is printed below?

```
      MAD=1
      TOT=0
    7 CONTINUE
      TOT=TOT+Y(MAD)
      MAD=MAD+2
      IF (MAD.LE.4) GO TO 7
      S=TOT/Y(1)
      S=S+Y(MAD-1)
      S=S+SQRT(Y(MAD-3))
      PRINT, S
```

Input and Output of Entire Arrays

If a subscripted variable name is used in a READ or PRINT statement with a subscript appended, then just the number stored in that location is read or printed. That is,

```
REAL XXX(5)
READ, XXX(3)
```

would result in the reading of just one number; it would be stored in XXX(3). However, if the statement

```
READ, XXX
```

were executed, the effect would be to instruct the computer to read in five numbers and store them in XXX(1), XXX(2), XXX(3), XXX(4), XXX(5) respectively. The same general rule applies to the PRINT statement but one must be doubly careful to assure that each of the variables in the entire array is defined before printing an entire array. In general, then, using a subscripted variable name in an input-output statement *without* appending a subscript results in the input or output of the entire array.

Other than in I/O statements, subscripted variables may be used in all statements covered thus far in every place that scalar variables were used, but only if the subscripted variable name is appended with a subscript. For example,

```
REAL X(20)
X=0.
```

is invalid because X is being used as both a subscripted and a scalar variable in the same program. In all but input-output statements, whenever a subscripted variable is used, it must be used with a subscript. If the above example were shown as

```
REAL X(20)
X(4)=0.
```

there is no violation. Can we write the following sequence?

```
REAL Q(5)
     •
     •
IF (Q.LT.7.0) GO TO 40
```

An Example

A program appears below which reads 38 test scores into an array called SCORE, computes the average, and prints the average. For input into the program each score is keypunched onto a separate data card. The variables K and L will be used as counters and are declared INTEGER.

```
  REAL SCORE(38),AVE,SUM
  INTEGER L,K
  SUM=0.
  L=0
  K=0
5 CONTINUE
  K=K+1
  READ, SCORE(K)
  IF(K.LT.38) GO TO 5
6 CONTINUE
  L=L+1
  SUM=SUM+SCORE(L)
  IF(L.LT.38) GO TO 6
  AVE=SUM/L
  PRINT,AVE
  RETURN
  END
```

Is it necessary to use the subscripted variable SCORE in this problem? Could you make SCORE a scalar variable and do the same job? How would you rewrite the program to do this?

Another Example

Suppose 16 storage locations to be used as counters (accumulators) are needed, each of which must be initialized before use; in this case zeros will be stored in each accumulator. (An example of an accumulator is the variable "S" in the Schematic Computer.)

We could name the accumulators A, B, C, D, E, F, G, H, AA, BB, CC, DD, EE, FF, GG, HH, for example. The process of initializing them requires 16 assignment statements:

```
 A=0.
 B=0.
 C=0.
 D=0.
 E=0.
 F=0.
 G=0.
 H=0.
AA=0.
BB=0.
CC=0.
DD=0.
EE=0.
FF=0.
GG=0.
HH=0.
```

Imagine the difficulty involved in setting 200 different accumulators to zero!

An alternative here is the use of subscripted variables. The few statements required to perform the same task are:

```
  INTEGER K
  REAL A(16)
  K=0
4 CONTINUE
  K=K+1
  A(K)=0.
  IF (K.LT.16) GO TO 4
        •
        •
```

What is even more impressive is that if we truly required 200 accumulators still only 7 statements would be required. The number 200 would simply be substituted for the number 16 whenever it occurred in the above statements.

Use of Data as Subscripts

As another example of the use of subscripts consider the following problem. A programmer is given a deck of cards which represent votes for four candidates in an election.

Each card, except the last, is punched with a single number of value 1, 2, 3, or 4, indicating a single vote for candidate 1, 2, 3, or 4. The last card is punched with the value -100 and is present simply to indicate the end of the data deck. The programmer is told to write a program which will count the number of cards punched with a 1, the number punched with a 2, etc.

If he/she were doing the job by hand, a person might designate four areas on a piece of paper as 1, 2, 3, 4 and begin looking at the cards, one at a time, making marks in the appropriate areas of the paper. After looking at all the cards the number of marks in the "1" area would represent the number of "1" cards, etc.

The technique we will use with the computer is not much different. Instead of four areas on a piece of paper we will use a subscripted variable, NVOTES, which will represent four locations in a machine. The machine will initialize the four areas by putting zeros in each location. The computer will then read each card and "make a mark" by adding a 1 to the appropriate location. If, for example, a card contains a 3, the NVOTES(3) will be increased by 1. At the termination of the card-reading phase, the machine will simply print out the values of the four locations as our answers. A program to use this procedure might look like this:

```
      INTEGER I,SUB,NVOTES(4)
      I=1
  101 CONTINUE
      NVOTES(I)=0
      I=I+1
      IF (I.LE.4) GO TO 101
  102 CONTINUE
      READ, SUB
      IF (SUB.EQ.-100) GO TO 103
      NVOTES(SUB)=NVOTES(SUB) +1
      GO TO 102
  103 CONTINUE
      I=1
  104 CONTINUE
      PRINT, I, NVOTES(I)
      I=I+1
      IF (I.LE.4) GO TO 104
      RETURN
      END
```

This program reads a number and uses that number as a subscript. If you have difficulty understanding the program, go through it using the following sample data:

```
   3
   4
   3
   1
-100
```

What results should be printed using these sample data? In the above program why were the four elements of NVOTES initially set to zero?

> When you use a datum as subscript you must make super sure that it lies within the proper range. If, by accident or keypunch error, a card were read by the above program which contained the number 5, either an incorrect answer would result or the program would end abnormally (ABEND). Think about what could be done by the programmer to prevent this situation, since erroneous data are not at all uncommon.

This program also illustrates a variation on looping technique. Here again, the data determined the number of times the input loop was executed. But instead of prescribing this number in advance, the data contained a trip value (-100) which, when sensed, terminated the input loop. A trip value should be one which could not possibly be a data value. Minus 100 is certainly safe in this case -- what politician would allow himself to be so designated?

Exercises

1. In each case below, determine whether the statement set is valid or invalid, and if invalid, why? Assume that the following Type Declaration Statement applies to "a" through "f" below and that none of the locations have been defined.

```
REAL XX(100),KLAM,CAT,RAT,MOUSE,HOUSE,A
```

a. `XX(3)=5.32`

b. KLAM=50*3
XX(KLAM)=0

c. CAT=426
RAT=695
MOUSE=CAT/RAT
XX(MOUSE)=CAT*2

d. HOUSE=22
XX=HOUSE

e. HOUSE=22
XX(HOUSE)=10.01

f. A=XX(5)

2. Assume that the following variables are declared by the Type Declaration Statement:

```
REAL Y(4), B, C, D, A
```

and the values stored in them are:

Y(1)	27.
Y(2)	30.
Y(3)	35.
Y(4)	39.
B	1.
C	2.
D	4.
A	

What value is stored in A in each case below?

a. A=Y(4)+Y(3)+A

b. A=Y(D)

c. A=Y(D/C)+C/D

d. `A=Y(Y(C)-Y(B))`

e. `A=Y(D*2)`

f. `A=2.*Y(D-B)`

g. `A=Y(D**C-Y(2)/2)`

<u>Subscripted Variables -- When to Use Them</u>

When does a programmer use a subscripted variable? It's not easy to generalize, but you should keep in mind the basic ability you have when using a subscripted variable: to allow the <u>calculation</u> of part of the variable name so as to make it unnecessary to name each variable explicitly at the time the source program is written. If you have an <u>aggregate of data</u> which consists of different numbers but which is generally of the same type, you should consider representing it with a subscripted variable. For example, several thousand license numbers of cars in a particular county might be candidates for elements of a subscripted variable.

Use of a subscripted variable or array is not without its price, however. Arrays take up memory space and it takes time to calculate the subscript. If you have an aggregate of data, you should ask yourself at least one question before deciding that a subscripted array is appropriate: does the problem require that all of these data be available to the program at any time or would it be possible to hold only one or two at a time and get the same job done? If the problem is such that the first datum could be read in, processed, replaced with the second, processed, etc., then a subscripted variable is not appropriate.

LABORATORY PROBLEM 08

Write a TSF program which will read in "m" numbers, where m is specified by the data but is not more than 200. For each of these m numbers print out the number itself and, beside it, the value of the difference between the number and the average of all the numbers.

> No computer program should ever be used to solve real problems without first having test data processed for which the programmer already <u>knows</u> the correct answers. All large computer programs initially contain programming errors; some very large programs have contained bugs which were not detected for years. It is ideal to test each possible logical path through a program. For very big, complex programs this is impossible. But it is important for the programmer to create test problems which exercise as many different logic paths as are reasonably possible, concentrating upon not only typical data, but atypical values also.

Draw a flowchart in the space below <u>before</u> you write the program:

LABORATORY PROBLEM 09

A formula for the standard deviation of a set of scores is as follows:

$$\hat{\sigma} = \sqrt{\frac{\sum_{i=1}^{n} (x_i - \bar{x})^2}{n - 1}}$$

where the symbols are as defined in the flowchart below.

> Suppose that a program which you write contains an expression involving division. Could the denominator ever be zero? Under what circumstances? Should some type of test be programmed to test for a zero divisor before the division takes place?

Use the computer to find the average and the standard deviation of a set of n scores. One flowchart might be:

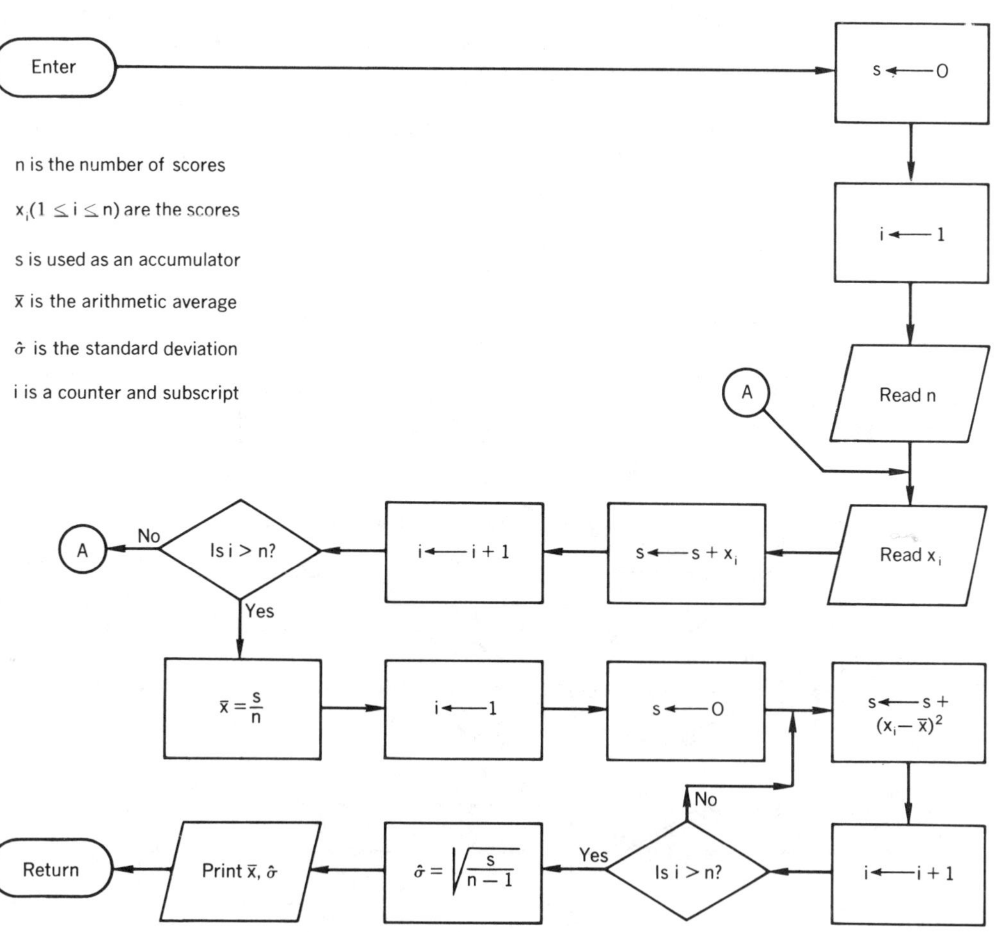
Enter
s ← 0
n is the number of scores
$x_i (1 \leq i \leq n)$ are the scores
s is used as an accumulator
$\bar{x}$ is the arithmetic average
$\hat{\sigma}$ is the standard deviation
i is a counter and subscript
i ← 1
Read n
A
Read x_i
s ← s + x_i
i ← i + 1
Is i > n?
No
A
Yes
$\bar{x} = \frac{s}{n}$
i ← 1
s ← 0
s ← s + $(x_i - \bar{x})^2$
i ← i + 1
Is i > n?
No
Yes
$\hat{\sigma} = \sqrt{\frac{s}{n-1}}$
Print $\bar{x}$, $\hat{\sigma}$
Return

LABORATORY PROBLEM 10

Use the computer to sort m numbers into ascending order using the sorting algorithm described below. Basically this algorithm sorts the numbers by what is called the tumble method. Each pair of adjacent numbers is compared. If the number in the first cell of the pair is larger than the number in the second cell, the numbers are exchanged with each other. The process is complete when each pair of cells contains numbers in the proper order. Understand completely how the algorithm works. If necessary, prepare a list of five numbers and, pretending you are the computer, follow the flowchart.

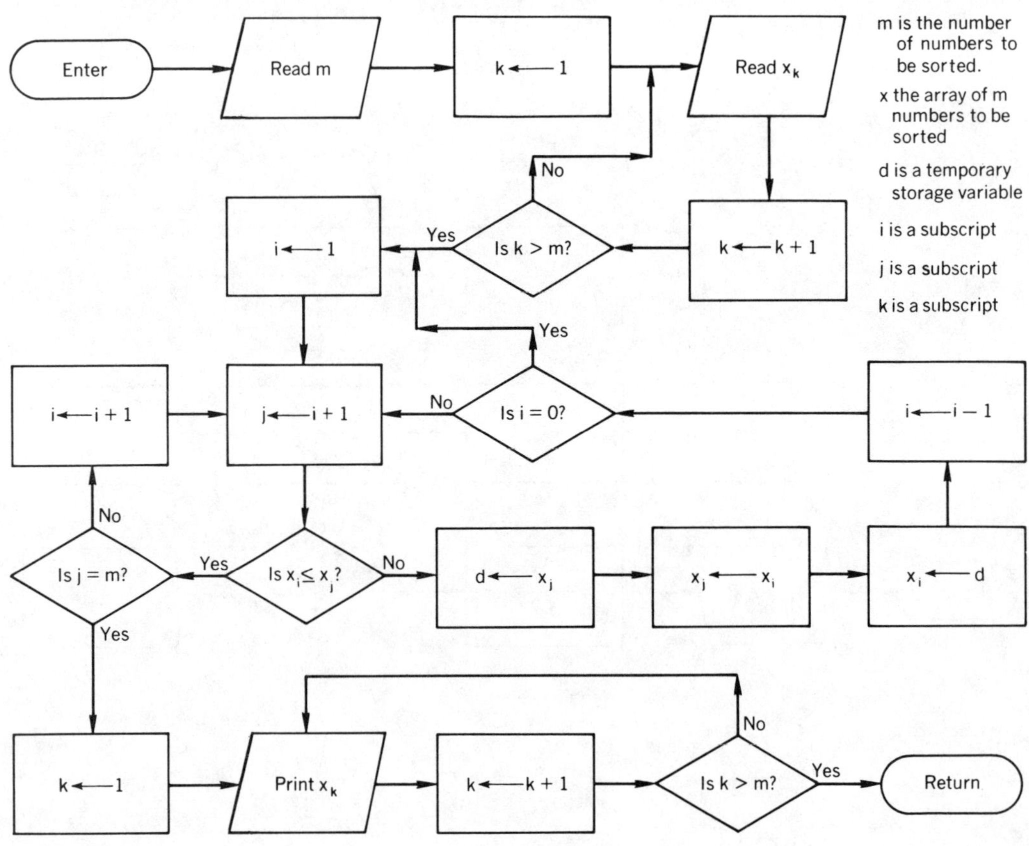

One element of a program desk check -- a careful examination of a program before its submission to the machine -- is a look at each subscript and an asking: under what conditions could this value be less than one, and under what conditions could it be greater than the limit specified by the Type statement? Subscripts which are out of the appropriate range are a common occurrence and a major nuisance. An IF statement before each subscript use is not a bad idea at all.

MULTIPLE SUBSCRIPTS

By now you can see the value of using subscripted variables for applications which require the storage of sets of data of similar types, such as the scores of several students on an exam. Storing these data under a subscripted variable allows great flexibility in performing arithmetic on and obtaining statistics from them.

It happens frequently, however, that simply numbering the locations of an array consecutively is not always the most convenient way to deal with the data. Suppose, for example, there existed a class of four students, each of whom took three exams during the term. This means we are dealing with twelve numbers. We could declare an array of these twelve numbers as

```
REAL GRADES(12)
```

which might appear as:

GRADES		Exam	Student
	GRADES(1)	1	1
	GRADES(2)	1	2
	GRADES(3)	1	3
	GRADES(4)	1	4
	GRADES(5)	2	1
	GRADES(6)	2	2
	GRADES(7)	2	3
	GRADES(8)	2	4
	GRADES(9)	3	1
	GRADES(10)	3	2
	GRADES(11)	3	3
	GRADES(12)	3	4

Here GRADES(1) is the grade of the 1st student on the 1st exam, GRADES(2) is the grade of the 2nd student on the 1st exam, and so on. If we want the average of all students on all exams we could simply add them together and divide by 12. But what if we want the average of each student or the average on each exam? Then we have to do some thinking. Which elements or cells relate to the third student? Which elements relate to the second exam? We have to contrive some scheme so that we can reference each variable if we know the exam number (1,2 or 3) and the student number (1, 2, 3 or 4). It's not too hard, actually. The reader can verify that, if I is the exam number and J is the student number, then the proper subscript value, K, is given by the formula

K=(I-1)*NS+J

where NS is the number of students. For example, the grade on the 2nd exam by the 3rd student is found in cell 7.

But there is a simpler way to think of these 12 data. Conceptualize them in "two-dimensional" fashion as three sets of four numbers each or four sets of three numbers each. Graphically, we might depict such a representation as:

SCORES

STUDENT SUBSCRIPT

EXAM SUBSCRIPT	1	2	3	4
1				
2			*	
3				

Here, for example, we would store the grade made on the second exam by the third student in the box marked *.

If we imagine the graphical representation above as an array in the machine, extending our concept of the subscripted variable a bit, we might call the location with the * by the name SCORES(2,3). Isn't that a more meaningful description of the grade on the second exam by the third student?

To declare a variable which would have twelve locations to be known as SCORES(1,1), SCORES(1,2), SCORES(1,3), SCORES(1,4), SCORES(2,1), ..., SCORES(3,4), you would write

STATEMENT NUMBER						STATEMENT
1	2	3	4	5	6	7 … 43
						REAL SCORES (3,4)

An array declared in this way is called a <u>two-dimensional array</u>, a <u>matrix variable</u>, or a <u>doubly subscripted variable</u>. Each time such a variable name is used it is appended with two subscripts, separated by a comma. The first of these indicates the row number and the second indicates the column number.

All the rules which applied to singly subscripted variables apply here.

Use of doubly subscripted variables is not much more difficult than singly subscripted variables. Consider an example using the array SCORES declared above. Here is a set of statements which would read in twelve numbers and define each member of the array SCORES.

```
      REAL SCORES(3,4)
      INTEGER I,J
      I=1
  101 CONTINUE
      J=1
  102 CONTINUE
      READ, SCORES(I,J)
      J=J+1
      IF (J.LE.4) GO TO 102
      I=I+1
      IF (I.LE.3) GO TO 101
        •
        •
        •
```

The operation of the program segment may not be immediately obvious; it involves a "loop within a loop" which, in flowchart language, might look like this:

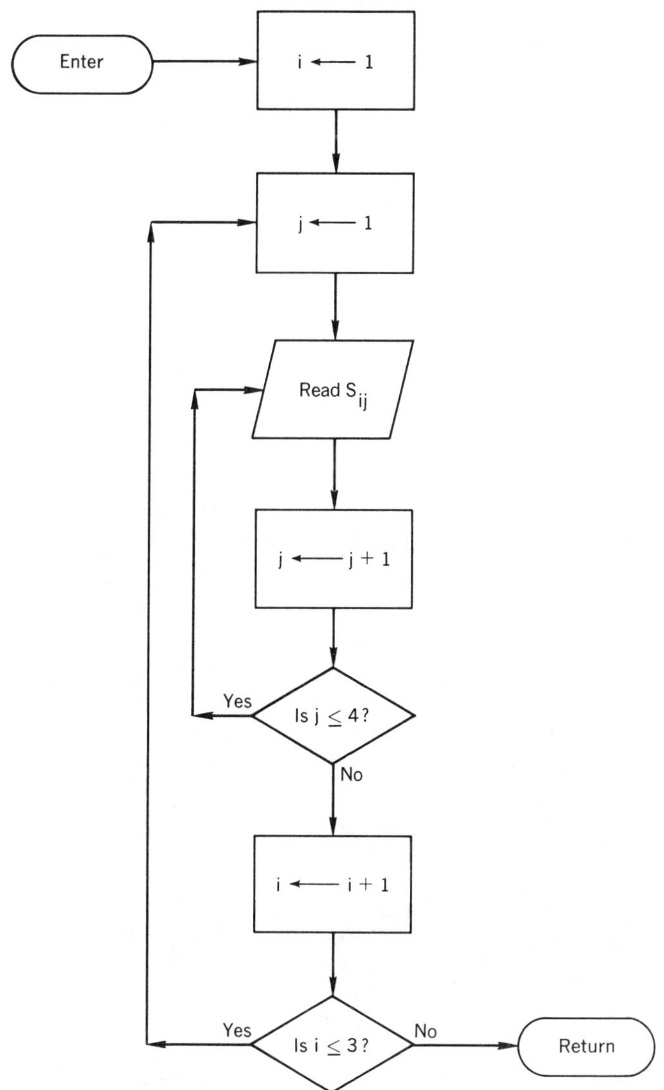
Enter
i ← 1
j ← 1
Read S_{ij}
j ← j + 1
Yes
Is j ≤ 4?
No
i ← i + 1
Yes
Is i ≤ 3?
No
Return

If you carefully follow the above algorithm through, you see that I and J take on the successive values:

I	J
1	1
1	2
1	3
1	4
2	1
2	2
2	3
2	4
3	1
3	2
3	3
3	4

which, of course, is what is desired.

If you are satisfied that you understand how the statements above define the values of the locations, we will now consider a slightly more complicated problem: assuming that twelve locations are already defined, instruct the computer to find the sum of the scores of each student. That is, we want four sums. The first represents the sum of the three numbers in the first column, etc. How might these four sums be stored? (If your answer is, "In a singly subscripted variable," give yourself ten points.) Let us declare the variable STUDNT:

```
REAL STUDNT(4)
```

Now we could write the statements to form the sums. When we were adding up several numbers in a loop using scalar variables we used a statement

```
S=S+X
```

to accumulate the values of X. Clearly such a procedure would work only if we defined S to be zero before we began the addition process.

In our present problem we are faced with a similar situation. Now we must define four accumulators to have the value zero. A previous example, using the variable NVOTES, showed how this could be accomplished. Assuming that this piece of housekeeping has been done, we write the statements that will actually form the four sums. As in reading numbers into the two-dimensional array, this process requires one loop <u>nested</u> inside another. In this example we will consider the scores in column-wise order. (Before, we operated on them in a row-wise order.)

```
            .
            .
            .
        J=1
    104 CONTINUE
        I=1
    105 CONTINUE
        STUDNT(J)=STUDNT(J)+SCORES(I,J)
        I=I+1
        IF (I.LE.3) GO TO 105
        J=J+1
        IF (J.LE.4) GO TO 104
            .
            .
            .
```

At the conclusion of this set of statements each number in the array will have been added into the appropriate accumulator; the singly subscripted array STUDNT could now be printed out to give the column sums.

Question: if we had operated on SCORES in row-wise order, would we have computed the same answer for the values of STUDNT(1), STUDNT(2), etc.?

The TSF language does not limit construction of arrays to only one or two dimensions. Arrays of 3, 4, 5 and more dimensions are available. Of course, as the number of elements in arrays increases, the amount of computer storage used grows also. Therefore, very large, multi-dimensional arrays are not practical.

To illustrate the declaration of a five-dimensional array, we could write

```
REAL X(5,7,10,20,9)
```

This statement attempts to reserve an array of five dimensions which contains a total of 63,000 variable locations, an amount not normally available to programmers.

Exercises

1. What, if anything, might be wrong with the following statements?

```
a.  RAT(LAND)=RAT(LAND,WATER)+5
b.  X(5)=X(SQRT(A+B))
c.  ABCDEFG(1)=88
d.  POT(0)=POT(1)*POT(3)
e.  ZEBRA=STRIP(1,2,5,KING)
f.  RRRRRR(AAAAAA,BBBBBB)=TTTTTT(RRRRRR,QQQQQQ)
g.  X(L)=X
```

2. Suppose that the values below reside in memory.

RUM

37.	.55	2.0
4.0	10.0	100.0

K	2
WW	1
VV	0.
UU	-4.
R	3

Using the above data, what value is stored in VV in each statement below?

```
a.  VV=RUM(2,K)
b.  VV=RUM(K,WW)*RUM(WW,K)
c.  VV=RUM(K,K)+UU
d.  VV=RUM(2,K+WW)/RUM(RUM(WW,R),K*WW+WW)
```

LABORATORY PROBLEM 11

Based on the previous example with the array SCORES, write a complete program which will find and print the average of the scores of each student, the average of the scores made on each of the three exams, and the average of all students on all exams. Supply the data for the problem and check the results.

Draw a flowchart in the space below before writing the program:

<u>Before</u> you run a set of test data, work out the answers you expect the computer to reproduce. It is too easy to be prejudiced toward the answers your program produces if you wait until after the run to work out the test results. Besides, you will probably learn something about your problem by actually getting your hands dirty with some data.

SUMMARY OF RULES FOR SUBSCRIPTED VARIABLES

1. Subscripted variables must be declared exactly once in a program, using a Type Declaration Statement which specifies the Type (REAL or INTEGER) and the number of locations to be reserved. For example,

```
REAL V(20)
```

or

```
INTEGER BATMAN(3)
```

2. Declaration does not define variables. Values are not stored in an array by simply declaring a variable as subscripted. For example,

```
REAL Q(5)
Q(2)=Q(2)+1
```

is an invalid sequence since Q(2) is undefined.

3. If the subscript is REAL any fractional portion is ignored and the INTEGER portion is used as the subscript. For example, in the statements

```
REAL A, X(20)
    .
    .
    .
A=3.96
X(A)=456.7
```

X(A) refers to the third location in the X array and consequently X(3) will take on the value 456.7.

> Subscripts may be INTEGER or REAL constants, variables, or expressions. However, using REAL numbers as subscripts wastes computer time since they are converted to INTEGERs prior to use.

4. The subscript may be any valid arithmetic expression, either INTEGER or REAL, as defined earlier, except that the non-fractional value of the subscript must be:

a. greater than or equal to one.
b. not greater than the constant specified in the Type Declaration Statement.

For example, assume X is an array with 8 locations declared REAL by REAL X(8). Then the various forms of X(subscript) are valid or invalid as shown below:

invalid	valid
X(-5)	X(1)
X(0)	X(4)
X(12)	X(8)
X(0.2)	X(1.3)
X(9.2)	X(8.7)

5. If a variable is used as a subscript it must have been previously defined either by a READ or an arithmetic assignment statement. For example,

```
REAL Y(4)
Y(I)=25.2
```

is invalid since the value of I has not been previously defined. If an expression is used as a subscript, all the variables in it must have been previously defined.

6. The value in parentheses in the Type Declaration Statement _must be an INTEGER constant_. The statement

```
REAL GG(33.4)
```

is invalid because 33.4 is not an INTEGER. The INTEGER constant which appears in the Type Declaration Statement is not a subscript; it is a memory reservation quantity. Do not confuse a subscript, which may be a constant, a variable, or an arithmetic expression, with the reservation quantity in a Type Declaration Statement, which may be _only an INTEGER constant_.

The Type Declaration Statement tells the computer, during the _translation_ or _compilation_ of the program, what variable names to expect and how many locations are to be devoted to each. But a statement such as

```
READ, M
```

does not define the value of M until the execution of the program, so the statement

```
REAL X(M)
```

could not inform the computer how many locations it should set aside for the array X at the time the program is compiled.

7. The name which is selected as a subscripted variable is arbitrarily chosen by the programmer just as names of scalar variables are chosen. The name can consist of from one to six capital letters.

Developing variable names which are short enough, meaningful, and unique is an art in itself. We won't suggest any techniques but advise simply that you develop one and stick to it. Most importantly, once you have decided on a variable name, write it down and write down what it means. Then refer to that definition whenever you use the name again if you have the slightest doubt that you are using the right name. Perhaps then you won't use both TTP and TPP for total population in the same program.

8. A program must not contain a scalar variable and a subscripted variable by the same name.

9. Of the FORTRAN statements covered thus far (except input or output statements) a subscripted variable name must be appended by a subscript which is enclosed in parentheses. For example,

```
REAL YAM(4)
YAM=0.
```

is invalid since we do not specify which location of YAM is to be changed.

10. A subscript is not a variable! A subscript is a number. You may use a constant to stand for that number or you may use a variable to stand for that number, but the subscript itself, at the time a program statement is executed, is a number.

In general, arithmetic involving INTEGER variables is faster. So when only whole numbers are required, using INTEGER variables can improve program run times. In Fortran, if REAL variables are employed as subscripts, the situation is even worse. Fortran will convert the REAL subscript to an INTEGER (to insure only integral values) before attempting to use it. This can significantly degrade program performance. A similar phenomenon occurs when INTEGER and REAL variables (or constants) are both employed in the same operation in an assignment statement. The INTEGER variables are first converted to REAL values and only then used in computation.

part ii

essential fortran iv

FROM TSF TO FORTRAN IV

If you solved the Laboratory Problems in Part I, you now have a practical understanding of Ten Statement Fortran and the tools to work almost any numerical problem amenable to solution by Fortran. The full Fortran IV Language, however, allows many statements which make it a more flexible language than TSF. In addition, Fortran IV allows the computer to handle non-numeric information. Fortran IV is a complex and powerful language, but if you have been able to master the concepts in Ten Statement Fortran, you should have little trouble in going further.

As a first step in expanding TSF into full Fortran IV, some simple language extensions are presented.

Variable Names

In TSF variable names can only consist of capital letters.

In full Fortran IV a variable name may consist of from one to six alphabetic <u>or</u> <u>numeric</u> characters (hereafter referred to as <u>alphanumeric</u> or <u>alphameric</u> characters) with the restriction that the first character of the name must be alphabetic.[1] No characters other than alphanumeric ones are legal in variable names. Hence the following are legal variable names:

```
A12345    ALP2D    I88888    Z1Y2X3    RS28P4
```

> Imbedding digits in variable names is not a very good idea. Particularly avoid using a zero in variable names; it looks too much like the letter O. You might think that a high-powered industry like the computing one could settle on a standard way of differentiating zero and the letter O, but no such luck. A slash through the character is a good differentiator, but some of us

---

[1] In IBM 360/370 Fortran, WATFOR, and WATFIV, the $ is defined as an alphabetic character. Names such as

```
ABC$        PZ$50
$2150       $$$$$$
```

are valid.

slash zeros and some of us slash the letter O. Stupid, huh?

The following names are illegal. Why?

a.	A38&P	b.	B2.GG3
c.	3ALPHA	d.	HASHISH
e.	X3/Y4	f.	I(BK@

Implicit or Default Typing

If a programmer fails to declare a scalar variable in a Type Declaration statement, it will automatically be typed as either REAL or INTEGER according to the following rule: if the first character of the variable name is one of the six letters I, J, K, L, M, or N, the variable is treated as an INTEGER quantity. Otherwise the variable is considered REAL.

Exercise

In a program devoid of Type Declaration statements, what types would be assigned to the following variable names?

a. IPQ
b. L
c. XYZ
d. AIBJ
e. IAJB
f. X5
g. NOT
h. MEAN
i. AVERAG

It is possible to change the rule for default typing by an IMPLICIT statement which is discussed in Module 10.

We strongly recommend the practice of listing each variable name used in a program in a Type Declaration Statement.

Statement Numbers

Some background first: non-executable statements are those statements which provide the computer with information which assists it in translating the program from Fortran to its own language during the compilation phase of the job. Executable statements are those which result in actual instructions to the machine to perform operations such as input, computation, etc., during the execution phase of the job. Thus far, the only statement which could be numbered has been the CONTINUE statement. However, Fortran allows the numbering of any executable statement in a similar manner but does not allow non-executable statements (with one exception to be discussed later) to be numbered. A full list of executable statements appears in Module 15.

The executable statements (any of which may be numbered in columns 1-5) which have been discussed thus far are:

```
      READ, list
      variable=expression
      PRINT, list
      RETURN
      IF(expression reop expression) GO TO stno
      GO TO stno
stno  CONTINUE
```

whereas the non-executable statements (which may not be numbered) which have been discussed thus far are:

```
      REAL list
      INTEGER list
      END
```

> The practice of numbering only CONTINUE statements has much to recommend it. It facilitates modifying programs, it helps find and correct errors in computer programs (debugging) and it simplifies some of the complexities which occur with other Fortran statements to be covered later.

Long Statements: Continuation

Fortran statements are punched in columns 7 through 72 and columns 1 through 5 are reserved for statement numbers.

Thus 66 columns are normally reserved for statements exclusive of the statement number. This leads to the question: what if the desired Fortran statement is longer than 66 characters? The answer is quite simple: the statement is "continued" on the following card starting in card column 7. This next card is called a continuation card and it is characterized by blanks in columns 1 through 5 and <u>any</u> character, except zero or blank, in card column 6. Normal Fortran statement cards, as you will remember, must be blank in card column 6. Up to 19 continuation cards are allowed to form a Fortran statement.

Statement Card Identification

Card columns 73 through 80 may contain any identifying alphanumeric information such as program name and card sequence numbers. The example shown next illustrates Fortran statements which span more than one actual card and also the use of columns 73 to 80 for identifying the sequence of the card deck in case the deck is accidentally scrambled.

STATEMENT NUMBER (1–5)	6	STATEMENT (7–72)	IDENTIFICATION SEQUENCE (73–80)
$JØB		NAME	
		REAL A,B,C,SUM	PGM A 10
		INTEGER I,J,K	PGM A 20
		READ,A,B,C	PGM A 30
		SUM= A*2 + B*2 + C*2 +	PGM A 40
	1	SQRT(A+B+C)	PGM A 50
		SUM=SUM+	PGM A 60
	1	B+C+	PGM A 70
	2	A*2.5	PGM A 80

There are two kinds of programmers in the world: those who have dropped an important deck of cards and those who are going to. Sequence numbers can make the difference between being able to put the deck back together again quickly -- perhaps with a card sorter -- and spending an evening with a huge pile of cards and a listing of the program. Incidentally, many computing centers have programs which will automatically punch a sequentially numbered deck for you.

An Extension of the Logical IF

In TSF the logical IF statement has the form:

```
IF (expression reop expression) GO TO stno
```

The logical IF statement was introduced in this form for simplicity. In the full Fortran IV language, the

```
GO TO stno
```

part of the statement (called a trailer) can be any executable Fortran statement except the DO statement (which is covered in the next section) or another logical IF statement.

Thus one might write logical IF statements such as:

```
IF (A.LT.B) PRINT,A,B
IF (LAST.EQ.99) RETURN
```

The basic idea of the statement has not changed, however. If the expression within the parentheses is TRUE, the trailer of the IF statement is executed. If the expression is FALSE, the trailer is skipped and the next statement in sequence is executed. If the expression is TRUE and the trailer does not transfer control (e.g., the trailer is an assignment, READ, or PRINT statement), the trailer is executed and then the statement after the IF is executed.

Examples:

a. In the program segment

```
INTEGER M,N,Q,R
M=0
N=1
Q=2
R=3
IF(M.LE.N)R=R+1
IF(N.GE.Q)R=R+5
IF(M.LT.R)R=R+10
PRINT,R
```

the value 14 would be printed.

b. In the segment

```
INTEGER M,N,Q,R
M=0
N=1
Q=2
R=3
IF(R*M-Q.LE.0)PRINT,R
IF(N.EQ.0)PRINT,Q
```

the value 3 would be printed.

Exercises:

1. If the INTEGERs M, N, Q, and R contained the values 1, 2, 3, and 4 respectively, which of the following statements would cause printing to occur?

   a. `IF(M*N*Q.EQ.R)PRINT,R`
   b. `IF(R/2*2-R.EQ.0)PRINT,Q`
   c. `IF(N*2.EQ.R)PRINT,M`

2. Which of the following statements contain errors? Why?

   a. `IF 3*N.EQ.M GO TO 7`
   b. `IF(M.LG.N) RETURN`
   c. `IF(T(3).LT.0) T(3)=0`
   d. `IF(A-B) GO TO 334`
   e. `IF(C*D.NE..5) PRINT,E`
   f. `IF(37..LE..75) IF(A.EQ.B)GO TO 8`
   g. `IF(RATS.LE.MICE) PRINT, A,B,C`
   h. `IF(A-B)*C.LE.100) GO TO 85`
   i. `7 IF(N.EQ.0) GO TO 7`

A SIMPLIFIED LOOPING STRUCTURE: DO INSTEAD OF IF

In previous examples the following flowchart structure was presented:

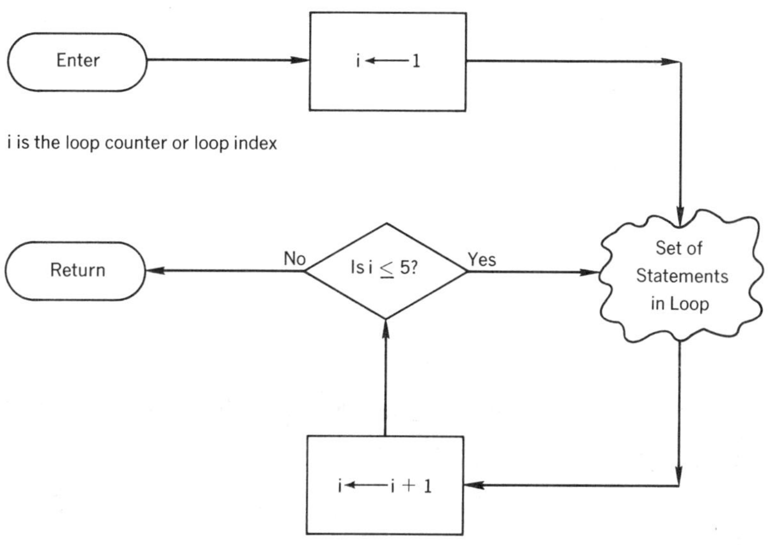

Figure 1

This structure will result in the "set of statements in loop" block being executed 5 times; i (for index) will take on the values 1, 2, 3, 4, 5.

A more general form of this structure follows, in which the constants in the above flowchart are replaced by variables.

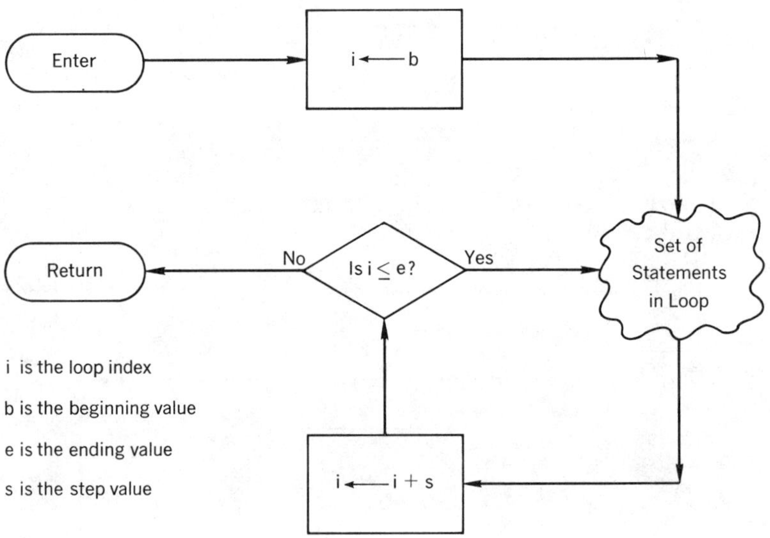

Figure 2

This would be identical to the previous example if b (for begin) were defined as 1, e (for end) were defined as 5, and s (for step) were defined as 1.

Consider an alternative flowchart for this structure.

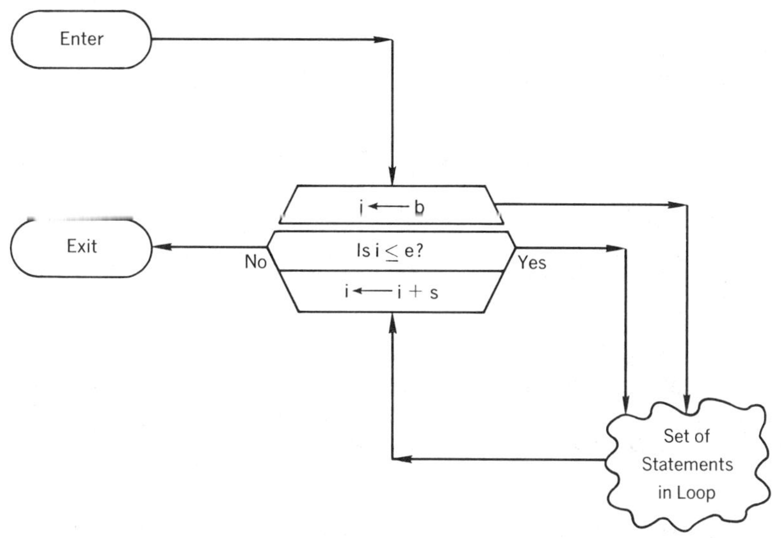

Figure 3

Using this notation, the hexagonal block is entered either at the top or bottom and the appropriate arithmetic replacement takes place (i.e., either i is set equal to b, or i is incremented by s). Control then passes to either the next block in sequence or to the center of the block where the question "is i≤e?" is asked.

The answer to this question dictates the next step of the program. It is important to understand the similarity between Figures 2 and 3 before continuing.

The DO Statement

To implement the flowchart of Figure 2 one might use the following coding which is sometimes called an IF loop. Assume that I, B, E and S have been declared INTEGER non-subscripted variables.

```
      I=B
    2 CONTINUE
      "set of statements in loop"
      I=I+S
      IF (I.LE.E) GO TO 2
```

Because this structure recurs so frequently in computer programming a special statement has been devised which accomplishes all the tasks outlined by the hexagonal block in Figure 3 plus the job of branching back to the beginning of the loop.

A statement of this type is called a DO statement. A programmer might use the DO statement (or DO loop) to code the flowchart in Figure 3 as follows:

```
      DO 2 I=B,E,S
      "set of statements in loop"
    2 CONTINUE
```

In words this DO statement means: set I equal to B. Execute all statements following the DO statement up to and including the statement

```
    2 CONTINUE
```

Increment I by S and test to see if I is less than or equal to E. If I is less than or equal to E then transfer to the statement <u>immediately following the DO statement</u>. Repeat the procedure of executing statements down to and including 2 CONTINUE, incrementing I, and testing I against E until I becomes greater than E. When I becomes greater than E, pass control to the statement <u>immediately following</u> 2 CONTINUE.

More rigorously, the general form of the DO statement is:

```
      DO stno i=b,e,s
```

where i is an INTEGER scalar variable, b, e, and s are INTEGER scalar variables or INTEGER constants such that

b is ≥ 1
e is $\geq b$ but $\leq 2147483647 - s$
s is ≥ 1

and stno is a statement number. The variable i is called the index of the loop; the quantities b, e, and s are called the parameters of the loop.

The range of the DO statement is defined to be all statements immediately following the DO statement down to, and including, the statement numbered stno. Thus the range of the DO contains those statements included within the bracket as follows:

```
        DO |stno| i=b,e,s
  ┌              .
  │              .
  │              .
  │              .
  └ |stno| CONTINUE
```

It is quite important to note that the DO statement itself is not within the range of the DO. Whenever a DO statement itself is encountered in the sequence of the program it causes initialization (or re-initialization) of the DO index i to the value b. Then the statements in the range of the DO are repeatedly executed while i takes on values b, b+s, b+2s, b+3s, b+4s,... until i becomes greater than e, at which point the execution of statements within the loop is completed. The path of control then goes to the first executable statement following the range of the DO. The completion of a DO loop in this manner is termed a normal exit.

Consider the program segment:

```
      INTEGER I
      REAL A                "I" is undefined in this part of
      A=1.                        the program.
      DO 3 I=1,5,1
  ┌   PRINT, I, A           This is the range of the DO where
  │   A=A*2.                      "I" takes on values
  └ 3 CONTINUE                    1, 2, 3, 4, and 5.
        .
        .                   "I" is undefined below the
        .                         statement "3 CONTINUE"
```

The segment would print 5 lines:

```
1     1.
2     2.
3     4.
4     8.
5    16.
```

The same effect could also be achieved with an IF loop, although less efficiently as far as programming effort is concerned.

```
      INTEGER I
      REAL A
      A=1.
      I=1
    4 CONTINUE
      PRINT, I,A
      A=A*2.
      I=I+1
      IF (I.LE.5) GO TO 4
```

Whether an IF loop or a DO loop is used, each new cycle through some or all of the statements in the loop is called an <u>iteration</u>.

Syntax of the DO Statement

The components of the DO statement are diagrammed below:

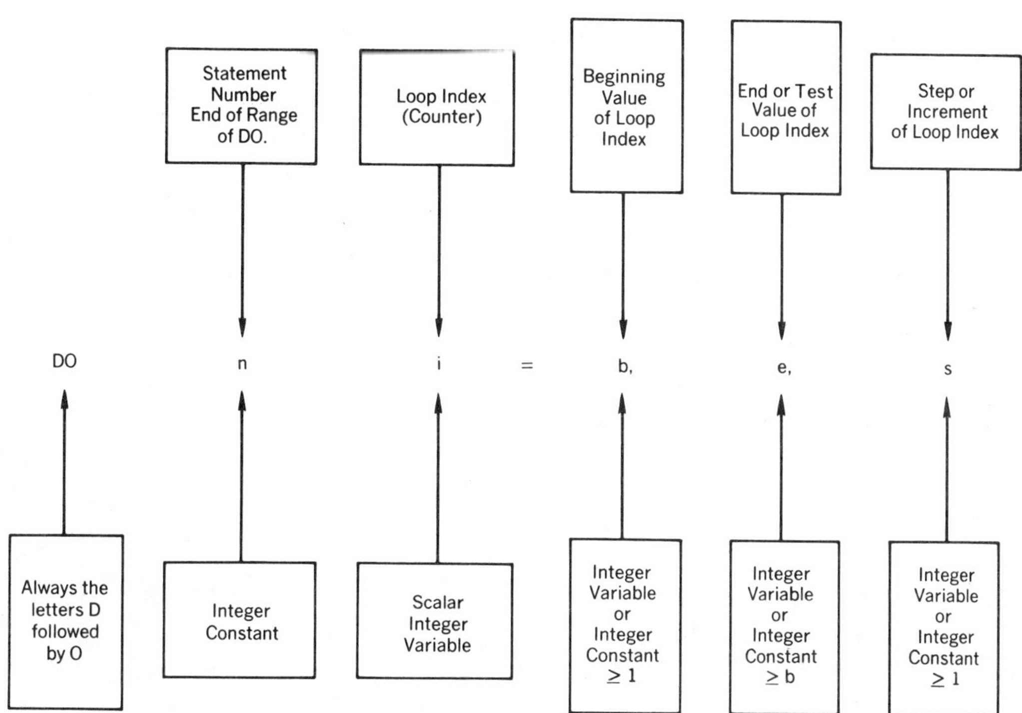

Figure 4

Exercises

1. In each of the following, what number, if any, would be printed? Assume implicit variable typing.

a.
```
      N=0
      DO 3 KLAM=1,12,1
      N=N+2
    3 CONTINUE
      PRINT, N
```

b.
```
      N=1
      NN=5
```

```
      DO 3 J=NN,11,2
      N=N+1
    3 CONTINUE
      PRINT, N
```

c.

```
      N=0
      NNN=10
      DO 3 JAY=1,NNN,1
      N=N+JAY
    3 CONTINUE
      PRINT, N
```

d.

```
      N=0
    2 CONTINUE
      DO 3 K=1,5,1
      N=N+K
      IF (N.LT.3) GO TO 2
    3 CONTINUE
      PRINT, N
```

2. What errors exist in each of the following?

a.

```
      N=0
      DO 3 K=1,5,1
      N=N+1
    3 CONTINUE
      PRINT, N, K
```

b.

```
      N=42
      NN=N/100
      BETA=7
      DO 3 A=NN,BETA,1
      N=N+2
    3 CONTINUE
      PRINT, N
```

c.

```
      DO 3 K=1,5,1
      K=K+1
    3 CONTINUE
      PRINT, K
```

d.

```
      N=0
      DO 5 K=10,1,-1
      N=N+1
    5 CONTINUE
      PRINT, N
```

Further Considerations Regarding the DO

A question might be asked now: what happens if s is not 1 and the value of the index does not ever become exactly e? Or, by example, how many lines would be printed by:

```
      DO 388 K=1,12,3
      PRINT, K
  388 CONTINUE
```

The answer comes quickly from examining the defining flowchart of Figure 3 using b as 1, e as 12, and s as 3. The printed lines would be:

```
 1
 4
 7
10
```

That is, the index takes on successively higher values up to the highest value which does not exceed the end (or test) value.[1]

There are certain rules to be followed in the use of the DO loop:

1. The programmer must not cause the values i, b, e, or s to be changed within the loop (the range of the DO). It would be incorrect to write:

   ```
         DO 15 I=1,10,1
         READ, I
      15 CONTINUE
   ```

   You'd give the machine a case of indigestion!

2. It is permissible to transfer out of the range of a DO at any time. The program:

---

[1] A DO loop will be executed [(e-b)/s]+1 times where the contents of [ ] means the greatest integer value contained in the expression. In the example of DO 388 K=1,12,3 we have [(12-1)/3]+1 = [3.67]+1 = 3+1 = 4. It might be easier to count on your fingers.

```
      REAL A
      INTEGER J
      A=10.
      DO 28 J=1,15,1
      A=A*.5
      IF (A.LT.1.)  GO TO 589
      PRINT, A
   28 CONTINUE
  589 CONTINUE
```

is perfectly permissible but will print only

```
5.
2.5
1.25
```

because the IF statement transfers control to a statement outside the range of the DO when A becomes less than 1, rather than when J surpasses 15. If the DO loop is ended in this manner, the value of the index J outside the loop retains the value it had at the time of the <u>abnormal exit</u>. In this case J would have the value of 4.

It is important to know that if the DO loop ends normally the index of the loop is not defined outside the loop; it cannot be used on the right side of an = symbol or in a PRINT statement without first having a value reassigned to it.

3. It is not permissible to transfer into the range of a DO from outside the range. That is:

```
      GO TO 96
      DO 944 KATS=IB,IE,IS
   96 CONTINUE
  944 CONTINUE
```

is illegal because statement 96 is within range of the DO. Would a transfer to statement 944 be legal? Why?

4. A DO statement may not be used as the trailer of a logical IF statement. For example, a statement such as

```
      IF(X.NE.Y) DO 15 I=1,3,1
```

is <u>not</u> legal.

When you put a statement in a loop it is usually going to be executed more than one time --

often many, many times. So you should be careful that you aren't repeatedly doing something within the loop that could be done outside. For a trivial example, say you want to write a loop to compute the areas of circles from their diameters:

$$a = \frac{\pi d^2}{4}$$

Don't write

```
         DO 101 I=1,N,1
         A(I)=3.141593*D(I)**2/4.
     101 CONTINUE
```

but compute outside of the loop that part of the arithmetic that doesn't change, e.g.,

```
         PIOVR4=3.141593/4.
         DO 101 I=1,N,1
         A(I)=PIOVR4*D(I)**2
     101 CONTINUE
```

Some people would suggest that you ought to compute pi over four independently of the computer program and put it in as a constant; we wouldn't. Computers do arithmetic faster and, more importantly in this case, with greater accuracy than do people.

<u>Nest of DOs</u>

We now look at the "set of statements in loop" block of Figure 2. Is it not possible for that block also to contain a loop? For example:

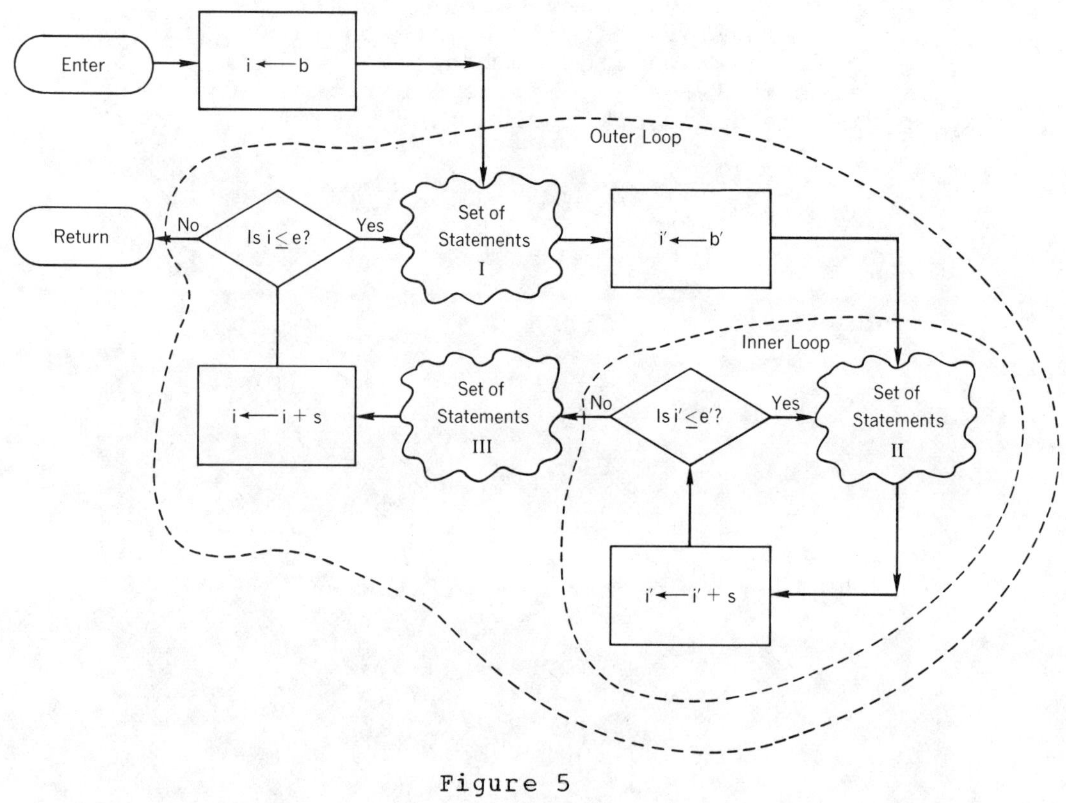

Figure 5

or, diagrammed by the new technique:

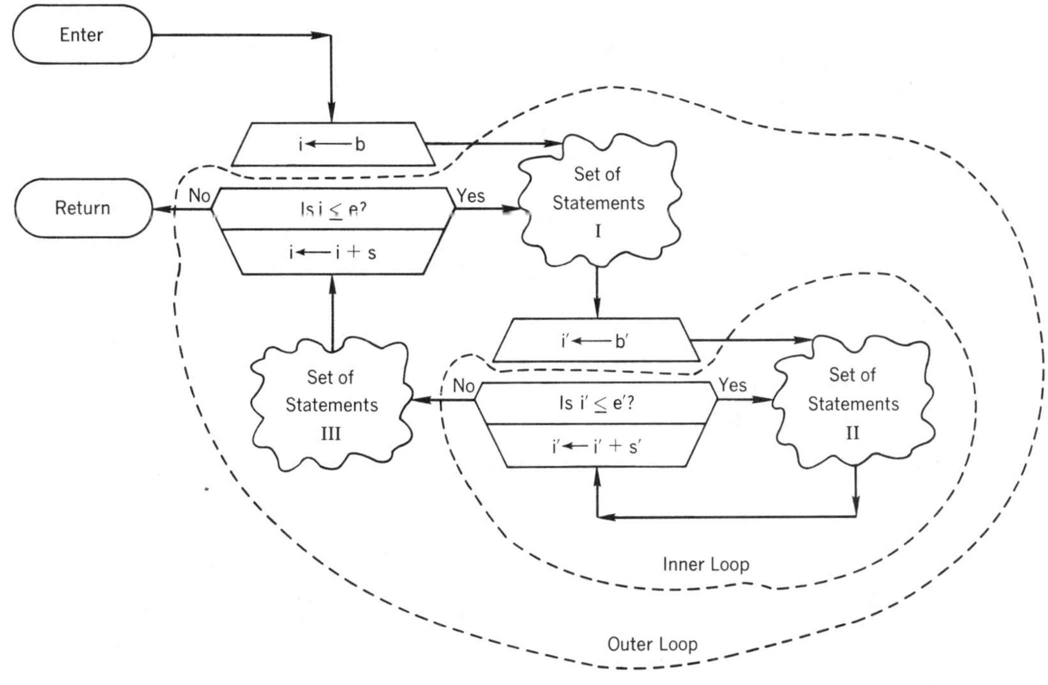

Figure 6

Programming for these two structures might appear as follows. First the structure appears without the use of the DO; this is diagrammed in Figure 5.

```
C THE VARIABLE NAMES IP, BP, EP AND SP RELATE
C TO IPRIME, BPRIME, EPRIME AND SPRIME IN THE
C FLOWCHART
      INTEGER I,B,E,S,IP,BP,EP,SP
        .
        .
        .
      I=B
   35 CONTINUE
        .
        .            set of statements I
        .
      IP=BP
   61 CONTINUE
        .
        .            set of statements II
        .
      IP=IP+SP
      IF (IP.LE.EP) GO TO 61
        .
        .            set of statements III
        .
      I=I+S
      IF (I.LE.E) GO TO 35
```

Using the DO loop, the structure appears as diagrammed in Figure 6.

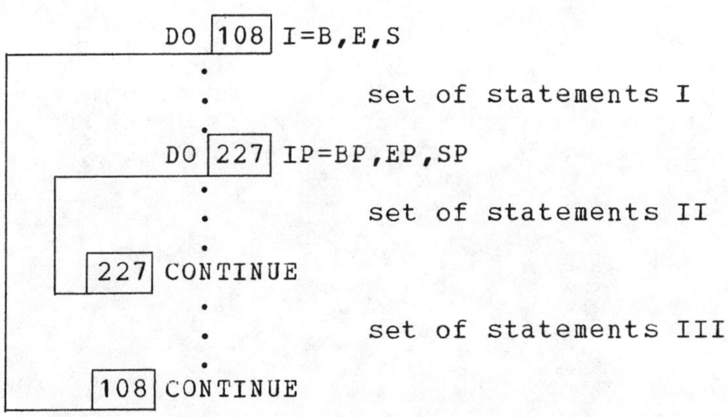

The arrangement of DO loops such as the one above is called, seriously, a <u>nest</u> or a <u>nested DO</u>.

How many lines would be printed by:

```
         DO 18 I=1,4,1
         DO 28 J=1,2,1
         DO 38 K=1,3,1
         PRINT, I,J,K
      38 CONTINUE
      28 CONTINUE
      18 CONTINUE
```

Analysis could proceed as follows: the innermost DO will, by itself, cause three lines to be printed.

The middle DO will cause the innermost DO to be executed two times, thus causing 2•3 or 6 lines to be printed.

The outermost DO will cause the middle DO to be executed four times, so the print statement will be executed 4•6 (4•2•3) times or 24 times. Specifically, the printed output would be:

```
1 1 1
1 1 2
1 1 3
1 2 1
1 2 2
1 2 3
2 1 1
2 1 2
2 1 3
2 2 1
2 2 2
2 2 3
3 1 1
3 1 2
3 1 3
3 2 1
3 2 2
3 2 3
4 1 1
4 1 2
4 1 3
4 2 1
4 2 2
4 2 3
```

A rule in the use of nested DO loops is that the inner loop(s) must be completely contained within the outer loop(s). That is,

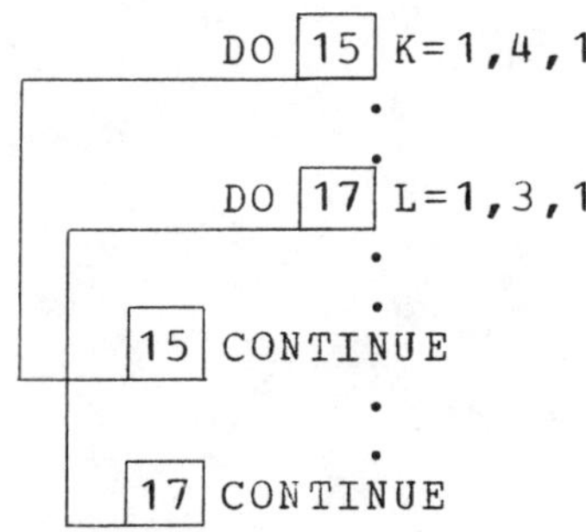

is not allowed. A further point is that although

```
      DO 22 M=1,6,1
            .
            .
      DO 22 N=1,5,1
            .
            .
   22 CONTINUE
```

will sometimes work properly, it is not good practice because it may produce unpredictable results. Preferable is

```
      DO 22 M=1,6,1
            .
            .
      DO 28 N=1,5,1
            .
            .
   28 CONTINUE
            .
            .
   22 CONTINUE
```

where the inner loop is totally contained within the outer loop.

> In fact, it is a good idea to have a unique statement number for <u>every</u> statement number reference in the program. Such a practice facilitates program modification and debugging.

DO Loops and Subscripted Variables

The DO statement performs the four required steps for looping:

1. Index initialization,

2. Index testing,

3. Index incrementing,

4. Transfer to the top of the loop.

The index of a DO can therefore be thought of as a counter which changes each time the loop has been executed.

Since the counter is being incremented each time through the loop, it is often convenient also to use this index as a subscript. For example, if you wanted to store zeros in each of 100 locations of an array named AXE it could be done as follows:

```
      INTEGER K
      REAL AXE(100)
      DO 23 K=1,100,1
      AXE(K)=0.
   23 CONTINUE
```

The following segment would read up to 25 numbers into the array SCORES.

```
      INTEGER I,K
      REAL SCORES(25),S
      READ, K
      DO 9991 I=1,K,1
      READ, SCORES(I)
 9991 CONTINUE
```

To find the sum of the 1st, 3rd, 5th, ..., 15th values one might add the statements:

```
      S=0.
      DO 55 K=1,15,2
      S=S+SCORES(K)
   55 CONTINUE
```

A nest of loops can be used to manipulate multi-dimensional arrays. For example:

```
      INTEGER I,J
      REAL COW(8,200) , S(8)
      DO 228 I=1,5,1
      S(I)=0.
      DO 339 J=1,120,1
      READ, COW(I,J)
      S(I)=S(I)+COW(I,J)
  339 CONTINUE
  228 CONTINUE
```

reads 600 numbers into the array COW and adds up each separate group of 120 placing the five sums in the array "S."

The rules regarding transfer in and out of DO loops apply as well to nested loops.

Some of the valid and invalid transfers are shown in the following example.

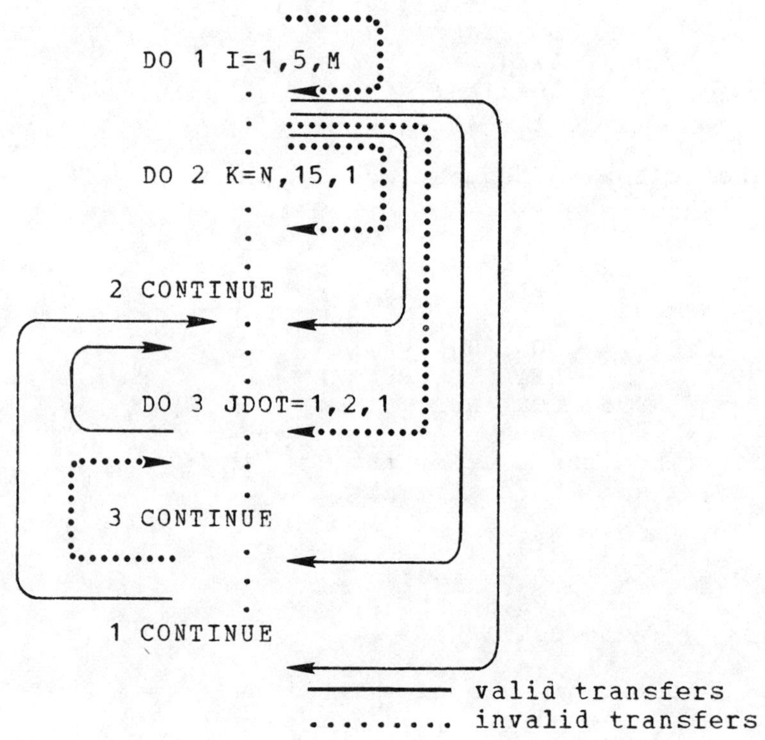

Array Use

Arrays come hard to some students, no doubt about it. But once a student has mastered the concept a new problem sometimes rears its head: overuse. The primary purpose of an array is to permit storage of like data in a way which facilitates processing it in various ways. But many times arrays are used when these requirements just don't exist -- when, for example, the data are simply used once in the order in which they are put in. As a trivial example, consider that

```
          REAL A,S,X(20)
          INTEGER I
          DO 101 I=1,20
          READ, X(I)
      101 CONTINUE
          S=0.
          DO 102 I=1,20
          S=S+X(I)
      102 CONTINUE
          A=S/20
          DO 103 I=1,20
          PRINT, X(I)
      103 CONTINUE
          PRINT, S,A
```

can be shortened to

```
          REAL A, S, X
          INTEGER I
          S=0.
          DO 101 I=1,20
          READ, X
          S=S+X
          PRINT, X
      101 CONTINUE
          A=S/20
          PRINT, S,A
```

Who, you ask, would be silly enough to write the program the first way? Even if the array were needed, who would use three loops instead of one? We'll tell you who. Some beginning students who became enamored of arrays and DO loops, that's who. And some pretty experienced programmers who just got into the habit of doing all the input, all the computation, and finally, all the output using arrays.

Before you use an array you should ask yourself several questions:

1) Would a scalar variable do the same job? That is, could a single location in the computer, used sucessively (as in the example above), produce the same effect?

2) If an array is necessary, is it possible to use a previously used array name which doesn't contain information necessary for subsequent calculation?

3) If the array you are about to declare is needed, how many dimensions does it need to have? Oftentimes problems are stated in terms which imply a greater number of dimensions than are actually needed for processing. If, for example, you were asked to add two matrices, element by element, you could declare them as two-dimensional arrays but you could accomplish the same task by simply pretending they were two vectors and adding those, element by element. This would not save space but it would save time, because two subscripts take longer to calculate than one does.

Implied Step Parameter

Many loops call for an increment (step) of one (1) for each iteration. To facilitate programming such loops, the form of the DO statement may be shortened from:

```
DO stno i=b,e,s
```

to

```
DO stno i=b,e
```

if you want s to be one (1).

Thus the statements

```
DO 15 J=K,L,1
```

and

```
DO 15 J=K,L
```

say precisely the same thing. Only the step parameter can be omitted--all others must always be present. If the step parameter is omitted, the preceding comma must also be omitted.

Summary of Rules for DO Statements

1. The parameters of the DO statement (b, e, and s) should not be changed by a statement within the range of the DO. Good programming practice also forbids changing the value of the loop index.

2. If DO statements are nested, all statements in the range of an inner DO must also be within the range of the outer DO.

3. A transfer out of the range of a DO is always permissible.

4. A transfer into the range of a DO from outside that range is not permissible. Entrance to the range of a DO may only be gained by the execution of the DO statement immediately above the range. In the diagrams below, transfers 1-3 are permissible while transfers 4-7 are not permissible.

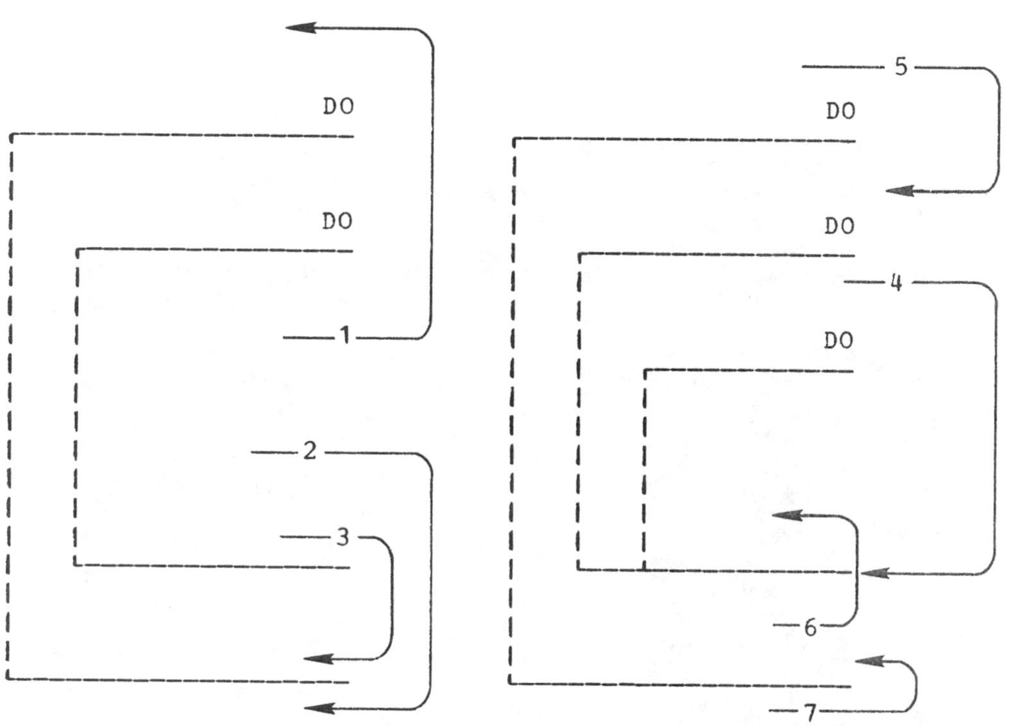

5. The last statement in the range of the DO implies a transfer of control to the first statement in the range of the DO. Therefore this last statement may not cause transfer of control by its own nature. For example, the last statement could not be a GO TO statement or a RETURN statement.

Of the Fortran statements covered thus far, the last statement in the range of a DO (the statement number referenced in the DO statement) must be one of the following:

a) assignment statement, or
b) READ statement, or
c) PRINT statement, or
d) CONTINUE statement, or
e) logical IF (as long as the IF trailer cannot itself transfer control).

6. The parameters (b,e,s) of the DO must be unsigned INTEGER constants greater than zero or non-subscripted INTEGER variables whose values are greater than zero. When using an IBM 360 or 370 computer, the end value (e) may not exceed 2147483647 (that's $2^{31}-1$) minus the value of s.

References to variables in an array usually require more time during the execution of a computer program than do references to scalar variables. If you are evaluating an expression which involves more than one or two references to a subscripted variable, it may be prudent to substitute a dummy variable. For example,

```
      DO 101 I=1,N,1
      A(I)=A(I)+SIN(A(I)-LOG(A(I))/A(I))
  101 CONTINUE
```

could be rewritten as

```
      DO 101 I=1,N,1
      B=A(I)
      B=B+SIN(B-LOG(B)/B)
      A(I)=B
  101 CONTINUE
```

and you will generally save execution time.

Exercises

1. In each case below, if the statement could possibly be correct write "OK"; otherwise correct the statement by rewriting the entire statement but changing only those portions that are not correct. Assume implicit variable typing.

   a. DO 6 K22-LAND
   b. DO 93 1,100,5
   c. DO666 DO 666=1,GO666
   d. DO N K=1,201,1
   e. DO 44 KKKKKK=LLLLL,MMMMMM,2
   f. DO 123 COUNT=1,10
   g. DO 923 INDEX=A,B

2. How many lines would be printed by the following? What numbers are printed?

```
      INTEGER NUM,K,J,I
      NUM=0
      DO 15 K=1,6
      NUM=NUM+1
      PRINT,K
      DO 13 J=1,4
      NUM=NUM+1
      PRINT,K,J
   13 CONTINUE
      DO 19 J=5,5,5
      NUM=NUM+1
      PRINT,J
   19 CONTINUE
      DO 1111 I=1,5,1
      DO 2222 J=1,2,1
      NUM=NUM+1
      PRINT, K,I,J
 2222 CONTINUE
 1111 CONTINUE
   15 CONTINUE
      PRINT, NUM
      RETURN
      END
```

3. What number is printed by:

```
      INTEGER N,K
      N=0
      DO 5 K=1,6
      N=N+K
      IF (N.GT.8) GO TO 7
      N=N+1
    5 CONTINUE
      N=N+100
    7 CONTINUE
      PRINT, N
```

4. Write the statements to store the number 43.8 into each of 3000 elements of an array named MOTHER.

5. Write the statements to sum the 400 elements of the array X and store that sum in the scalar variable named TOTAL.

6. Write the statements to store zeros in all 120 elements of the two-dimensional array declared by the statement:

```
      REAL XXX(4,30)
```

7. What value is stored in C in each of the following?

   a.

```
      INTEGER KAB
      REAL B(10),A,C
      A=0.
      DO 88 KAB=1,10
      B(KAB)=KAB
   88 CONTINUE
      DO 38 KAB=1,10,2
      A=A+B(KAB)
   38 CONTINUE
      C=A
      RETURN
      END
```

b.

```
      INTEGER J,K,N(10),C,E
      E=0
      DO 5 J=1,10
      K=11-J
      N(K)=J/2
    5 CONTINUE
      DO 6 K=1,10
      E=E+N(K)
    6 CONTINUE
      C=E
      RETURN
      END
```

8. The largest INTEGER value an IBM 360/370 can hold is 2,147,483,647. What would be the effect of the following statement?

```
      DO 1 K=1,2147483647
```

FORMATTED INPUT AND OUTPUT

In this section we undertake to make input and output (I/O) more complicated. But we will also make it more powerful. So far we have been concerned only with two I/O devices: the card reader and the line printer. There are other devices -- for example, a card punch -- and we will lay the groundwork for being able to use them.

Just as important, we will introduce ways to systematize both input and output of information. We will introduce methods the programmer can use to read information packed tightly on input cards. We will show how the programmer can adorn the output listing with alphabetic information to identify or explain the answers.

Up to this point the student has used format-free input and output. This meant that the numbers used as input data could be in any card columns, separated by blanks. This approach is somewhat wasteful of space. Using what we call FORMAT, a programmer can read information from cards or other input media which do not contain blank columns. We illustrate by introducing a modification of an old acquaintance, Revised Lab Problem 02.

```
      REAL HEIGHT,WIDTH,PI,RAREA,SAREA,AREA
      PI=3.141593
      READ (5,501) HEIGHT, WIDTH
  501 FORMAT (F5.0,F4.0)
      IF (HEIGHT.LT.WIDTH/2.)  GO TO 23
      RAREA=HEIGHT*WIDTH
      SAREA=PI*WIDTH**2/8.
      AREA=RAREA-SAREA
      WRITE (6,601) HEIGHT,WIDTH,AREA
  601 FORMAT(' H IS',F6.1,'   W IS',F5.1,'   AREA IS',F12.2)
      RETURN
   23 CONTINUE
      WRITE (6,602) HEIGHT, WIDTH
  602 FORMAT(' *ERROR* HEIGHT',F6.1,' IS < HALF WIDTH',F5.1)
      RETURN
      END
```

First examine the change in the input statement. Instead of

```
          READ, HEIGHT, WIDTH
```

we have

```
        READ (5,501)HEIGHT, WIDTH
```

The "5" is an I/O unit number or device code and indicates that the reading is to be done from the card reader. At most computing installations, the standard codes are:

5 - card reader
6 - line printer
7 - card punch

The "501" is a statement number. Locating statement 501 in the program -- here it turns out to be the next statement -- we find that it says

STATEMENT NUMBER		STATEMENT
1 2 3 4 5	6	7 8 9 10 11 12 13 14 15 16 17 18 19 20 21 22 23 24 25 26 27 28 29 30 31 32 33 34 35 36 37 38
501		FORMAT(F5.0,F4.0)

Using this statement is the programmer's way of telling the computer where it should expect to find the card columns containing the two variables it is going to read. In particular, the first variable will be found within the first 5 columns of the card and the second variable will be located in the next 4 columns The characters "F5.0" and "F4.0" are called FORMAT <u>field specifications.</u> For the time being we will ignore the "F" and the ".0".

The major point we are attempting to make is that the I/O statement still indicates what is to be read or written; the associated FORMAT statement indicates what positions the data occupy.

The FORMAT statement, though numbered, is not an executable statement. You may not branch to a FORMAT statement. Its number is strictly for reference by an I/O statement.

Looking now briefly at the output statements we discover that

```
PRINT, HEIGHT, WIDTH, AREA
```

has been changed to

```
WRITE(6,601) HEIGHT, WIDTH, AREA
```

WRITE is used here instead of PRINT because the computer has the capability of writing on several output devices other than the PRINTer. "6", as you already know, indicates the line printer, however, so that the effect is the same. "601" is the associated FORMAT statement and it is sort of a mess:

```
601 FORMAT(' H IS',F6.1,'   W IS',F5.1,'   AREA IS',F12.2)
```

If HEIGHT were 100, WIDTH were 40, and AREA were 3371.682, the WRITE and FORMAT statements would work jointly to print out:

```
H IS 100.0   W IS 40.0   AREA IS     3371.68
```

A FORMAT statement contains specifications within its parentheses. These specifications may or may not be associated with variables in the I/O statement that the FORMAT Statement serves. In the above example, the specifications F6.1, F5.1 and F12.2 are associated with the variables HEIGHT, WIDTH, and AREA respectively.

The "6" in F6.1 is the number of positions in the line of output reserved for printing the value of the variable HEIGHT. The ".1" indicates that the computer should use one of those positions for a single decimal place. Isn't it nice not to have to look at 0.100000E 03 for a simple number like 100.0?

The specifications ' H IS', '   W IS', and '   AREA IS' are not associated with variables in the I/O statement but are there to identify answers on the printed output listing.

Again, the I/O statement indicates what variable values are to be printed out and the FORMAT statement indicates the form of the output.

What we have just presented contains most of the "concept" part of FORMAT. Much of what follows is niggling but necessary detail. We start by defining, or redefining, some terms.

Field--a field is a sequence of one or more meaningful characters. An example of a field might be the number

-258.117

in which case the field consists of eight characters. A field might also contain blanks, alphabetic or special characters. The field width is the number of characters, including blanks, contained in the field. As an example, the field width of a field in a punched card is the number of columns occupied by the field.

Record--a record is simply a set of fields in sequence on some medium, such as cards, printer paper, magnetic tape, or magnetic disk. The number of characters in a record, called the record length, is a fixed quantity for some external media and a varying quantity for others. For example, a record stored on a punched card is always 80 characters long even though many of these characters may be blank. Similarly, the number of characters in a printed line is also of a fixed length which depends on the number of print positions allowed by the line printer. On the other hand the record length on magnetic tape has no such well defined limits.

Block--a block is made up of several records put together without spaces between them; the term block usually pertains to magnetic storage devices such as tapes or disks, although one might consider a deck of cards as a block of records.

READ Statement

The READ statement causes data from some external storage medium (such as cards, magnetic tape, magnetic disk) to be read into memory and stored in desired locations. The usual form is

READ (u,f) list

In this statement, u represents the input device number and can be an INTEGER constant or an INTEGER scalar variable. The unit numbers usually have the following meaning:

1 - magnetic tape or disk unit
2 - magnetic tape or disk unit
3 - magnetic tape or disk unit
4 - magnetic tape or disk unit
5 - card reader
6 - printer
7 - card punch

The method used to assign units 1, 2, 3, and 4 as disks, tapes, or even other devices is beyond the scope of this book. For illustrative purposes they will all be considered to be tapes here. The letter f represents a FORMAT statement number, is always INTEGER and is usually a constant. The list of variable names is simply one or more names, each of which must be separated from the next by a comma. The statement

```
READ(5,3) A,B
```

means read a <u>card</u> (unit 5 is the card reader) and store two numbers from that card in the locations called A and B. The precise location of the numbers on the card is specified in statement number 3 which must be a FORMAT statement.

```
READ (3,5) W, X, Y, Z
```

means: read four values from magnetic tape unit number 3 according to the FORMAT statement numbered 5 and store them in locations W, X, Y, and Z.

What is meant by

```
READ (4,333) Q,R,S
```

What is meant by

```
READ (2,7) NAT, T(2), T(3)
```

WRITE Statement

The WRITE statement causes information from computer memory to be recorded onto some external storage medium such as a card, paper or magnetic tape. The general form is

```
WRITE (u,f) list
```

where u is the unit number and f is the statement number of the corresponding FORMAT statement. The statement

```
WRITE (6,44) MOP,TOP,DROP
```

causes three values (which are internally stored in the computer memory in locations MOP, TOP, and DROP) to be printed (unit 6 is the printer) according to the specifications of the FORMAT statement numbered 44. The statement

```
WRITE (3,5) V(2),LAD
```

causes two values (stored in locations named V(2) and LAD) to be written onto tape unit number 3 according to the arrangement specified in the FORMAT statement which is numbered 5.

What is meant by

```
K=2
WRITE(K,5) W,X,Y,Z
```

> Whenever you use a constant in a program, ask yourself: are there any conditions under which I might want a variable here? Frequently programmers needlessly restrict the flexibility of their programs by using constants.

FORMAT Statement

A FORMAT statement, which is always numbered in columns 1-5, specifies the location and the form of data in input or output records. The FORMAT statement describes one or more records. A record can be:

- one 80-column card, or
- one line on a printed page, or
- a length of magnetic tape, or
- a sequence of characters on magnetic disk.

While other forms of records exist, only these are covered here.

The general form of the FORMAT statement is

```
stno FORMAT (a1,a2,a3,...)
```

where stno represents some unique statement number in the program, and a1, a2, a3,... represent field specifications.

A field is a contiguous section of a record which might contain information such as a number or a word; a field might also be blank.

Records are composed of fields. A set of field specifications describes a record. For example, we can think of the card below as a record composed of several fields.

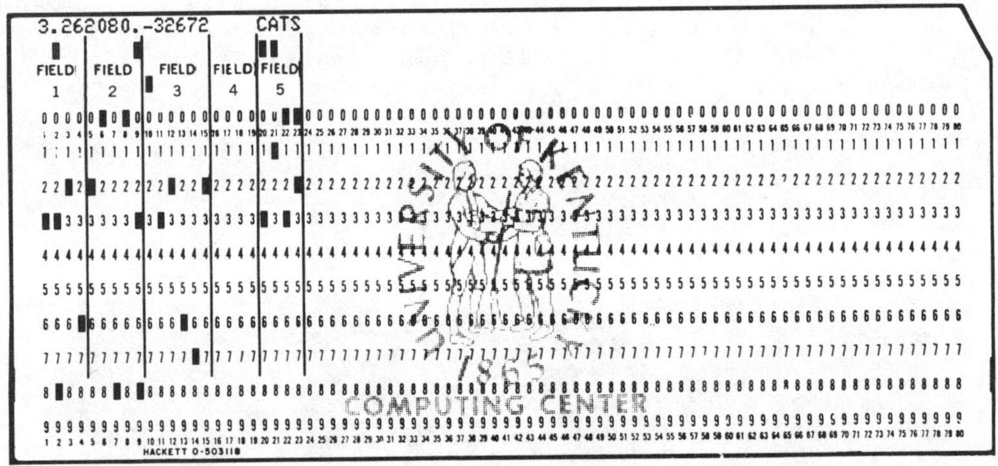

Field 1 contains a REAL number; it is 4 columns wide and has 2 decimal digits. Field 2 contains another REAL number; it is 5 columns wide and has no decimal digits. Field 3 contains an INTEGER number and it is 6 columns wide. Field 4 contains blanks (4 of them). Field 5 contains alphabetic characters, and is 4 columns wide.

Every variable in the list of a WRITE or READ statement has an associated field specification. The FORMAT statement, however, may contain field specifications which are not associated with any variable name. If the number of variables to be input or output is the same as the number of field specifications, the first variable name in the list of the READ or WRITE statement refers to the first field specification in the FORMAT statement, the second variable name in the list refers to the second field specification in the FORMAT statement, and so on.

Five field specifications will be covered here. (Others exist and are covered later in the text.) Each field specification type specifies two things:

1. the field type, and

2. the field width.

In addition, in the case of the F field for REAL numbers, the field specification denotes another attribute:

3. the location of an implied decimal point.

INTEGER Fields (I)

The I field specification has the form:

Iw

where I indicates that the field contains an INTEGER number and w is an INTEGER constant which specifies the width of the field in columns.

For example, look at the READ and FORMAT statements shown below:

STATEMENT NUMBER		STATEMENT
		INTEGER MAD,J,K
		READ(5,37) MAD,J,K
37		FØRMAT(I3,I2,I4)

The READ statement says: Read a record from unit number 5 according to FORMAT statement number 37; the record will contain three numbers which are to be stored in locations MAD, J, and K. The FORMAT statement describes the placement of the numbers within the record; in this case the first number resides in the first 3 columns of the record, the next number is recorded in the next two columns of the record and the third number is to be found in the next four columns of the record. The letter "I" means that the numbers are INTEGERs. In general, the READ verb instructs the computer <u>what</u> data to take in and the FORMAT statement tells <u>how</u> the data are arranged within the record.

REAL Fields (F)

The F field specification has the form:

Fw.d

where F indicates that the field contains a REAL number, w specifies the total field width in columns, and d relates to the number of decimal places in the number.

The example below illustrates the use of the I and F fields.

```
      REAL A
      INTEGER B,C,D
      READ (5,39) A,B,C,D
   39 FORMAT (F5.2,I3,I2,I3)
```

This sequence means: read a card (since the unit number is 5) containing four numbers which are to be stored in the locations A, B, C, and D. The REAL number to be stored in A is contained in the first 5 columns of the card (columns 1-5), with columns 4 and 5 containing digits assumed to be to the right of the decimal point; the INTEGER which is to be stored in B is found in the next three columns (6-8); the INTEGER in field 3 of the data card (the next two columns: 9 and 10) is to be stored in the location named C; and the INTEGER to be found in the next three columns (columns 11-13) is to be stored in the location named D. Suppose that the card to be read is as follows:

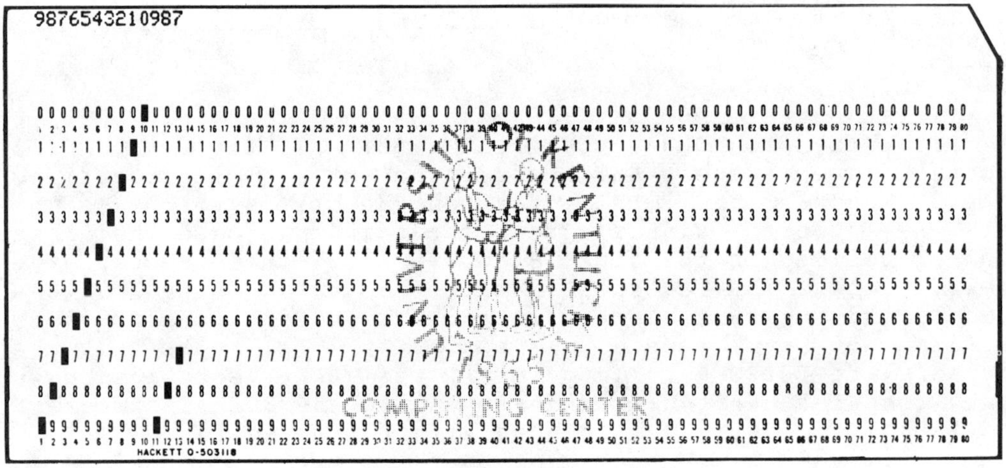

9876543210987

What values are stored in A, B, C, and D? The answer is

A=987.65   B=432   C=10   D=987

Suppose that the card above is read by the READ statement above, except that the FORMAT statement (number 39) is

```
39 FORMAT(F5.2,I1,I5,I1)
```

In this case what values are stored? The answer is

A=987.65   B=4   C=32109   D=8

Notice that since the FORMAT only included columns 1-12, column 13, which contained a 7, is ignored and the 7 is not stored anywhere.

The above is a dramatic illustration of the fact that a FORMAT statement can radically alter the input data accidentally. It is one more reason why input should be printed out and checked. The truly idiot-proof program is a rarity. You must assume that any other person who uses your program is going to be somewhat intelligent and knowledgeable. But most programmers assume much too much about the quality of use and, especially, the quality of data their programs will be subject to. So make your programs with narrow eyes and a suspicious nature.

F FORMAT and Output

With output, the d in Fw.d represents the number of decimal digits in the field. That is, if location A contained the number 6.1236 and statements

```
   WRITE (7,33)A
33 FORMAT(F5.2)
```

were executed, the number

b6.12

would be punched (unit 7 is the card punch), since the FORMAT says, "output the number in a field five columns wide with two decimal places." The digits would actually appear in columns 2, 4, and 5; a decimal point would be punched in column 3; and a blank would appear in column 1. The blank in column one illustrates that numbers are placed at the right side of the space allowed for them. They are said to be _right-adjusted_ or _right-justified_.

Incidentally, REAL numbers are rounded on output. If A had contained the number 2.2370 and had been punched with the statement above, the resulting output field would have appeared in card columns 1-5 as:

b2.24

When you construct a format specification for writing out the value of a variable, you must leave enough room (i.e., make w large enough) to accommodate the total of the following:

1. the maximum number of whole number digits which might exist in the number,

2. the number of decimal digits you want in the number,

3. a decimal point, which requires one column or print position,

4. a space for a minus sign if the number might be negative,

5. the number of blanks which you want to precede the first non-blank character of the number.

F FORMAT and Input

On _input_, the d portion of Fw.d has a slightly different meaning than on output. It means: if the data field contains _no_ actual decimal point, store the number _as if_ the last d columns of the field were to the right of the decimal point; if a decimal point is actually recorded in the field, store the number exactly as it appears on the input medium _and_ ignore the d portion of the field specification. To illustrate this, if

```
      REAL A,B
      READ (5,3) A,B
    3 FORMAT(F4.4,F3.3)
```

is executed and the card read is

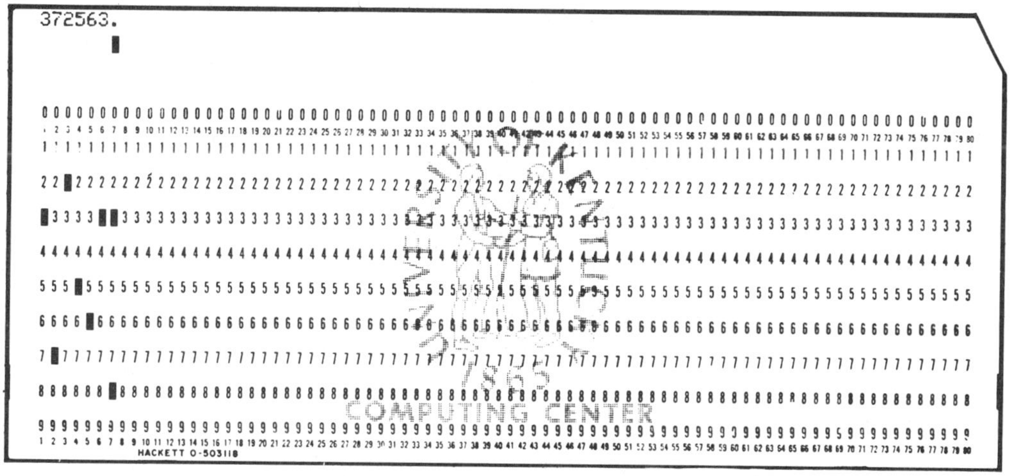

```
372563.
```

the number stored in A will be .3725, since the field specification F4.4 says, "if no decimal is actually recorded in the field, treat the number as if the last four digits in the field were to the right of the decimal point." On the other hand, the number stored in B would be 63.0 since a decimal point actually exists on the input medium. The number is stored as recorded and the decimal portion of the field specification is overridden (ignored).

In general, blanks on input are considered the same as zeros.

Exercise

Suppose that the following statements are executed:

```
      REAL A,B
      INTEGER C
      READ (5,2) C,B,A
    2 FORMAT (I2,F3.0,F2.1)
```

If each line below represents a different data card, what values will be stored in C,B, and A?

card columns--->	1	2	3	4	5	6	7	8	9	10	11	12	13	14	15
a.	9	8	7	6	5	4	3	2	1	0	9	8	7		
b.	6	2	2	8	9	8	7	6							
c.	-	7	.	2	5	3	.								
d.	9	8	7	6	.	1	2								
e.	4	4	4	4	4	4	4								
f.															
g.	K	E	N	T	U	C	K	Y							
h.	2	5	-	.	3	-	2	6							
i.		6	2	2	8	9	8	7	6						
j.	7	.	2	1	2	1	2								

Skipped Field (X)

The facility exists to ignore or skip over fields by using the X field specification. Its general form is

wX

where the w is the number of columns in the record to be skipped over and X represents the field type. There are two important differences between the X field and the others mentioned thus far:

1. the X field has no corresponding variable name in the READ or WRITE list, and
2. the field width precedes the field type, X, instead of following it as is the case with I and F fields.

Example: If

```
      REAL A,B
      READ (5,32) A,B
   32 FORMAT (2X,F6.1,4X,F2.0)
```

were executed, the value stored in A would be taken from card columns 3-8 (since the 2X means skip over or ignore 2 columns) and the value stored in B would be taken from card columns 13-14 (since the 4X means ignore four columns: 9-12). Again, X fields do not possess corresponding variable names in the READ statement; thus the field specification for A is F6.1 and the field specification for B is F2.0.

Example: In the case below

```
      INTEGER A,B
      READ (5,5) A,B
    5 FORMAT (I3,3X,I1)
```

if the following card is read

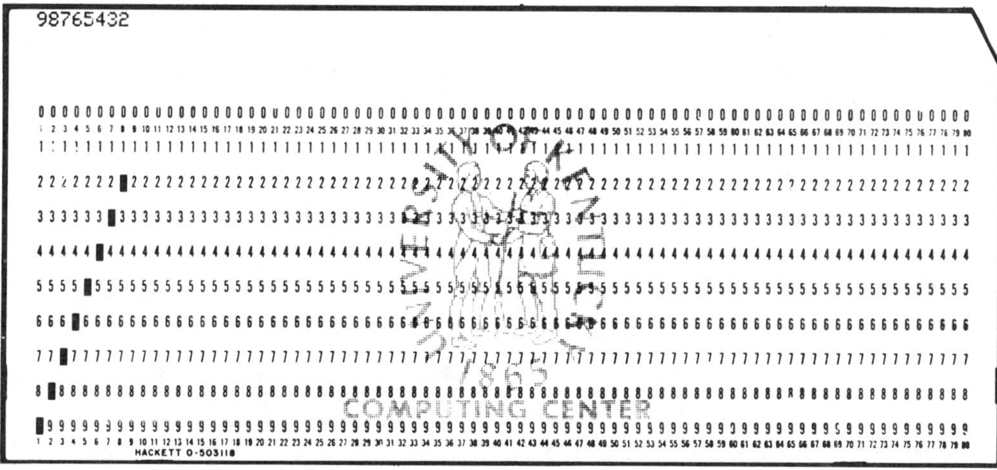

the value 987 is stored in A, card columns 4-6 are ignored, and the value 3 is stored in B.

<u>Exercise</u>

If the statements

```
      REAL A
      INTEGER B
      READ (5,20) A,B
```

are executed, and the card read is

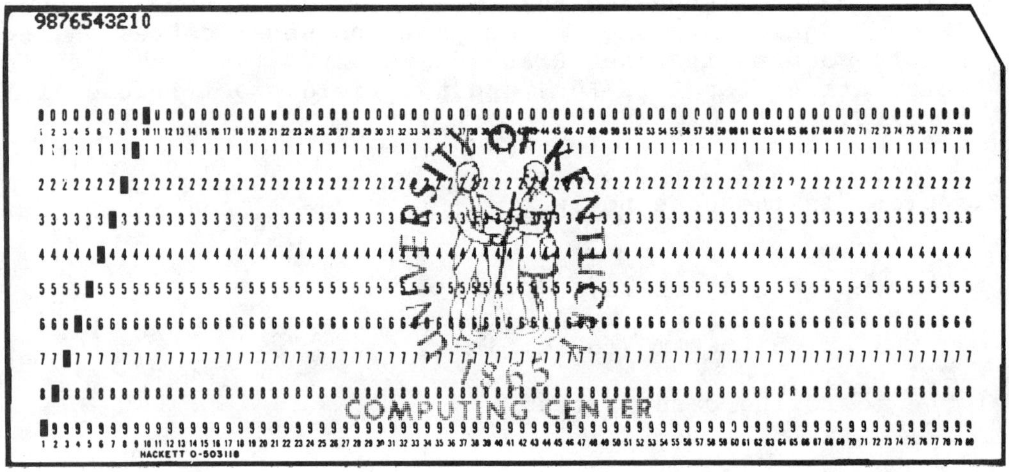

```
9876543210
```

what values are stored in A and B for each FORMAT statement shown below?

a. 20 FORMAT (1X,F3.1,I2)

b. 20 FORMAT (F3.0,3X,I1)

c. 20 FORMAT (3X,F2.0,I2)

d. 20 FORMAT (2X,F1.1,3X,I1)

e. 20 FORMAT (F1.1,2X,I5)

f. 20 FORMAT (1X,F3.1,I2,2X)

Non-Numeric Information

Computers, despite the name, are not just big calculating machines. They are, in fact, symbol manipulators. The symbols which they can read, compare, transform, write, etc., are usually those which can be punched on a keypunch machine plus some others such as lower case letters. In all, the IBM 360/370 has the power to operate on any of 256 distinct symbols besides its ability to handle numbers. (You may have already guessed that the computer you've been working with could deal with symbols which represented non-numeric information, since you've been handing it alphanumeric information, in the form of program statements, for some time now.)

The Fortran language was originally developed to do mathematical computation, and its ability to handle non-numeric data is clumsy and limited. There are other languages designed to manipulate symbols in more general ways than Fortran, and they do a good job of it. But even if Fortran is not a language you'd choose to do non-numeric data manipulation, it needs some of this capability just to produce output which can be easily read and understood. Besides, alphanumeric data frequently accompanies numeric data, such as names on paychecks, so the ability to handle it must be present.

In order to be able to do alphanumeric character manipulation in Fortran, you ought to know something about the "innards" of the machine you are dealing with. We've tried to avoid talking too much about the machine itself, since part of the idea of a high-level language like Fortran is to allow the person to solve problems with a computer without understanding, or even liking, computers. But using Fortran with non-numeric information tends to be somewhat machine dependent -- that is, the characteristics of the language vary with the type of computer being used -- so we now introduce some information about the hardware of the particular machine we are dealing with: the IBM 360/370.

We have talked about locations within the memory of the machine. In the schematic computer of Part I we showed locations, with variable names attached, holding numbers. The numbers could be INTEGER or REAL. Each such variable location we will now call a computer word. A computer word can be logically subdivided into four equally sized parts. We call each such part a byte. A byte, at any given time, can store any one of the 256 possible symbols that we referred to earlier. That is, we could store the letter "W" in a byte, the symbol "$" in another byte, and so on. Since there are four bytes in a word, it follows that a word or location of computer storage, as we have previously discussed it, can hold up to four alphanumeric characters.

Alphanumeric Fields (A)

Alphanumeric (or alphameric) fields on data cards contain any valid alphabetic characters, numeric characters or special characters such as

(* /) . $,

IBM 360 or 370 computers store such fields with up to four alphanumeric characters in one location or word. The <u>variable</u> location so used can be declared as either REAL or INTEGER. The <u>field</u> specification in the FORMAT statement must have the form:

Aw

where A denotes alphanumeric and w is the field width. The quantity w can usually be 1,2,3, or 4. If w<4 then the <u>rightmost</u> remaining positions of the computer word are filled with blanks. Once information is internally stored in alphanumeric form, it cannot be used in arithmetic computations even if it consists of numbers. The following illustrates the use of the A field:

```
      INTEGER A,B,C
      READ(5,2)A,B,C
    2 FORMAT(A4,2X,A2,I2)
```

Suppose that the card read contained:

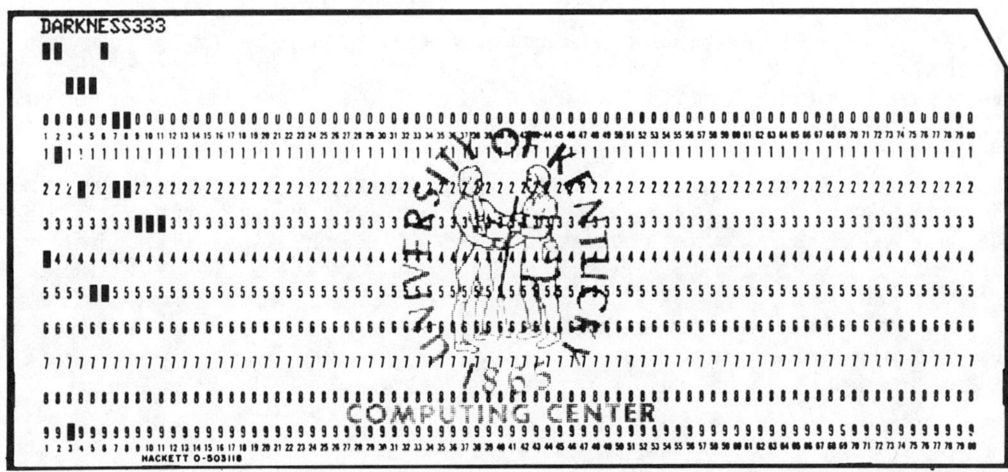

Then the values stored in the variables A, B, and C would be:

```
    ┌───────┐
A   │ DARK  │
    ├───────┤
B   │ SSbb  │
    ├───────┤
C   │   33  │
    └───────┘
```

where b indicates a blank character. The value in C is an arithmetic INTEGER and can be used for computation. Suppose the card had been:

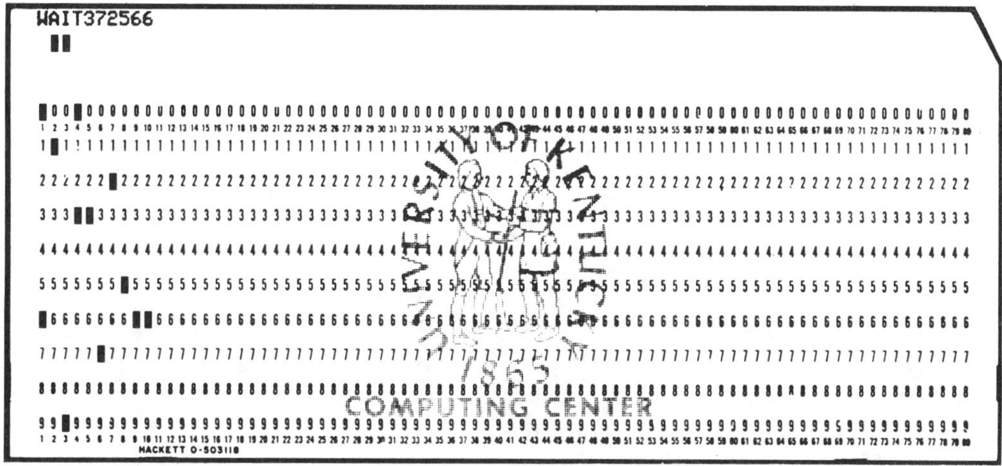

The values stored would have been:

```
    ┌───────┐
A   │ WAIT  │
    ├───────┤
B   │ 25bb  │
    ├───────┤
C   │   66  │
    └───────┘
```

It is clear that the value in A cannot be used in arithmetic computation. There just aren't rules for adding letters together and getting other letters. What may prove confusing at first is that the value stored in B likewise cannot be used for computation but the value in C could be.

What makes the difference? The FORMAT specification that dictated the input does. A and B were both read in under an A specification while C was read in under an I specification. The fact that all three were read into locations declared to be INTEGER makes no difference.

Furthermore, if the programmer wanted to write out A, B, and C he/she would have to write out A and B under an A specification and C under an I specification.

A major difference between alphanumeric quantities and numeric ones is that alphanumeric quantities are left-justified, whereas numeric ones are right-justified.

Exercise

If the card

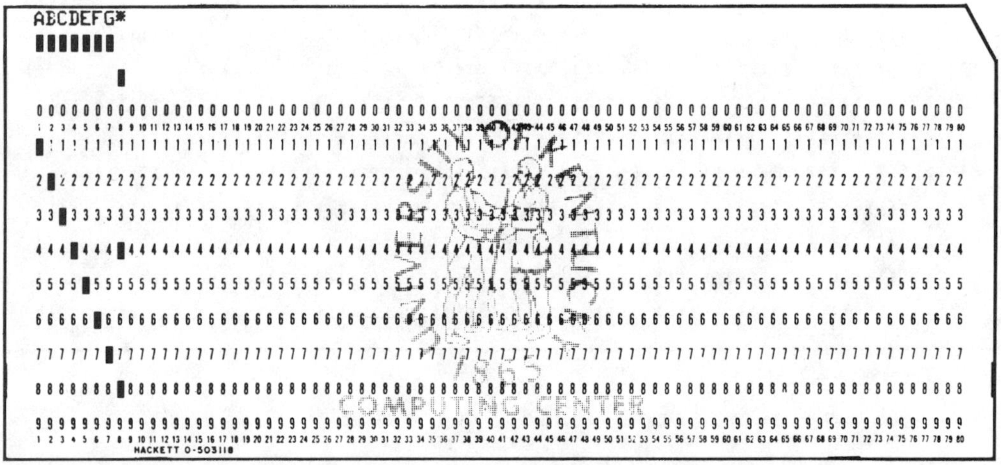

```
ABCDEFG*
```

is read by

```
INTEGER A
REAL B
READ (5,9) A,B
```

what values are stored in A and B if the FORMAT statements are as follows?

a) 9 FORMAT (A4,A2)
b) 9 FORMAT (A3,A1)
c) 9 FORMAT (A1,A4)

```
d)   9 FORMAT (A2,A2)
e)   9 FORMAT (A4,A4)
f)   9 FORMAT (2X,A4,A1)
g)   9 FORMAT (A3,I2)
```

Literal Fields

Literal fields are contained in FORMAT statements and are usually used only for output; they allow you to produce headings or other identifying information. Literal fields are simply characters enclosed in single quotes: a single quote symbol appears at both the beginning and end of the field. Literal fields appear in FORMAT statements and, like the X field, do not correspond to any variable name in the list. The statements

```
    WRITE (7,333)
333 FORMAT('SALES REPORT')
```

would result in

```
SALES REPORT
```

being punched on one card in columns 1 through 12. Literal fields may be combined with other fields as in the case below.

```
  INTEGER V
  V=25
  WRITE (7,3) V
3 FORMAT ('TOTAL=',I2)
```

Here one card would be produced with

```
TOTAL=25
```

being punched in card columns 1-8.

The relative position of the literal field in the FORMAT statement determines the relative position of the literal information on the output medium. This is illustrated by the following where

```
  INTEGER V
  V=25
  WRITE (7,3) V
3 FORMAT (I2,'TOTAL=')
```

would produce

25TOTAL=

on a punched card in columns 1-8.

Example

Write the statements necessary to punch John Doe's age (eighteen) and his name on a card as

AGE=18 JOHN DOE

This can be done at least two ways:

a)
```
      WRITE (7,3)
    3 FORMAT ('AGE=18 JOHN DOE')
```

b)
```
      INTEGER A
      A=18
      WRITE (7,3) A
    3 FORMAT ('AGE=',I2,' JOHN DOE')
```

Summary of Field Specifications

Field Specification Type	Is There A Corresponding List Variable	Type of Variable In list	Maximum Value of w
Iw	Yes	INTEGER	Any length, but maximum value stored will be 2147483647
Fw.d	Yes	REAL	Any length, but only the 7 most significant digits are retained
Aw	Yes	REAL or INTEGER	Usually 4
wX	No	None	w≥1
Literal	No	None	Size≥1

Leading Zeros and Output

On output, whether to cards, printer, tape, or disk, the leading zeros in each numeric field written with FORMATted output are converted to blanks. For example, if the number 26.5 is printed as F6.1, the output would appear as bb26.5, where b indicates a blank character.

Blanks and Input

On input of numeric data under FORMAT control, blank columns are treated as zeros. That is, all blank columns in a numeric field are considered to be zeros if they are found before, after, or _between_ non-zero digits. If the number "23b4b5" is read as an I6 field, the number stored is 230405 (b denotes a blank column). Only when reading data with an A field specification is a zero distinguished from a blank.

Field Specification Repetition

The ability exists to indicate that several _identical_ field specifications are wanted by simply placing an unsigned INTEGER constant (sometimes called a _repetition count_) before the field specification. To specify that three I4 fields occur, we could write

```
12 FORMAT (I4,I4,I4)
```

or more simply

```
12 FORMAT (3I4)
```

The two FORMAT statements above are identical in meaning.

Parentheses may be used to set off parts of the FORMAT statement. Repetition of those parts in parentheses is also allowed and is achieved by placing an unsigned INTEGER constant in front of the left parenthesis. For example, the two following FORMAT statements are identical in effect.

```
99999 FORMAT(I2,3(F3.1),2(I4,F5.5),I8)
99999 FORMAT(I2,F3.1,F3.1,F3.1,I4,F5.5,I4,F5.5,I8)
```

Parentheses cannot be nested indefinitely, however. The limit is probably best shown by an example.

```
FORMAT( ( ( ) ) )
```

is legal, while

```
FORMAT( ( ( ( ) ) ) )
```

and more extensive nesting of parentheses is not legal.

The A Field Specification and Arrays

Arrays are often convenient storage for alphanumeric information. Recall that if no subscript is associated with an array name in an I/O statement, the entire array is read or written. Thus, if you want to tell the computer to read an entire card (80 columns) of alphanumeric information, you could do so by writing

```
      REAL XYZ(20)
      READ(5,8) XYZ
    8 FORMAT(20A4)
```

since one storage location can hold only 4 alphanumeric characters.

If each card column requires individual examination, you might write

```
      REAL XYZ(80)
      READ(5,8) XYZ
    8 FORMAT(80A1)
```

In the latter case, each symbol on the card would be stored in a separate element of the array XYZ as a character followed by three blanks. In terms of efficiency, it takes the computer about four times as long to READ the 80 single-character fields as it does to READ the 20 four-character fields.

Printing and Carriage Control

The printer is a unique output device in that there is vertical movement of the paper to control as well as the contents of printed lines. Fortran allows control of the vertical paper movement through the printer by use of a carriage control character. This character is part of the output record and always precedes the characters which are actually printed. This first character <u>is not</u> actually printed, but it performs the control function. The carriage control characters are

blank	-	single space before printing (used for single-spaced output)
0	-	double space before printing (used for double-spaced output)
+	-	do not space before printing (used when overprinting is desired)
1	-	skip to the top of the next page before printing.

The best way to designate carriage control is to use a literal field with the above characters. The carriage control designation must be the first field specification of any FORMAT statement which describes a printed line. The carriage control character is not used with any device other than the printer.

The following FORMAT statement specifies that the paper is to be single-spaced (the normal case) vertically before the line is printed:

```
328 FORMAT(' ',I3,F10.2)
```

The following specifies that the paper on the printer is to be double-spaced before the line is printed:

```
444 FORMAT ('0',I3,F10.2)
```

The blank or zero literals above are not printed. Every time a line is printed, the first character of the record, whether it be part of a number to be printed or specified by a literal, is used for carriage control and is not printed. Carelessness regarding the carriage control character can cause unexpected results. For example, if the following statements are executed,

Example 1:

```
    INTEGER K
    K=133
    WRITE (6,303)K
303 FORMAT (I3)
```

the digit 1 (in 133) would be used for carriage control (skipping to the top of the next page to be printed) and the number 33 would actually be printed there. In pictorial form:

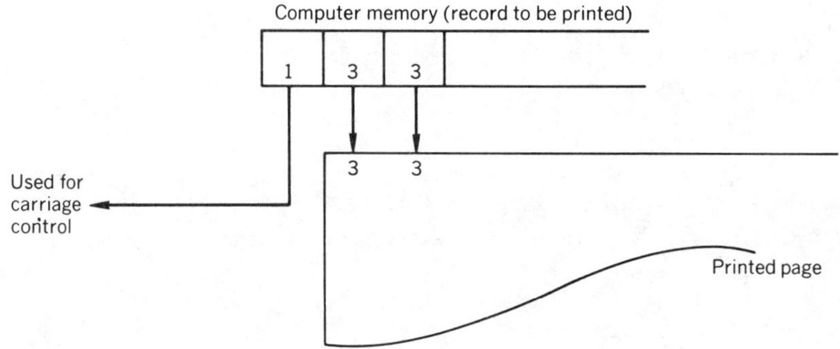

Since the zeros preceding any number (called *leading zeros*) are converted to blanks by Fortran, this problem could be avoided by providing a larger field specification than is required by the number. A better way, however, is to insert the literal explicitly.

Example 2:

```
          INTEGER K
          K=133
          WRITE (6,303) K
      303 FORMAT (' ',I3)
```

would result in a single vertical space of the printed page and the entire number 133 being printed. In pictorial form:

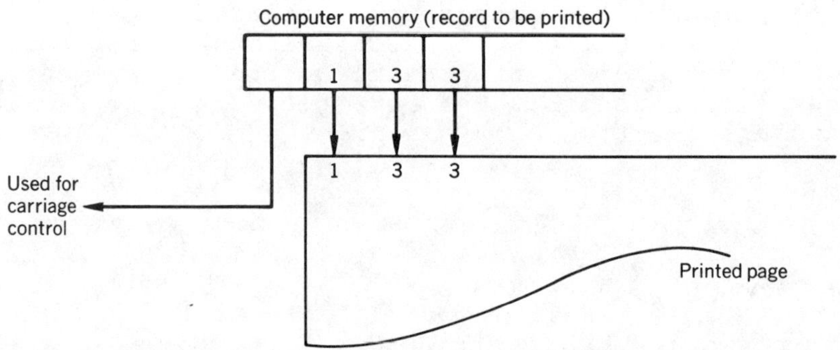

It is a good programming practice to use an explicit literal carriage control character at the beginning of a FORMAT statement describing a line to be printed.

The number of allowable printer positions varies from computer to computer. Many printers allow up to 132 characters per line, plus an additional character for carriage control.

Magnetic Tape

Magnetic tape is similar to cards in concept, except that cards always contain 80 columns per record and magnetic tape may contain a variable number of "columns" or characters per record. Magnetic tape recording can be thought of schematically as

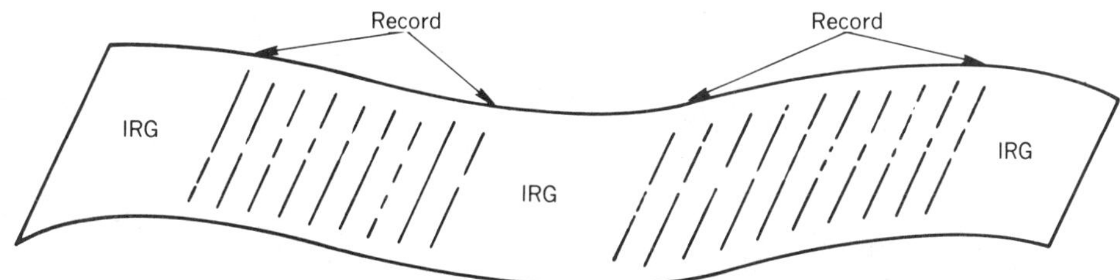

where each record is composed of columns and each record is separated from the next by an inter-record gap (IRG). An IRG is simply a short bit (about one-half inch) which is blanked out by the magnetic tape unit between each pair of records. It signals the magnetic tape unit when to stop reading a record on input. A great advantage of magnetic tape is that a large amount of information can be stored in a small amount of space. Typically, just one inch of magnetic tape could store a record of 1600 columns or characters. That is the equivalent of 20 cards.

Conceptually, a programmer treats magnetic tape almost exactly the same as cards with two exceptions.

1. Each record can be less than, greater than, or equal to 80 columns depending upon what you want, and

2. You can rewind a magnetic tape back to its beginning by issuing the Fortran statement:

```
REWIND u
```

where u is an INTEGER constant or variable and designates the unit containing the tape to be rewound.

To illustrate the use of tape, assume that tape unit 4 contains a reel of magnetic tape with 100 records and each record contains one five-digit INTEGER.

The objective of the program is to sum these 100 numbers and print the average with an F14.2 field specification. It could be done as follows:

```
  INTEGER A(100), K
  REAL B,C
  B=0.
  REWIND 4
  DO 6 K=1,100
  READ (4,2) A
2 FORMAT (I5)
  B=B+A
6 CONTINUE
  C=B/100.
  WRITE (6,3) C
3 FORMAT (' ',F14.2)
  RETURN
  END
```

Magnetic Disk

As a device for writing and reading sequential records, disks can be used in the same way that magnetic tapes are used. The REWIND instruction can be used to allow input or output to start at the beginning of the portion of the disk designated by the unit number specified. Non-sequential disk input and output are covered in Module 6.

Exercises

1. Write the Fortran statements to read the 3 numbers indicated from the following card, compute the average, and print the average:

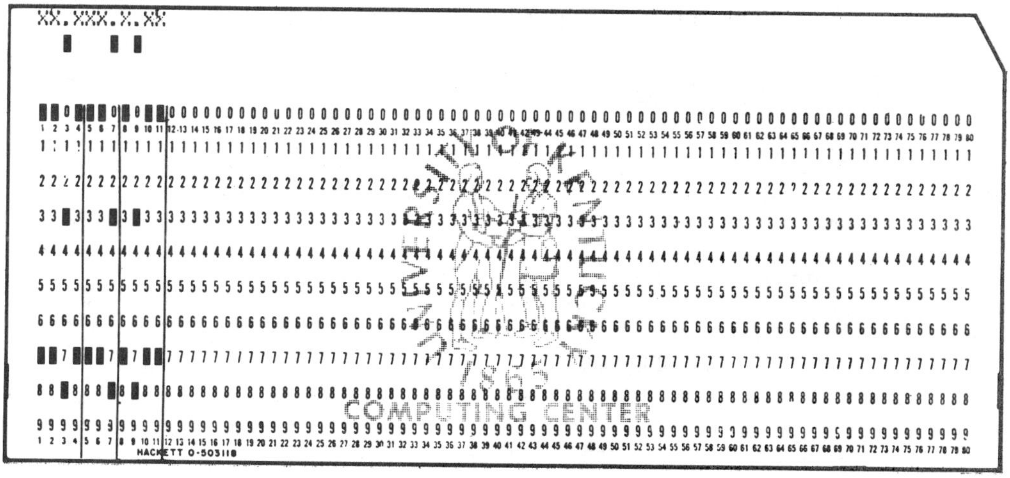

XX.XXX.X.XX

where X=any numeric digit. (Print result as 10 digits with 3 decimal places.)

2. Twenty records are recorded on magnetic tape and the tape reel is mounted on tape unit 4. Each record contains

   Col. 1-20 Worker's name
   Col. 21-22 Worker's age

   For each record on magnetic tape, print one line, single spaced, showing worker's name (print columns 2-21) and worker's age (print columns 25-26). Then print one line, double-spaced with the letters AVERAGE in columns 2-8 and the average age of all twenty workers in print columns 21-24 as F4.1.

Multiple Records and Input-Output

A question is now posed: "what events can cause either the reading or the writing of a new record?" There are three such events.

First, whenever an input or an output statement is encountered during the execution of the program a new record is triggered--that is a new card is read, a new line is printed, a new record is served up on a magnetic tape unit, etc.

The second event that can cause an input or output (I/O) device to serve up a new record is a slash "/" in a FORMAT statement. Usually the slash makes its appearance in the place of a comma. For example,

```
WRITE(7,678) AAA,BBB,CCC,DDD
```

when used with the statement

```
678 FORMAT(I1,I2,I3,I4)
```

would produce four fields on one card in columns 1 through 10. However, if the statement

```
678 FORMAT(I1,I2/I3,I4)
```

were used, two cards would be produced. The first would contain the values of AAA in column 1 and BBB in columns 2-3; the second card would contain the values CCC in columns 1-3 and DDD in columns 4-7.

Third, if a READ or WRITE list dictates the input or output of more values than there are data-related FORMAT specifications in the FORMAT statement, then a new record is triggered. For example, the statement pair

```
WRITE(7,555) AA,BB,CC

555 FORMAT(F5.1,F4.2)
```

would cause two cards to be punched. On the first card would be the values corresponding to AA and BB in card columns 1-5 and 6-9 respectively. Since the FORMAT statement is "exhausted" but there is still a value to be punched, a new record (card) is begun. But under what specification should CC be punched? It seems logical to return to the beginning of FORMAT statement 555 and print CC under specification F5.1, and in this particular case that is what happens. In the general case, however, a new record is triggered and FORMAT specifications are reused starting with the repetition count (if any) of the group of FORMAT specifications terminated by the last right parenthesis that precedes the right parenthesis ending the FORMAT statement. An example is demanded. Suppose that a large number of data elements are to be written out. The FORMAT statement

```
23456 FORMAT(I2,2(I4,5X),I6)
```

is equivalent to

```
23456 FORMAT(I2,I4,5X,I4,5X,I6/I4,5X,I4,5X,I6/I4,5X,I4...)
                                 ----------------------------
                                                ============
```

where the single underline indicates the first repeat of the specifications, and the double underline indicates the second repeat. Repeats of the specifications would continue until the list being read or written was exhausted. Incidentally, if the list is exhausted before the FORMAT specifications have all been used the remainder of the FORMAT statement is ignored.

READing with END and ERRor Transfers

The complete general form of the READ statement is:

```
READ(u,f,END=x,ERR=y) list
```

where u and f are the unit and FORMAT numbers as before. END=x is optional and if used, x is the number of the Fortran statement to which control is *immediately* given if the end of data is encountered. That is, if one attempts to read more data than actually exist, control is transferred to statement x. ERR=y is optional and if used, y is the number of the Fortran statement to which control is transferred if an error occurs on the input device. An example of the full form of the READ is:

```
READ(3,301,END=666,ERR=888) list
```

This statement performs normally except under two conditions. If the end of the data set is encountered when the statement is being executed, control is immediately transferred to statement 666. If an error occurs during the READ operation, control is transferred to statement 888; this transfer might allow a message to be printed or some totals to that point printed. If either the END of the data or an error is encountered during reading and the READ statement does not contain the END and/or ERR parameters, the job is terminated.

IMPLIED DO: INPUT AND OUTPUT STATEMENTS

The DO notation can be used in READ and WRITE (or PRINT) statements. It is similar to the DO statement except the word DO is not used and the entire notation must be enclosed in parentheses. A form of the implied DO is:

```
READ(u,f) (list,i=b,e,s)
```

or

```
WRITE(u,f) (list,i=b,e,s)
```

where b, e, and s mean beginning value, ending value, and step value as in a DO loop. If s and its preceding comma are omitted, the step value is assumed to be 1. Symbols u and f are unit and FORMAT designators, as explained previously. The word "list" designates a list of variable names.

A set of parentheses must enclose that portion of the input or output statement for which iteration is intended. To read the first 6 elements of an array named A, a programmer might write:

```
      REAL A(35)
      INTEGER M
      READ(5,78) (A(M),M=1,6)
   78 FORMAT(6F10.2)
```

The READ statement above is equivalent to

```
      READ (5,78)A(1),A(2),A(3),A(4),A(5),A(6)
```

but simpler to write. This sequence would read a single card.

The preceding statements form a very different situation in terms of the number of records read than does the sequence

```
      REAL A(35)
      INTEGER M
      DO 999 M=1,6
      READ(5,78) A(M)
   78 FORMAT(6F10.2)
  999 CONTINUE
```

in which one number is read from columns 1-10 of each of six cards. Why? Because a new record is triggered each time a READ or WRITE statement is encountered during the execution of a program. The 6F10.2 could have just as easily been F10.2 since only one variable appears in the input list, and thus only one field was read from each card.

Suppose the sequence

```
      REAL A(35)
      INTEGER M
      READ(5,78) (A(M),M=1,6)
   78 FORMAT(F10.0)
```

were executed. Six cards would be read in this case as well. Only one READ statement is executed and it calls for six numbers but the FORMAT statement is exhausted five times thus triggering five more records.

REMEMBER: three events cause a new record to be read or written:

1. the execution of an I/O statement,

2. a slash in the FORMAT statement,

3. exhausting the FORMAT statement while reading or writing remains to be done.

As a second example, to define only the even elements of an array named B, one might write:

```
      REAL B(100)
      INTEGER N
      READ (5,20) (B(N),N=2,100,2)
```

where 20 is an appropriate FORMAT statement.

As a third example, to print a table as

```
1          XXXX
2          XXXX
3          XXXX
4          XXXX
.            .
.            .
100        XXXX
```

where XXXX represents the contents of Q(1),Q(2),...,Q(100), we could write:

```
      INTEGER Q(100),IVAN
          .
          .
      WRITE (6,305) (IVAN,Q(IVAN),IVAN=1,100)
  305 FORMAT(' ',I3,15X,I4)
```

There is an advantage to writing out entire arrays rather than using implied DO's: it's much faster for the same number of items. On the other hand it may limit the flexibility of your program.

Nested Implied DO's

The implied DO notation can also be used in a nested form where more than one index is operative. This nested form is similar to a nested set of DO statements. To print a matrix which contains ten rows and fifteen columns, one row to a line, a programmer can write:

```
      REAL X(10,15)
            .
            .
            .
      WRITE(6,11) ((X(I,J),J=1,15),I=1,10)
   11 FORMAT(' ',15F8.2)
```

Notice that each set of implied DO parameters is enclosed in its separate set of parentheses. The innermost DO notation iterates most rapidly. In the above sequence, why is it that the machine doesn't attempt to write all 150 values on one line?

Exercises

1. Print the odd elements of the array Q which is declared as REAL Q(100).

2. What is wrong with each statement below:

    a. WRITE (6,3) A(M),M=1,20

    b. READ(5,4) (A(M),R(M),M=1,40),S

c. READ(5,1) (AM(M),AM=1,20)

d. WRITE(6,3) K,(A(M),M=1,25

e. WRITE(6,6) (I,X(I,J),J=1,10),I=1,30)

f. WRITE(6,1) (((X(I,J,K),I=1,9),J=1,9),K=1,9)))

g. READ(5,1)B,E,S,(A(M),M=B,E,S)

3. How many cards would be punched by each of the following, assuming that an array named A is declared as REAL A(20) and is defined?The output statement is:

```
WRITE(7,9)(A(I),I=1,10)
```

a. 9 FORMAT(10F6.2)
b. 9 FORMAT(5F6.2)
c. 9 FORMAT(3F6.4/5F8.3)

4. Answer question 3 using the following program segment:

```
      DO 8 I=1,10
      WRITE(7,9)A(I)
    8 CONTINUE
```

INITIALIZATION, EXTENDED PRECISION, AND MORE ON TYPING

A Type Declaration Statement (or Type statement) is a non-executable statement which informs the computer that variable names are going to stand for certain types of quantities. Two Type statements have been covered thus far: REAL and INTEGER. The Type statement can also specify the numbers of dimensions and numbers of elements in subscripted arrays.

For example, the statement

```
REAL A,X(5)
```

tells the computer that the variable name A is a REAL variable and further declares that there shall be a REAL one-dimensional array named X composed of five elements.

Initialization by Type Statement

It has been stressed, ad nauseam, that the Type Declaration Statement does not define the values of the quantities it declares; this function has been left to other statements.

A modification of the Type Declaration Statement is now presented, however, which allows it both to declare variables and to give them *initial* values.

Suppose in the preceding example the programmer wished to initialize the variable A with a value of 3.141593 and to initialize all the values of the array X to zero. He could write

```
REAL A/3.141593/,X(5)/0.,0.,0.,0.,0./
```

In general, the values to be used for initialization follow the variable or array name and are set off by slashes; if there is more than one initialization value, commas are used to separate the values. If several initialization values are identical, an integer repeat number followed by an asterisk may be used. Therefore, the example could be written

```
REAL A/3.141593/,X(5)/5*0./
```

The Type statement can also be used to initialize variables with alphanumeric data. If a programmer wanted the words CARD and DECK stored initially in the two locations of an INTEGER array named GAME he/she could write

```
INTEGER GAME(2)/'CARD','DECK'/
```

In this newly extended form, the Type Declaration Statement is:

```
type a(k1)/x1/, b(k2)/x2/...
```

where a and b are variable names; each k is an optional set of up to seven integer constants specifying the dimensions and sizes of an array; each x is an optional set of initial values for the variables.

The Type statement still remains a non-executable statement and cannot define values of variables except during the compilation (translation) phase of the job. If these values are changed by a READ or arithmetic assignment statement the original values are lost and could only be restored by an executable statement.

Another statement which performs essentially this same function of variable iniialization is the DATA statement. It will not be covered in this text because it offers no significant power in initializing variables over a Type statement.

> Only the most judicious use should be made of this method of defining values of variables. Using a Type statement to define values of variables is one of the primary reasons programs fail to run properly on a second iteration. It is much safer to have initialization done by executable statements. Furthermore, using a Type statement to do initialization increases both the time required to compile the program and the bulk of the compiled program.

Extended Precision REAL

In an IBM 360 or 370 computer, variables typed REAL occupy one word of storage (4 bytes) and can hold either four alphanumeric characters or a number with from 1 to 7 significant decimal digits (approximate magnitude: 16^{-63} to 16^{63} or zero). Now we introduce a variation.

The REAL Type statement can be written in three ways:

```
REAL   list
REAL*4 list
REAL*8 list
```

The first two forms are identical in meaning, but the third form (REAL*8) reserves two words of storage (8 bytes). If a variable is so typed, it can hold either eight alphanumeric characters or a number with from 1 to 16 significant decimal digits (again with magnitude: 16^{-63} to 16^{63} or zero). For example:

```
REAL*8 A,B,CAT(10)
```

declares A, B, and all ten elements of CAT as "extended precision" REAL variables, each of which can contain up to 16 significant decimal digits.

These are the only options available for REAL variables. Another statement, DOUBLE PRECISION, performs the same task as REAL*8; it will not be described in this text.

> A REAL*8 takes up twice as much storage as a regular REAL variable. It also slows execution time down -- even by a factor of 4 sometimes. Don't use it unless you have to but be aware that there are many situations when you might. Furthermore, the tipoffs that you need to go to REAL*8 are usually subtle: wrong answers. See Appendix H on Numerical Considerations in Computing and Module 12 on Fortran Data Forms.

Space-Saving INTEGER

Three forms of the INTEGER type statement are possible:

```
INTEGER list
INTEGER*4 list
INTEGER*2 list
```

Both INTEGER and INTEGER*4 are identical in meaning: each variable so declared is four bytes in length and can contain up to four alphanumeric characters, or a whole number with a maximum magnitude of 2147483647, i.e., $2^{31}-1$.

The statement

```
INTEGER*2 list
```

declares variables as two bytes in length which can hold up to two alphabetic characters or a number with a maximum magnitude of 32767, i.e., $2^{15}-1$. Examples:

```
INTEGER C,EACH(200)
INTEGER*2 A,B,DOGGIE(3,6)
INTEGER*4 F,G,LOOT(4,3,7)
```

The need to conserve memory space might suggest using INTEGER*2 if you are certain that your variable will never need to hold a number larger than $2^{15}-1$.

> Some time is usually lost during execution in using INTEGER*2, but it is frequently more than offset by the saving in storage which can result. For example, if you have an INTEGER array of 10000 elements, each of which holds a number between 0 and 100, there is some point to considering INTEGER*2.

Summary of Type Statements

The table below shows the number of storage bytes required and allowed for each Type statement.

TYPE STATEMENT	LENGTH	VALUES
REAL or REAL*4	4	4 alphabetic characters or up to 7 significant digits
REAL*8	8	8 alphabetic characters or up to 16 significant digits
INTEGER or INTEGER*4	4	4 alphabetic characters or 9 decimal digits
INTEGER*2	2	2 alphabetic characters or 4 decimal digits

The length specification can be combined with the initialization information in the Type Declaration statement. For example:

```
REAL*8 A/3.95632147/,B/'REGULARS'/,C(50)/50*0./
```

or

```
INTEGER*2 Q/23/,R/'IN'/,S/1234/
```

A further discussion of Typing appears in Module 10.

As a general rule, remember that in most computer programs there is a trade-off between the amount of storage required for the program and data, and the amount of time required to execute the program. You can frequently conserve one at the expense of the other. For example, suppose that you have an array of 1000 X's. As the program progresses you repeatedly need some function of these values. If you wanted to save time you could compute the function of each X and store the results in 1000 additional array positions, say Y. On the other hand, to save memory space, you could compute each value of Y as you need it. For most applications of any complexity, the programmer should weigh the two factors relating to speed and program size before selecting an algorithm. Sometimes the choice will be forced upon the programmer based upon the computing installation, the management, and the equipment.

SUBPROGRAMS

Thus far we have generally considered a program to be a single set of instructions which tell the computer to perform a set of tasks. It is often convenient to divide a program into a set of subprograms, all of which work together to instruct the computer. In Fortran there is always exactly one main program (the kind written in every case so far). In addition, one or more subprograms may exist.

You have already had experience with subprograms in the form of FUNCTIONs such as SQRT which are part of the Fortran language. We review and extend such subprograms first.

FUNCTIONs

A Fortran FUNCTION is invoked (called into action) on the right side of an assignment statement. It may specify one or more arguments (inputs to the function) and it produces one output value. Fortran contains many built-in (Fortran-supplied) FUNCTIONs. The inputs to a FUNCTION are called arguments and the output is the FUNCTION value.

Fortran-Supplied FUNCTIONs

Nearly one hundred FUNCTIONs are supplied to the user by the Fortran system. The FUNCTION name with the associated argument(s) is used in an assignment statement and the proper value is returned in that statement. For example, if we write:

```
A=144.0
B=SQRT(A)
```

the value 12.0 will be stored in B. SQRT is one of the built-in FUNCTIONs in Fortran. To invoke a FUNCTION one writes the FUNCTION name followed by a left parenthesis followed by the argument(s), followed by a right parenthesis. If a FUNCTION reference contains two or more items, each is separated from the next by a comma.

Several FUNCTION references may exist in one assignment statement. For example:

```
X=SQRT(A)*SIN(B)+ABS(C)
```

If several FUNCTION references do exist in one assignment statement, they are invoked in the order specified by the hierarchy of the expression.

Some of the built-in FUNCTIONs, together with the required argument types, are listed below. A complete list of FUNCTIONs may be found in Module 14.

Some Commonly Used Fortran-Supplied FUNCTIONs

Each of the following FUNCTIONs has only one argument.

FUNCTION USE	FUNCTION NAME	TYPE ARGUMENT	TYPE VALUE RETURNED
Exponential (e to the x power)	EXP DEXP	REAL*4 REAL*8	REAL*4 REAL*8
Natural Logarithm	ALOG DLOG	REAL*4 REAL*8	REAL*4 REAL*8
Common Logarithm	ALOG10 DLOG10	REAL*4 REAL*8	REAL*4 REAL*8
Square Root	SQRT DSQRT	REAL*4 REAL*8	REAL*4 REAL*8
Absolute Value	IABS ABS DABS	INTEGER*4 REAL*4 REAL*8	INTEGER*4 REAL*4 REAL*8
Trigonometric Sine(argument in radians)	SIN DSIN	REAL*4 REAL*8	REAL*4 REAL*8
Trigonometric Cosine(argument in radians)	COS DCOS	REAL*4 REAL*8	REAL*4 REAL*8
Trigonometric Tangent (argument in radians)	TAN DTAN	REAL*4 REAL*8	REAL*4 REAL*8
Trigonometric Cotangent (argument in radians)	COTAN DCOTAN	REAL*4 REAL*8	REAL*4 REAL*8
Float	FLOAT DFLOAT	INTEGER*4 INTEGER*4	REAL*4 REAL*8
Fix	IFIX HFIX	REAL*4 REAL*4	INTEGER*4 INTEGER*2

It is also possible, however, to write your own FUNCTIONs. Further, you can write another kind of subprogram called a SUBROUTINE. A third type of subprogram exists in Fortran: it is called a Statement FUNCTION. It is shown in the Summary of Fortran Statements but, because it is of so little value, it is not discussed in this text.

User-Created Subprograms -- An Example

To illustrate how subprograms might be used we return to Revised Lab Problem 02, which calculated the area of a geometric figure. Here, for convenience, is a copy of a Fortran program which solves that problem:

```
      REAL HEIGHT,WIDTH,PI,RAREA,SAREA,AREA
      PI=3.141593
      READ,HEIGHT,WIDTH
      IF (HEIGHT.LE.WIDTH/2.) GO TO 23
      RAREA=HEIGHT,WIDTH
      SAREA=PI*WIDTH**2/8.
      AREA=RAREA-SAREA
      PRINT,HEIGHT,WIDTH,AREA
      RETURN
   23 CONTINUE
      PRINT,HEIGHT,WIDTH
      RETURN
      END
```

Even after you know about subprograms you would probably still write this program pretty much in this way because it is short and simple. But suppose that each of its several tasks -- reading HEIGHT and WIDTH, computing the semicircle area, etc. -- were more complicated. Then you might want to break the problem up into parts. Your program, with the subprograms you wrote, might look like this:

```
      REAL HEIGHT,WIDTH,AREA
      REAL RECT,SEMI
      CALL GET(HEIGHT,WIDTH)
      IF(HEIGHT.LE.WIDTH/2.) GO TO 23
      AREA=RECT(HEIGHT,WIDTH)-SEMI(WIDTH)
      CALL PUT(HEIGHT,WIDTH,AREA)              Main Program
      RETURN
   23 CONTINUE
      CALL PUTERR(HEIGHT,WIDTH)
      RETURN
      END

      REAL FUNCTION RECT(HEIGHT,WIDTH)
      REAL HEIGHT,WIDTH
      RECT=HEIGHT*WIDTH                       FUNCTION RECT
      RETURN
      END

      REAL FUNCTION SEMI(DIAMTR)
      REAL DIAMTR,PI/3.141593/
      SEMI=PI*DIAMTR**2/8.                    FUNCTION SEMI
      RETURN
      END

      SUBROUTINE GET(HEIGHT,WIDTH)
      REAL HEIGHT,WIDTH
      READ, HEIGHT,WIDTH                      SUBROUTINE GET
      RETURN
      END

      SUBROUTINE PUT(A,B,C)
      REAL A,B,C
      PRINT, A,B,C                            SUBROUTINE PUT
      RETURN
      END

      SUBROUTINE PUTERR(Y,Z)
      REAL Y,Z
      PRINT, Y,Z                              SUBROUTINE PUTERR
      RETURN
      END
```

Well, we only made it about twice as long and four times as confusing. But reconsider! What we have written, in addition to the main program, are five little subprograms -- RECT, SEMI, GET, PUT, PUTERR -- which are virtually independent of the main program, could have been written at different times by different people, and could be tested separately.

The statements in each subprogram are activated by a FUNCTION reference or a CALL statement in the main program. The variables in parentheses after the subprogram names provide the communications link between the main program and the subprogram.

Let's look at the FUNCTIONs first. There are two of them: RECT and SEMI. They are declared as REAL <u>scalar variables</u> in the main program. When they are used in the main program, in the statement

```
AREA=RECT(HEIGHT,WIDTH)-SEMI(WIDTH)
```

each is followed by <u>arguments</u> in parentheses. As with FUNCTIONs like SQRT, the arguments supply information to the FUNCTION subprogram which does some calculation and returns the answer to the main program via the FUNCTION name. In this case RECT(HEIGHT,WIDTH) produces the area of a rectangle as the product of HEIGHT and WIDTH, just as SQRT(W) produces the square root of the number stored as W.

The primary difference between SQRT and RECT is that SQRT is supplied to programmers within the context of the Fortran language. Here the programmer has written the subprogram RECT. Let's examine the REAL FUNCTION RECT in detail.

First notice that it is a separate program with its own Type Declaration statement and its own END statement. The first statement of the FUNCTION

```
REAL FUNCTION RECT(HEIGHT,WIDTH)
```

does several things:

1. It tells the name of the FUNCTION. This name must be identical to the name used in the main program.

2. It declares the Type of the FUNCTION name. Thus REAL FUNCTION RECT in the subprogram corresponds to the declaration of RECT as REAL in the main program.

3. It specifies the <u>parameters</u>, in this case, HEIGHT and WIDTH, of the FUNCTION. You can consider that the parameters are the "input" values from the main program with which the FUNCTION will operate.

The second statement in FUNCTION RECT declares and Types all the variables that the FUNCTION will work with except the FUNCTION name itself.

The third statement is simply an arithmetic replacement statement,

```
RECT=HEIGHT*WIDTH
```

which defines the FUNCTION name, RECT, to have the value that is to be returned by the FUNCTION.

The fourth statement is an old friend employed in a new context. RETURN means to transfer control back to the program which activated the FUNCTION, since the work of the FUNCTION is completed. Control is transferred back to the main program at precisely the point the reference to the FUNCTION was made.

As with all good Fortran programs, the last statement is END.

The REAL FUNCTION SEMI, which computes the area of a semicircle based on its diameter, is similar to RECT. Some differences are apparent. The first is that the FUNCTION reference in the main program has only one argument and, correspondingly, the first statement of the FUNCTION subprogram

```
REAL FUNCTION SEMI(DIAMTR)
```

has only one parameter. The second difference is that the <u>argument</u> name is WIDTH but the <u>parameter</u> name is DIAMTR. The ability to use different names in this situation contributes to the independence of the subprogram from the main program. This is the same property which allows you to use SQRT(W) and SQRT(ABCDEF) in the same program. There must be certain agreement between arguments and parameters (e.g., same number of arguments as parameters, corresponding arguments and parameters must be of the same Type and length) but the variable names used need not be identical.

A third thing to notice about SEMI is that it contains a variable PI which is not in the main program. This variable, since it is not a parameter (and also is not the subprogram name), is completely independent of the main program. If there were a variable named PI in the main program it would <u>not</u> be the same variable as PI in the subprogram.

We turn our attention now to the other variety of subprogram illustrated: the SUBROUTINE. There are three here: GET, PUT, and PUTERR. There are great similarities between FUNCTIONs and SUBROUTINEs. It is easier to just talk about the differences. Take GET for example:

1. It is activated by a separate statement, CALL, rather than being referenced or invoked within an expression.

2. It has no Type. It is simply SUBROUTINE GET.

3. Its name is not used to return a value to the main program. All communication with the main program takes place through arguments and parameters. In the case of GET, the statements in the subprogram cause two REAL variables to be read and the values transmitted to the main program via the argument/parameter linkage.

Now you should go through the example program step by step to get a feel for how subprograms operate. After that read below to understand the details and to find out the power and advantages of using subprograms.

For the remainder of this chapter the words FUNCTION and SUBROUTINE will often be used alone instead of appending the word subprogram each time.

Rationale

There are several reasons for breaking a task into subprograms. Some are:

1. A large program can be written by various people if each person writes one subprogram. (Take a look at Lab Problem 41, the Magic Square.)

2. A large program can be tested and, if necessary, debugged more easily if it is written as a set of subprograms.

3. Subprograms often contain instructions that are to be executed many times. Rather than including these instructions in the main program each time the set is to be used, memory space can be conserved if these instructions are in the form of a subprogram and re-used each time.

4. A program can be logically segmented into subprograms.

5. Once a subprogram is written, it can be reused later with another calling program.

To illustrate some of these reasons for using subprograms assume that a program requires the calculation of factorials at several different points. N factorial is defined as

N!=N*(N-1)*(N-2)*. . .*1

For example,

4!=4*3*2*1=24
6!=6*5*4*3*2*1=720

Our old approach would involve writing the instructions to compute the factorial at each point of the program where it was needed. A better approach, however, involves calculation of the factorial by a subprogram each time. A reduction in computer storage required to do the job would result.

The diagram below shows schematically the factorial subprogram being used twice. The pair of solid lines shows the first transfer from the main program to the subprogram and RETURN; the dotted lines show the second CALL and RETURN.

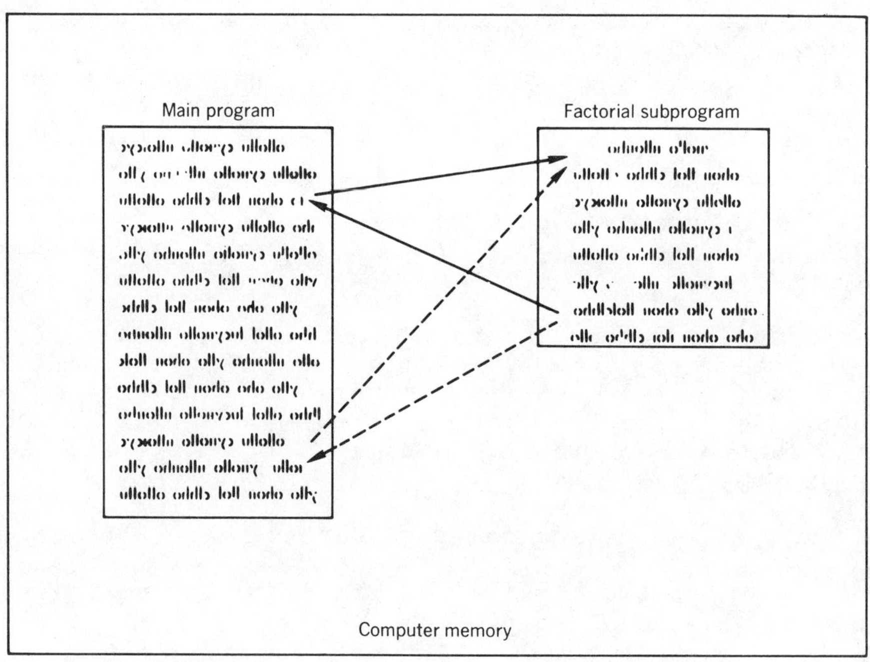

User-Created Functions

The programmer can use his/her own FUNCTIONs by performing two steps:

1. writing statements which invoke the FUNCTION, and

2. writing the FUNCTION subprogram.

He first decides upon a unique name which follows the rules for naming Fortran variables (i.e., it contains from 1-6 alphanumeric characters, the first of which must be alphabetic; no special characters are allowed). Whenever the FUNCTION value is desired, he writes the FUNCTION name followed by the argument(s).

Suppose that the programmer decides upon the name NFACT for the FUNCTION to compute a factorial. Whenever he wants to compute the factorial of a value, he simply writes a statement like this:

```
K=NFACT(N)
```

where N contains the value for which he wishes to compute the factorial. The factorial will be stored in K. Suppose he decides that the FUNCTION is to return (or produce) an INTEGER value. He would declare NFACT to be INTEGER in his main, or calling, program.

A program using NFACT could look like this:

```
INTEGER NFACT,K,N
N=6
K=NFACT(N)
PRINT, N, K
RETURN
END
```

which should print

```
6        720
```

assuming the subprogram NFACT is properly written.

The FUNCTION subprogram is a separate program which returns a single value to the invoking or calling program.

The first statement of the FUNCTION subprogram is:

```
REAL FUNCTION name(a1,a2,a3,....)
```

or

```
INTEGER FUNCTION name(a1,a2,a3,....)
```

where "name" is the name chosen for the FUNCTION and parameters a1, a2, a3... are nonsubscripted variables or array names. REAL is used if the FUNCTION is to return a REAL value to the calling program and INTEGER is used to return an INTEGER value.

Since the FUNCTION is a separate program, the variables and statement numbers within it are independent of any other program, except for those names which appear in its set of parameters.

The parameters in the FUNCTION must agree with the arguments in the calling program in number, order, type, and length.

Following is an example of how the NFACT FUNCTION subprogram could be written.

```
C ROUTINE PROVIDES FACTORIALS OF POSITIVE INTEGERS
      INTEGER FUNCTION NFACT(NUMBER)
      INTEGER NUMBER,L,ACCUM
      IF (NUMBER.LE.2) GO TO 101
      ACCUM=2
      DO 102 L=3,NUMBER
      ACCUM=ACCUM*L
  102 CONTINUE
      NFACT=ACCUM
      GO TO 103
  101 CONTINUE
      NFACT=NUMBER
  103 CONTINUE
      RETURN
      END
```

Consider the following:

1. The variable N in the calling program in the preceding section corresponds to the variable NUMBER in the FUNCTION. The variables L and ACCUM are unique to the FUNCTION. They exist only in the FUNCTION.

2. The INTEGER FUNCTION statement is always the first

statement of the FUNCTION subprogram.[1]

3. The name of the FUNCTION is set equal to the value to be returned to the calling program. This happens either with the statement NFACT=ACCUM or NFACT=NUMBER.

4. Return to the calling program takes place when the RETURN statement is executed.

Storage Locations of Arguments and Parameters

It is important now to conceptualize the locations in memory which are used to store the arguments and parameters. For scalar variables the story is this: the value of an argument in the calling program which corresponds to a parameter in the subprogram is located in one and only one memory location. This location is part of the data area of the main program. The preceeding statement is true even if different names are used for the argument and parameter. The subprogram "figures out" where in the calling program the argument value is located at the time the subprogram is invoked ,or called, and uses the value in that location as a parameter. An example is demanded.

Calling Program

```
REAL R,S,T,A,X
R=3.
S=4.
T=100.
A=X(R,S,T)
    •
    •
END
```

FUNCTION Subprogram

```
REAL FUNCTION X(A,B,C)
REAL A,B,C,Q
Q=A*(B-C)
X=Q/100.
RETURN
END
```

The value returned to the calling program and stored in A will be -2.88. Verify that this is true.

---

[1] If the name of a FUNCTION is not explicitly typed as either REAL or INTEGER, the FUNCTION name chosen determines the Type value returned to the calling program. If the name begins with a letter I-N then the value returned is INTEGER, otherwise the value is REAL. The first statement in the FUNCTION subprogram could be FUNCTION NFACT(NUMBER) instead of INTEGER FUNCTION NFACT(NUMBER) and NFACT would still return an INTEGER value, because its name begins with an N.

The variables A, B, and C in the FUNCTION subprogram really refer to R, S, and T in the calling program. The variable A in the calling program is unique to it and has no similarity to A in the FUNCTION subprogram. The variable Q in the FUNCTION subprogram is unique to it. For all the variables used in the two programs -- R, S, T, A, A, B, C, and Q -- only 5 actually occupy memory space: R, S, T and A in the calling program and Q in the subprogram.

Using Arrays in Subprograms

This matter of the location of the variables which are arguments and parameters is quite important when arrays are being shared between programs. By analogy with the preceding section, such arrays occupy space only once -- in the calling program. For example, suppose we want a FUNCTION which will provide the sum of the elements of an array. We could write:

Calling Program

```
      REAL EL(25),S,T,SUM
      INTEGER NUMELE
      NUMELE=18
    8 CONTINUE
      S=SUM(EL,NUMELE)
      NUMELE=12
      T=SUM(EL,NUMELE)
      RETURN
      END
```

FUNCTION Subprogram

```
      REAL FUNCTION SUM(A,N)
      INTEGER N,J
      REAL A(25),B
      B=0.
      DO 8 J=1,N
      B=B+A(J)
    8 CONTINUE
      SUM=B
      RETURN
      END
```

In this coding, the array EL, which is dimensioned 25, holds in its first "NUMELE" positions the numbers which are to be summed by the FUNCTION. EL(25) corresponds to the array A(25) in the FUNCTION; in fact, they are the same array and the locations they occupy are part of the data storage area of the main program.

There is a statement number 8 in the main program and a statement number 8 in the subprogram. They are independent. The fact that the variable names and statement numbers are independent of each other makes it possible for one person to do part of a programming project by writing a main program and delegating the writing of a subprogram to another person. Neither needs to be concerned about the variable names and statement numbers the other uses. They only need to agree on the order, number, type, and length of the arguments.

Variable-Sized Arrays

A rule from the beginning has been that only INTEGER *constants* may be used to specify array sizes in Type Declaration Statements. This remains true when one is considering main or primary programs. However, the facility exists in subprograms to use variable names in Type Declaration Statements instead of constants for arrays which are parameters of a subprogram. In this case the array has been actually declared to have a given size by a Type Declaration Statement in the calling program; the array size values in the subprogram must agree with those set up in the calling program even though they may be expressed as variables. For example, consider a rewrite of FUNCTION SUM and its calling program:

Calling Program

```
      REAL EL(25),S,T,SUM
      INTEGER NUMELE, ARSIZE
      ARSIZE=25
      NUMELE=18
          .
    8 CONTINUE
          .
      S=SUM(EL,NUMELE,ARSIZE)
          .
          .
          .
      NUMELE=12
          .
          .
      T=SUM(EL,NUMELE,ARSIZE)
          .
          .
      RETURN
      END
```

FUNCTION Subprogram

```
      REAL FUNCTION SUM(A,N,DIM)
      INTEGER N,J,DIM
      REAL A(DIM),B
      B=0.
      DO 8 J=1,N
      B=B+A(J)
    8 CONTINUE
      SUM=B
      RETURN
      END
```

Here the purpose of the FUNCTION SUM is to add together N elements of an array named A which has length DIM. Thus the calling program passes three arguments to the FUNCTION. First the array itself which is named EL in the calling program; second, the number of elements that are to be added; and third, the length of the array in the calling program. Why is this ability to use a variable name in the

Type Declaration Statement in a subprogram useful? Because it makes the subprogram more general and allows it to be used with other calling programs. Thus our FUNCTION SUM might also be used as a subprogram for a calling program like this:

```
      REAL EX(53),UUUUUU,SUM
      INTEGER NNN,SIZ
      SIZ=53
         .
         .
         .
      UUUUUU=1.888/SUM(EX,NNN,SIZ)
         .
         .
         .
      END
```

without making any changes in the subprogram. If the length of the array in the subprogram had been stated as a constant such as

```
      REAL A(25)
```

instead of

```
      REAL A(DIM)
```

then the subprogram would not have worked for the calling program containing EX regardless of whether variable-sized or fixed-sized arrays were used. When an array is shared between a calling and a called program, it must be declared to have the same dimensions (and number of dimensions) in each. For example, an array in a calling program which was Typed as

```
GEORGE(2,8,6)
```

and which is used as an argument in a FUNCTION reference must match up with another array in the FUNCTION, e.g.,

```
OTHER(2,8,6)
```

<u>The dimension information must be the same in the subprogram as in the calling program</u>.

Sample Deck Set-up with Subprograms

You may use the following deck setup with programs written for compilation by WATFOR/FIV.

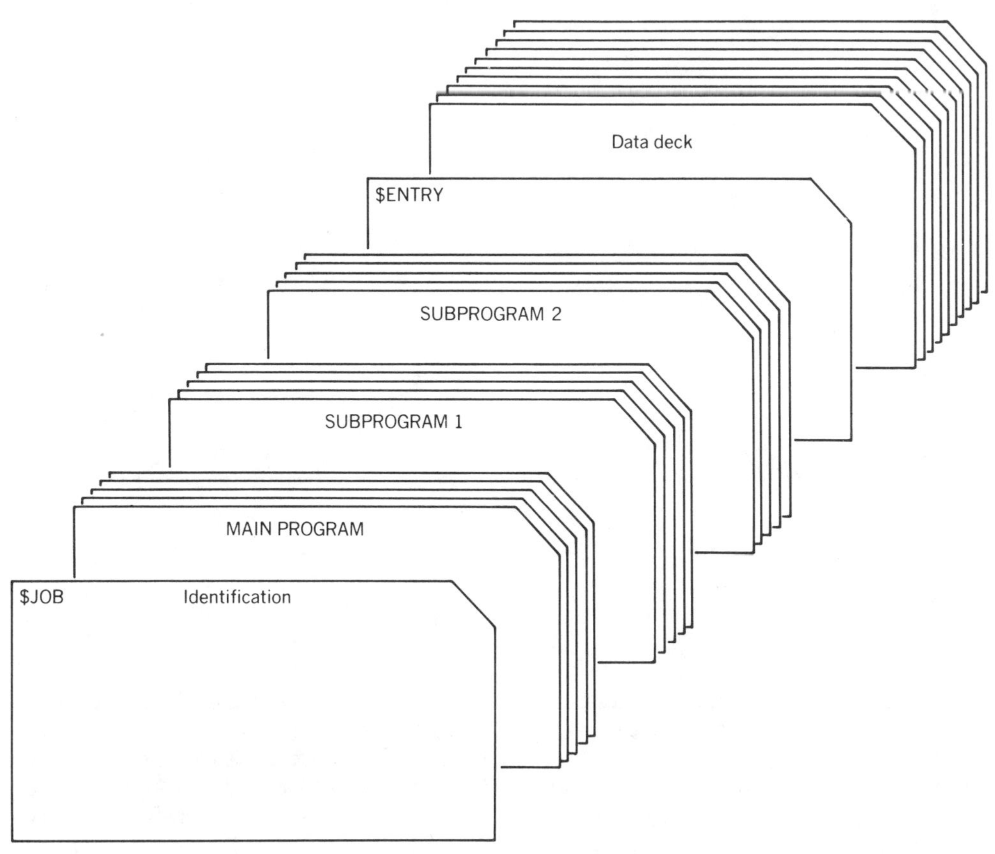

The main program and the subprograms have END statements to tell the compiler when each deck has been read in. The main program and the subprogram are separate Fortran programs.

> One advantage of using subprograms is that sometimes they can be compiled separately from the main program and the resulting machine language programs, called object decks, can simply be included with the main program when it is run. The operating system of the computer sets up the necessary linkages between the two programs. In WATFOR, however, this advantage does not exist.

All programs presented to WATFOR must be in source (Fortran) program form. WATFIV allows machine language programs to be included with Fortran decks. To make use of object decks, check the procedures of your particular computing installation.

Exercises

What might be wrong with the following?

Calling Program	FUNCTION Subprogram
REAL A,B,C,D,E	REAL FUNCTION MPY(G,H,I)
•	REAL G,H,I,R
•	R=G*H(I)
D=MPY(A,B,C)	MPY=R
•	RETURN
•	END
E=MPY(D,A)	
•	
•	
END	

Mites on the Fleas

It is not only main programs which can call or invoke subprograms. Subprograms can invoke other subprograms, which can in turn call other subprograms, almost without limit. A subprogram may not call itself, however. Nor may a subprogram call another subprogram which is itself under the influence of a call. That is, if A calls B and B calls C, C may not call either A or B.

User-Written SUBROUTINE Subprograms

A SUBROUTINE subprogram is invoked by a FORTRAN statement

```
CALL name (a1,a2,a3,...)
```

where "name" is the SUBROUTINE name chosen by the programmer and a1, a2, a3... are arguments. No specific value is returned via the subprogram name to the calling program as in the case of the FUNCTION subprogram. Hence the programmer does not assign a Type to the SUBROUTINE name.

The SUBROUTINE can store results in the arguments. The SUBROUTINE and FUNCTION are quite similar and most of what has been said before applies here.

The first statement of a SUBROUTINE is the statement

SUBROUTINE name (a1,a2,a3,...)

where "name" is the name chosen by the programmer and a1, a2, a3... are parameters.

Example 1

<u>Calling Program</u>

```
  REAL EL(25),S,T,ANS
  INTEGER NUMELE, ARSIZE
  ARSIZE=25
      •
      •
8 CALL SUM(EL,18,ARSIZE,ANS)
  S=ANS
      •
      •
  CALL SUM(EL,NUMELE,25,T)
      •
      •
  END
```

<u>SUBROUTINE Subprogram</u>

```
  SUBROUTINE SUM(A,N,DIM,AN)
  INTEGER N,J,DIM
  REAL A(DIM),B,AN
  B=0.
  DO 8 J=1,N
  B=B+A(J)
8 CONTINUE
  AN=B
  RETURN
  END
```

Example 1 performs the same job as the FUNCTION SUM earlier. Notice the differences:

1. The first statement is different (SUBROUTINE SUM rather than REAL FUNCTION SUM). The name of a SUBROUTINE is not typed as either INTEGER or REAL in the CALLing program because the name of a SUBROUTINE does not stand for a value.

2. A <u>CALL statement</u> is used to invoke the subprogram.

3. The SUBROUTINE stores the value directly in a parameter (AN), and hence in the corresponding argument in the CALL statement (ANS or T), rather than transmitting the value by means of a FUNCTION name.

Example 2

Another example will point out a case in which a FUNCTION should not be used. Suppose that a programmer wants to create a subprogram which will divide every element of a square matrix by a specific value. That is, an entire matrix is to be returned rather than a single scalar value.

Here the SUBROUTINE named DIV divides every element of the matrix X by the third argument in the CALL statement, V.

<u>Calling Program</u>

```
REAL X(30,30),V
    •
    •
    •
CALL DIV(X,30,V)
    •
    •
    •
END
```

<u>SUBROUTINE Subprogram</u>

```
  SUBROUTINE DIV(R,K,T)
  REAL R(K,K),T
  INTEGER K,M,N
  DO 3 M=1,K
  DO 4 N=1,K
  R(M,N)=R(M,N)/T
4 CONTINUE
3 CONTINUE
  RETURN
  END
```

The program above brings up an interesting point: you have to be awfully careful when invoking any subprogram if you use a constant as an argument. We stop just short of saying "don't do it." The danger is illustrated by the results of the following program:

```
INTEGER I
I=13
PRINT, I
CALL BADSUB(13)
J=13
PRINT, J
RETURN
END
SUBROUTINE BADSUB(M)
INTEGER M
M=-65
RETURN
END
```

What would be printed? If the compiler lets you get away with this idiocy -- and some do -- the printed results will be

```
 13
-65
```

The value of the constant 13 will have been changed to -65. So don't ever invoke a subprogram with a constant as an argument without first checking that the subprogram doesn't change the corresponding parameter.

Calling and Dummy Arguments -- A Nasty Exercise

What we present now is slightly simplified, but it should increase your understanding of subprograms. When a CALL statement is executed, control is transferred to a subprogram. At the same time, actions are performed regarding the arguments of the CALL; the discussion which follows is a description of those actions.

A SUBROUTINE begins with a SUBROUTINE statement

```
SUBROUTINE name (a1,a2,a3,...)
```

where parameters a1, a2, a3,... are sometimes termed dummy arguments because they simply stand in place of the actual arguments in the CALL statement. At the time the subprogram was compiled, the addresses or location references of the dummy variables were "left blank."

When the CALL statement is executed, the actual addresses of the dummy arguments are "filled-in" with addresses of the arguments within the calling program. To illustrate, suppose the following main and sub- programs were written:

Calling Program	SUBROUTINE Subprogram
A=5.	SUBROUTINE SUB(T,W)
B=10.	•
•	•
•	S=2.5
CALL SUB(A,B)	Q=50.
•	•
•	•
S=B	T=Q*S
•	W=Q*T
•	•
•	•
RETURN	RETURN
END	END

Variables A, B, and S occupy locations in the data storage area of the calling program, and variables Q and S occupy locations in the data storage area of the subprogram. The variables T and W are dummy arguments; their names refer to storage locations in the calling (in this case, main) program.

References to the variable T in the subprogram actually refer to the variable A in the main program and references to the variable W in the subprogram actually refer to the variable B in the main program. The variables S and Q in the subprogram are not dummy variables; they actually exist in the subprogram and are different from any variables in the main program. The variable S in the main program has no similarity to S in the subprogram; they represent two different locations. The diagram below shows a representation of computer storage before the program is executed. We suggest that you pretend you are a computer and follow through the program and subprogram to gain further insight into what actually occurs when a CALL statement is executed. You should fill in the blanks for locations 602, 603, 604, 846, 847 and three sets of parentheses.

COMPUTER STORAGE

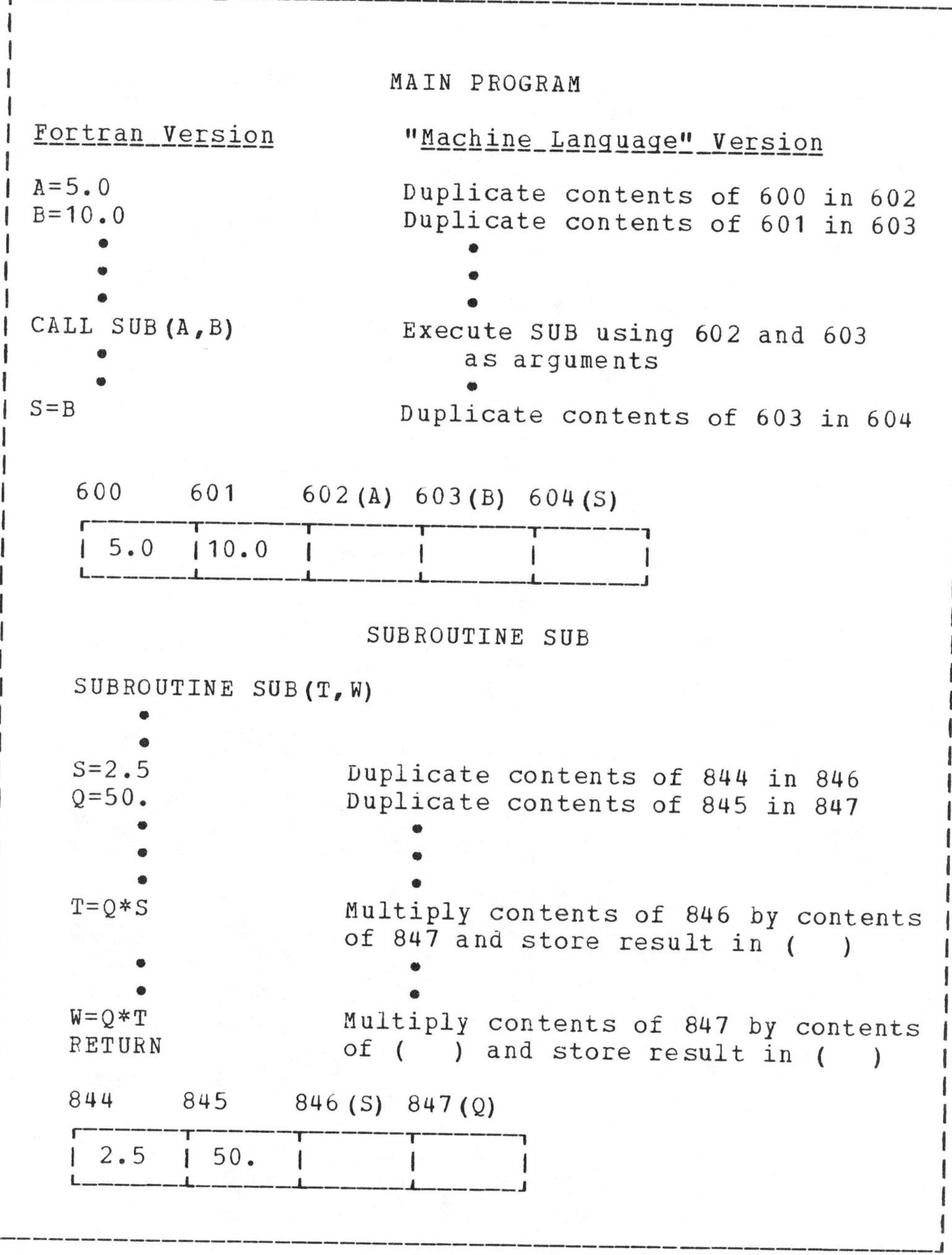

The completed exercise is in Appendix P. But don't look yet. And don't try to figure out what the purpose of the program is. Just follow the instructions, looking first at the Fortran, then at the "machine language."

Every algorithm of any complexity at all involves decisions. If you are drawing a flowchart or writing a program and come to a point where the machine must make a decision, then you too must make a decision: which branch of the coding should you do first? If the branch you select also has a decision in it, the problem is compounded. One suggestion is to code the shorter branch first -- you are less likely to forget the longer one.

A situation in which one branch can be disposed of quite quickly is when you are testing for an error of some sort. Presumably you want to print out a signal on the printed output, should an error occur. One technique for doing this is to write a subroutine similar to OUCH below:

```
      SUBROUTINE OUCH(N)
      INTEGER N
      WRITE (6,601) N
  601 FORMAT('0**WOOPS**',6X,'ERROR#',I4)
      RETURN
      END
```

Now suppose you are at a point in the program at which you want to signify an error if a variable, WEIGHT, is negative. You simply write

```
      NUMERR=23
      IF (WEIGHT.LT.0) CALL OUCH(NUMERR)
```

and dutifully write down on your documentation notes, which are ever by your side, that error number 23 refers to a value of WEIGHT less than zero.

Using subroutine OUCH is not a perfect solution, but it is vastly superior to reflecting momentarily on the probable impact of WEIGHT being negative and then saying, "Heck, that won't happen," because it's too much trouble to diagnose and announce it.

> Subroutine OUCH could, of course, have more arguments, such as telling it whether to RETURN or stop execution, or to set some flag in the program to signify that an error has occurred. A really sophisticated OUCH could have arrays of explanatory error messages. But regardless of the form you choose to use, you would be wise to employ some neatly packaged method of dealing with errors which occur during the execution of your programs.

COMMON Data Storage

If subprograms are invoked often, a great deal of computer time can be used in passing the addresses of arguments back and forth between calling programs and subprograms. A method of eliminating this passing back and forth has been devised and included in Fortran. It is called COMMON storage. The concept is simply that one or more COMMON areas can be established in which variables are stored. If the location of the contents of COMMON are known to both the calling program and the subprogram, no passing of argument addresses is required. COMMON is established by including statements of the form:

```
COMMON /name/a,b,c,d,...
```

in both the calling program and the subprogram. Here name refers to a COMMON block name and a, b, c, d,... are the variable or array names which make up the block of locations.

In this form of the COMMON statement the name, which is always imbedded in slashes, follows the same rules as do variable names but it is not the name of a variable; rather it is the name of a block of variables or arrays which may be of any Type. To illustrate, consider the program and subprogram below:

Calling Program

```
REAL CAT,COW,DOG,TOTAL
COMMON/AAA/CAT,COW,DOG
READ, CAT,COW,DOG
CALL ADDUM(TOTAL)
PRINT, TOTAL
RETURN
END
```

SUBROUTINE Subprogram

```
SUBROUTINE ADDUM(SUMIT)
REAL HORSE,MOOSE,PIG,SUMIT
COMMON/AAA/HORSE,MOOSE,PIG
SUMIT=HORSE+MOOSE+PIG
RETURN
END
```

Here the subprogram (ADDUM) deals with four quantities (SUMIT, HORSE, MOOSE, PIG). Only one of these quantities is passed to the subprogram; the others are in a COMMON storage area named AAA under different names. Both the calling program and the subprogram know where COMMON block AAA is located. Within the COMMON block there is a one-to-one correspondence between the variables. Thus, CAT is the same variable as HORSE, COW the same as MOOSE, etc.

The above discussion pertains to what is called <u>labeled COMMON</u>. There is another kind of COMMON called <u>blank COMMON</u>. Blank COMMON is similar to labeled COMMON except that it is not given a name by the programmer. There can be several labelled COMMON areas, each with a different name; there is only one blank COMMON area.

Example

<u>Calling Program</u>

```
REAL A(30),B(6),C,D
COMMON A,B,C,D
     .
CALL XX
     .
     .
     .
     .
END
```

<u>Subprogram</u>

```
  SUBROUTINE XX
  REAL E(30),F(6),G,H
  INTEGER K
  COMMON E,F,G,H
  H=0.
  DO 8 K=1,30
  H=H+E(K)
8 CONTINUE
  RETURN
  END
```

The COMMON storage area has been described as containing 38 locations. The first 30 are an array, the next 6 are another array, the next two locations are each scalar variables. In the example above, the array called A in the calling program is identical to E in the subprogram; this array consists of 30 locations. The sum of this array is stored in the location called D in the calling program (H in the subprogram) since it is the 38th location in COMMON.

Notice that a SUBROUTINE may be CALLed and defined without arguments; this is not true for a FUNCTION which must have at least one argument. FUNCTIONs may, however, use COMMON storage.

Computer memory containing subprograms and COMMON blocks might be thought of as being segmented as shown below:

```
┌──────────────────┐
│ MAIN PROGRAM     │
├──────────────────┤
│ SUBPROGRAM 1     │
├──────────────────┤
│ SUBPROGRAM 2     │
├──────────────────┤
│       .          │
├──────────────────┤
│ SUBPROGRAM n     │
├──────────────────┤
│       .          │
├──────────────────┤
│       .          │
├──────────────────┤
│ COMMON/name1/    │
├──────────────────┤
│ COMMON/name2/    │
├──────────────────┤
│ blank COMMON     │
└──────────────────┘
```

Restrictions

If a variable appears in a COMMON block, it may not be included in the arguments of a CALL statement or in the dummy arguments of a subprogram. Furthermore, if a name is used as the name of a COMMON block, it must not be used as a variable name.

BLOCK DATA

In most Fortran dialects, if a variable or array name appears in COMMON, it may not be given an initial value in a Type Declaration statement in a main or subprogram. That is, it would be incorrect to write:

```
REAL A/0./,B/100./,C(2)/'AGE1','AGE2'/
COMMON A,B,C
```

If a variable name appears in a labeled COMMON block, it may be initialized by a Type Declaration Statement, but this statement must appear in a separate, special, "subprogram" called a BLOCK DATA subprogram. A BLOCK DATA subprogram is not named and cannot contain any executable statements. The subprogram begins with the statement:

and it must end with an END statement. The BLOCK DATA subprogram can be used to initialize variables in <u>labeled</u> COMMON blocks but cannot be used to initialize variables in <u>blank</u> COMMON blocks in Fortran.

> It is interesting to note that BLOCK DATA subprograms are not necessary in WATFOR/FIV, where a Type Declaration Statement can initialize variables in either blank or labeled COMMON.
>
> We say "interesting" rather than "worthwhile" because one of the best ways to get into trouble doing programming is to use some of the nifty features that some compilers use which are not standard on other compilers. If you write a program which you might someday want to use on another machine (you move to another city, perhaps) or with another compiler (for better execution efficiency), you may have boxed yourself in. Our advice is to avoid special features like the plague. If you must use non-standard features, use Comments to document them.

Only the following statements are allowed in a BLOCK DATA subprogram:

```
IMPLICIT statement (not yet discussed)
COMMON statement
Type Declaration Statements
DATA statement (not discussed in this text; also not
END statement                              important)
```

Any particular labeled COMMON block may be initialized by only one BLOCK DATA subprogram. A BLOCK DATA subprogram, however, can initialize values in several different labeled COMMON blocks.

For an example, suppose that you wanted to initialize a variable in COMMON to have the value 12345. You might write the following:

```
REAL A
COMMON/BLK1/A
```

and in a subprogram:

```
REAL X
COMMON/BLK1/X
```

and in another subprogram (BLOCK DATA) as follows:

```
BLOCK DATA
COMMON/BLK1/P
REAL P/12345./
END
```

Above we showed a variable which had three different names: A, X, and P. We used the different names so you would realize the flexibility which existed. It is best, however, to use the same names in main and subprograms when you can.

Really bad things can happen if the variables in COMMON blocks aren't lined up in the various subprograms in exactly the same way as each other and in the Main program. The simplest and most idiot-proof way of assuring correct alignment is to use a keypunch to make multiple, identical, sets of cards for each COMMON block of each subprogram. A set is then inserted into each subprogram regardless of whether each variable mentioned is used in each subprogram. It doesn't waste any space for data and it sure saves a lot of debugging time on occasion.

Exercises

1. What location is defined or re-defined in the calling program by the subprogram? What is its new value?

Calling Program

```
REAL A,B,C,Y
A=3.
B=2.
C=10.
CALL S(A,B,C,Y)
    .
    .
```

Subprogram

```
SUBROUTINE S(Y,C,B,A)
REAL A,B,C,Y
A=Y*C-B
RETURN
END
```

```
      .
RETURN
END
```

2. What location is changed in the calling program by the subprogram? What is its new value?

<u>Calling Program</u>

```
REAL A,B,C,Y
COMMON/LABEL/A,B,C,Y
A=0.
B=3.
C=27.
Y=40.
CALL S
      .
      .
      .
RETURN
END
```

<u>Subprogram</u>

```
SUBROUTINE S
REAL Q,R,S,T,W
COMMON/LABEL/Q,R,S,T
W=Q+R+S+T/2
Q=W**2
RETURN
END
```

Before you undertake to write a computer program, you should ask yourself if it is likely that someone else has faced this same problem, with different data perhaps, and written a program to solve it. Ask questions of the consultants at your local computing center about your problem and possible "canned" programs to solve it. If you want to solve a set of linear equations, tabulate the responses to a questionnaire, or compute the FICA (Social Security) tax on salaries, the chances are pretty good that someone has faced the problem before and may be able to hand you a program to do it. His/her program may not work, may not be documented so that you can use it, or may not run on your machine without modifications, but at least you have more options than if you never asked yourself the question: am I re-inventing the wheel?

part iii

selected fortran iv topic modules

MODULE 1

OPERATIONS WITH LOGICAL QUANTITIES

Prerequisites: Parts I and II

The capabilities of FORTRAN in handling numeric quantities (the arithmetic assignment statement, arithmetic constants, arithmetic variables, arithmetic operations, and input-output of arithmetic quantities) are old friends now.

We now turn our attention to a simpler but less familiar system in which Fortran also has capabilities.

This system involves "logical" quantities, i.e., those that can take on _only_ the values "true" and "false". The logical system has constants, variables, and operators just as its arithmetic counterpart does. The basic features of the logical system in Fortran will now be presented.

Logical Constants

Constants are fixed quantities in a program. Arithmetic constants can take on values such as

```
 6.2    -1.9531
15        3.141493
 0         .3815E+08
```

Logical constants, on the other hand, can take on only two values:

```
.TRUE.
.FALSE.
```

Logical Variables

Arithmetic variables are names that stand for numbers, or, put another way, they are names of locations where numbers are stored. They are typed, for example, as REAL or INTEGER. Logical variables are names which stand for one of the two values "true" or "false." All logical variables must be typed as LOGICAL. The names of logical variables, like other variable names, are from one to six characters; the first character must be alphabetic.

If it is desired to have the variable names A, B, and LOG1 and the array name XPR of 28 elements declared as logical variables, one would write:

```
LOGICAL A,B,LOG1,XPR(28)
```

This declaration statement restricts the variables A, B, LOG1, and <u>all</u> of the elements of the array XPR to take on only the values true or false. To define these variables, one might write

```
      INTEGER I
      A=.TRUE.
      B=.FALSE.
      LOG1=.TRUE.
      DO 15 I=1,28
      XPR(I)=.FALSE.
   15 CONTINUE
```

This shows how variables in the logical system might be given initial values in a manner equivalent to the arithmetic system's initialization of variables by setting them to constant values.

The statement

```
LOGICAL list
```

is a Type Declaration statement and follows the rules for such statements.

Three forms of the LOGICAL type statement are allowed:

```
LOGICAL
LOGICAL*1
LOGICAL*4
```

In the first and third cases, each logical variable occupies four bytes (one word) of storage. Optionally, (as in case two) a logical variable can be declared as using only one byte of storage. This form is space saving but increases the execution time of a program, whereas the first and third forms use more storage space but enable the program to execute faster. In most programs the difference is small. If a program requires extensive use of logical variables, however, (either because they are used frequently or there are many) a large difference in execution time or storage space can occur.

Examples:

```
LOGICAL P,Q,R(300)
LOGICAL*1 ABLE,BAKER,W(3,4)
LOGICAL*4 S,T(3,3,3)
```

Logical Operators

By now the student is familiar with the arithmetic operators **, *, /, +, and -. Usually each of these operators is a binary operator which combines the two quantities on either side of it according to some rule. For example,

```
F=D*X
```

means combine D and X to form a third quantity F according to the rule of multiplication.

In addition, the operator "-" can serve as a unary operator which means "change the quantity to the right of the operator according to some rule." For example,

```
K=-M
```

means to form the quantity K by changing the sign of M.

In similar fashion there are three operations in the logical system. ".AND." and".OR." are two binary logical operators and ".NOT." is a unary logical operator.

The rules for these operators are simpler than those for the arithmetic system but are probably not familiar. The unary operator ".NOT." will be explained first. Its function is simply to change a "true" to a "false" or a "false" to a "true". Consider the following example:

```
LOGICAL X1,X2,Y1,Y2
X1=.TRUE.
X2=.FALSE.
Y1=.NOT.X1
Y2=.NOT.X2
```

At the end of this program segment "Y1" would have the value "false". What value would "Y2" have?

A table summarizes the .NOT. operator:

Value of P	Value of .NOT.P
T	F
F	T

where T stands for .TRUE. and F for .FALSE.

The binary logical operator .AND. has essentially the same meaning as it does in English. It combines two separate expressions which each have <u>truth value</u> (that is, is either true or false) into a third quantity which has truth value. For example, the statement

"Tom is more than six feet tall AND Jim weighs at most 150 pounds."

is true <u>if and only if</u> the statements about Tom and Jim are both true. It is false if Tom is less than (or exactly) six feet. It is false if Jim weighs more than 150 lbs. It is also false if both of the statements about Tom and Jim are false.

The program segment

```
LOGICAL TOM,JIM,VALUE
TOM=.TRUE.
JIM=.FALSE.
VALUE=TOM.AND.JIM
```

would produce a false value for VALUE.

In tabular form the .AND. operator is summarized:

Value of P	Value of Q	Value of P.AND.Q
T	T	T
T	F	F
F	T	F
F	F	F

Given that the .NOT. operator has precedence over the .AND. operator, what value has VALUE after the following sequence:

```
LOGICAL K,Z,VALUE
K=.TRUE.
Z=.NOT.K
VALUE=K.AND..NOT.Z
```

The operator .OR. has a slightly different meaning in Fortran than in English. For those with a background in logic, the operator .OR. is the inclusive "or". The truth table for the .OR. operator is

Value of P	Value of Q	Value of P.OR.Q
T	T	T
T	F	T
F	T	T
F	F	F

The difference between Fortran and English is in the first line of the table which shows both operands as true and the resultant value as true; consider first the other three lines of the table. For example, the statement

"Hamlet was written by Shakespeare OR Hamlet was written by Bacon."

is true in English if Hamlet was written by either of the men of letters. If Hamlet was written by Schmaltz instead, the statement would be false according to English usage.

However, in the first line of the table, Fortran's treatment differs from that of English. English would consider that statement false if Hamlet were written by <u>both</u> Shakespeare and Bacon. But Fortran considers the statement true if either operand is true <u>or if both operands are true.</u>

<u>Logical Expressions</u>

Logical expressions, like arithmetic expressions, are strings of operators, operands, parentheses and FUNCTION references. The value of a logical expression is either .TRUE. or .FALSE.

It should be clear that operator .NOT. must be followed by a logical expression and the operators .AND. and

.OR. must be preceded by and followed by logical expressions.

The order of hierarchy (in the absence of parentheses) of the operators is:

```
.NOT.
.AND.
.OR.
```

For example,

```
LOGICAL A,B,C,D,E,F
    •
    •
    •
```

```
1)    E = A.AND.B.OR..NOT.C
      means
      E = ((A.AND.B).OR.(.NOT.C))

2)    E = A.OR.B.AND.C.OR..NOT.D
      means
      E = ((A.OR.(B.AND.C)).OR.(.NOT.D))
```

Exercises

If P and Q have values of true and R and S have values of false, then what value does each expression below have?

1. P.AND.Q
2. P.AND.R
3. P.AND.Q.AND.R
4. P.AND.S
5. P.OR.Q
6. P.OR.R
7. P.OR.Q.OR.R
8. P.AND.R.OR.Q
9. P.OR.R.AND.Q
10. P.AND..NOT.R
11. P.AND..NOT.R.AND..NOT.Q
12. .NOT.P.OR..NOT.R
13. P.AND.Q.OR.R.OR.S
14. P.OR.R.AND.Q.OR.S
15. (P.OR.R).AND.(Q.OR.S)

Logical Assignment Statements

Like the arithmetic assignment statement, the logical assignment statement consists of a variable on the left of an "=" sign and an expression on the right. In the logical assignment statement both the variable on the left of the "=" sign and the expression on the right must be logical quantities and, as such, may take on only the values true and false.

For example,

```
LOGICAL RAT,COW,MAT(55),PILL
INTEGER K
K=15
COW=.TRUE.
RAT=.FALSE.
MAT(K)=RAT.OR..NOT.COW
PILL=RAT.AND.COW
```

The last four statements above are logical assignment statements. The third statement "K=15" is an arithmetic assignment statement. Why is the following set of statements invalid?

```
LOGICAL P,Q
INTEGER K,L
K=15
Q=.FALSE.
P=Q.OR.K
```

The Logical IF Statement

The reader may be surprised to find that one of the original ten statements he learned was a statement from the logical system: the logical IF. Consider the statement in this new light. It says:

IF (something true or false) is true do such and such

Up to this point, contact with the logical IF statement has been the use of the relational operators:

```
.GT.
.GE.
.EQ.
.NE.
```

```
.LE.
.LT.
```

But it is now clear that things other than questions about the relationship between two numbers can have truth value. For example,

```
REAL XNUM, YNUM, ZNUM
    •
    •
IF (XNUM.GT.YNUM) ZNUM=28.
    •
```

has a rough equivalence to:

```
LOGICAL XLOG, YLOG, ZLOG
    •
    •
IF (XLOG.AND.YLOG) ZLOG = .TRUE.
    •
```

The important point to note is that in each of the IF statements the quantity within the parentheses has <u>truth value</u>: it is either true or false.

Of the relational operators only .EQ. and .NE. can be used between LOGICAL quantities. The results of such comparisons are obvious.

Expressions of Arithmetic and Logical Operators

In this section a hierarchy will be established for all of Fortran's operators. Specifically, the hierarchy for all operators in Fortran is shown by the following list.

Natural Hierarchy Without Parentheses
First: FUNCTION reference
Second: **
Third: *,/
Fourth: +,-
Fifth: .GT.,.GE.,.EQ.,.NE.,.LE.,.LT.
Sixth: .NOT.
Seventh: .AND.
Eighth: .OR.

Consider the logical IF statement in the sequence

```
REAL T,J
     •
     •
IF (T.GT.6..AND.J.LE.150.)  GO TO 28
```

Since the relational operators ".GT." and ".LE." take precedence over the logical operator ".AND." it should be clear that the expression in parentheses has truth value. The statement above is an example of a statement involving both arithmetic and logical operators. A transfer to statement 28 will take place if both T is >6 and J is ≤150. Note that a double period ".." appears because of the "6." and the ".AND." in the expression.

Notice that certain of the operators can only appear in certain contexts. For example, arithmetic operators can separate only arithmetic quantities, relational operators can separate only arithmetic quantities, and logical operators can separate only logical quantities. It is important to remember not to attempt to store an arithmetic quantity in a logical variable.

If variables are typed as

```
LOGICAL P,Q,R
REAL A,B,C
```

verify that the following replacement statements are correctly shown as valid or invalid.

<u>VALID</u>

```
A=B*C+100.3
P=B*C.GT.1009.
P=Q.AND.R
P=A.LT.B.OR.C.GE.3.0
```

<u>INVALID</u>

```
A=P.OR.Q
P=B*C
P=Q+R
P=A.OR.B.LT.100.
```

Exercises

If the following declarations are made:

```
LOGICAL P,Q,R,S,T
INTEGER K,L,M
```

and the variables contain the following values:

```
P  true
Q  true
R  false
S  false
K  10
L  20
M  30
```

what value would be stored in T in each case below? (Some statements are invalid and would therefore store no value in T. In these cases determine why the statements are invalid).

```
 1.  T=P.OR.S
 2.  T=R.OR.S
 3.  T=K.EQ.10.OR.K.EQ.20
 4.  T=K.EQ.10.OR.20
 5.  T=P.AND.L.LE.M
 6.  T=P.OR.Q.OR.M
 7.  T=K.LT.M.OR.L.GT.400
 8.  T=S.AND.P.OR.K.EQ.10
 9.  T=K.EQ.10.OR.P.AND.S
10.  T=M
11.  T=110/3.LT.K
12.  T=M-K*L.OR.P
13.  T=P.AND.M-K*L.LT.K**2.OR.Q
14.  T=P.AND.Q.AND.K.AND.L
15.  T=.NOT.M.LT.K
16.  T=.NOT.M*3
17.  T=.NOT.M.GT.K.OR.P.GT.S
18.  T=.OR.P.AND.S
19.  T=M+K.GT.L.AND.S
20.  T=K.GT.L.OR.K.GT.M.OR.S.OR.R
```

Input and Output of Logical Quantities

The output of logical quantities is handled by the usual WRITE statement together with the FORMAT specification, Lw. The L denotes that the quantity to be transferred is logical and the w is the field width desired as in the Iw FORMAT specification. If the quantity being output is true, a "T" is placed in the output field at the extreme right-hand end. If the quantity to be written is false, an "F" is transmitted. Consider the following example:

```
      REAL XREAL,YREAL
      INTEGER XINTG,YINTG
      LOGICAL XLOG,YLOG
          •
          •
      XREAL=15.
      YREAL=XREAL
      XINTG=12
      YINTG=XINTG/4
      XLOG=.FALSE.
      YLOG=.NOT.XLOG
      WRITE(6,501) XREAL,XINTG,XLOG,YREAL,YLOG,YINTG
  501 FORMAT (' ',F10.2,I5,L4,F8.0,L2,I3)
```

would produce

```
bbbbb15.00bbb12bbbFbbbbb15.bTbb3
```

where the character "b" is used to indicate a blank position.

Input is similar to output for logical quantities. However, the "T" or "F" may be anywhere within the field indicated by the FORMAT specification. If both a "T" and an "F" exist in an input field of width w, the first T or F encountered is used. No characters other than "T" or "F" may be the first non-blank character in a field. If the field is completely blank, the variable is assigned the value "false," except in WATFOR, which gives an error message. Consider the following example which reads and writes an entire logical array:

```
      LOGICAL LOGARY(7)
      READ (5,502) LOGARY
      WRITE (5,502) LOGARY
  502 FORMAT (7L4)
```

If the input data are:

bbbTbbbFbbbbTFTFTbbbFbbbbbFb

the output will be:

bbbTbbbFbbbFbbbTbbbTbbbFbbbF

Logical Subprograms

Logical variables and constants may be transmitted in the calling sequence of FUNCTIONs and SUBROUTINEs. If the programmer wants to write a FUNCTION subprogram which will return a logical value, he must use the statement

```
LOGICAL FUNCTION name(a1,a2,...)
```

as the first statement of his subprogram. And, of course, the variable "name" must be declared as LOGICAL in the calling program.

Sample Problem

A programmer is presented with a deck of n cards, each of which is punched with a pair of INTEGER numbers. Each number is in the range $1 \le k \le 25$. He is to write a program to read each card and determine if both of the numbers are prime or if neither is prime. He decides to prepare a singly subscripted logical array, P, in the machine such that if j is a prime, Pj will be true and if j is not a prime, Pj will be false. He will then check each pair of numbers he reads against the table to determine whether they are both prime or not.

Fortunately, he has at his disposal a deck of cards with the prime numbers less than 25 punched one to a card. The last card is punched 9999 to signify the end of the deck.

The Fortran program might be as follows:

```
      INTEGER I,J,K,L,N
      LOGICAL P(25)
      DO 11 I=1,25
      P(I)=.FALSE.
   11 CONTINUE
   13 CONTINUE
      READ,J
      IF (J.EQ.9999) GO TO 12
      P(J)=.TRUE.
      GO TO 13
   12 CONTINUE
      READ,N
      DO 14 I=1,N
      READ,K,L
      IF (P(K).AND.P(L)) GO TO 15
      IF (.NOT.P(K).AND..NOT.P(L)) GO TO 16
      WRITE (6,501) K,P(K),L,P(L)
  501 FORMAT (' ',I5,L2,I5,L2)
      GO TO 14
   15 CONTINUE
      WRITE(6,502) K,L
  502 FORMAT (' ',2I5,2X,'BOTH')
      GO TO 14
   16 CONTINUE
      WRITE(6,503) K,L
  503 FORMAT(' ',2I5,2X,'NEITHER')
   14 CONTINUE
      RETURN
      END
```

Try the program with the following data. What happens?

```
   2
   3
   5
   7
  11
  13
  17
  19
  23
9999
   4
   3   5
   4   9
   4  10
   7  20
```

MODULE 2

OPERATIONS WITH COMPLEX NUMBERS

Prerequisites: Parts I and II
Knowledge of complex arithmetic

The following section is intended for those who are already familiar with complex numbers in the mathematical sense.

Complex Variables

Since a complex number can be represented as an ordered pair of real numbers, Fortran reserves two words of computer memory for each complex number which is declared.[1] The Type Declaration statement is of the form:

```
COMPLEX  list
```

For example, the statement

```
COMPLEX AX,CRT,RLIM,IJK,SP(35),AMNZ(10,10)
```

would declare as complex quantities four simple variables, the elements of one vector, and the elements of one matrix AMNZ. 278 words of computer memory would be reserved. Why?

Complex Constants

A complex constant in Fortran is of the form (a,b) where "a" and "b" are each REAL constants. Examples of complex constants and their mathematical equivalents are:

(1.,3.)	$1+3i$
(-8.2,18.4)	$-8.2+18.4i$
(.12E+07,0.2)	$.12\times10^{7} + .2i$
(0.,-.7)	$-.7i$

The enclosing parentheses must always be present.

---

[1] Complex numbers can also be extended precision; see Module 10.

Complex Expressions

Complex numbers can be added, subtracted, multiplied, and divided. In addition, complex numbers can be raised to INTEGER powers; however, complex numbers cannot be raised to REAL powers and complex numbers cannot be used as exponents.

Arithmetic with complex quantities (constants and variables) is accomplished with the same operators as are used in operating with REAL and INTEGER quantities.

For example, the program segment

```
COMPLEX ACX,BCX,XCX,YCX,ZCX
ACX=(2.,3.)
BCX=(5.,-1.)
XCX=ACX+BCX
YCX=ACX-BCX
ZCX=ACX*BCX
```

would produce

```
XCX as 7+2i
YCX as -3+4i
ZCX as 13+13i
```

If a complex quantity exists in an expression involving REAL or INTEGER quantities, the expression will be evaluated as though the REAL or INTEGER quantities were complex quantities and the expression will produce a complex number.

As with REAL and INTEGER quantities, one must be careful when mixing types within an expression. For example, it would be inadvisable to write

```
REAL A,B
COMPLEX C
B=5.2
C=(3.1,0.0)
A=B+C
```

because the quantity B+C is evaluated as a complex number, and since A is REAL, only the REAL portion of the expression (value 8.3) is stored in A; the imaginary portion is lost.

Functions Involving Complex Quantities

Several functions are available in Fortran to assist the programmer in handling complex quantities. If only the first of the ordered pair of real numbers which make up the complex number is desired, the FUNCTION

REAL(cexp)

may be used where cexp is a complex expression. That is, the FUNCTION named REAL extracts the real part of the complex number. In a similar way the FUNCTION

AIMAG(cexp)

extracts the second number of the ordered pair. These two FUNCTIONs provide a means for "breaking" the complex number into its two real parts. For example,

```
COMPLEX X,Y
REAL A,B
X=(5.1,3.2)
Y=(2.2,3.5)
A=REAL (X+Y)
B=AIMAG (X+Y)
PRINT,A
PRINT,B
```

would print

```
7.3
6.7
```

Clearly, the argument of each FUNCTION must always be a complex number or expression. Don't confuse the Type Declaration REAL with the FUNCTION REAL.

A FUNCTION which serves to perform the opposite task from REAL and AIMAG is the COMPLEX FUNCTION CMPLX which puts two REAL numbers or expressions into a complex number. This FUNCTION is called by

CMPLX (rexp1,rexp2)

where rexp1 stands for one real expression and rexp2 stands for another real expression.

As a simple example consider

```
REAL A,B
COMPLEX X
A=5.5
B=6.6
X=CMPLX(A,B)
```

which stores in X the complex number (5.5,6.6i). Notice that while one may write

```
X=(5.5,6.6)
```

to store a complex number, one unfortunately may not write

```
X=(A,B)
```

but rather must write

```
X=CMPLX(A,B)
```

In short, a complex constant is defined as two REAL <u>constants</u> in parentheses. But a complex number may not be defined simply by putting two REAL variables in parentheses. In the latter case the FUNCTION CMPLX must be used.

Other FUNCTIONs exist in Fortran for handling complex quantities. For example, the function CSQRT has a complex expression or number for an argument and produces a complex number as a result. CSQRT(cexpr) produces as a result the complex number which when squared gives cexpr.

In contrast, the FUNCTION CABS (the absolute value of a complex number) is a REAL FUNCTION, and therefore produces a REAL number as a result. It is called by

```
CABS(cexp)
```

where cexp is a complex expression.

Thus

```
REAL A
COMPLEX X
X=(3.,4.)
A=CABS(X)
```

would produce the REAL number 5.0 for A.

A list of complex FUNCTIONs can be found in Module 14.

A warning: there are instances when built-in functions in WATFOR/FIV must be explicitly Typed. To be on the safe side you should probably include the name of any built-in function in WATFOR/FIV which does not return either an INTEGER*4 or REAL*4 value. For example, if you use the built-in function CMPLX, you will get an error message -- SR-9, Library Program was not assigned the correct Type -- unless you include a Type declaration: COMPLEX CMPLX.

Input and Output of Complex Quantities

Complex quantities are read and written just as REAL quantities are with F, D, or E FORMAT. See Module 3 for a discussion of D and E FORMAT specifications. The difference is simply that each complex variable written or read will cause the transfer of two REAL quantities.

For example, two identical lines would be written by the following:

```
    REAL A,B
    COMPLEX X, CMPLX
    A=1.2
    B=-8.9
    X=CMPLX(A,B)
    WRITE(6,501) A,B
    WRITE(6,501) X
501 FORMAT(' ',F10.2,F10.2)
```

Complex numbers are not enclosed in parentheses when they are read (e.g., from cards) as data or written (e.g., on the printer) as output; they must, however, be enclosed in parentheses when used in a program as constants.

MODULE 3

MORE TOPICS IN FORMAT

Prerequisites: Parts I and II

In addition to the FORMAT specifications

```
 Iw
 Fw.d
 Lw
 Aw
wX
```

several other specifications are permissible.[1] Most of these are covered here.

E FORMAT Specifications

The E specification is used in transmitting REAL data. Its general form is

```
rEw.d
```

where r is optional and is an unsigned integer constant used to specify the number of times the specification is to be repeated. If omitted, it is assumed to be 1.

w is the field width in columns.

d is the number of significant digits.

An E field is composed of two parts: the number and the exponent and can be written as:

$\pm$.xxxxxxxxE$\pm$yy

The plus signs are optional.

The E can be thought of as denoting the number multiplied by 10 raised to some power. Therefore the number

.34567E+3

is equivalent to 345.67, because E+3 means to interpret the number as being multiplied by 10 raised to the power of 3;

---

[1] Discussion of the L specification is found in Module 1.

or, put another way, move the decimal point 3 places to the right. The number

.34567E-2

is equivalent to .0034567; to interpret an E-notation number which has a negative exponent, move the decimal point to the left. Shown below are numbers in E notation and their equivalences in F notation.

Number in E notation	Equivalent Number
32.E4	320000.
4.E-8	.00000004
.865E11	86500000000.
-325.E6	-325000000.
-325.E-5	-.00325

On output, the first significant digit appears just to the right of the decimal point and therefore the d portion of the field specification controls the number of significant digits in the output. Digits in excess of d are dropped after rounding from the right.

One of the frequent errors programmers make using the E specification on output is failing to make the number w in Ew.d sufficiently large. An E form number will always require that the value of w be at least 7 larger than the value of d. In general an E form number will appear on output as

±0.xxxxxxxE±yy

and space must be provided for

±0.   E±yy

which consists of seven characters regardless of the value of d. Thus w must be at least 7 greater than d.

Number Stored in Computer	Field Specification	Actual output
123.456	E13.6	0.123456E 03
123.456	E13.5	0.12346E 03
123.456	E13.4	0.1235E 03
-123.456	E13.3	-0.123E 03
-123.456	E13.2	-0.12E 03
-123.456	E13.1	-0.1E 03
.0000456	E13.6	0.456000E-04
.0000456	E13.5	0.45600E-04
.0000456	E13.2	0.46E-04

D FORMAT Specifications

The D specification is identical to the E specification except that it is used for variables declared as REAL*8 and therefore can specify up to 16 significant digits.

Number Stored in Computer	Field Specification	Actual Output
12345678.9386	D19.12	0.123456789386D 08
12345678.9386	D19.11	0.12345678939D 08
12345678.9386	D19.10	0.1234567894D 08

G FORMAT Specifications

The G denotes a generalized field specification. Its form is

rGw.d

where r, w, and d have the same meanings as with E and D specifications on input. On output, however, the value of d is the number of significant digits desired in the answer rather than the number of digits to the right of the decimal.

It can be used to transmit REAL, INTEGER, COMPLEX or LOGICAL data depending upon the declaration of the variables in the input-output list. The .d portion of the field specification can be omitted for INTEGER or LOGICAL variables. If not omitted, it is ignored in these cases. On output of REAL numbers, if the number is between .1 and 10**d in absolute value, the number is output in the F type FORMAT; otherwise it is output in the E or D type FORMAT.

Number in Computer Storage	Type	Field Specification	Actual Output
123.456	REAL*4	G20.10	123.4560000
123.456	REAL*4	G20.8	123.45600
123.456	REAL*4	G20.6	123.456
123.456	REAL*4	G20.4	123.5
123.456	REAL*4	G20.3	123.0
123.456	REAL*4	G20.2	0.12E 03
.123456	REAL*4	G20.10	0.1234560000
.123456	REAL*4	G20.8	0.12345600
.123456	REAL*4	G20.6	0.123456
.123456	REAL*4	G20.5	0.12346
.123456	REAL*4	G20.4	0.1235
.123456	REAL*4	G20.3	0.123
.123456	REAL*4	G20.2	0.12
1234567.	REAL*4	G20.10	1234567.000
1234567.	REAL*4	G20.8	1234567.0
1234567.	REAL*4	G20.7	1234567.0
1234567.	REAL*4	G20.6	0.123457E 07
1234567.	REAL*4	G20.4	0.1235E 07
1234567.	REAL*4	G20.2	0.12E 07
1234567.	REAL*8	G20.6	0.123457D 07
1234567.	REAL*8	G20.4	0.1235D 07
1234567.	REAL*8	G20.2	0.12D 07
100	INTEGER*4	G20.5	100
.TRUE.	LOGICAL*4	G20.5	T
.FALSE.	LOGICAL*4	G20.5	F

T FORMAT Specifications

The T specification denotes the position in the Fortran record where the transfer of data will begin. The general form is:

```
Tw
```

where w is an unsigned INTEGER constant between 1 and 255.

To print

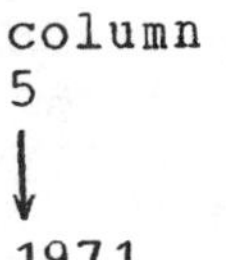

```
column                                          column          column
5                                               35              50
|                                               |               |
v                                               v               v
1971                                            ANNUAL REPORT   XYZ CORP
```

any of the following FORMAT statements could be used with the print statement, WRITE (6,42). The blank literal (' ') specification at the beginning of each FORMAT specification provides the blank for carriage control.

```
42 FORMAT(' ',T35,'ANNUAL REPORT',T50,'XYZ CORP',T5,'1971')
42 FORMAT(' ',T50,'XYZ CORP',T5,'1971,T35,'ANNUAL REPORT')
42 FORMAT(' ',T5,'1971',T35,'ANNUAL REPORT',T50,'XYZ CORP')
42 FORMAT(' ',3X,'1971',26X,'ANNUAL REPORT',2X,'XYZ CORP')
```

All of the FORMAT statements above will print exactly the same information in exactly the same order.

The T specification can also be used on input to read numbers from columns in orders other than left to right. For example,

```
  INTEGER K,L,M
  READ(5,2) K,L,M
2 FORMAT(T70,I5,T6,I4,T31,I6)
```

would read K from card columns 70-74, L from card columns 6-9, and M from card columns 31-36.

Z FORMAT Specifications

There is no procedure in Fortran which allows the programmer to place binary information, as such, in the memory of the computer nor to get binary numbers out. There is, however, a method by which he can insert and retrieve numbers which are much more closely related to the binary numbers than are the base 10 integers you have dealt with so far. These numbers, which are in some senses a shorthand for binary numbers, are base sixteen or hexadecimal numbers. The table below shows the relationships of decimal, hexadecimal, and binary numbers.

decimal	hexadecimal	binary
0	0	0000
1	1	0001
2	2	0010
3	3	0011
4	4	0100
5	5	0101
6	6	0110
7	7	0111
8	8	1000
9	9	1001
10	A	1010
11	B	1011
12	C	1100
13	D	1101
14	E	1110
15	F	1111

Since a byte of computer storage, in the IBM 360/370 computer, contains eight bits, it could be thought of as containing two hexadecimal digits. Thus a computer word, four bytes, could contain a hexadecimal number of eight hexadecimal digits. Since a hexadecimal number can be translated into a binary number by simply converting each of its digits according to the above table and stringing the resultant conversions together (see Appendix G), the programmer can decipher what binary number is being represented. For example, the hexadecimal number 15AF is equivalent to the binary number 0001 0101 1010 1111.

To read in or write out hexadecimal data the programmer uses a FORMAT specification of the form

rZw

where r is the repeat number, Z denotes hexadecimal data, and w is the field width of the number to be transmitted. On input the integer constant w must not be more than twice the number of bytes of the storage location in which the hexadecimal number is to be stored; if it is, the leftmost, or most significant, digits of the number will be lost. If w is less than twice the number of bytes in the location, then hexadecimal zeros are placed in the leftmost digits of th number in memory.

On output, if the number of characters in the hexadecimal number is greater than the width allowed, w, the leftmost portion will be lost; if w is greater than the number of digits, blanks are supplied on the left.

Other Specifications

There are two other FORMAT specifications which will not be discussed in this text but of whose existence you should be aware. They are the H specification, which can be used instead of quotes to transmit literal data, and the P specification, which can change the position of a decimal point in a number as it is transmitted into or out of the computer.

Object Time FORMATs

This text has stressed generality in program writing so that you will get in the habit of writing programs which can be reused by modifying only the inputs to the program rather than the program itself. One way in which this can be accomplished is to refrain from putting constants in programs when it is possible that the program could solve a wider range of problems if those quantities were made variables and read in as data.

Another way in which Fortran programs can be more general is by specifying FORMAT information at execution time rather than compile time. First consider an example of the usual method of employing FORMAT specifications: the FORMAT statement.

```
      REAL A, B
      INTEGER I
      READ(5,501) A,I,B
  501 FORMAT(F10.2,I10,F10.2)
```

where the data might be

CARD COLUMNS

1	2	3	4	5	6	7	8	9	10	11	12	13	14	15	16	17	18	19	20	21	22	23	24	25	26	27	28	29	30	31	32	33	34	35	36	37	38	39	40	41	42	43
						5	.	1									3	8	8					-	2	.	2	2	2													

Given this program segment certain things are specified about the data: there will be three quantities in the first record, the first and third will be REAL, the second will be INTEGER, each datum will occupy 10 columns and the data will be adjacent. The restrictions expressed in the underlined part of the preceding statement can be removed; those restrictions are imposed by the FORMAT statement and, as will be demonstrated, the FORMAT description can be deferred until the data are read in during the execution phase of the program. This is accomplished by declaring an array in the program, reading the FORMAT specifications into that array at execution time, and then referencing that array (instead of a FORMAT statement number) when other data are read in. For example, the preceding example could be rewritten as

```
      REAL A,B
      INTEGER I,FMTSPC(20)
      READ(5,999) (FMTSPC(I),I=1,20)
  999 FORMAT(20A4)
      READ(5,FMTSPC) A,I,B
```

where the data would now be on two cards

CARD COLUMNS

1	2	3	4	5	6	7	8	9	10	11	12	13	14	15	16	17	18	19	20	21	22	23	24	25	26	27	28	29	30	31	32	33	34	35	36	37	38	39	40	41	42	43
(	F	1	0	.	2	,	I	1	0	,	F	1	0	.	2	)																										
							5	.	1								3	8	8						-	2	.	2	2	2												

In the example above the first few elements of the array FMTSPC would contain:

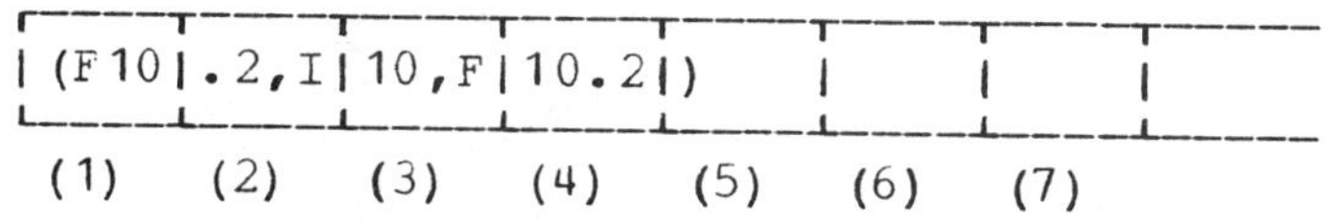

The advantage of this procedure is that if the data were in a different FORMAT, say in five rather than ten column fields, the user of the program could simply change the first data card (containing the FORMAT specifications) and use the program without modification.

There are two important points about this feature which need to be emphasized.

1. The form of the FORMAT specifications read in as data should be such that a left parenthesis is in the left-most position of the array containing the FORMAT specifications, the specifications themselves should follow as they would in a FORMAT statement, and a right parenthesis should end the set of specifications. The word FORMAT should not be read in nor should any statement number.

2. The array chosen must be of sufficient length to hold the complete specification. In the example an array of length twenty was used so that an entire card could be read under A4 specification. The array may be of any Type but the FORMAT specification must be read in under A FORMAT.

MODULE 4

READ AND WRITE USING NAMELIST

Prerequisites: Parts I, II, (Module 1)

The NAMELIST statement allows the use of READ(u,n) and WRITE(u,n) without a list or FORMAT statement, where u is a Fortran I/O unit number and n is a NAMELIST name. The general form of the NAMELIST statement is:

```
NAMELIST/n1/a,b,c/n2/d,e,...
```

where n1,n2,... are NAMELIST names and a,b,c,d,e,... are scalar variable names or array names. NAMELIST names follow the same naming conventions as variables. Variables used in a NAMELIST statement may appear in more than one NAMELIST but may not be dummy variables in a SUBROUTINE or FUNCTION statement.

The input associated with the READ statement which utilizes a NAMELIST is prepared in a very special way. When the READ with NAMELIST statement is executed, the computer begins searching through input data until the NAMELIST name is found. The first column of each data card is blank. Column 2 of the first card of a set contains &(ampersand), followed by the NAMELIST name, followed by a blank. Then a variable or array name appears, followed by an equals sign, followed by a value, then a comma, variable name, equals sign, value, etc. Values of an array may be included by separating each value with a comma. After the last comma on the input data for that NAMELIST are the characters "&END". Not all the names in the NAMELIST need be in the NAMELIST data and those data that are on the cards do not need to be in any particular order.

Example:

```
REAL A,B(3)
INTEGER I,J(2)
LOGICAL L,M(4)
NAMELIST/ABC/A,B,I,J,L,M
READ(5,ABC)
WRITE(6,ABC)
    •
    •
```

Data cards might appear as follows:

CARD COLUMNS

1–6	7–
$ENTRY	
&ABC	J=4,235,B=3.1,3.75,3.,L=.TRUE.
M=F,	3*T,A=3.001,I=0,&END

The statement WRITE(6,ABC) would produce the values shown above on the printer in the order they were mentioned in the NAMELIST statement.

Notice that if an array is printed with NAMELIST but all elements have not had numbers stored in them, the output will contain meaningless numbers for those elements. Also, it is illegal to include the name of one <u>element</u> of an array in the NAMELIST statement. While only a single element of an array may be included in the data, the array name and not the single element must appear in the NAMELIST statement. On output, the values are printed with sufficient space to include all digits.

MODULE 5

UNFORMATTED I/O FOR INTERMEDIATE DATA

Prerequisites: Parts I and II

Sometimes you want to write out information in some machine-readable medium such as cards, tape, or disk so that the information can be read in later by the same or some other program. In these cases the FORMAT used is unimportant so long as the FORMAT used to write out the information is consistent with the FORMAT used to read it back in.

In these cases a considerable amount of time is saved by using a WRITE statement of the form

```
WRITE(u) list
```

where u is an I/O device number represented as either INTEGER constant or unsubscripted INTEGER variable. Time is also saved in reading the information back unFORMATted by

```
READ(u) list
```

Suppose, for example, the elements of two large arrays are unneeded for a time during the execution of program and the space in the array is needed for something else. The programmer can write the elements unFORMATted, and later read them back.

```
REAL X(10000), Y(5000)
    •
    •
REWIND 2
WRITE (2) X, Y
    •
    •
REWIND 2
READ(2) X, Y
    •
    •
```

He/She could have done the same thing using FORMATted WRITE and READ specifying the same FORMAT for both I/O operations but nothing would have been gained and time would have been lost.

Use unformatted READ or WRITE statements whenever possible. It's <u>much</u> faster. When is this possible? Whenever the machine is writing out data for input at a later time via tape or disk rather than writing out information for the consumption of the user.

MODULE 6

DIRECT-ACCESS INPUT, OUTPUT, and STORAGE

Prerequisites: Parts I, II, (Modules 3,5)

Data records are usually processed sequentially; that is, the first data record is read or written, then the second, then the third, etc. Direct-access, on the other hand, refers to processing data records in any order desired. That is, the seventh record can be processed first, the fifty-third record processed next, etc. The ability to READ or WRITE records in any order desired creates the necessity to add some new statements to the Fortran language, since all input and output covered to this point has been of a sequential nature.

Direct-access input and output are implemented in IBM 360 /370 Fortran and WATFIV. They are not implemented in WATFOR. The physical device usually used for implementing direct-access storage is a magnetic disk. (See Appendix E.)

The DEFINE FILE Statement

The first step in utilizing the direct-access features involves declaring information about the direct-access files (units from which records are to be read or onto which records are to be written). This is accomplished through the use of a new Fortran statement of the form:

```
DEFINE FILE u(m,r,c,v)
```

where: u represents an INTEGER constant that is the data set or file reference number (Fortran unit number).

m represents an INTEGER constant that specifies the number of records in the data set associated with u.

r represents an INTEGER constant that specifies the maximum size of each record associated with u. The unit of measurement is either characters or words (a word is 4 characters) depending upon the value given to c.

c specifies that the data set is to be read or written with or without FORMAT control; c may have the value L, E, or U.

L indicates that the data set is to be read or written either with _or_ without FORMAT control. In this case the unit of measurement of r is characters.

E indicates that the data set is to be read or written _under_ FORMAT control. In this case r is measured in characters.

U indicates that the data set is to be read or written _without_ FORMAT control. In this case r is measured in words.

v represents a non-subscripted INTEGER variable called an _associated variable_. At the conclusion of each READ or WRITE operation, v is set to a value that points to the record that immediately follows the last record transmitted. The associated variable cannot appear in the list of a READ or WRITE statement for a data set associated with the DEFINE FILE statement.

Example

```
DEFINE FILE 1(500,80,E,N)
```

This statement describes the FILE to be used for direct-access input or output to be:

unit number 1,
500 records in size,
made up of 80-character records,
read or written under FORMAT control,
associated with the variable N.

An appropriate control card called a Data Definition or DD card (not covered in this text), must also be created which relates to the DEFINE FILE statement. The exact details concerning the DD card should be obtained at your computing center.

The READ Statement

The form of the direct-access READ statement is almost identical to the READ statement covered in sequential input. Its form is:

```
READ(u'r,f,ERR=stno) list
```

where: u is the data set reference number (unit number) declared in the DEFINE FILE statement; u is an INTEGER constant or an INTEGER variable that is of length 4; u must be followed by an apostrophe ('),

r is an INTEGER expression that represents the relative position of a wanted record within the data set associated with u,

f is optional (depending upon the DEFINE FILE statement) and, if specified, is an INTEGER constant representing the FORMAT statement or an array name where an object-time FORMAT is stored,

ERR=stno is optional and, if specified, indicates the statement number to which control is transferred in the event of an error while reading a record.

Consider the statement

```
READ(1'26,10) A, B, C
```

which says READ A, B, and C from the twenty-sixth record of data set number 1 (unit 1) under the control of FORMAT statement number 10.

The statement

```
READ(2'N,125) M
```

says READ M from the Nth record of data set number 2 under control of FORMAT statement number 125. The contents of N will determine which record is read.

The WRITE Statement

The direct-access WRITE statement is almost the same as the form previously covered. It has the form:

```
WRITE(u'r,f) list
```

where the notation is the same as in the direct-access READ statement.

Examples

The following program READs 100 cards and stores the contents of each entire card into data set number 4. It then READs the card images from the data set in reverse order, printing each card image on the printer. order, printing each card image on the printer. Data set 4 is declared to contain as many as 100 records, each of which can be up to 80 characters in length. In addition, records are to be read or written under FORMAT statement control and the variable ASVAR is the associated variable for the data set.

```
      INTEGER ASVAR,IMAGE(80),K
      DEFINE FILE 4(100,80,E,ASVAR)
      ASVAR=1
      DO 6 K=1,100
      READ(5,1) IMAGE
    1 FORMAT(80A1)
      WRITE(4'ASVAR,1) IMAGE
    6 CONTINUE
      DO 7 K=1,100
      ASVAR=100-K+1
      READ(4'ASVAR,1) IMAGE
      WRITE(6,2) IMAGE
    2 FORMAT(' ',80A1)
    7 CONTINUE
      RETURN
      END
```

Notice that, since ASVAR always automatically points to the record in the data set following the record previously processed, it is quite easy to process data in a sequential fashion; the associated variable is automatically incremented as in the DO 6 loop above.

The following sample program reads cards; from each card a three-digit number is extracted and stored into NUM. Then the record designated by NUM in data set number 2 is retrieved and stored in VALUE. Finally this VALUE is printed along with the original number NUM. Data set 2 contains 999 records. Retrieval of data from data set 2 is under FORMAT control.

```
      INTEGER VALUE, NUM,REL
      DEFINE FILE 2(999,10,E,REL)
    4 READ(5,502,END=9) NUM
  502 FORMAT(I3)
      READ(2'NUM,835) VALUE
  835 FORMAT(I10)
      WRITE(6,66) NUM, VALUE
   66 FORMAT(' ',2I10)
      GO TO 4
    9 RETURN
      END
```

MODULE 7

ADDITIONAL DECISION-MAKING ELEMENTS
Prerequisites: Parts I, II, Appendix D

You have already encountered several FORTRAN statements which aid in decision-making or control of the program: logical IF, unconditional GO TO, CONTINUE, DO and RETURN. Several others are allowed by the Fortran language. Each of these is concerned with modifying the path of control through the program.

The Arithmetic IF

The general form of the arithmetic IF statement is as follows:

```
IF (e) a1,a2,a3
```

where e is an arithmetic expression and a1, a2, and a3 are statement numbers of executable Fortran statements.

Just as the DO statement and the computed GO TO statement combined the functions of several flowchart boxes into one, the arithmetic IF statement does also. It could be diagrammed as follows:

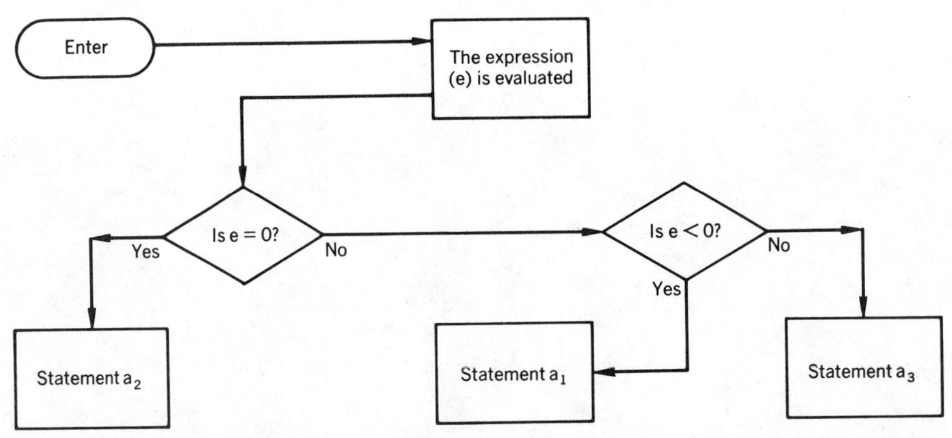

The arithmetic IF says: if the value of the arithmetic expression "e" is less than zero, pass control to the statement numbered a1; if "e" is equal to zero, pass control to a2. Suppose "e" is greater than zero. What statement is executed next? The statement immediately following the arithmetic IF must be numbered. Why?

As an example of the use of the arithmetic IF consider:

```
      IF (B**2-4.*A*C) 31,588,9001
   22 CONTINUE
        •
  588 CONTINUE
      PRINT,A
        •
 9001 CONTINUE
      PRINT,B
        •
   31 CONTINUE
      PRINT,C
```

If A, B, and C are such that the expression in parentheses is less than zero, control will pass to statement number 31 which will print C. If the expression is equal to zero, control will pass to statement 588 so A will be printed. If the value of the expression is greater than zero, control is transferred to statement 9001 and the value of B is printed. If A is 29.0, B is 5.0, and C is 3.0, what will be printed?

The Computed GO TO

A cousin to the unconditional GO TO statement is the computed GO TO statement, which may cause transfer of control to one of several numbered statements. Its general form is:

```
GO TO (a1,a2,a3,...),i
```

where each of the a1, a2, a3,... is a statement number (INTEGER constant form) of a statement within the program, and "i" is a non-subscripted scalar INTEGER variable. The value of "i" determines the statement to which control will pass after the execution of the computed GO TO. If "i" has value 1, control will pass to the statement numbered a1; if "i" has value 2, control will pass to the statement a2; etc.

If "i" is less than one or greater than the maximum permissible value (the number of statement numbers in parentheses), control passes to the statement immediately following the computed GO TO.

Suppose, for example, a program segment is as follows:

```
      REAL A,B,C,D
      INTEGER ICNTRL
        •
      READ, ICNTRL
      GO TO (13,58,86),ICNTRL
      READ,A
        •
   58 CONTINUE
      READ,B
        •
   86 CONTINUE
      READ,C
        •
   13 CONTINUE
      READ,D
```

If ICNTRL is read in as less than 1 or more than 3, the next value read in would be placed in A. If ICNTRL is read in as 1, control would pass to a1, which is statement number 13 in this case; thus D would be read. If ICNTRL is 2, then control passes to the second statement number in parentheses, a2, or 58, so B would be read. What is the result if ICNTRL is read as 3?

Diagrammatically, the computed GO TO statement might be viewed as a series of decision boxes.

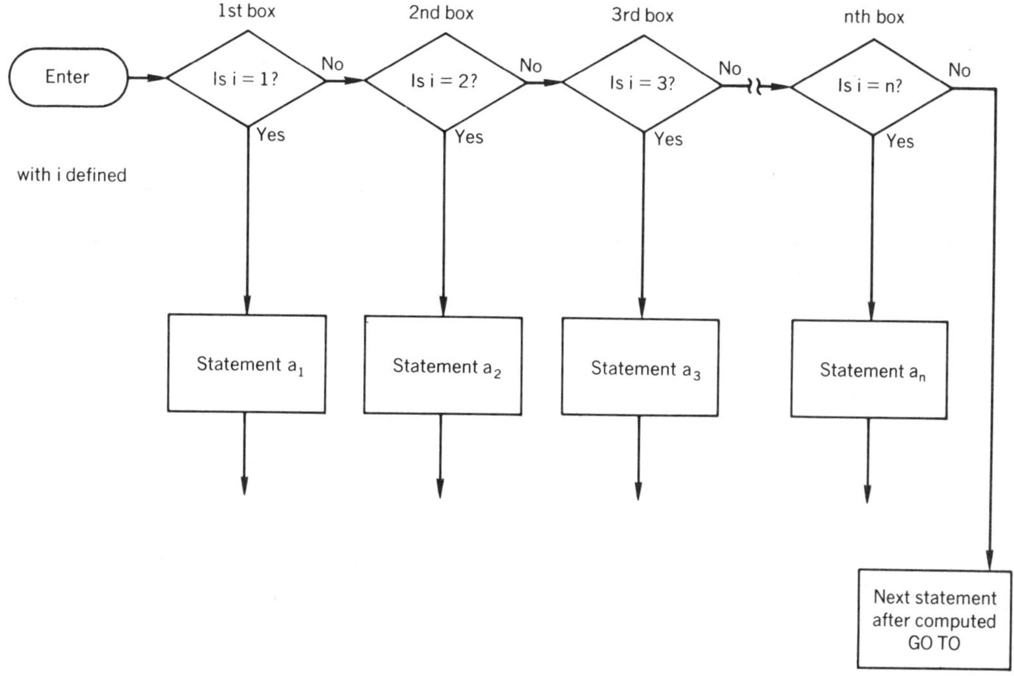

The Assigned GO TO

The student may have wished at some time to be able to write statements such as:

```
BLAZES=585
   •
   •
GO TO BLAZES
```

While such a statement as GO TO BLAZES is invalid, though sometimes not inappropriate, a statement similar to this exists and is called the assigned GO TO.

The general form of this statement is:

```
GO TO variable,(stno1,stno2,stno3,...)
```

where the variable[1] is an INTEGER, and stno1, stno2, stno3, ... are numbers of statements in the program in INTEGER constant form. The statement passes control to one of the previously assigned values of stno1, stno2, stno3, ...

Suppose, for example, the variable ICNTRL had been previously assigned the value 8. Then the statement

```
GO TO ICNTRL, (3,16,999,8,4)
```

would pass control to the statement numbered 8. It must be emphasized that the assigned GO TO may not pass control to any statement number which is not contained in the parentheses following the variable name.

Thus, in the example, it would be illegal to execute the assigned GO TO with ICNTRL having any value other than 3, 16, 999, 8, or 4.

Unfortunately, it is not, repeat not, permissible to assign the value of the INTEGER variable in an assigned GO TO statement with an arithmetic assignment statement. That is, one may not say

```
ICNTRL=8
```

or

```
ICNTRL=I+J*K
```

Rather, one must say

```
ASSIGN 8 TO ICNTRL
```

and one may not assign anything other than an INTEGER constant to such a variable. The general form then of the ASSIGN statement is:

```
ASSIGN stno TO variable
```

where stno is one of the INTEGER constant form numbers listed in the parentheses in the assigned GO TO statement and variable is the INTEGER variable used in the assigned GO TO statement.

Thus the use of the assigned GO TO statement in a program implies the existence of (usually) two or more ASSIGN statements.

---

[1] The variable must be 4 bytes long.

If the student is still interested in the application of this awkward pair of statements he/she might consider the example which follows.

Here we want to execute a certain program segment (A) only once and to skip it thereafter.

```
          .
          .
          ASSIGN 333 TO KLUDGE
          .
          .
       26 CONTINUE
          .
          GO TO KLUDGE, (123,333)
      333 CONTINUE
          .
          .
          .                       program segment A
          ASSIGN 123 TO KLUDGE
      123 CONTINUE
          .
          .
          GO TO 26
```

STOP Statement

A control statement whose use is rarely recommended is the STOP statement. In a Main program it serves the same purpose as the RETURN statement. When executed in a subprogram it halts the execution of the entire job. The STOP statement, in most computing centers, does not actually stop the computer, but rather tells it to go on to another job. STOP might be used in a subprogram when things have become so bad that you want to abort the run rather than RETURN control to the calling program.

MODULE 8

THE EQUIVALENCE STATEMENT

Prerequisites: Part I and II

There is a feature in Fortran which makes it possible for the programmer to refer to a location in memory by more than just one name. In fact, he can have as many names for one location as he desires. This feature is implemented by use of the EQUIVALENCE statement whose general form is

```
EQUIVALENCE (a,b),(c,d,e),...
```

where a, b, c, d, and e are variable names, array names, or names of specific members of an array to be made equivalent.

The concept of EQUIVALENCE is quite simple. Here is an example of one of its applications. A programmer discovers that he has inadvertently referred to a single quantity by the variable name SUM seven times in his program and by the variable name TOTAL nine other times. He can either repunch several cards to correct his error or he can write the statement

```
EQUIVALENCE (SUM,TOTAL)
```

so that the program treats the variable names SUM and TOTAL as names of the same location in memory, and he is extricated from his difficulty.

Another example: a programmer has written a program which is cramped for storage space. He discovers that he has two arrays, EDGAR and OSCAR, which are never in use at the same time. He simply writes

```
REAL EDGAR (100,50)
INTEGER OSCAR (3000)
EQUIVALENCE (EDGAR,OSCAR)
```

and thus saves 3000 positions. He could have also written

```
EQUIVALENCE (EDGAR(1,1),OSCAR(1))
```

to produce the same effect. Since matrices are stored with the first subscript varying most rapidly (column-wise), this implies the equivalence of locations between

```
EDGAR(1,1)  and OSCAR(1)
EDGAR(2,1)  and OSCAR(2)
EDGAR(3,1)  and OSCAR(3)
    •
    •
EDGAR(1,2)  and OSCAR(101)
    •
    •
EDGAR(100,30)  and OSCAR(3000)
```

It would also be possible for the programmer to have written

```
EQUIVALENCE (EDGAR(1,2),OSCAR(101))
```

which would have equivalenced the two arrays in exactly the same way.

How can a programmer get into trouble with the EQUIVALENCE statement? Oh, lots of ways:

1. He can provide contradictory information. For example,

   ```
   REAL A,B,X(2)
   EQUIVALENCE (A,X(1)),(B,X(2)),(A,B)
   ```

2. He can EQUIVALENCE two variables in the same or different COMMON blocks and create chaos.

3. In the IBM 360/370 he can EQUIVALENCE variables in such a way as to slow down the execution of the program considerably by not ensuring that variables fall on proper full and double-word boundaries.

4. He can put the statement in the wrong place in the program (see Module 13, Physical Order of Fortran Statements). In WATFOR/FIV there is danger if the EQUIVALENCE statement precedes the Type statement as well as if it doesn't precede any data initialization statement.

The programmer who wants to use the EQUIVALENCE statement is well advised to obtain a set of language specifications of the particular Fortran compiler he is using and to study them carefully.

The COMMON and EQUIVALENCE statements can be used together in an interesting way to cut down the number of items in an I/O list and hence decrease the time required to write the list. For example, suppose you wanted to write out the scalar variable X, the arrays Y (declared as REAL Y(30)), and Z (declared as REAL Z(10,10)). You could write the I/O statement as

```
WRITE (some I/O device) X,Y,Z
```

But it would be much faster if we could name only one quantity in the I/O list instead of three. So we will make W such a quantity. We write

```
REAL X,Y(30),Z(10,10),W(131)
COMMON /some block name/ X,Y,Z
EQUIVALENCE (X,W(1))
```

and then just

```
WRITE (some I/O device) W
```

MODULE 9

MORE DETAILS OF WATFOR AND WATFIV

Prerequisites: Parts I, II, Modules 1,2,3,4,5

The WATFOR and WATFIV compilers are not completely compatible with IBM Fortran compilers. This module will point out some of the differences and features which are not part of Fortran. The term WATFOR/FIV will refer to both the WATFOR (version 0) compiler and the WATFIV (version 1) compiler, both of which were developed at the University of Waterloo, Ontario, Canada.

FORMAT-free Input and Output

The WATFOR/FIV compilers allow the statements

```
READ,list
PRINT,list
PUNCH,list
```

which are not part of the Fortran language, although several universities and some manufacturers have implemented them into their versions of Fortran.

The READ,list statement causes one or more cards to be read. WATFOR/FIV will read at least one card each time this statement is executed and will continue reading cards until all list variables have received a value. Each data item in a data card must be separated from the next item by one or more blanks and/or a comma. Unused data items punched into data cards are ignored. Data items may be punched anywhere on the data cards. A data item cannot be continued onto another data card although as many data cards as desired may contain the data for the READ.

The FORMAT-free READ statement can read REAL, INTEGER, LOGICAL, or COMPLEX numbers. In addition, hexadecimal data are permitted. The implied DO notation may be used in the READ,list statement. CHARACTER data, covered later in this module, can be read in WATFIV only.

FORMAT-free Input Data Forms

A REAL data item can be punched into a data card with or without a decimal point in I, F, E, or D notation. The data item may possess a leading algebraic sign.

An INTEGER data item is punched without a decimal point. The data item may possess a leading algebraic sign.

A COMPLEX data item is punched within a set of parentheses with the REAL and imaginary parts separated by a comma. Each part may possess a leading algebraic sign.

A LOGICAL data item can be punched into a data card as one or more characters. A "T" will result in .TRUE. being stored, an "F" will result in a .FALSE. being stored. The first "T" in the field results in .TRUE. or the first "F" results in .FALSE. Here WATFOR and IBM Fortran differ slightly. In WATFOR if none of the characters in the field is "T" or "F" an error results. In IBM Fortran the absence of either character results in .FALSE.

A hexadecimal data item is punched with a preceding "Z".

FORMAT-free Output Data Forms

The PRINT,list statement can be used in WATFOR/FIV to print the values of variables, constants, or expressions; literal constants, or variables containing CHARACTER data, cannot be printed with this statement in WATFOR but they can in WATFIV. The PRINT,list statement will print variables, constants, or expressions as follows:

number type	printed as
REAL*4	E16.7
REAL*8	D28.16
INTEGER*2	I12
INTEGER*4	I12
COMPLEX*8	E16.7 (each part)
COMPLEX*16	D28.16 (each part)
LOGICAL*1	L8
LOGICAL*4	L8

When printing occurs, as many output items are printed on a line as will fit. If the list cannot be printed on one line, WATFOR/FIV prints as many lines as are required. The implied DO notation may be used in this statement. Some examples of valid PRINT,list statements are shown below.

```
LOGICAL L
REAL R
INTEGER I
COMPLEX C
L=.TRUE.
```

```
R=37.5
I=3
C=(3.3,-2.2)
PRINT,L,R,I,C
PRINT,1,2,3,4
PRINT,SQRT(R),I**2,.NOT.L
PRINT,.TRUE.,3.75
PRINT,'ANSWER=',X (in WATFIV only)
```

The PUNCH,list statement operates as the PRINT,list statement does except that output is placed on punched cards instead of paper.

In WATFIV an asterisk can be used instead of a FORMAT statement number in a READ or WRITE statement. This results in the READ or WRITE statement being treated as a FORMAT-free statement, but it allows the use of the END= or ERR= options as well as input and output unit numbers. For example,

```
READ(N,*,END=375,ERR=987)A,B,C
```

The following pairs of statements are logically identical:

```
READ(5,*) A,B,C
READ, A,B,C

WRITE(6,*) D,E,F
PRINT, D,E,F

WRITE(7,*) G,H,I
PUNCH, G,H,I
```

I/O Unit Designations

A variable used to denote an input or output unit number must be declared as a full-word INTEGER (that is, INTEGER or INTEGER*4 and not INTEGER*2) in IBM Fortran and WATFIV.

Multiple Statement Cards

Multiple statements per card are permitted in WATFIV. This is done by following a statement number with a colon and ending a Fortran statement with a semi-colon. Only columns 7-72 may be used for statements; normal continuation conventions apply. FORMAT statements must be punched one to a card as usual. Examples of multiple statement cards are:

```
READ,AA,BB,CC; DD=AA+BB; PRINT,DD;
A=33.5;B=100.5;23:IF(C.EQ.D)GO TO 3;
```

Nested DO's

Nested DO statements in WATFOR are limited to a depth of twenty. Neither WATFIV nor IBM Fortran limit the depth.

CHARACTER Variables

CHARACTER variables and constants are allowed in WATFIV only. Here the CHARACTER Type Declaration statement is implemented. It is

```
CHARACTER*s a*s1(k1)/x1/,b*s2(k2)/x2/...
```

where the s's, k's and x's are optional. Each s represents a length specification; a,b,... represent variable or array names; each k is composed of from 1 to 7 unsigned INTEGER constants separated by commas representing array specifications; the x's represent initial values. An example is

```
CHARACTER*80 ALPHA,BETA*3(2)/'ABC','DEF'/
```

Here ALPHA is an eighty CHARACTER scalar variable, BETA is an array with two elements, each of which is three CHARACTERS in length. BETA(1) is initialized with the value ABC and BETA(2) is initialized with the value DEF. If the *3 had been omitted after BETA, then all elements of BETA would have been 80 CHARACTERs in length, since the first length specification applies to all variables without a different length specification.

The CHARACTER variable can be used in an assignment statement with other CHARACTER variables or CHARACTER (literal) constants. CHARACTER variables and constants can also be used in IF, READ, and WRITE statements.

Example

```
      CHARACTER*9 DOG
      READ(5,1)DOG
    1 FORMAT(A9)
      IF(DOG.EQ.'ABCDEFGHI') GO TO 4
      WRITE(6,2)DOG
    2 FORMAT(' ',A9)
    4 RETURN
      END
```

The CHARACTER variable name may also be used instead of a unit number in a READ or WRITE statement. If this is done, information is read from or written to the variable in memory rather than from or to some device.

You must be quite careful when you use the neat features a compiler has to offer over and above basic Fortran. If you should ever want to run the program under a different compiler, you could have difficulty.

Other Features

NAMELIST (covered in Module 4) and direct-access input and output (covered in Module 6) are implemented in WATFIV and IBM Fortran but not in WATFOR.

WATFIV allows multiple assignments in a single assignment statement. For example,

```
D=C=B=A=expression
```

is valid in WATFIV and has the same meaning as the set of statements:

```
A=expression
B=A
C=B
D=C
```

WATFIV contains fewer incompatibilities with IBM Fortran than WATFOR. This allows better use as a debugging tool. Since the WATFOR and WATFIV compilers translate so rapidly, programs can be tested using them and later re-translated using IBM Fortran, which usually executes object programs faster and conserves memory better, for production work.

MODULE 10

VARIABLE TYPING: THE GENERAL CASE

Prerequisites: Parts I, II, (Modules 1, 2)

There are four basic variable types in Fortran IV: INTEGER, REAL, COMPLEX, and LOGICAL. The reader is now familiar with Type Declaration statements such as:

```
REAL list
LOGICAL list
```

If a variable name, whether subscripted or not, appears in a Type Declaration statement, its type is fixed by that statement. If the variable is subscripted then it must appear in a Type Declaration statement to specify the array size.[1]

The IMPLICIT Statement

If a variable name is not mentioned in a Type Declaration statement then its type is determined by an IMPLICIT statement if there is one in the program. An IMPLICIT statement tells the computer to assign a certain Type to a variable name on the basis of the first alphabetic character of that name. The basic form of the statement is

```
IMPLICIT type (a,b,c), type (d,e-f,g), ...
```

where "type" is one of the four words--INTEGER, REAL, COMPLEX, or LOGICAL--and a, b, c, d, e, f, g represent single capital alphabetic characters. Variables whose names begin with those characters will be typed according to the variable type name preceding the parentheses. If the characters are separated by a hyphen rather than a comma (e.g., R-W), then the type applies to both the characters _and to all other characters which fall between them alphabetically_. Thus the effect of the statement:

```
IMPLICIT INTEGER (A,P,R-W)
```

---

[1] There is a statement, DIMENSION list, included in most Fortran IV dialects for compatibility with Fortran II, which allows designation of array size but does not type the variable; its use is not recommended.

is the same as the statement

```
IMPLICIT INTEGER (A,P,R,S,T,U,V,W)
```

That effect is to assign the type INTEGER to any variable name which begins with A,P,R,S,T,U,V, or W provided that the variable name in question is not specifically listed in a Type Declaration Statement.

As an illustration, the statements

```
IMPLICIT REAL(S,T)
INTEGER SONG,TONG
```

would result in SONG and TONG being considered as INTEGER quantities, but SANG and TANG, for example, would be typed as REAL.

Only one IMPLICIT statement may be used in a program and it must invariably be the first statement in a main program and the second statement in a subprogram. Care must be taken not to allow conflicts within the IMPLICIT Typing statement. It would be incorrect, for example, to write

```
IMPLICIT INTEGER (I-Z),REAL(P,Q)
```

If a variable name is not mentioned explicitly in a Type Declaration statement and if it does not begin with a letter which is mentioned in an IMPLICIT statement, then it is typed according to a default typing rule: if the first character of the name is any of the characters I,J,K,L,M, or N, the variable is typed as INTEGER: otherwise it is typed as REAL.

> If you declare each variable in a Type Declaration statement, as good programming practice dictates, then the IMPLICIT statement is superfluous.

Exercises

Suppose a program began

```
$JOB            NAME
      IMPLICIT INTEGER(A,C,E),
     1REAL(G,I,K),COMPLEX(M,O,Q),
     2LOGICAL(S-Z)
      INTEGER ABE,BOY,GIRL(20),
     1HAT,MAN
      REAL ABLE,BAKER(35)
      COMPLEX ALACK,QUOTE,LEO
      LOGICAL ADCAT,IGLO,OUENT
```

What type would be assigned to each of the following variables? Why?

1. ABE
2. UNIT(28)
3. BIG
4. ABLE
5. ALAS
6. ALACK
7. AUTO
8. BOY
9. SOUTH(2,2,2)
10. CLEO
11. JAM
12. QUEST
13. QUOTE
14. ADCAT

Alternate Length Capability for Variables

One other feature exists in the area of variable typing for some dialects of Fortran. It is a machine-dependent feature and will be described for the IBM 360/370.

Normally Fortran assigns four bytes of computer memory for each INTEGER, REAL, and LOGICAL variable location; eight bytes are assigned to each COMPLEX variable, since a COMPLEX variable is essentially an ordered pair of two real numbers, each occupying four bytes. Thus the statement

```
LOGICAL X, YOUNG(50), ZULU
```

would reserve 208 bytes of memory. (See Module 12 for a more detailed discussion of the organization of computer memory.) There exists, however, a feature which allows the programmer to tell the computer to assign an alternate number of bytes to each variable; he/she may specify two bytes for selected INTEGER variables, one byte for selected LOGICAL variables (using only 52 bytes instead of 208 in the above example), eight bytes for selected REAL variables, and sixteen bytes for selected COMPLEX variables. In tabular form:

variable type	normal # of bytes	alternate # of bytes
INTEGER	4	2
REAL	4	8
LOGICAL	4	1
COMPLEX	8	16

An INTEGER variable which is two bytes in length instead of four can only contain a number of magnitude $2^{15}-1$ or 32767. But frequently only numbers of that magnitude or smaller are needed. If, for example, a programmer needs an INTEGER array of 10000 elements and each element will be used for storing a number that is no larger than 100, he might well consider saving space by allocating only two bytes to each element instead of four. The program may require a bit more time in the execution phase but the saving of 20000 bytes of storage may well be worth it. In some cases this saving might spell the difference between being able to get the program into the machine and failing to do so. Similar statements may be made about the fourfold saving in storage space when using one byte LOGICAL variables.

The feature which allows an alternate number of bytes is not always provided for space saving, however. In fact, one of its most important uses is to allow computation to be done with increased precision.

Sometimes seven or eight significant digits are not enough to do computation (See Appendix H on numerical considerations of using REAL numbers.) Assigning eight bytes to each REAL number used in "sensitive" computations will often eliminate or reduce the problem, because an 8-byte REAL number can have 15 or 16 significant digits. Eight-byte REAL numbers will increase the storage requirements of the program and will cut into its execution speed but may be the only way to obtain correct or nearly correct answers. Using eight bytes for REAL variables is sometimes known as using "double precision" and earlier versions of Fortran actually had a DOUBLE PRECISION statement; in Fortran IV the DOUBLE PRECISION statement is included mainly for compatibility with earlier Fortran versions and will not be discussed.

Assigning sixteen bytes to a COMPLEX variable has the effect of assigning eight bytes to each of its two parts; thus it is similar to two extended precision REAL locations.

To assign alternate lengths to COMPLEX and LOGICAL variables you follow the patterns previously set for REAL and INTEGER variables. The list now includes:

```
INTEGER
INTEGER*2
REAL
REAL*8
LOGICAL
LOGICAL*1
COMPLEX
COMPLEX*16
```

These eight variable types may be used in Type Declaration Statements and IMPLICIT statements.

For example, the statements

```
IMPLICIT REAL*8 (A,C,Z),REAL(B,D,E-G), LOGICAL*1(Y)
INTEGER*2 GEORGE,BETA(200),CAN(3,3,3,3,12)
REAL*8 DOUBPV(500,2)
COMPLEX*16 XIY,ABI(14)
```

are legal.

Incidentally, the variable types INTEGER*4, REAL*4, LOGICAL*4, and COMPLEX*8 are also valid (if useless) and have the same effect as INTEGER, REAL, LOGICAL, and COMPLEX. That is, writing

```
INTEGER*4 DUMDUM
```

is identical in effect to writing

```
INTEGER DUMDUM
```

The question now arises: "what happens when variables of different lengths are used together in an arithmetic expression?" (Logical variables, of course, may not be part of an arithmetic expression.) The table below shows what results when INTEGER numbers (shown as I2 for length 2 variables and I4 for length 4 variables), REAL numbers (R4 and R8), and COMPLEX numbers (C8 and C16) are added, subtracted, multiplied, and divided. The type and length of the result is shown at the row and column intersection of the types of the two operands. For example, a number designated as REAL length 8 multiplied by a number designated as INTEGER length 4 would result in a number that was REAL length 8.

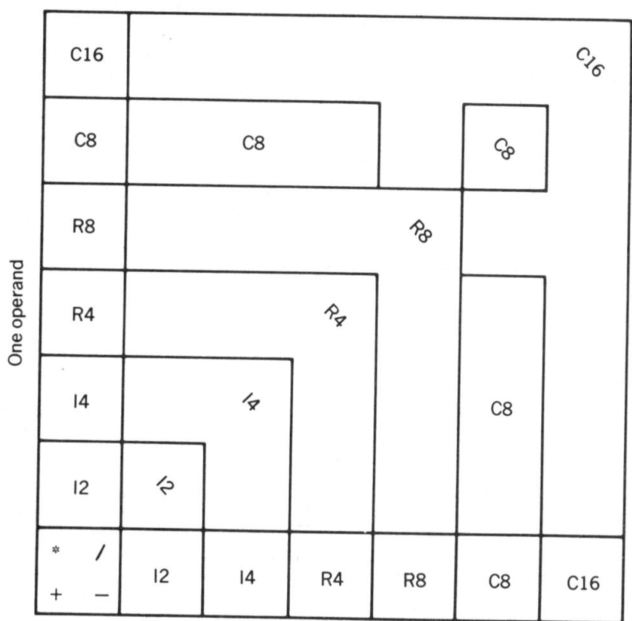

The table above is almost regular; the exception is that an R8 number combined with a C8 number produces a C16 number. This is done so that no significance contained in the R8 number will be lost in the operation. The rule here is that an extended precision number combined with a single precision number results in an extended precision number.

In the matter of exponentiation the same general rules hold: the operands of the greatest length take priority, and the order of hierarchy, from greatest to least, is COMPLEX, REAL, and INTEGER. The only exceptions occur with COMPLEX numbers which may only be raised to INTEGER powers and may not be used as exponents. A table is presented for completeness.

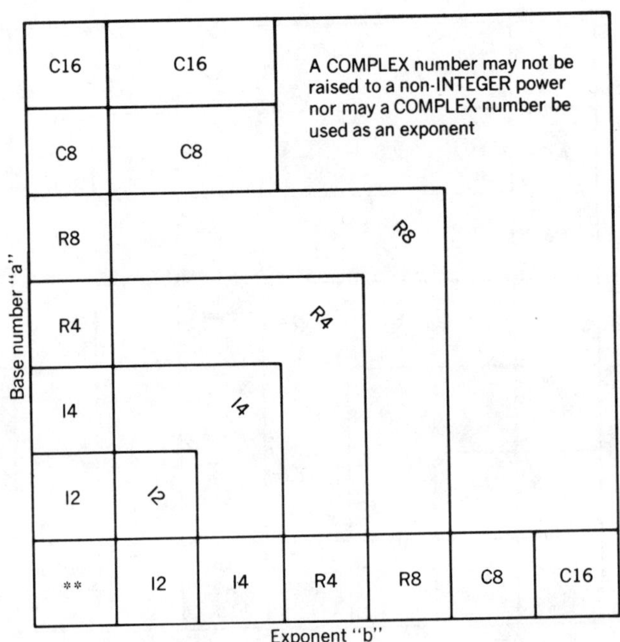

Here the resulting type is shown for all valid combinations of "a" raised to the "b" power.

Exponentiation can be performed by any of four different combinations of REAL and INTEGER values. Using an INTEGER value as the exponent usually produces two advantages: speed and the ability to have a base number which is negative. An examination of the two possibilities for the type of the exponent shows why.

If the exponent is REAL, the base number is converted to its logarithm, the exponent is multiplied by the logarithm, and then the antilogarithm of this product is used as the result. This is a very time-consuming process requiring a great many more computations, all of which use more computer time. If the exponent is REAL, the base must be positive, because negative numbers do not possess logarithms.

On the other hand, if the exponent is INTEGER, the computation is performed through multiplication, usually in a highly efficient manner. For example, X**17 would require only 5 multiplications with many compilers.

Choice of Variable Type

In many cases, the programmer may make a choice among data types employed in a program. For each variable type, at least two lengths are available.

As you know, INTEGER variables can be declared as either 2 bytes in length or 4 bytes in length. The INTEGER*2 (or 2-byte) variables can hold a number as large as +32767 or as small as -32768. INTEGER*2 variables require only half as much computer memory as INTEGER*4 variables. So you might believe that you should employ 2-byte INTEGERs whenever possible. Right? Wrong!

In some cases, while INTEGER*2 variables can save computer memory, their use can require more computer time. So if memory space is not a problem, the use of INTEGER*4 variables is recommended even if numbers larger than 32767 are not required.

The same considerations apply to LOGICAL variables. LOGICAL*1 variables require only 1 byte of storage each while the other possibility, LOGICAL*4, requires 4 bytes each. But use of LOGICAL *4 generally saves computer time because the process of individually selecting one byte of storage can be more time-consuming than selecting 4 bytes at a time.

However, the choice between REAL*4 and REAL*8 is different. REAL*8 usage requires additional computer storage and additional computer time. Where more than seven digits of floating-point significance is required, REAL*8 is necessary. These same considerations apply to a choice between COMPLEX and COMPLEX*16 variables.

Mixed Mode

In the olden days, a decade or so ago, programmers could not mix REAL and INTEGER numbers in a Fortran expression. "Mixed mode" was one of the most common errors. If you wanted to add 1 to X (a REAL number), and if you wrote

```
X=X+1
```

you might get an error message at compilation time. You could correct it to

```
X=X+1.
```

and it would be accepted.

Things are different now. Mode mixing has gone underground. Instead of causing a program not to compile, mode mixing simply makes things take longer, either in compilation or execution of a program, because the computer must convert each member of almost every pair of quantitites it deals with to the same type before it can do the indicated arithmetic operation on them.

This story has two morals: (1) try to do arithmetic operations exclusively on numbers of equivalent type, especially if many operations are concerned, as within a highly iterative loop, and (2) when you do mix modes, be sure you understand what the results are going to be.

MODULE 11

NON-NUMERIC DATA: STORING, SORTING, SEARCHING

Prerequisites: Parts I, II, (Modules 1,2)

While Fortran is used heavily to manipulate numeric information, it can also be used to input, store, process and output non-numeric information. Non-numeric information is generally input and output through the use of alphanumeric format specifications (A fields).

Computer storage locations (variables) in which non-numeric data are stored can be of any type using any of the length attributes.[1] When using an IBM Fortran compiler or WATFOR/FIV, the maximum FORMAT specification field widths for each type of variable are as shown below:

VARIABLE TYPE	MAXIMUM FIELD WIDTH
LOGICAL*1	1
LOGICAL	4
INTEGER*2	2
INTEGER	4
REAL	4
REAL*8	8
COMPLEX	8
COMPLEX*16	16

Data read by A-field FORMAT specifications are stored left-adjusted, and unused characters are filled with blanks. For example, if the letter "A" were read into the INTEGER

---

[1] The WATFIV compiler makes the CHARACTER variable available. While this feature can be extremely useful, it is not recommended because the feature is unique to WATFIV; programs which employ the CHARACTER variable cannot be run with other Fortran compilers. The CHARACTER variable is explained in Module 9.

variable XYZ with an A1 FORMAT field specification, XYZ would appear as

```
        ┌─┬─┬─┬─┐
    XYZ │A│b│b│b│
        └─┴─┴─┴─┘
```

where b indicates a blank character. Each byte of XYZ would contain a series of 8 binary bits. The bit structure of XYZ would be

```
        ┌────────┬────────┬────────┬────────┐
    XYZ │11000001│01000000│01000000│01000000│
        └────────┴────────┴────────┴────────┘
```

The identical bit structure would result if the value "A" were read into a REAL or an INTEGER variable. However, after non-numeric data are read into a variable, the computer "forgets" this fact and treats the contents of the variable as a numeric quantity in any comparisons, assignments, or computations. Only if the variable is employed for input or output using A-field FORMAT specifications does the machine treat its value as non-numeric.

It is important, therefore, that any assignments or comparisons between variables with non-numeric data be of the same type. If this is not the case, the computer will convert one of the values prior to the assignment or comparison. For example, if a REAL*4 variable named RDATA and an INTEGER*4 variable named IDATA each contained the letters ABCD, an IF statement comparing them would result in an unequal condition. This would occur because the computer, not knowing that the "value" of IDATA is alphanumeric, will convert IDATA to a REAL value prior to the comparison. The process of conversion, of course, temporarily changes the bit structure of IDATA. Two variables are equal only if they have identical bit structures.

LOGICAL variables can be used nicely to store non-numeric data which is to be simply input and later output. But if we need to determine whether one non-numeric field is either larger or smaller than another, then LOGICAL variables cannot be used, because the only valid relational operators for use with LOGICAL variables are equal (.EQ.) and not equal (.NE.).

A good practice is to store alphabetic data _only_ in INTEGER variables when comparison is involved.

Variables can also be initialized with non-numeric data in Type statements. For example, suppose that we need to create a variable named CK which contains the letter S in the first byte. This can be done as follows:

```
INTEGER CK/'S'/
```

Suppose that we want to initialize an array of variables with various names. We can do this as follows:

```
REAL*8 NAME(3)/'JANE','BETSY','MARGARET'/
```

Rationale for Using INTEGER Variables

Alphabetic characters or numbers read by A fields into REAL or INTEGER variables are actually stored as negative numbers. The table below shows the IBM 360/370 numeric values of the various characters if they were read by an A1 FORMAT and printed as Z8, E20.7 and I10. (In each case, the character is followed by three blank characters in computer storage; that is, A is stored as Abbb where b is a blank character, 3 is stored as 3bbb, etc.) We use one alphanumeric character per array element here for illustration. The concepts are identical if 2, 3, or 4 characters per element are used.

CHARACTER	HEX VALUE	NUMERIC VALUE REAL*4	NUMERIC VALUE INTEGER*4
A	C1404040	-.4015686E01	-1052753856
B	C2404040	-.6425098E02	-1035976640
C	C3404040	-.1028016E04	-1019199424
D	C4404040	-.1644825E05	-1002422208
E	C5404040	-.2631720E06	- 985644992
F	C6404040	-.4210752E07	- 968867776
G	C7404040	-.6737203E08	- 952090560
H	C8404040	-.1077953E10	- 935313344
I	C9404040	-.1724724E11	- 918536128
J	D1404040	-.7407633E20	- 784318400
K	D2404040	-.1185221E22	- 767541184
L	D3404040	-.1896354E23	- 750763968
M	D4404040	-.3034167E24	- 733986752
N	D5404040	-.4854667E25	- 717209536
O	D6404040	-.7767466E26	- 700432320
P	D7404040	-.1242795E28	- 683655104
Q	D8404040	-.1988471E29	- 666877888

R	D9404040	-.3181554E30	- 650100672
S	E2404040	-.2186347E41	- 499105728
T	E3404040	-.3498156E42	- 482328512
U	E4404040	-.5597049E43	- 465551296
V	E5404040	-.8955279E44	- 448774080
W	E6404040	-.1432845E46	- 431996864
X	E7404040	-.2292551E47	- 415219648
Y	E8404040	-.3668082E48	- 398442432
Z	E9404040	-.5868932E49	- 381665216
0	F0404040	-.1575429E58	- 264224704
1	F1404040	-.2520687E59	- 247447488
2	F2404040	-.4033099E60	- 230670272
3	F3404040	-.6452959E61	- 213893056
4	F4404040	-.1032473E63	- 197115840
5	F5404040	-.1651957E64	- 180338624
6	F6404040	-.2643132E65	- 163561408
7	F7404040	-.4229011E66	- 146784192
8	F8404040	-.6766418E67	- 130006976
9	F9404040	-.1082627E69	- 113229760
blank	40404040	+.2509804E00	+1077952576

Notice an interesting aspect of these values. Those stored in INTEGER form will compare properly. That is, if the letter D is compared with the letter R, the D possesses a smaller value (i.e., larger negative). If the letter D were stored in the INTEGER variable LTR(1), and the letter R were stored in the INTEGER variable LTR(2), and the statement

```
IF (LTR(1).LT.LTR(2)) GO TO 40
```

were encountered, the transfer to statement 40 would take place, since the numeric value of LTR(1) is less than that of LTR(2).

However, the numeric values of letters stored in REAL variables become smaller as we go through the alphabet. That is, the numeric value of an R stored in a REAL variable is smaller than that of the letter D.

It becomes particularly important to know this if, for example, names of people are to be sorted into alphabetical order. If non-numeric values are always stored in INTEGER variables, comparisons operate as one would expect: letters farther through the alphabet possess larger values. Even when 2, 3, or 4 characters are stored in an INTEGER variable this property holds. With REAL variables the opposite is true: letters farther through the alphabet possess smaller values. Unfortunately the blank character is larger than all letters or numbers stored by A-field FORMAT specifications, whether stored in REAL or INTEGER variables, and usually must be checked for separately in any sorting operation.

Sorting Example

Once non-numeric data are stored within the computer they can be manipulated in a manner analogous to numeric data. For example, if our task were to read a set of names (no more than 1000, none longer than 4 characters, no blanks in the first character position), sort them in ascending order, and print the list, we could proceed as follows:

```
C PROGRAM TO READ UP TO 1000 4-CHARACTER NAMES
C PUNCHED ONE TO A CARD, ALPHABETIZE AND PRINT THEM.
      INTEGER V(1000), TEMP
      INTEGER J,K,L,M,N
C READ NAMES INTO V AND COUNT THE NUMBER
C OF THEM IN N.
      N=0
      DO 2 K=1,1000
      READ (5,101,END=3) V(K)
    2 N=N+1
C SORT INTO ASCENDING ORDER (ALPHABETIZE)
    3 L=N-1
      DO 5 J=1,L
      M=J+1
      DO 4 K=M,N
      IF (V(J).LE.V(K)) GO TO 4
      TEMP=V(J)
      V(J)=V(K)
      V(K)=TEMP
    4 CONTINUE
    5 CONTINUE
C PRINT NAMES
      DO 6 K=1,N
    6 WRITE(6,102)V(K)
  101 FORMAT(A4)
  102 FORMAT(' ',A4)
      RETURN
      END
```

Notice in the above program that if TEMP were not typed as INTEGER, an unwanted conversion would have been made in the statements TEMP=V(J) and V(K)=TEMP. The conversions would have added to the running time of the program and would have risked the possibility that, in conversion and reconversion, some bits might have been changed.

Larger Non-numeric Groupings

The Fortran language does not provide for sizable numbers of non-numeric characters to be stored in a single variable. (The table at the beginning of this section indicates how many characters each of the various Types may contain.) Therefore, it is usually necessary to utilize arrays of elements to process such data. Suppose, for example, that we wanted to process fields of alphanumeric data which were up to 32 characters in length. (As previously indicated, there is some danger in using any but INTEGER variables.) We could declare an array of 32 characters by:

```
          INTEGER NAMES(8)
```

The array named NAMES is composed of eight elements, each four bytes or characters in length. Consequently, we could read a name punched into card columns 1-32 by a FORMAT statement such as

```
      3   FORMAT(8A4)
```

To read a set of, say, up to 200 such names, we could declare an array as:

```
          INTEGER NAMES(200,8)
```

so that each of the 200 rows of the matrix stored one name. To read up to 200 names, we could write

```
          DO 8 K=1,200
          READ (5,3,END=9) (NAMES(K,J),J=1,8)
      3   FORMAT(8A4)
      8   CONTINUE
              •
              •
              •
      9   CONTINUE
```

Another Sorting Example

Sorting such an array involves comparing up to eight elements of a row to determine which is larger. Suppose the names have been read into memory. Assume they are in an

INTEGER array called NAMES which contains 200 rows and eight columns, and assume I, J, K, L, M, N, and TEMP are INTEGER. If N contains the number of names to be sorted, we could write:

```
      M=N-1
      DO 8 I=1,M
      J=I+1
      DO 7 K=J,N
      DO 4 L=1,8
      IF (NAMES(I,L).LT.NAMES(K,L)) GO TO 7
      IF (NAMES(I,L).GT.NAMES(K,L)) GO TO 5
4     CONTINUE
5     DO 6 L=1,8
      TEMP=NAMES(I,L)
      NAMES(I,L)=NAMES(K,L)
      NAMES(K,L)=TEMP
6     CONTINUE
7     CONTINUE
8     CONTINUE
```

This program will work provided there are not blanks at differing character positions among the 32 characters. If there are no blanks, or if the blanks in each occur at the same positions in each set of 32 characters, or if no blanks happen to fall in the first byte of any word, the sort will be accurate.

If these conditions do not exist and one is forced to do the sort in Fortran, then a procedure which would work is to read each character into a separate word with A1 format and do the sort as above, checking separately for the occurrence of a blank. Painful and slow -- but that's Fortran in non-numeric gear.

Methods of Searching

Computer programs are often used to read a transaction record, search through an array of items and match some value on the transaction, called a search argument, with some value in an array to find a second value which is associated with the first. An example of this task might be to read a record showing a social security number, search through an array in the computer memory, and find the person's name or address.

While there are many techniques of computer searching, three will be discussed here. All three relate to searching within the memory of the computer as opposed to searching for information on tape or disk.

Brute Force

The most obvious method of computer searching involves placing a table of information items in memory and searching through the list, item by item, until a match is found or until the end of the list is reached without finding a match.

For example, suppose that we place a table of social security numbers and names in the computer memory. The task will be to read a card with a social security number, find the person's name, and print the name and number for each card. Computer memory might appear as follows:

	Array N	Array NAME
(1)	246883021	Jones, J
(2)	507322108	Smith, F
(3)	404556811	Steinem, G
(4)	321541729	Lovelace, L
(5)	107326855	Welch, R
•	•	•
•	•	•
•	•	•

We could read the social security number from the card, compare it with N(1). If a match occurs, then we know that NAME(1) contains the correct name. If no match occurs, we compare with N(2), and so on. Without any further information, we would search through about half of the list, on the average, for each look-up operation.

Probabilistic Ordering

Clearly we can reduce the search time of the program if the most likely social security numbers appeared early in the array. Probabilistic ordering may be useful in part-number searches where we know that certain parts are more frequently ordered or used. Another area of use could be searching for job titles where certain titles are more prevalent than others.

Binary Search

The binary search technique consists of first sorting the array of items to be examined during the look-up process into alphanumerical order. During the sorting process, any associated values must also be exchanged. That is, if we move the social security number in N(3) to N(11) we must also move the associated name from NAME(3) to NAME(11).

Once the sorting is completed, the binary search method consists of dividing the list of search arguments in half on each search. We start at the approximate middle of the list. If the value that we are looking for is larger than the middle value, then we can eliminate from further consideration all values in the list smaller than the middle value. That is, on the first look-up, half of the list or table is eliminated. Then we examine the middle value of the remaining half of the list and eliminate another 25% of the list from examination. This "halving" continues until either the desired value is found or it is determined that it is not in the list at all. Very large lists of arguments can be searched in a relatively small number of comparisons -- doubling the length of the list only increases the maximum number of searches by one. Assuming that a table of 500 social security numbers and names resides in memory, the maximum number of searches required to find any one of them is nine. If the list contained 1000 values, the maximum number of searches would be only ten.

Given that NA contained the search argument (value of the variable for which a match is to be found) and that the variable N contained the number of elements in a search array named SA (sorted in ascending order), the following routine could be used to perform a binary search. (Notice that N, L, U, and I are INTEGER. SA and NA should both be of the same type.)

```
C BINARY SEARCH ROUTINE
      L=1
      U=N
   22 IF(U.LT.L)GO TO 98
      I=(L+U)/2
      IF(NA-SA(I))24,99,25
   24 U=I-1
      GO TO 22
   25 L=I+1
      GO TO 22
        •
        •
```

In the routine above, if control reaches statement 99, then a match occurs and I contains the subscript of the matched argument. If control reaches statement 98, then the argument was not found in the list. Notice that L (the lower limit) and U (the upper limit) continue to bound the potentially equal value. Each check results in about half of the elements being eliminated. The maximum number of comparisons required is approximately m, where the number of elements in the search array is 2 to the m power. The table below shows the maximum number of comparisons required for a successful search. If all elements have an equally likely chance of being the object of a search, then the maximum number of comparisons will be required about 50% of the time and one less than the maximum will be required most of the rest of the time.

Elements in a search array	Maximum number of comparisons
60000	16
15000	14
4000	12
1000	10
250	8
60	6
30	5

One may use a binary search in Fortran on a set of elements which has been "sorted" in Fortran. The comments above about the manner Fortran handles blanks, etc. do not apply so long as the search regimen is identical to the sort regimen. It is very dangerous to sort according to one method -- say a card sorter -- and search according to another -- e.g., a Fortran program. Be certain that there is no chance for inconsistency between the two methods.

It should be emphasized that many algorithms for searching exist. For an extensive treatment of these techniques see Donald Knuth, Sorting and Searching, Reading, Mass.: Addison-Wesley, 1973.

MODULE 12

FORTRAN DATA FORMS IN IBM 360/370

Prerequisites: Parts I, II, Appendices E, G
(Modules 1, 2)

In Parts I and II of this book we talk loosely about "locations" in computer memory. You know that we can store REAL numbers in locations, INTEGER numbers in locations, alphanumeric characters in locations, and so on. Now we want to tighten up these ideas a bit so that you can understand the complexities and difficulties of operations between, principally, numbers. But we begin at the beginning, with bits. For completeness, we include some material which has been previously covered.

The idea of a binary digit (bit) has already been introduced. One way of looking at the memory of a computer is simply to consider it as being made up of a large number of these bits. But a bit can store only the minimum of information: yes or no; on or off; one or zero. So it is useful to consider aggregates of bits which can store larger elements, such as numbers or characters. For the IBM 360/370 it is probably most useful to look first at a group of 64 bits because almost all numeric data forms which can be represented are based on 64 bits or some division thereof. We could think of the memory of the computer as being composed of a large number of these groups of 64 bits. Figure 1 shows such a configuration.

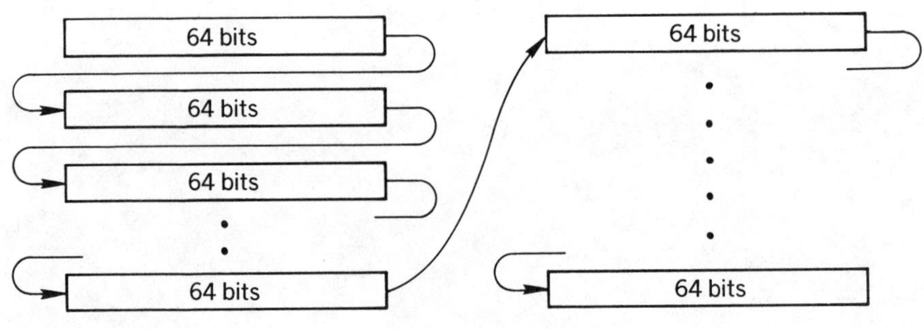

Figure 1

If we isolate one of these groups of 64 bits and number each bit according to the standard convention, we would have:

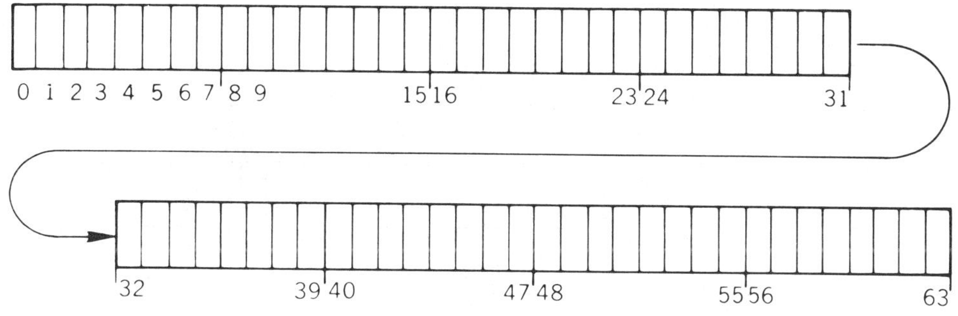

Figure 2

Each small rectangle can hold either a one or a zero. You will immediately perceive what you may regard as insanity, mindlessness, or a mixture of both in the numbering system of the 64 bits in Figure 2. The first bit is numbered zero, the second is called one, the third, two and on ad stupiditatem. It turns out that there are good reasons for this numbering system, in terms of the way the machine must reference information, even though it's a bit hard on the humans who have to deal with it.

Alphanumeric Characters

Characters are stored by using groups of eight adjacent bits. Each of the alphanumeric characters used in Fortran has its own unique code of bits. For example, an A is 11000001, a B is 11000010, a $ is 01011011, and a 7 (when stored alphanumerically, not numerically) is 11110111. Each character which is stored in memory starts in bit location 0, 8, 16, 24, 32, 40, 48, or 56.

An aggregate of bits which starts in locations 0, 8, 16,...56 is called by a special name: byte. In fact, when we talk about the memory size of an IBM 360/370 computer we generally talk not about the number of bits it can remember but rather the number of characters or bytes. So we can look at our aggregate of 64 bits in a new way:

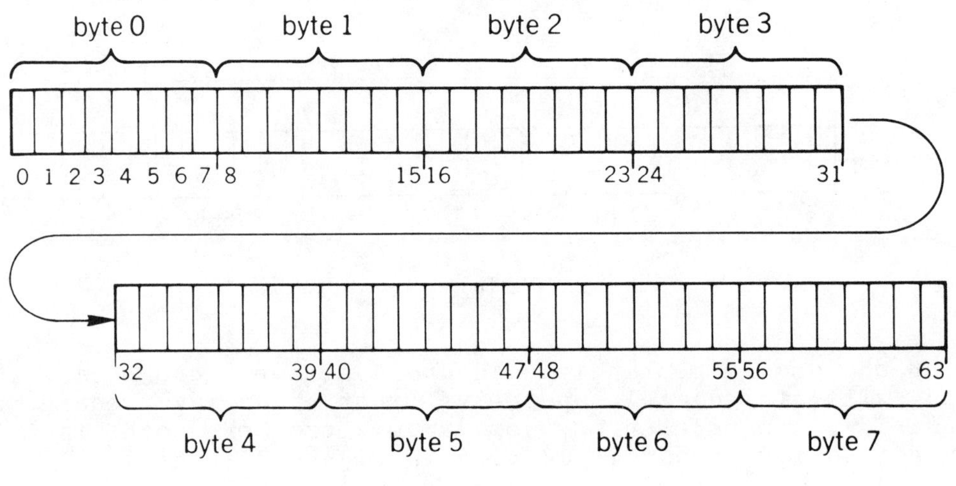

Figure 3

For more details see Module 11, Non-Numeric Data.

INTEGER*4

We have used variables typed as INTEGER or INTEGER*4 when we wanted an integer which was greater than or equal to -2,147,463,648 but less than or equal to 2,147,483,647. These limits correspond to -2^{31} and $2^{31}-1$ respectively. To explain why, we introduce the concept of a word of computer storage. A word is a sequence of four adjacent bytes which starts in either byte 0 or byte 4 (bit 0 or bit 32). We would represent two words in our aggregate of bits as:

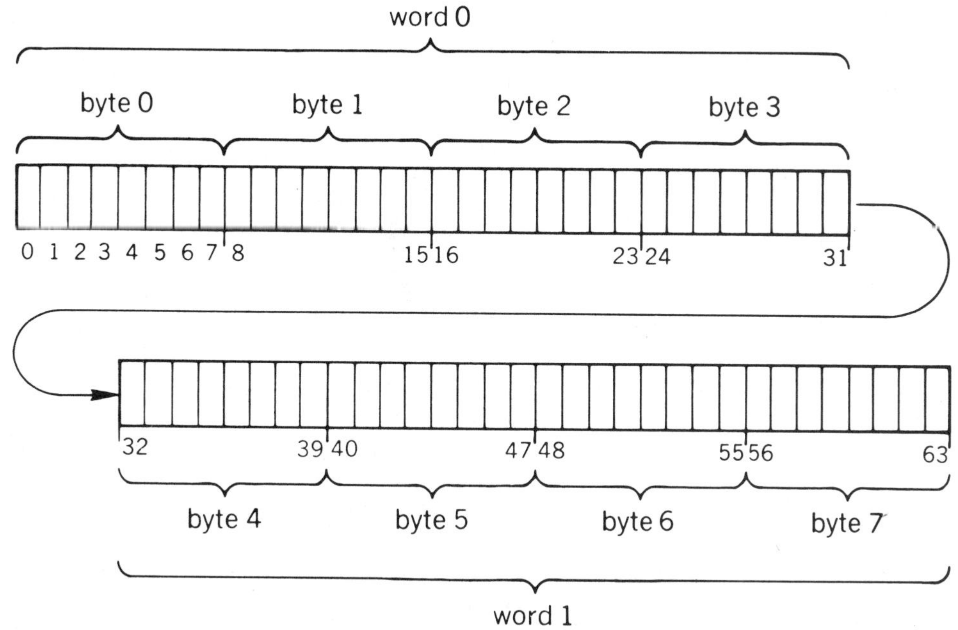

Figure 4

Suppose an INTEGER variable were located in word zero of our aggregate of 64 bits. Then bits 1 through 31 would be used to represent the number in binary form. Bit 0 would represent the sign. If bit 0 contains a zero, the sign of the number is positive; if bit 0 contains a one, the sign is negative. The absolute value of the smallest negative number a word can store is one greater than the value of the largest positive number, because two's-complement notation, explained below, is used for storing negative numbers.

INTEGER*2

Variables typed as INTEGER*2 use only two bytes (sometimes called a *half word*) to store the number whose value must lie between -32,768 and 32,767. These variables may only begin on bytes 0, 2, 4, or 6. We say, then that INTEGER*2 variables must be aligned on *halfword* boundaries in the IBM 360.

INTEGER*2 Examples

Examine the following numbers and their binary equivalents.

Base Ten Number	INTEGER*2 Contents
2	0000000000000010
5	0000000000000101
64	0000000001000000
513	0000001000000001

If the number is negative (the left-most bit is a one), the number is stored in its two's-complement form. To compute the two's-complement of a number, simply write the binary value, "not" each bit (that is, if the bit is a one, convert it to a zero; if the bit is a zero, convert it to a one) and then add one. The result is the two's-complement, and this is how negative INTEGERs are stored in Fortran. For example, the INTEGER representation of -12 would be formed as follows:

value	bit value
12	0000000000001100
not 12	1111111111110011
(not 12)+1	1111111111110100

Therefore the bit value 1111111111110100 is the Fortran INTEGER*2 value of -12.

INTEGER*4 values follow the same rules except that there are 32 binary bits in a variable instead of 16. In either case, the left-most bit is the sign.

What is the base ten value of the smallest number which can be represented in INTEGER*2? The largest? What binary value represents -1?

REAL*4

The situation becomes more complicated with REAL variables (sometimes called floating-point variables), since both a mantissa and an exponent must be stored. REAL variables require four bytes and are aligned on fullword boundaries. Most of the first byte is devoted to the exponent of the number and the remaining three bytes (24 bits) to the mantissa.

REAL numbers are stored as an exponent and a mantissa. The following scheme is used:

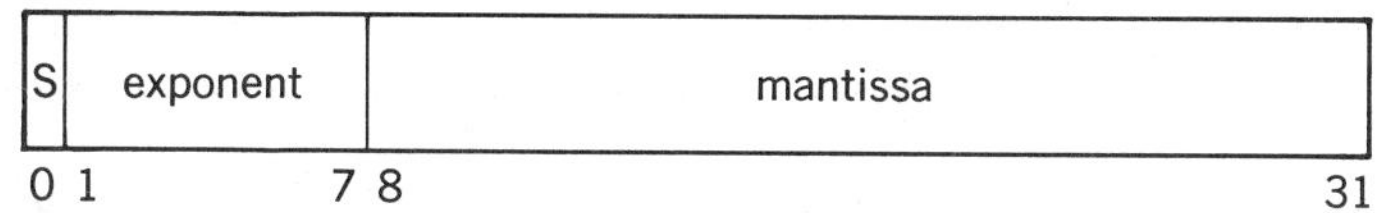

Figure 5

The sign "s" is the sign of the mantissa. The mantissa is treated as a binary fraction -- a set of bits with the decimal point assumed to be at the left end. The left-most bit represents .5, the next 0.25, then 0.125, etc. Each bit represents a value which is one-half the value of the one on its left.

Twenty-four bits are devoted to the representation of the mantissa, although the actual precision is 21. This is because the three leftmost bits of the mantissa are zero for some numbers. If you want an effective significance greater than 21 bits you must go to REAL*8 variables.

The exponent of the number is stored in 7 bits as a straight binary number between zero and 127 without a sign; an exponent always represents some power of 16. Its value is reduced by 64 to determine the power of 16 to be used. This method is called excess-64 notation.

For example, if the exponent contained

1000001

(the binary value of 65), then to evaluate the value of the variable, the mantissa is multiplied by 16 (because 65-64=1 and 16 raised to the power of 1 equals 16).

If the exponent value were

1000010

(the binary value of 66), then to evaluate the variable, the mantissa is multiplied by 256 (16 raised to the 66-64 power). The following examples serve to illustrate:

base 10 number	bit values REAL*4
.5	01000000100000000000000000000000
-.5	11000000100000000000000000000000
8.0	01000001100000000000000000000000
-8.0	11000001100000000000000000000000

REAL*8

When more precision is needed the programmer can specify REAL*8. In this case all 8 bytes (64 bits) are used to represent the number. This representation, sometimes called double precision (though, in fact, it is more than double), is aligned on double word boundaries. Again, most of the first byte is used for the exponent and the remaining seven bytes are used for the mantissa.

REAL*8 variables follow the same format as REAL*4, except that the numeric portion contains 56 bits instead of 24, providing for about 16 significant decimal digits instead of about 7. The graphic representation would be:

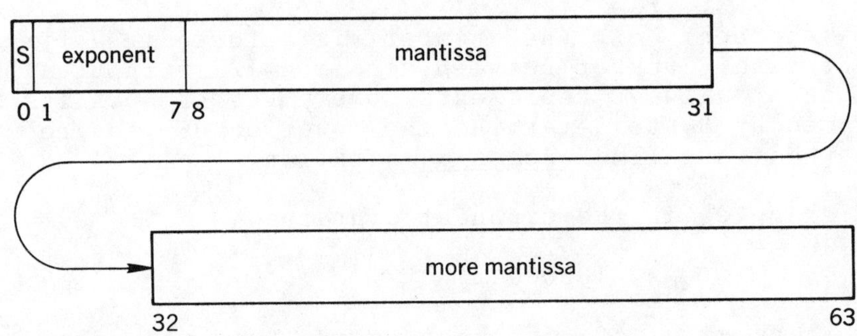

Figure 6

COMPLEX

COMPLEX*8 variables consist of two REAL locations, the first for the real portion of the COMPLEX number and the second for the imaginary portion. Each separate portion follows the format of REAL variables. They are aligned on double word boundaries.

COMPLEX*16 variables use essentially two REAL*8 locations. The total number of bits used is 128.

LOGICAL

A variable typed LOGICAL usually stores data with value .TRUE. or .FALSE. Fortran uses a convention of storing all one-bits in the first byte (character) of the variable if the value is true and all zero-bits in the first byte if the value is false. If a LOGICAL variable is used for storage of alphanumeric data, then the variable contains the standard alphanumeric representation.

MODULE 13

PHYSICAL ORDER OF FORTRAN STATEMENTS

The physical order of statements in IBM Fortran, WATFOR, or WATFIV may be as follows, and if it is so, it will prevent difficulties from occurring because of incorrect order:

1. SUBROUTINE, FUNCTION, or BLOCK DATA statement, if any.

2. IMPLICIT statement, if any;

3. Specification statements, if any (COMMON, COMPLEX,DIMENSION,DOUBLE PRECISION, EQUIVALENCE, EXTERNAL, INTEGER, LOGICAL, or REAL);

4. Arithmetic statement FUNCTION definitions, if any;

5. Executable statements, if any;

6. END statement.

FORMAT statements can appear anywhere after the IMPLICIT statement and before the END statement. If DATA statements are used, they must appear after any declaration statements which name the variables to which they refer. They may appear after executable statements, if the variable(s) concerned has(have) not yet been used in an executable statement.

In WATFOR/FIV, if a variable is used in a COMMON or EQUIVALENCE statement and is initialized with a value in a Type Declaration statement, then the initialization statement must appear after the EQUIVALENCE or COMMON statement.

NAMELIST and DEFINE FILE statements must logically precede any input or output related to them.

FORTRAN-SUPPLIED SUBPROGRAMS[1]

Function	Entry Name	Definition	In-Line (I) Out-of-Line (O)	No. of Arg.	Type of Arguments	Type of Function Value
Exponential	EXP	e^{arg}	O	1	Real *4	Real *4
	DEXP	e^{arg}	O	1	Real *8	Real *8
	CEXP	e^{arg}	O	1	Complex *8	Complex *8
	CDEXP	e^{arg}	O	1	Complex *16	Complex *16
Natural Logarithm	ALOG	ln (Arg)	O	1	Real *4	Real *4
	DLOG	ln (Arg)	O	1	Real *8	Real *8
	CLOG	ln (Arg)	O	1	Complex *8	Complex *8
	CDLOG	ln (Arg)	O	1	Complex *16	Complex *16
Common Logarithm	ALOG10	$\log_{10}$(Arg)	O	1	Real *4	Real *4
	DLOG10	$\log_{10}$(Arg)	O	1	Real *8	Real *8
Arcsine	ARSIN	arcsin (Arg)	O	1	Real *4	Real *4
	DARSIN	arcsin (Arg)	O	1	Real *8	Real *8
Arccosine	ARCOS	arccos (Arg)	O	1	Real *4	Real *4
	DARCOS	arccos (Arg)	O	1	Real *8	Real *8
Arctangent[1]	ATAN	arctan (Arg)	O	1	Real *4	Real *4
	ATAN2	arctan (Arg_1/Arg_2)	O	2	Real *4	Real *4
	DATAN	arctan (Arg)	O	1	Real *8	Real *8
	DATAN2	arctan (Arg_1/Arg_2)	O	2	Real *8	Real *8
Trigonometric Sine (Argument in radians)	SIN	sin (Arg)	O	1	Real *4	Real *4
	DSIN	sin (Arg)	O	1	Real *8	Real *8
	CSIN	sin (Arg)	O	1	Complex *8	Complex *8
	CDSIN	sin (Arg)	O	1	Complex *16	Complex *16
Trigonometric Cosine (Argument in radians)	COS	cos (Arg)	O	1	Real *4	Real *4
	DCOS	cos (Arg)	O	1	Real *8	Real *8
	CCOS	cos (Arg)	O	1	Complex *8	Complex *8
	CDCOS	cos (Arg)	O	1	Complex *16	Complex *16
Trigonometric Tangent (Argument in radians)	TAN	tan (Arg)	O	1	Real *4	Real *4
	DTAN	tan (Arg)	O	1	Real *8	Real *8
Trigonometric Cotangent (Argument in radians)	COTAN	cotan (Arg)	O	1	Real *4	Real *4
	DCOTAN	cotan (Arg)	O	1	Real *8	Real *8
Square Root	SQRT	$(Arg)^{1/2}$	O	1	Real *4	Real *4
	DSQRT	$(Arg)^{1/2}$	O	1	Real *8	Real *8
	CSQRT	$(Arg)^{1/2}$	O	1	Complex *8	Complex *8
	CDSQRT	$(Arg)^{1/2}$	O	1	Complex *16	Complex *16

[1]Two arguments must be supplied for ATAN2 and DATAN2.

---

[1] Reprinted by permission from FORTRAN IV LANGUAGE © (1968) by International Business Machines Corporation.

Function	Entry Name	Definition	In-Line (I) Out-of-Line (O)	No. of Arg.	Type of Arguments	Type of Function Value
Hyperbolic Tangent	TANH DTANH	tanh (Arg) tanh (Arg)	O O	1 1	Real *4 Real *8	Real *4 Real *8
Hyperbolic Sine	SINH DSINH	sinh (Arg) sinh (Arg)	O O	1 1	Real *4 Real *8	Real *4 Real *8
Hyperbolic Cosine	COSH DCOSH	cosh (Arg) cosh (Arg)	O O	1 1	Real *4 Real *8	Real *4 Real *8
Error Function	ERF DERF	$\frac{2}{\sqrt{\pi}}\int_0^x e^{-u^2}\,du$	O O	1 1	Real *4 Real *8	Real *4 Real *8
Complemented Error Function	ERFC DERFC	1-erf (x)	O O	1 1	Real *4 Real *8	Real *4 Real *8
Gamma	GAMMA DGAMMA	$\int_0^\infty u^{x-1} e^{-u}\,du$	O O	1 1	Real *4 Real *8	Real *4 Real *8
Log-gamma	ALGAMA DLGAMA	$\log_e \Gamma(x)$	O O	1 1	Real *4 Real *8	Real *4 Real *8
Modular Arithmetic[2]	MOD AMOD DMOD	Arg_1 (mod Arg_2)= Arg_1-[x]*Arg_2 Where: [x] is the largest integer whose magnitude does not exceed the magnitude of Arg_1/Arg_2. The sign of the integer is the same as the sign of Arg_1/Arg_2.	I * I * I *	2 2 2	Integer *4 Real *4 Real *8	Integer *4 Real*4 Real *8
Absolute value	IABS ABS DABS	|Arg|	I * I * I *	1 1 1	Integer *4 Real *4 Real *8	Integer *4 Real *4 Real *8
	CABS CDABS	$\sqrt{(a^2+b^2)}$ for a+bi	O O	1 1	Complex *8 Complex *16	Real *4 Real *8
Truncation	INT	Sign of Arg times largest integer ≤|Arg|	I *	1	Real *4	Integer *4
	AINT IDINT		I * I *	1 1	Real *4 Real *8	Real *4 Integer *4
Largest value[3]	AMAX0 AMAX1 MAX0 MAX1 DMAX1	Max(Arg_1,Arg_2,...)	O * O * O * O * O *	≥2 ≥2 ≥2 ≥2 ≥2	Integer *4 Real *4 Integer *4 Real *4 Real *8	Real *4 Real *4 Integer *4 Integer *4 Real *8

[2]MOD and AMOD are not defined when the value of the second argument is zero.
[3]For the FORTRAN IV (H) compiler, these functions are in-line.
*USA FORTRAN IV intrinsic function

Function	Entry Name	Definition	In-Line (I) Out-of-Line (O)	No. of Arg.	Type of Arguments	Type of Function Value
Smallest value[3]	AMIN0 AMIN1 MIN0 MIN1 DMIN1	$\text{Min}(\text{Arg}_1,\text{Arg}_2,\ldots)$	O * O * O * O * O *	≥2 ≥2 ≥2 ≥2 ≥2	Integer *4 Real *4 Integer *4 Real *4 Real *8	Real *4 Real *4 Integer *4 Integer *4 Real *8
Float	FLOAT DFLOAT	Convert from integer to real	I * I	1 1	Integer *4 Integer *4	Real *4 Real *8
Fix	IFIX HFIX	Convert from real to integer	I * I	1 1	Real *4 Real *4	Integer *4 Integer *2
Transfer of sign[4]	SIGN ISIGN DSIGN	Sign of Arg_2 times $\lvert\text{Arg}_1\rvert$	I * I * I *	2 2 2	Real *4 Integer *4 Real *8	Real *4 Integer *4 Real *8
Positive difference	DIM IDIM	$\text{Arg}_1-\text{Min}(\text{Arg}_1,\text{Arg}_2)$	I * I *	2 2	Real *4 Integer *4	Real *4 Integer *4
Obtaining most significant part of a Real *8 argument	SNGL		I *	1	Real *8	Real *4
Obtain real part of complex argument	REAL		I *	1	Complex *8	Real *4
Obtain imaginary part of complex argument	AIMAG		I *	1	Complex *8	Real *4
Express a Real *4 argument in Real *8 form	DBLE		I *	1	Real *4	Real *8
Express two real arguments in complex form	CMPLX DCMPLX	$C=\text{Arg}_1,+i\text{Arg}_2$	I * I	2 2	Real *4 Real *8	Complex *8 Complex *16
Obtain conjugate of a complex argument	CONJG DCONJG	C=X-iY For Arg=X+iY	I * I	1 1	Complex *8 Complex *16	Complex *8 Complex *16

[3]For the FORTRAN IV (H) compiler, these functions are in-line.
[4]SIGN, ISIGN, and DSIGN are not defined when the value of the second argument is zero.
*USA FORTRAN IV intrinsic function

Function	CALL Statement	Argument Information
Alter status of sense lights	CALL SLITE(i)	i is an integer expression. If i = 0, the four sense lights are turned off. If i = 1, 2, 3, or 4, the corresponding sense light is turned on.
Test and record status of sense lights	CALL SLITET(i,j)	i is an integer expression that has a value of 1, 2, 3, or 4 and indicates which sense light to test. j is an integer variable that is set to 1 if the sense light was on, or to 2 if the sense light was off.
Dump storage on the output data set and terminate execution	CALL DUMP (a_1,b_1,f_1, ...,a_n,b_n,f_n)	a and b are variables that indicate the limits of storage to be dumped. (Either a or b may be the upper or lower limits of storage, but both must be in the same program or subprogram or in common.) f indicates the dump format and may be one of the following: 0 - hexadecimal 1 - logical*1 2 - logical*4 3 - integer*2 4 - integer*4 5 - real*4 6 - real*8 7 - complex*8 8 - complex*16 9 - literal
Dump storage on the output data set and continue execution	CALL PDUMP (a_1,b_1,f_1, ...,a_n,b_n,f_n)	a, b, and f are as defined above for DUMP.
Test for divide check exception	CALL DVCHK(j)	j is an integer variable that is set to 1 if the divide-check indicator was on, or to 2 if the indicator was off. After testing, the divide-check indicator is turned off.
Test for exponent overflow or underflow	CALL OVERFL(j)	j is an integer variable that is set to 1 if an exponent overflow condition was the last to occur, to 2 if no overflow condition exists, or to 3 if an exponent underflow condition was the last to occur. After testing, the overflow indicator is turned off.
Terminate execution	CALL EXIT	None

MODULE 15

A FORTRAN IV SUMMARY[1]

IBM Fortran IV Character Set

The 49 characters shown below constitute the components of every Fortran IV statement except characters found within a literal field (enclosed in quotes) where any characters are valid.

ALPHABETIC CHARACTERS ABCDEFGHIJKLMNOPQRSTUVWXYZ$

NUMERIC CHARACTERS 0123456789

SPECIAL CHARACTERS

+ (plus)	. (decimal point)	((left parenthesis)
(blank)	= (equal sign)	' (apostrophe)
/ (slash)	* (asterisk)	& (ampersand)
- (minus)	, (comma)	) (right parenthesis)

Definitions

The definitions below apply to models of the IBM 360/370.

---

[1] Some of this material is reprinted by permission from FORTRAN IV LANGUAGE © (1968) by International Business Machines Corporation.

Definitions

The definitions below apply to models of the IBM 360 System.

Integer Constant - a whole number written without a decimal point. It occupies four locations of storage (i.e., four bytes). Maximum Magnitude: 2147483647 (i.e., $2^{31}-1$).

Real Constant -- has one of three forms: a basic real constant, a basic real constant followed by a decimal exponent, or an integer constant followed by a decimal exponent. A basic real constant is a string of decimal digits with a decimal point. If the string contains fewer than eight digits, the basic real constant occupies four storage locations (bytes); if the string contains eight or more digits, the basic real constant occupies eight storage locations (bytes). The storage requirement (length) of a real constant can also be explicitly specified by appending an exponent to a basic real constant or an integer constant. An exponent consists of the letter E or the letter D followed by a signed or unsigned 1- or 2-digit integer constant. The letter E specifies a constant of length four; the letter D specifies a constant of length eight. Magnitude: (either four or eight locations) 0 or 16^{-65} (approximately 10^{-78}) through 16^{63} (approximately 10^{75}) Precision: (four locations) 6 hexadecimal digits (approximately 7.2 decimal digits) (eight locations) 14 hexadecimal digits (approximately 16.8 decimal digits)

Symbolic Name - from 1 through 6 alphameric (i.e., numeric, 0 through 9, or alphabetic, A through Z and $) characters, the first of which must be alphabetic.

Literal Constant - a string of alphameric and/or special characters, delimited as follows:

1. The string can be enclosed in apostrophes.

2. The string can be preceded by wH where w is the number of characters in the string.

Complex Constant - an ordered pair of signed or unsigned real constants separated by a comma and enclosed in parentheses. A complex constant may assume one of two forms:

1. From 1 through 7 decimal digits with a decimal point, optionally followed by an E decimal exponent. In this form, each number in the pair occupies 4 storage locations.

2. Either 1 through 7 decimal digits with a decimal point, followed by a D decimal exponent or 8 through 16 decimal digits optionally followed by a D decimal exponent. In this form each number in the pair occupies 8 storage locations.

Magnitude: (either form) 0 or 16^{-63} through 16^{63} (i.e., approximately 10^{75}) for each real constant in the pair.

Logical Constant - a constant that specifies a logical value. There are two logical values:

.TRUE.
.FALSE.

Each occupies four storage locations. The words TRUE and FALSE must be preceded and followed by periods as shown above.

Hexadecimal Constant - the character Z followed by a hexadecimal number formed from the set 0 through 9 and A through F.

Statements

Below are the general forms of the statements of the Fortran IV language in alphabetical order. Included are statements not covered in the text as well as some not operational in WATFOR or WATFIV; appropriate notations are made in these cases. The executability of each statement is given.

ARITHMETIC ASSIGNMENT STATEMENT (see ASSIGNMENT STATEMENT)

<u>Conversion Rules for Arithmetic Assignment Statement: a=b</u>

<table>
<tr><th>Type of b / Type of a</th><th>INTEGER*2
INTEGER*4</th><th>REAL*4</th><th>REAL*8</th><th>COMPLEX*8</th><th>COMPLEX*16</th></tr>
<tr><td>INTEGER*2
INTEGER*4</td><td>Assign</td><td colspan="2">Fix and assign</td><td colspan="2">Fix and assign real part; imaginary part not used.</td></tr>
<tr><td>REAL*4</td><td>Float and assign</td><td>Assign</td><td>Real assign</td><td>Assign real part; imaginary part not used.</td><td>Real assign real part; imaginary part not used.</td></tr>
<tr><td>REAL*8</td><td>DP Float and assign</td><td colspan="2">Assign</td><td colspan="2">Assign real part; imaginary part not used.</td></tr>
<tr><td>COMPLEX*8</td><td>Float and assign to real part; imaginary part set to zero.</td><td>Assign to real part; imaginary part set to zero.</td><td>Real assign real part; imaginary part set to zero.</td><td>Assign</td><td>Real assign real and imaginary parts.</td></tr>
<tr><td>COMPLEX*16</td><td>DP float and assign to real part; imaginary part set to zero.</td><td colspan="2">Assign to real part; imaginary part set to zero.</td><td colspan="2">Assign</td></tr>
</table>

<u>Notes</u>:

1. <u>Assign</u> means transmit the resulting value, without change. If the significant digits of the resulting value exceed the specified length, results are unpredictable.
2. <u>Real Assign</u> means transmit to <u>a</u> as much precision of the most significant part of the resulting value as REAL*4 data can contain.
3. <u>Fix</u> means transform the resulting value to the form of a basic real constant and truncate the fractional portion.
4. <u>Float</u> means transform the resulting value to the form of a REAL*4 number, retaining in the process as much precision of the value as a REAL*4 number can contain.
5. <u>DP Float</u> means transform the resulting value to the form of a REAL*8 number.
6. An expression of the form E=(A,B), where E is a complex variable and A and B are real variables, is invalid. The mathematical function subprogram CMPLX can be used for this purpose. See Appendix C.

ARITHMETIC IF STATEMENT - executable

```
IF (a) x1,x2,x3

Where:  a is any arithmetic expression except complex.

        x1,x2,x3 are executable statement numbers.
```

ASSIGN STATEMENT - ASSIGNED GO TO STATEMENT - executable

```
ASSIGN i TO m
        .
        .
        .
GO TO m, (x1,x2,x3,...,xn)

Where:  i is an executable statement number.  It must be one of the
        numbers x1,x2,x3,...,xn.

        x1,x2,x3,...,xn are executable statement numbers in the pro-
        gram unit containing the GO TO statement.

        m is a nonsubscripted integer variable of length 4 which is
        assigned one of the statement numbers:  x1,x2,x3,...,xn.
```

ASSIGNMENT STATEMENT - executable

```
a = b

Where:  a is a subscripted or nonsubscripted variable.

        b is an arithmetic expression or logical expression.
```

BACKSPACE STATEMENT - executable - not covered in the text - used with sequential data sets such as tape or disk

```
BACKSPACE a

Where:  a is an unsigned integer constant or integer variable that
        is of length 4 and represents a data set reference number.
```

BLOCK DATA SUBPROGRAM - non-executable - used to initialize values of variables in labeled COMMON - valid but not necessary in WATFOR

```
BLOCK DATA
   .
   .
   .
END
```

CALL STATEMENT - executable

```
CALL name (a1,a2,a3,...,an)

Where:  name is the name of a SUBROUTINE subprogram.

        a1,a2,a3,...,an are the actual arguments that are being sup-
        plied to the SUBROUTINE subprogram.  Each may be of the form
        &n where n is a statement number
```

COMMON STATEMENT - non-executable - data initialization feature not covered in the text

```
COMMON /r/a (k1),b(k2),.../r/c(k3),d(k ),...
```

Where: a,b,...,c,d... are variable names or array names that cannot be dummy arguments.

$k_1,k_2,\ldots k_3,k$ ... are optional and are each composed of one through seven unsigned integer constants, separated by commas, representing the maximum value of each subscript in the array.

/r/... represent optional common block names consisting of one through six alphameric characters, the first of which is alphabetic. These names must always be embedded in slashes.

COMPUTED GO TO STATEMENT - executable

```
GO TO (x1, x2, x3, ...,xn), i
```

Where: $x_1,x_2,\ldots,x_n$, are executable statement numbers.

i is a nonsubscripted integer variable whose current value is in the range: $1 \leq i \leq n$

COMPLEX STATEMENT (see TYPE DECLARATION STATEMENT)

CONTINUE STATEMENT - executable

```
CONTINUE
```

DATA STATEMENT - non-executable - not covered in the text - used as another way to initialize variable values at compile time

```
DATA    k1/d1/,k2/d2/,...,kn/dn/

Where:  Each k is a list containing variables, subscripted variables
        (in which case the subscripts must be integer constants), or
        array names.  Dummy arguments may not appear in the list.

        Each d is a list of constants (integer, real, complex, hexa-
        decimal, logical, or literal), any of which may be preceded
        by i*.

        Each i is an unsigned integer constant.  When the form i*
        appears before a constant, it indicates that the constant is
        to be specified i times.
```

DEFINE FILE STATEMENT - non-executable - implemented in WATFIV but not WATFOR

DEFINE FILE $\underline{a}_1(\underline{m}_1,\underline{r}_1,\underline{f}_1,\underline{v}_1),\underline{a}_2(\underline{m}_2,\underline{r}_2,\underline{f}_2,\underline{v}_2),\ldots,\underline{a}_n(\underline{m}_n,\underline{r}_n,\underline{f}_n,\underline{v}_n)$

Where: $\underline{a}$ represents an integer constant that is the data set reference number.

$\underline{m}$ represents an integer constant that specifies the number of records in the data set associated with $\underline{a}$.

$\underline{r}$ represents an integer constant that specifies the maximum size of each record associated with $\underline{a}$. The record size is measured in characters (bytes), storage locations (bytes), or storage units (words). (A storage unit is the number of storage locations divided by four and rounded to the next highest integer.) The method used to measure the record size depends upon the specification for $\underline{f}$.

$\underline{f}$ specifies that the data set is to be read or written either with or without format control; $\underline{f}$ may be one of the following letters:

L indicates that the data set is to be read or written either with or without format control. The maximum record size is measured in number of storage locations (bytes).

E indicates that the data set is to be read or written under format control (as specified by a format statement). The maximum record size is measured in number of characters (bytes).

U indicates that the data set is to be read or written without format control. The maximum record size is measured in number of storage units (words).

$\underline{v}$ represents a nonsubscripted integer variable called an associated variable. At the conclusion of each read or write operation, $\underline{v}$ is set to a value that points to the record that immediately follows the last record transmitted. At the conclusion of a find operation, $\underline{v}$ is set to a value that points to the record found.

DIMENSION STATEMENT - non-executable - not covered in the text - used to reserve memory for subscripted variables

DIMENSION $\underline{a}_1(\underline{k}_1)$,$\underline{a}_2(\underline{k}_2)$, $\underline{a}_3(\underline{k}_3)$,...,$\underline{a}_n(\underline{k}_n)$

Where: $\underline{a}_1$, $\underline{a}_2$, $\underline{a}_3$,..., $\underline{a}_n$ are array names.

$\underline{k}_1$, $\underline{k}_2$, $\underline{k}_3$,...,$\underline{k}_n$ are each composed of one through seven unsigned integer constants, separated by commas, representing the maximum value of each subscript in the array. $\underline{k}_1$ through $\underline{k}_n$ may be integer variables of length 4 only when the DIMENSION statement in which they appear is in a subprogram.

DO STATEMENT - executable

	End of Range	DO Variable		Initial Value	Test Value	Increment
DO	$\underline{x}$	$\underline{i}$	=	$\underline{m}_1$,	$\underline{m}_2$,	$\underline{m}_3$

Where: $\underline{x}$ is an executable statement number appearing after the DO statement.

$\underline{i}$ is a nonsubscripted integer variable.

$\underline{m}_1$, $\underline{m}_2$, and $\underline{m}_3$, are either unsigned integer constants greater than zero or unsigned nonsubscripted integer variables whose value is greater than zero. $\underline{m}_2$ may not exceed $2^{31}-2$ in value. $\underline{m}_3$ is optional; if it is omitted, its value is assumed to be 1. In this case, the preceding comma must also be omitted.

DOUBLE PRECISION STATEMENT - non-executable - not covered in the text - used as an alternate way to declare variables as REAL*8

DOUBLE PRECISION $\underline{a}(\underline{k}_1),\underline{b}(\underline{k}_2),\ldots,\underline{z}(\underline{k}_n)$
Where: $\underline{a},\underline{b},\ldots,\underline{z}$ represent variable, array, or function names
$(\underline{k}_1),(\underline{k}_2),\ldots,(\underline{k}_n)$ are optional. Each $\underline{k}$ is composed of one through seven unsigned integer constants, separated by commas, that represent the maximum value of each subscript in the array.

END STATEMENT - non-executable

END

END FILE STATEMENT - executable - not covered in the text - used to close sequential data file.

END FILE $\underline{a}$
Where: $\underline{a}$ is an unsigned integer constant or integer variable that is of length 4 and represents a data set reference number.

ENTRY STATEMENT - non-executable - not covered in the text - provides for additional entries into subprograms

ENTRY $\underline{name}$ $(\underline{a}_1,\underline{a}_2,\underline{a}_3,\ldots,\underline{a}_n)$
Where: $\underline{name}$ is the name of an entry point
$\underline{a}_1,\underline{a}_2,\underline{a}_3,\ldots,\underline{a}_n$ are the dummy arguments corresponding to an actual argument in a CALL statement or in a function reference.

EQUIVALENCE STATEMENT - non-executable

```
EQUIVALENCE (a, b, c, ...), (d, e, f,...)

Where:  a, b, c, d, e, f,...  are variables (not dummy arguments)
        that may be subscripted.  The subscripts may have two forms:
        If the variable is singly subscripted, it refers to the
        position of the variable in the array (i.e., first variable,
        25th variable, etc.).  If the variable is multi-subscripted,
        it refers to the position in the array in the same fashion
        as the position is referred to in an arithmetic statement.
```

EXTERNAL STATEMENT - non-executable - not covered in the text - used to identify names of subprograms passed to other subprograms as arguments

```
EXTERNAL a,b,c,...

Where:  a,b,c,...  are names of subprograms that are passed as argu-
        ments to other subprograms.
```

FIND STATEMENT - executable - implemented in WATFIV but not in WATFOR - not covered in text

```
FIND (a'r)

Where:  a is an integer constant or unsigned integer variable that
        is of length 4 and represents a data set reference number; a
        must be followed by an apostrophe (').

        r is an integer expression that represents the relative
        position of a record within the data set associated with a.
```

FORMAT STATEMENT - non-executable - wH specification is not covered in the text (see next page)

FORMAT STATEMENT - non-executable - wH specification is not covered in the text

```
xxxxx   FORMAT (c1,c2,...,cn)

Where:      xxxxx is a statement number (1 through 5 digits).

            c1,c2,...,cn are format codes.

The format codes are:

aIw         (Describes integer data fields.)
paDw.d      (Describes real data fields.)
paEw.d      (Describes real data fields.)
paFw.d      (Describes real data fields.)
aZw         (Describes hexadecimal data fields.)
paGw.s      (Describes integer, real, complex, or logical data fields.)
aLw         (Describes logical data fields.)
aAw         (Describes alphameric data fields.)
'Literal'   (Transmits literal data.)
wH          (Transmits literal data.)
wX          (Indicates that a field is to be skipped on input or filled
              with blanks on output.)
Tr          (Indicates the position in a FORTRAN record where transfer
              of data is to start.)
a(...)      (Indicates a group format specification.)

Where:      a is optional and is an unsigned integer constant used to
            denote the number of times the format code is to be used.
            If a is omitted, the code is used only once.

            w is an unsigned nonzero integer constant that specifies the
            number of characters in the field.

            d is an unsigned integer constant specifying the number of
            decimal places to the right of the decimal point; i.e., the
            fractional portion.

            s is an unsigned integer constant specifying the number of
            significant digits.

            r is an unsigned integer constant designating a character
            position in a record.

            p is optional and represents a scale factor designator of
            the form nP where n is an unsigned or negatively signed
            integer constant.

            (...)  is a group format specification.  Within the paren-
            theses are format codes separated by commas or slashes.
            Group format specifications can be nested to a level of two.
            The a preceding this form is called a group repeat count.
```

Notes:

1. Complex data fields in records require two successive D, E, F, G, or A format codes. These codes may be grouped within parentheses.

2. Both commas and slashes can be used as separators between format codes.

FUNCTION STATEMENT - non-executable

```
Type FUNCTION name*s (a1,a2,a3,...,an)

Where:  Type is INTEGER, REAL, DOUBLE PRECISION, COMPLEX, or LOGIC-
        AL.  Its inclusion is optional.

        name is the name of the FUNCTION.

        *s represents one of the permissible length specifications
        for its associated type.  It may be included optionally only
        when Type is specified.  It must not be used when DOUBLE
        PRECISION is specified.

        a1,a2,a3,...,an are dummy arguments.  They must be nonsub-
        scripted variable, array, or dummy names of SUBROUTINE or
        other FUNCTION subprograms.  (There must be at least one
        argument in the argument list.)
```

GO TO STATEMENT (see ASSIGN statement, COMPUTED GO TO statement, or UNCONDITIONAL GO TO statement)

IF STATEMENT (see ARITHMETIC IF or LOGICAL IF)

IMPLICIT STATEMENT - non-executable

```
IMPLICIT type*s(a1,a2,...),...,type*s(a1,a2,...)

Where:  type is one of the following:  INTEGER, REAL, COMPLEX, or
        LOGICAL.

        *s is optional and represents one of the permissible length
        specifications for its associated type.

        a1, a2,...  are single alphabetic characters separated by
        commas, or a range of characters drawn from the set A, B,
        ...Z, $, in that order.  The range is denoted by the first
        and last characters of the range separated by a minus sign
        (e.g., (A-D)).
```

INTEGER STATEMENT (see TYPE DECLARATION STATEMENT)

LOGICAL ASSIGNMENT STATEMENT (see ASSIGNMENT STATEMENT)

LOGICAL IF STATEMENT - executable

```
IF(a)s

Where:  a is any logical expression.

        s is any executable statement except a DO statement or
        another logical IF statement.
```

NAMELIST STATEMENT - non-executable - implemented in WATFIV but not in WATFOR

```
NAMELIST/x/a,b...c/y/d,e,...f/z/g,h,...i

Where:    x,y, and z,...  are NAMELIST names.

          a,b,c,d,...  are variable or array names.
```

PAUSE STATEMENT - executable - not covered in the text - causes a machine halt with an optional message to the operator. In WATFOR/FIV the PAUSE statement is treated as a CONTINUE.

```
PAUSE
PAUSE n
PAUSE 'message'

Where:  n  is a string of 1 through 5 decimal digits.

        'message' is a literal constant of one form only:  specific-
        ally, a string of alphameric and/or special characters
        enclosed in apostrophes.
```

PRINT STATEMENT - executable - use of FORMAT reference with this statement not covered in the text

```
PRINT b, list

Where:  b is the statement number or array name of the FORMAT state-
        ment describing the data.

        list is a series of variable or array names, separated by
        commas which may be indexed and incremented.  They specify
        the number of items to be written and the locations in
        storage from which the data is taken.
```

PUNCH STATEMENT - executable - not covered in the text

```
PUNCH b, list

Where:  b is the statement number or array name of the FORMAT state-
        ment describing the data.

        list is a series of variable or array names, separated by
        commas, which may be indexed and incremented.  They specify
        the number of items to be written and the locations in
        storage from which the data is taken.
```

READ STATEMENT - executable

```
READ(a,b,END=c,ERR=d) list

Where:   a is an unsigned integer constant or an integer variable
         that is of length 4 and represents a data set reference
         number.

         b is optional and is either the statement number or array
         name of the FORMAT statement describing the record(s) being
         read, or a NAMELIST name.

         END=c is optional and c is the number of the statement to
         which transfer is made upon encountering the end of the data
         set.

         ERR=d is optional and d is the number of the statement to
         which transfer is made upon encountering an error condition
         in data transfer.

         list is optional and is an I/O list.
```

READ STATEMENT - executable - use of FORMAT reference with this statement not covered in text

```
READ b,list

Where:  b is the statement number or array name of the FORMAT state-
        ment describing the data.

        list is a series of variable or array names, separated by
        commas, which may be indexed and incremented.  They specify
        the number of items to be read and the locations in storage
        into which the data is placed.
```

READ STATEMENT - executable - implemented in WATFIV but not in WATFOR

```
READ (a'r, b, ERR=d) list

Where:  a is an integer constant or unsigned integer variable that
        is of length 4 and represents a data set reference number; a
        must be followed by an apostrophe (').

        r is an integer expression that represents the relative
        position of a record within the data set associated with a.


        b is optional and, if given, is either the statement number
        of the FORMAT statement that describes the data being read
        or the name of an array that contains an object time format.

        ERR=d is optional and d is the statement number to which
        control is given when a device error condition is encoun-
        tered during data transfer from device to storage.

        list is optional and is an I/O list.
```

REAL STATEMENT (see TYPE DECLARATION STATEMENT)

RETURN STATEMENT - executable - RETURN i feature not covered in the text

```
RETURN

RETURN i

Where:  i is an integer constant or variable of length 4 whose
        value, say n, denotes the nth statement number in the argu-
        ment list of a SUBROUTINE statement; i may be specified only
        in a SUBROUTINE subprogram.
```

REWIND STATEMENT - executable

```
REWIND a

Where:  a is an unsigned integer constant or integer variable that
        is of length 4 and represents a data set reference number.
```

STATEMENT FUNCTION - executable - not covered in the text - provides limited (one statement limit) subprogram capability *within* a program

```
name(a1,a2,a3,...,an) = expression

Where:     name is the statement function name


           a1,a2,a3,...,an are dummy arguments.  They must be unique
           (within the statement) nonsubscripted variables.

           expression is any arithmetic or logical expression that does
           not contain subscripted variables.  Any statement function
           appearing in this expression must have been defined
           previously.
```

STOP STATEMENT - executable - causes the computer program to terminate execution. In WATFOR/FIV the STOP i is treated as STOP

```
STOP
STOP n

Where:  n is a string of 1 through 5 decimal digits.
```

SUBROUTINE STATEMENT - non-executable

```
SUBROUTINE name (a1,a2,a3,...,an)
    .
    .
    .
RETURN
    .
    .
    .
END
```

Where: name is the SUBROUTINE name

$a_1, a_2, a_3, \ldots, a_n$ are dummy arguments. (There need not be any.) Each argument used must be a nonsubscripted variable or array name, the dummy name of another SUBROUTINE or FUNCTION subprogram, or of the form * where the character "*" denotes a return point specified by a statement number in the calling program.

TYPE DECLARATION STATEMENT - non-executable

Type*s $a*s_1(k_1)/x_1/, b*s_2(k_2)/x_2/, \ldots, z*s_n(k_n)/x_n/$

Where: Type is INTEGER, REAL, LOGICAL, or COMPLEX.

$*s, *s_1, *s_2, \ldots, *s_n$ are optional. Each s represents one of the permissible length specifications for its associated type.

a,b,...,z are variable, array, or function names

$(k_1), (k_2), \ldots, (k_n)$ are optional and give dimension information for arrays. Each k is composed of one through seven unsigned integer constants, separated by commas, representing the maximum value of each subscript in the array. Each k may be an unsigned integer variable of length 4 only when the type statement in which it appears is in a subprogram.

$/x_1/, /x_2/, \ldots, /x_n/$ are optional and represent initial data values.

UNCONDITIONAL GO TO STATEMENT - executable

```
GO TO xxxxx

Where:  xxxxx is an executable statement number.
```

WRITE STATEMENT - executable

```
WRITE(a,b) list

Where:     a is an unsigned integer constant or an integer variable
           that is of length 4 and represents a data set reference
           number.

           b is optional and is either the statement number or array
           name of the FORMAT statement describing the record(s) being
           written, or a NAMELIST name.

           list is optional and is an I/O list.
```

WRITE STATEMENT - executable - implemented in WATFIV but not WATFOR

```
WRITE (a'r,b) list

Where:  a is an integer constant or unsigned integer variable that
        is of length 4 and represents a data set reference number;
        a must be followed by an apostrophe (').

        r is an integer expression that represents the relative
        position of a record within the data set associated with a.

        b is optional and, if given, is either the statement number
        of the FORMAT statement that describes the data being writ-
        ten or the name of an array that contains an object time
        format.

        list is optional and is an I/O list.
```

part iv

laboratory problems

LABORATORY PROBLEMS

Laboratory problems to be run on a computer comprise this part. There are three general sections, denoted by the "footers" on each page; those of general interest, those of interest to students in mathematics and science areas, and those of interest principally to students in business areas.

The text requirements for each problem are indicated at the beginning of the problem. If a section of Part I or II is required, it means that the previous text up through the named part is required. When data are to be read from an input unit other than the card reader, an indication is shown as I/O unit ___ where you can fill in the proper unit number at your computer installation.

After a student has learned programming fundamentals, a "real life" problem can be one of the most interesting. The student is encouraged to select problems from other sources for his/her particular area of study and write programs to solve them.

A very good additional source of provocative problems is the RAND Corporation publication Problems for Computer Solution by Fred Gruenberger and George Jaffray.

Laboratory Problem 12 - Calculating Factorials

Text Required: TSF (Part I), no subscripts

Problem: Calculate the factorials for the integers 1 through 10.

Procedure: N factorial is represented as N!, and is calculated as N•(N-1)•(N-2)• ... •1

For example,

6 factorial=6!=6•5•4•3•2•1

and

4 factorial=4!=4•3•2•1

Input: None

Output: Print out in tabular form each integer (1-10) and its factorial value.

```
1     1
2     2
3     6
4    24
etc.
```

Laboratory Problem 13 - Scanning an Array

Text required: TSF (Part I) with subscripts

Problem: Given a set of numbers keypunched one per card, find the one closest to the average (arithmetic mean). There will be fewer than 100 numbers. Your program should also determine how many times each distinct number occurs in the input.

Input: The first card contains a two-digit number, punched in columns 1-2, which specifies the number of cards which follow the first card. The remaining cards each contain one number punched in columns 1-10 with the decimal point recorded in the number.

Output: The arithmetic mean, the number in the set closest to it, a list of the different numbers, and the frequency of of occurrence of each.

Laboratory Problem 14 - Loop Exercise

Text Required: FORMAT; Module G

Problem:

a. Write a program to implement the following flowchart. If each execution of the output box results in a single line, how many lines should it print? Use a value for n which is less than or equal to 7.

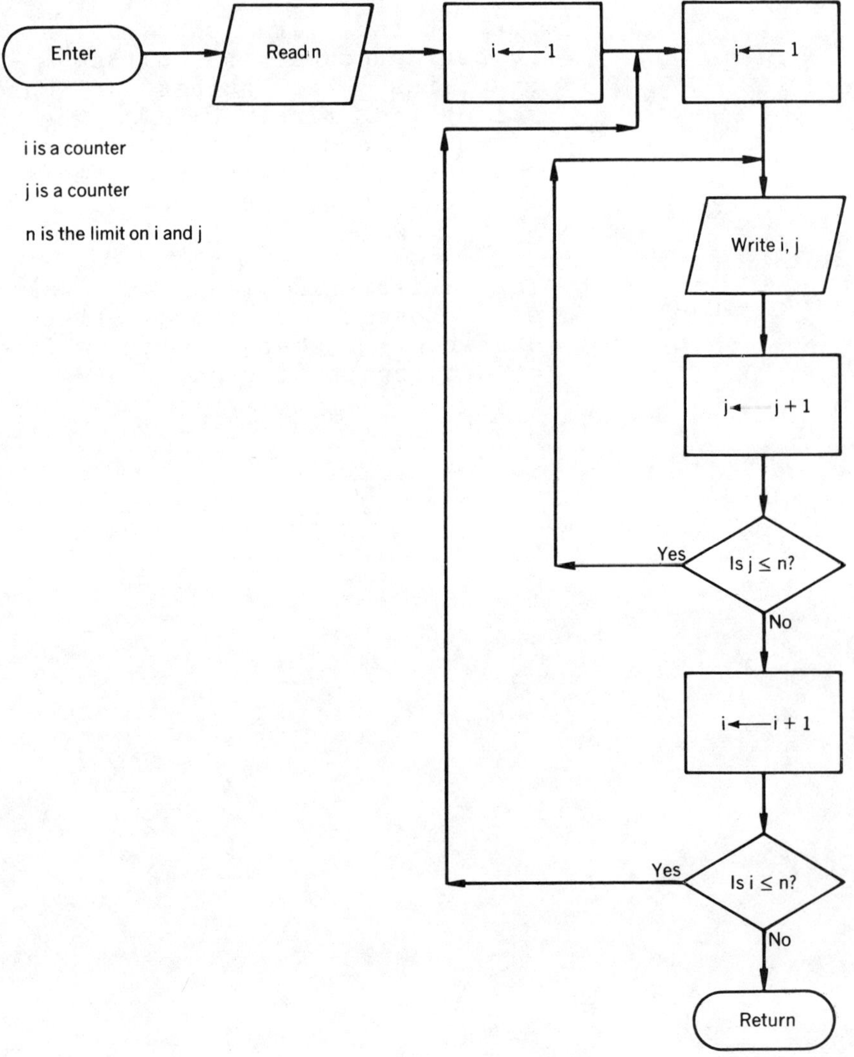

b. Rewrite this problem using DO loops; draw a flowchart. Consider each pair of numbers on each line as a single number. Does the resulting sequence of numbers suggest anything about the construction of a base (n-1) number system?

Laboratory Problem 15 - Array Manipulation

Text Required: FORMAT

Problem: Write a Fortran program which will read in an array of m (m<100) numbers (X(n), n=1,m) and which will then write out the following five lists:

1. The m numbers and their subscripts as they were read.

2. The 1st, 3rd, 5th,. . . numbers (i.e., the numbers with odd subscripts) and their subscripts.

3. The m numbers and their subscripts in reverse order.

4. All the numbers that are divisible by 2 and their subscripts.

5. All the numbers that are greater than the number that follows them in the original list.

Input: The data are written on I/O unit ___.

The format of each record is I4.

1st record m
2nd record X(1)
3rd record X(2)
.
.
m+1 record X(m)

Output: Print a descriptive heading on each of the five lists and leave a blank line between lists. Be sure to leave several blank spaces between the number and its subscript.

Laboratory Problem 16 - Triangle Area Subprogram

Text Required: Subprograms

Problem: Given a, b, and c as the lengths of the three sides of a triangle, the area (A) of the triangle is given by

$$A = \sqrt{s(s-a)(s-b)(s-c)}$$

where s is the semi-perimeter

$$\frac{(a+b+c)}{2}$$

Write a subprogram to compute the area of the triangle and return this value to a calling program. Write a main program to read in the lengths of the sides, call the subprogram, and print the results.

Laboratory Problem 17 - Random Number Generation

Text Required: TSF (Part I) with subscripts

Problem: Many computer applications require the use of random numbers. Uniformly distributed random numbers all have the same probability of occurrence just as the different faces of a die all have equally probable chances of occurrence. The power residue method of random number generation is quite popular. It consists of computing

M(i+1) = M(i) * L

where M(i) is the ith random number, M(i+1) is the next random number and L is a constant multiplier. This generator will produce random numbers from a rectangular distribution, i.e., one in which each number has the same chance of occurrence.

To construct a generator, choose M(0) that is not divisible by 2 or 5. Choose as a constant multiplier an integer of the form L=200t±r, where t is any integer and r is any of the values:

3,11,13,19,21,27,37,53,61,67,69,77,83,91

A value of L close to 10**(D/2) is a good choice, where D is the number of digits that the computer can hold in one word (9 for the IBM 360/370). . The low order one or two digits produced by this method are not random. Therefore, do not use the two low order digits in the random number, but retain them for computation.

Using the above method, write a program that will generate 100 random digits; count the frequency with which each digit occurs. Then perform a chi-square test to determine if the numbers generated are sufficiently random.

Procedure:

So that each program produces identical answers, use M(0) = 28437 and L = 52283. Produce a series of 100 random digits by using the digit in the ten thousands position of each M(i). Do not use subscripted variables to produce these random numbers; use simple (scalar) variables instead. Count the number of 0,1,2,3,4,5,6,7,8 and 9's generated. Select the first random digit from M(1), not M(0). When all random digits have been generated and counted, compute the value of chi-square from the formula:

$$\chi^2 = \sum_{i=0}^{9} [(o(i) - e(i))^2 / e(i)]$$

where o(i) is the number of times the digit i occurred and e(i) is the number of times the digit i was expected to occur (10 in this case). A value of chi-square less than 2.7 or greater than 19.0 would indicate that the numbers generated are not truly random.

Input:

None.

Output:

Write a table showing the digits 0-9 and the frequency with which each occurred. Also print the value of chi-square.

Laboratory Problem 18 - A Coded Message

Text Required: FORMAT

Problem: A secret message written in code has been received. You are to write a program to decode this message. The message may consist of all 26 letters of the alphabet and special characters. The special characters are to be left unchanged. The letters are to be decoded as follows:

Letter in Message	A	B	C	D	E	F	G	H	I	J	K	L	M
Decoded Letter	R	C	G	U	I	A	D	W	X	T	H	N	M

Letter in Message	N	O	P	Q	R	S	T	U	V	W	X	Y	Z
Decoded Letter	P	B	Z	L	E	Q	S	Y	K	O	J	V	F

Input: The data are written on I/O unit ___. The first record is a three-digit integer which specifies how many records make up the message. The rest of the records make up the message itself, with 30 characters per record.

Output: Write the original message as read. Then write the decoded message. Put 30 characters on each line. Provide appropriate titles for each message.

Laboratory Problem 19 - Loops or Logs

Text Required: FORMAT

Problem: For every number x greater than 1 there corresponds a number n such that

$$2^{**}(n-1) \le x < 2^{**}n$$

Draw a flow chart for a procedure which would:

1. read a number m
2. read a number x
3. determine the value of n such that $2^{**}(n-1) \le x < 2^{**}n$
4. write x and n
5. determine if m numbers [x(i),i=1,m] have been processed.
6. if m numbers have not been processed, return to step 2.

Express the flow chart as a Fortran program using data as shown below.

Input:

Data on unit ___.	FORMAT
m	I5
x(i) (i=1,m)	E20.8

Output:

On printer	FORMAT
x(i) , n(i)	E20.8,i9

Laboratory Problem 20 - Schedules

Text Required: FORMAT

Problem: You wish to get the faculty of your school (no more than 200 people) together at an all school meeting to discuss student complaints. You want to pick a time when all the faculty can be present.

Procedure: The registrar has given you permission to scan the file on which is located a record for each faculty member. The record contains the name and other information regarding whether or not he/she has a class at a certain hour. Classes may begin at ten times during each of the five week days: 8 a.m., 9 a.m., etc.

Input: The information for each faculty member is written as one record on I/O unit ___. The format of each teacher's information is as follows:

first 20 cols.--name
next 9 cols.--social security number
next 10 cols.--ones or zeros for each class on Monday. A one in the first position would indicate an 8 a.m. Monday class. A zero in the second position would indicate no 9 a.m. Monday class, etc.
next 10 cols.--schedule for Tuesday
etc.

Output: Write a program which will select the hours during the week when none of the faculty have classes. If no such time(s) exist, find the hour(s) at which the fewest faculty have classes and print names of those who do. You are not permitted to know the social security numbers of the faculty members; your program must not read these data.

Laboratory Problem 21 - Numerical Inaccuracies

Text Required: TSF, no subscripts; Appendix H is a reference

Problem: To demonstrate various arithmetic manipulations which give rise to numerical inaccuracies.

Procedure: Perform the following operations and produce the indicated output. If you know how, provide appropriate headings to distinguish one answer from another.

1. Add up .1 fifty times and print out the sum. Is the answer 5.? If not, why not?

2. Find the sum of 1+1/2+1/3+. . . +1/99 + 1/100. (Add the terms in the order indicated!) Write the result.

3. Find the sum of 1/100 + 1/99 + 1/98 + . . . +1/3 +1/2 + 1. (Add the terms in the order indicated!) Write the result. Are the answers to 2 and 3 the same? If not, why not?

4. The value of the number e is given by the infinite series,

$$e = (1/0!)+(1/1!)+(1/2!)+(1/3!)+(1/4!)+...$$

where $0! = 1$

Implement the following flowchart to find the value of e. Write c, t and e. Since t never becomes zero, why does the process stop?

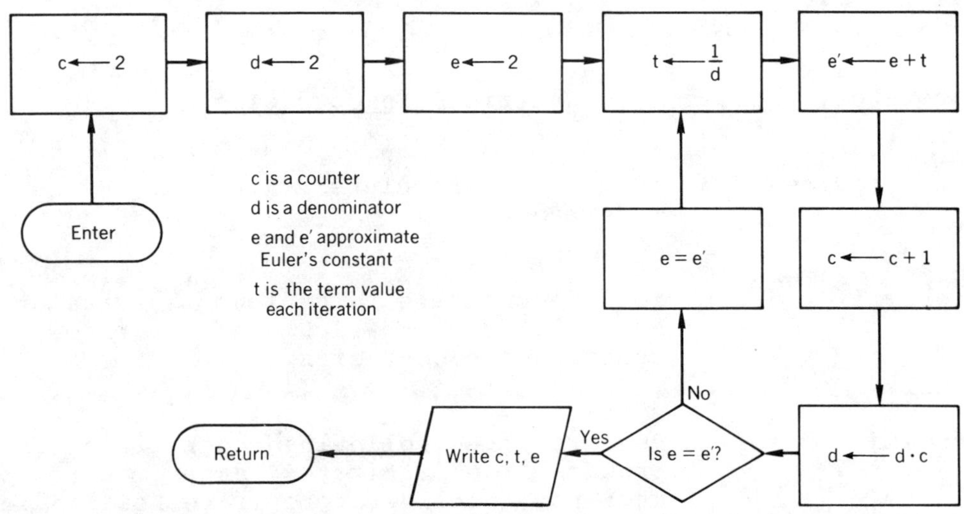
c ← 2
d ← 2
e ← 2
t ← 1/d
e′ ← e + t
Enter
c is a counter
d is a denominator
e and e′ approximate Euler's constant
t is the term value each iteration
e = e′
c ← c + 1
No
Yes
Return
Write c, t, e
Is e = e′?
d ← d · c

Laboratory Problem 22 - Calendar Model

(Contributed by Dr. J. W. Atwood, Sir George Williams University, Montreal, Canada)

Text Required: MOD Function, Module 14; FORMATted Input and Output

Input: A punched card contains a four-digit positive integer n (indicating a year such as 1975), a two-digit month number m and a number x of value 1 through 7. The number x indicates that January 1 of year n falls on weekday x.

Problem: Using this information, write a program to print a calendar for year n, month m. A typical calendar should look like this:

NOVEMBER 1984

Sun	Mon	Tue	Wed	Thur	Fri	Sat
					1	2
3	4	5	6	7	8	9
10	11	12	13	14	15	16
17	18	19	20	21	22	23
24	25	26	27	28	29	30

The program should take into account that February has 29 days if either

1) MOD(n,4)=0 <u>and</u> MOD(n,100)≠0 or

2) MOD(n,400)=0

Laboratory Problem 23 - The Automatic Change Maker

(Contributed by Dr. J. W. Atwood, Sir George Williams University, Montreal, Canada)

Text Required: TSF with subscripts

Procedure: We frequently observe the cashier "make change" as we pay our bill at a restaurant or shop, taking for granted the actual process of making change. The computer can be programmed to simulate a cashier in the process of making change. In this simulation the act of handing the cashier the waitress' check together with the cash payment is the <u>input</u>, and the cashier handing over the change containing a <u>minimum</u> number of bills and/or coins is the <u>output</u>.

Problem: Write and test a computer program which will perform the following steps:

(1) Accept any number of sets of two data items per set of parameters. (The amount of a customer's bill and the cash payment.)

(2) For each pair compute the number of each denomination in the change returned to the customer. Use ten common U.S. currency values (penny, nickel, dime, quarter, half-dollar, dollar bill or coin, five-dollar bill, ten-dollar bill, twenty-dollar bill, and fifty-dollar bill). These ten values should be stored in a type INTEGER array.

Output: For each set of data print out the value of the waitress' bill, cash payment and change on one line, followed by a list of denomination type and number. For example, if the bill was \$1.35 and \$5.00 was tendered, the output would appear as follows:

135	500	365
3	100	
1	50	
1	10	
1	5	

If the change is negative (i.e., if an insufficient amount of money is paid to the cashier), simply print out the bill, cash payment, and change (negative).

Laboratory Problem 24 - Parsing I

Text Required: Parts I, II, Modules 3 and 11

Problem: Data cards contain various keypunched information between card columns 2 and 72 (inclusive). Your task, as a programmer, is to write a computer program to search through the cards looking for the following words:

DOG

CAT

FROG

BULL

RICK

ARCH

After searching through all of the data cards, print a list of each of the words with the number of occurrences of each beside it. Rules that the data must observe are that words cannot be split between data cards and that words cannot contain imbedded blank characters.

Laboratory Problem 25 - Parsing II (Difficult Problem)

Text Required: Parts I, II, Modules 3 and 11

Problem: You are to write a program which uses as input data a Fortran program. For each data card, print on the same line the eighty columns of the card followed by the statement type if it is one of the types shown below:

```
INTEGER
REAL
assignment statement
RETURN
END
IF
```

If it is not one of the above, print "OTHER".

Notice that you should be able to correctly identify statements which use keywords above as variable names. For example,

IF=6 is an assignment statement.

IF(J+K)=R is an assignment statement.

DO 5 L=1 is an assignment statement.

DO 5 L=1,3 is not an assignment statement.

Also remember that blank spaces are allowed anywhere in any of these statements. For example,

```
ABC=3
A BC=3
A   B  C =3
```

are all identical statements in Fortran.

Laboratory Problem 26 - Evaluation of e to the x Power

Text Required: TSF, no subscripts

Problem: We wish to find the value of e to the x power, where e is Euler's constant, and e to the x power =

$$1+(x/1!)+(x^2/2!)+(x^3/3!)+\ldots$$

Procedure: Note that each term can easily be calculated from the preceding one. For example:

1st term = 1

2nd term = $x/1! = (x^0/0!)\bullet(x/1) =$ (1st term)$\bullet(x/1)$

3rd term = $x^2/2! = (x^1/1!)\bullet(x/2) =$ (2nd term)$\bullet(x/2)$

4th term = $x^3/3! = (x^2/2!)\bullet(x/3) =$ (3rd term)$\bullet(x/3)$

This should suggest an algorithm similar to that used in calculating factorials. The program should be designed to continue calculating e to the x power for different values of x until it encounters an x=-99. Thus, the last data card must always have the value -99. punched on it. This is the "trip value." Stop calculating terms for a particular value of x when the terms of the series become less than 10^{-4}.

Input: Read in the following values of x: 3.5, 0.0, -2.31, and .13; do not forget to include the trip value.

Output: For each x write, on the same line, the value of x, the final value of e to the x power and the number of terms in the series that were used in the calculation.

Laboratory Problem 27 - Calculating Square Roots

Text Required: TSF, no subscripts

Problem: Compute the square root of a REAL positive number.

Procedure: The square root of A can be computed by using an algorithm based on the formula

$$y = (1/2) \bullet (x + A/x)$$

This method utilizes an iteration process. A starting value of x is arbitrarily selected and is used to compute y. This computed value, y, will be more nearly equal to the true square root of A than was the arbitrarily selected x. We can compute a still better estimate of the square root of A by replacing the value of x with that of y and recomputing y. This process may be repeated as many times as we wish in order to give improved estimates of the square root of A.

Taking a value of A (say 25) for which the square root is known, and performing the previously explained procedure will make the algorithm clear. If 2 were used as a starting estimate, then:

1st approximation: y=1/2(2+25/2)=7.25
2nd approximation: y=1/2(7.25+25/7.25)=5.35
3rd approximation: y=1/2(5.35+25/5.35)=5.01

Terminate the iterative procedure when the absolute value of the difference between two successive estimates is less than some positive number, say, one ten-thousandth.

Input: Find the square root of the following three numbers: 16.0, 73.315 and .0025.

Output: Print the value of A, the final value of y, and the square root of A found by using the SQRT function.

Laboratory Problem 28 - FUNCTION Exercise

Text Required: TSF with built-in FUNCTIONs

Problem: Calculate the value of r for 4 sets of data.

$$r = 16.78 \bullet \text{COS } 2\pi \text{ x} + (y + 1.667)^{i}$$

Procedure: Read the following values from cards:

Input:

card	x	y	i
1	77.538	-1.0	2.
2	-.3862	.125E-07	6.2
3	12.5E13	-52.0	-3.3
4	2.56E-2	.0735E06	5.

Output: If y+1.667≥0, print x, y, i and r. If y+1.667<0, do not attempt to calculate r; instead print x, y, and i. An attempt to calculate A**B if A is negative will result in an error condition.

Note: Use the value 3.14159 for the value of pi.

Laboratory Problem 29 - Prime Numbers

Text Required: DO loops

Problem: Write a program to print the prime numbers between 2 and 100 inclusive. (A prime number is an integer number greater than 1 which cannot be divided evenly by any positive integer except itself and one.) Use the DO statement.

Laboratory Problem 30 - Sorting

Text Required: FORMAT

Problem: To read in REAL numbers (maximum of 14 significant digits, each with decimal point recorded) and print them in ascending order.

Input: Data are on I/O unit ___. Each record in the file contains one number in columns 1-16. There are fewer than 500 numbers.

Output: Print n lines, one for each number, printing the numbers in ascending order.

Procedure: Read all numbers into an array, sort the array into ascending order, and print the array.

Many sorting algorithms exist: two are shown below. Each assumes X is an array of values to be sorted, N is the number of elements in the array, and T is an element variable with the same attributes as any element of X. The following algorithm will rearrange the elements of X into ascending order.

```
C TUMBLE SORT
      NM=N-1
      DO 5 I=1,NM
      IP1=I+1
      DO 6 J=IP1,N
      IF (X(I).LE.X(J)) GO TO 6
      T=X(I)
      X(I)=X(J)
      X(J)=T
    6 CONTINUE
    5 CONTINUE
```

Another algorithm to do the same thing is:

```
C BUBBLE SORT
      ND=N
      NM=N-1
      DO 5 I=1,NM
      ND=ND-1
      DO 6 J=1,ND
      IF (X(J).LE.X(J+1)) GO TO 6
      T=X(J)
      X(J)=X(J+1)
      X(J+1)=T
    6 CONTINUE
    5 CONTINUE
```

Laboratory Problem 31 - Matrix Symmetry

Text Required: FORMAT

An n by n matrix is symmetric if, for each r ($1 \le r \le n$) and each s ($1 \le s \le n$), the element a(r,s) is the same as the element a(s,r).

Problem: Write a program to determine for a series of m matrices whether or not each is symmetric.

Input: The data are arranged on I/O unit ___ as follows (each line constitutes one record):

DATA				FORMAT
m				(I3)
n1	k1			(I2,I2)
a(1,1)	a(1,2)	a(1,3)	... a(1,n1)	(5(F5.2))
a(2,1)	a(2,2)	a(2,3)	... a(2,n1)	(5(F5.2))
•				
•				
a(n1,1)	a(n1,2)	a(n1,3)	... a(n1,n1)	(5(F5.2))
n2	k2			(I2,I2)
b(1,1)	b(1,2)	b(1,3)	... b(1,n2)	(5(F5.2))

and so on, where:

m is the number of matrices in the series
n is the order number of the ith matrix (n is $\le$ 5)
k is the identification number of the ith matrix
a(r,s),b(r,s) ... are the elements of the matrices

Output: For each matrix print the message:

MATRIX k IS SYMMETRIC
or
MATRIX k IS NOT SYMMETRIC

Lab Problem 32 - Quadratic with Square Root Subprogram

Text Required: Subprograms, Lab Problems 05 and 27

Problem: Solve the quadratic equation using a FUNCTION subprogram for square roots.

Rewrite Laboratory Problem 05 for solving the quadratic equation, using a FUNCTION subprogram to calculate the square root of b^2-4ac. The method used for calculating the square root is to be the iteration method used in Lab Problem 27. The name of the FUNCTION is to be FSQRT. Do not use the SQRT built-in FUNCTION in this program.

Use the same input and output that you used in Lab Problem 5.

Laboratory Problem 33 - Dot Product

Text Required: Subprograms

Problem: Write a FUNCTION subprogram to calculate the scalar product of two vectors (one-dimensional arrays).

The scalar product is

$$S = \sum_{i=1}^{N} A(i) \bullet B(i)$$

Write this as an extended precision (REAL*8) FUNCTION.

The FUNCTION should have 3 arguments: the names of the two arrays and the number of numbers in each. For example, assuming the name SCALAR for the function: SCALAR (A,B,N)

The function should be able to accept a value of N of any size.

Label your output "SCALAR PRODUCT= "

The data to be read by the calling program are:

N=15

A	B
-14.012	360.000
200.013	88.555
-200.132	-777.777
11.111	3.333
21.212	6.667
.001	9.999
10.345	-0.010
-60.789	-1.712
3.141	1024.255
57.322	550.055
-2.782	-1.872
999.314	11.412
1000.215	8.315
0.000	3.815
4.777	2.782

Laboratory Problem 34 - Polynomial Evaluation

Text Required: Subprograms

Problem: Write a subprogram to evaluate the polynomial function

$$y = a0+a1\bullet x+a2\bullet x^2+a3\bullet x^3+\ldots+an\bullet x^n$$

where x, the coefficient (a), and n are to be given.

Procedure: Compute the value of the polynomial by considering it in factored form. That is, taking a third degree polynomial, for example,

$$a0+x(a1+x(a2+xa3))$$

which is equivalent to

$$a0+a1x+a2x^2+a3x^3$$

Using the factored polynomial for computation is better for two reasons: speed and accuracy.

Input: Write a main program to read the data and invoke the subprogram. Store the coefficients of the polynomial as an array in COMMON. The input is on I/O unit ___. The first record contains x in columns 1-10 with decimal point recorded and n in columns 11-12 without decimal. Following this record are n+1 records, in order, each containing a coefficient (a) in columns 1-9 with decimal point recorded.

Output: Return the answer, y, to the driving (or calling) program. Write out the data and answer with the main program.

Laboratory Problem 35 - Integration

Text Required: FORMAT

Problem: Find the area under a curve between two values X=A and X=B, using the trapezoid method. Given are the beginning point A, the ending point B, and the number of small trapezoids into which that area is to be divided. The function used in this problem will be

$$X^2+25X+3$$

Input: Consists of REAL numbers (with decimal points recorded) on one record on I/O unit ___.

Columns 1-10 A
Columns 11-20 B
Columns 21-23 N (the number of trapezoids to use)

Procedure: The trapezoid algorithm is given below:

```
  H=(B-A)/N
  X=A
  S=0
  NP1=N+1
  DO 5 I=1,NP1
  W=1
  IF (I.EQ.1.OR.I.EQ.NP1) W=0.5
2 S=S+(X*X+25.*X+3)*W
  X=X+H
5 CONTINUE
  S=S*H
```

In the algorithm above the larger the value of N, the closer is the approximation to the true area under the curve, but at the same time, the more costly is the computer run. Notice that this algorithm can be used with functions of your own by substituting the function expression within the parentheses of the statement numbered 2.

Laboratory Problem 36 - Fibonacci Sequence

Text Required: Data Initialization, Subprograms

Problem: Write a FUNCTION subprogram that will return to the main program a given term in the series of Fibonacci numbers. A Fibonacci series is one in which each term in the series is equal to the sum of the previous two terms, given the first two terms are 0 and 1. The beginning terms would, therefore, be

0,1,1,2,3,5,8,......

For example, the number 0 is the 0th term and the number 8 is the 6th term.

Write the FUNCTION to have one argument. This argument is the number of the term that you wish to be returned.

Write the FUNCTION such that the first time it is invoked, it will generate the first 40 terms and store them in an array and return the term specified by the argument. On subsequent calls to the FUNCTION, it will only require that the term be looked up from the array of numbers.

In the main program write out the number M given by

$$M=[F(n-1) \bullet F(n+1)]-F(n)^2$$

for n ranging from 2 to 40, where F(n) refers to the nth term in the series of Fibonacci numbers. Put appropriate labels on the output. Each of the 39 lines of output should have 4 numbers printed: first M, then F(n-1), F(n+1), and finally F(n).

Laboratory Problem 37 - Monte Carlo Technique

Text Required: Subprograms, Lab Problem 17

Problem: Suppose you have a sewing needle of length x. Suppose also you are in a room with a hardwood floor and the width of each board in the flooring is length 2x. Suppose further that you need to know the value of pi. No difficulty. You simply drop the needle on the floor a few times and note how many times the needle crosses the lines between the flooring. In particular, if you drop the needle n times and it crosses a line m times, the quantity n/m will approach pi as n approaches infinity. Write a program to simulate the dropping of the needle on the floor.

Procedure: You will need two random numbers for each toss of the needle: one for the position of a point on the needle and one for its angle with respect to the flooring. Either fabricate the 6-digit random numbers from random digits generated by using Lab Problem 17 as a subprogram, or use some other random number generator.

Output: Drop the needle 1000 times; print out the approximation to pi after each 100 trials.

Laboratory Problem 38 - Lowest Terms Fractions

Text Required: Subprograms

Problem: Given a pair of numbers which represent the numerator and denominator of a fraction, write a subprogram to reduce each fraction to its lowest terms, i.e., the denominator of the final answer is a prime number. Write a calling program which reads inputs and prints answers.

Input: Each card contains a numerator in card columns 1-2 and a denominator in card columns 3-4.

Output:

cols 1-4 original numerator
cols 5-9 original denominator
cols 15-18 integral portion of answer
cols 19-22 new numerator
cols 24-27 new denominator

Note 1: The original numerator may be larger than the original denominator.

Note 2: The program should print an error message if the denominator is zero.

Laboratory Problem 39 - Counting Binary Digits

Text Required: Number Systems: An Overview; FORMAT

Problem: Each card in a deck contains one positive number in card columns 1-10. For each input card print one line with the number of one-bits contained in the binary representation of the number; print also the hexadecimal representation of the number. For example, if the number punched into a card were 29, the binary representation of the number would be 11101 and, therefore, the number of one-bits would be 4. The hexadecimal representation would be 1D.

Laboratory Problem 40 - Gaussian Elimination (Matrices)

(Contributed by Dr. J. W. Atwood, Sir George Williams University, Montreal, Canada)

Text Required: TSF

Background:

Systems of equations frequently arise during the formulation or the attempted solution of various problems from the physical and biological sciences, engineering, applied mathematics and the social sciences. A solution to a set or system of equations is a simultaneous solution, in that it must satisfy each equation individually. Thus x=3 and y=-2 provide a solution to the system:

$$2x+y=4 \qquad (1)$$

$$x+y=1$$

Linear systems of equations can usually be solved successfully either by hand or on a computer. A method that most people have met already is the Gaussian elimination technique. This is the method most frequently used to solve sets of linear equations and can easily be implemented on a computer. First a review of the method is given by showing the solution of a small problem, step by step, and following this a flowchart for implementing the general procedure on a computer.

Consider the system:

$$2X(1)+2X(2)-4X(3)=4 \qquad (2)$$

$$X(1)-X(2)+2X(3)=4$$

$$4X(1)-2X(2)-2X(3)=20$$

The first stage of the method consists of eliminating X(1) from the second and third equations. This is accomplished by subtracting a suitable multiple of the first equation from the second and third equations. These multipliers are just the ratios of the coefficients of X(1) in each equation to the coefficient of X(1) in the first equation: in this case they are 1/2 and 2, respectively. Thus the system becomes

$$2X(1)+2X(2)-4X(3)=4 \qquad (3)$$

$$-2X(2)+4X(3)=2$$

$$-6X(2)+6X(3)=12$$

The second stage of the method eliminates X(2) from the third equation. This involves only the second and third equations, and the necessary multiplier is (-6)/(-2)=3. The system is rewritten as

$$2X(1)+2X(2)-4X(3)=4 \qquad (4)$$

$$-2X(2)+4X(3)=2$$

$$-6X(3)=6$$

Thus, the third equation yields

$$X(3)=6/(-6)=-1$$

$$X(2)=(2-4(-1))/(-2)=-3$$

$$X(1)=(4+4(-1)-2(-3))/2=3$$

The solution (X(1),X(2),X(3)) to (2) obtained by back substitution is therefore (3,-3,-1).

The Gaussian elimination method is thus a step by step triangularization followed by a back substitution as the final stage.

An <u>apparent</u> pitfall for the method is the possible occurrence of a zero coefficient of the first variable in the first equation of the orginal system, or the second variable of the second equation at the next stage, etc. (Why?) More specifically, in our example if either the coefficient of X(1) in the first equation of (2) had been zero, or the coefficient of X(2) in the second equation of (3) had been zero, how could we have formed the multipliers necessary for the eliminations? This problem can be avoided by simply interchanging the first equation with any other equation for which the coefficient of X(1) is not zero, and repeating this process where necessary throughout the successive stages of the method. Moreover, since any computer program for Gaussian elimination must include this safeguard feature, you are required to make a row interchange wherever necessary to ensure that the coefficient with largest absolute value is always employed when forming the multipliers for that stage.

Thus in the example above the first and third equations of (2) should be interchanged so that the coefficient 4 is used to form the multipliers for the first stage. This modification improves the accuracy of the elimination method when it is implemented on a computer, since the overall effect of rounding errors can thereby be reduced for most problems.

The general system of n linear equations is:

```
A(1,1)*X(1)+A(1,2)*X(2)+...+A(1,n)*X(n)=B(1)      (5)
A(2,1)*X(1)+A(2,2)*X(2)+...+A(2,n)*X(n)=B(2)
                    •
                    •
                    •
A(n,1)*X(1)+A(n,2)*X(2)+...+A(n,n)*X(n)=B(n)
```

You should invent an algorithm or make a search of existing algorithms or flowcharts for the solution of the general system (5) by Gaussian elimination.

Write a program to solve a system of up to 20 equations. Then punch the data and solve the following two systems for the values of the X's:

```
 X(1)+2*X(2)+3*X(3)+4*X(4)=30      (A)
-X(1)+  X(2)-  X(3)+  X(4)= 2
      10*X(2)+2*X(3)+8*X(4)=58
         X(2)-  X(3)+6*X(4)=23
```

```
    X(1)+2X(2)+0X(3)= 25      (B)
   2X(1)- X(2)-3X(3)=-45
   6X(1)-3X(2)+ X(3)= 15
```

Laboratory Problem 41 - Magic Squares (a problem for three students)

(Contributed by Dr. J. W. Atwood, Sir George Williams University, Montreal, Canada)

Text Required: Parts I and II

Background:

A Magic Square consists of a number of integers arranged in the form of a square, so that the sum of the numbers in every row, in every column, and in each diagonal is the same. If the integers are the consecutive integers from 1 to n^2, the square is said to be of the nth order, and the sum of the numbers in every row, column and diagonal is equal to $n(n^2+1)/2$.

Thus the first 25 integers, arranged in the form of Figure 1, represent a magic square of the fifth order.

17	24	1	8	15
23	5	7	14	16
4	6	13	20	22
10	12	19	21	3
11	18	25	2	9

Figure 1
Magic Square

The formation of these squares is an old amusement, and in times when mystical ideas were associated with particular numbers it was natural that such arrangements should be studied. Magic squares were constructed in China before the Christian era; their introduction into Europe appears to have been due to Moschopulus in the early part of the fifteenth century. A magic square engraved on a silver plate was sometimes prescribed as a charm against the plague. The mathematical theory of the construction of these squares was taken up in France in the seventeenth century, and since then it has been a favorite subject with writers in many countries.

A magic square of the nth order, where n is odd (i.e., $n=2m+1$, where m is an integer), can be constructed as follows. First, the number 1 is placed in the middle cell of the top row. The successive numbers are then placed in their natural order in a diagonal line which slopes upwards to the right, except that

1) when the top row is reached, the next number is written in the bottom row, one column to the right;

2) when the right-hand column is reached, the next number is written in the left-hand column, one row up;

3) if a number, say k, is written in the upper right hand cell, the number k+1 should be written in the cell immediately underneath it; and

4) if a number, say j, cannot be written in a cell because the cell is occupied by another number, then j should be written in the cell immediately beneath the cell containing the previous number j-1.

A check of Figure 1, showing the construction of a square of the fifth order, should make the rules clear.

Magic squares of the nth order, where n is even and $n=2(2m+1)$ -- i.e., n is twice an odd number -- can also be constructed by a rule. Determine m by the formula $m=(n/2-1)/2$. Divide the square into four equal quarters: A, B, C, D, as in Figure 2. Construct in A, by the method above for an odd n, a magic square with the numbers 1 to u^2, where $u=n/2$.

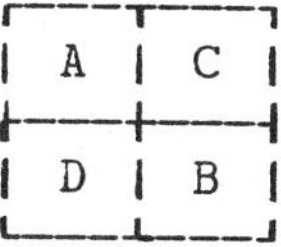

Figure 2
Subdivision of Magic Square

Construct by the same rule, in B, C, D, similar magic squares with the numbers u^2+1 to $2u^2$, $2u^2+1$ to $3u^2$, and $3u^2+1$ to $4u^2$. The resulting composite square is magic in columns only (see Figure 3).

8	1	6	26	19	24
3	5	7	21	23	25
4	9	2	22	27	20
35	28	33	17	10	15
30	32	34	12	14	16
31	36	29	13	18	11

Figure 3
Initial Quarter-Squares

In the middle row of A take the set of m cells next but one to the left-hand side; in each of the other rows of A take the set of m cells nearest to the left-hand side. The numbers in these cells are underlined in Figure 3. Now, interchange the numbers in these cells with the numbers in the corresponding cells of D.

Next, interchange the numbers in the cells in each of the m-1 columns next to the right-hand side of C with the numbers in the corresponding cells of B. Of course, the resulting square remains magic in columns, and it is now also magic in rows and diagonals as seen in Figure 4.

35	1	6	26	19	24
3	32	7	21	23	25
31	9	2	22	27	20
8	28	33	17	10	15
30	5	34	12	14	16
4	36	29	13	18	11

Figure 4
Final Square, n=6

In the example of Figure 3 and Figure 4, m=1, so m-1=0 and therefore no interchanges were made between blocks C and B. In general, however, there would be interchanges of the corresponding m-1 columns on the right-hand side of blocks B and C. For instance, when n=14, then m=3 and m-1=2, so that the two most right-hand columns of block B must be interchanged with the two corresponding columns of block C.

Procedure:

Write a SUBROUTINE to compute a magic square of any order. Call the subroutine MAGSQR. MAGSQR should call a second SUBROUTINE to compute the magic square of any <u>odd</u> order. Call this routine ODDSQR. Write a driving program to call MAGSQR, print the results, and print checks of the sums of the rows, columns and diagonals. The driver should be able to handle a magic square of order 15.

Three students should cooperate on this project. One writes the driver, one writes MAGSQR, and one writes ODDSQR.

Laboratory Problem 42 - Compound Interest

Text Required: TSF, no subscripts

Problem: Compute and print out a table for money in a savings account where the interest is compounded annually, semi-annually, quarterly, and daily (assume 365 days per year). Assume all of the principal is deposited at the beginning of the first year.

Procedure: The needed equations can be derived from the general compound interest formula:

$$An = P\left(1 + i/m\right)^{m \bullet n}$$

where

- An is the amount at the end of n years
- P is the principal
- i is the interest rate expressed as a decimal
- n is the number of years
- m is the number of times per year that interest is compounded

Input: Read the values of P and i from cards. The end of the data deck will be identified by a negative value of P. This last card is not to be used in calculations. When a negative value of P is found, the program should terminate.

Supply four data cards punched as follows:

```
  500.    .05
 1000.    .03
13000.    .045
   -1.    .0
```

Output: For each set of data, print P and i. Then print on a single line n and An for each of the four methods of paying interest. Let n take on the values 1, 2, 3, . . . , 10.

Laboratory Problem 43 - The $24 Question

Text Required: TSF without subscripts

Background: The proceeds of money invested in a bank for one year are

P(1)=Amount*(1+r)

where r is the annual interest rate. The value after the second year is

P(2)=P(1)*(1+r)

This process is known as compounding interest on an annual basis. The bank computes the interest and rounds it to the nearest cent at the end of each year.

Speculation: It is widely reported that in 1626 Peter Minuit, the Governor of the Dutch West India Company, bought Manhattan Island from Indians for $24 worth of trinkets.

Problem: Write a computer program to compute the proceeds of $24 if it were invested in a bank in 1626 at 6% interest compounded yearly and held until this year. If the Indians had so invested the $24, do you think they would have enough money now to repurchase Manhattan at its current value? (Note: assume that no interest accrues for either this year or 1626.)

Laboratory Problem 44 - Array Search

Text Required: TSF with subscripts

Problem: You are given a deck of cards in which each card contains a positive integer in the first 4 columns followed by a single card at the end of the deck which contains a negative integer in the first four columns. Write a program to find the different positive integer numbers in this group.

For example, assume the set of numbers is as follows:

```
 2
 3
 2
 1
 4
 9
 4
-9
```

Then the output might look like the following:

```
 2
 3
 1
 4
 9
```

Laboratory Problem 45 - The Registrar's Problem

Text Required: TSF with subscripts

Problem: The Registrar's Office has a tabulating card for each student. Write a program to count the total number of students, the number of each sex and the number from each state. Although only a small set of data is provided, write the program so that it could process a data deck of any size.

Input: The data cards from the Registrar's Office are punched as follows:

cols.	1- 5	student ID number
	7	sex code (0=female,1=male)
	9-10	state code (ranges from 1-50)

The last card will be a trip card with a negative ID number. For this program, punch an input data deck as follows:

```
31625   0   21
68261   1   15
53812   1    7
12953   0   21
68532   0   49
73861   1   15
26385   0   21
63998   1   33
82138   1   50
93189   0    1
   -1   0    0
```

Output: Print the total number of students on the first line and the number of males and the number of females on the second line. On each following line, print the state code and the number of students from that state if the number of students from that state is non-zero.

Laboratory Problem 46 - Questionnaire Analysis

Text Required: FORMAT

Complete the following questionnaire by filling in the blanks at the right with the appropriate numbers or numeric code. Notice that each blank has a number below it. After filling in the questionnaire, keypunch your responses in the card column indicated by the number under the line. As an example, punch your age in card columns 1 and 2, punch your sex code in column 3, etc. Submit the punched card to your instructor. The responses will be written on I/O unit ___. Write a program to tabulate the responses as outlined below.

1. Age ___ ___ (1, 2)

2. Sex (female=1, male=2) ___ (3)

3. Academic year (fr=1, soph=2, jr=3, sr=4, grad=5, special student=6) ___ (4)

4. Overall grade point average ___ . ___ ___ (5, 6, 7)

For Questions 5-11, no=0, and yes=1

Have you taken or are you currently taking:

5. Two years of high school algebra or a year of college algebra? ___ (8)

6. First semester calculus? ___ (9)

7. Second semester calculus? ___ (10)

8. Third semester calculus? ___ (11)

9. Differential equations? ___ 12

10. Applied calculus? ___ 13

11. Had you ever written a computer program before enrolling in this class? ___ 14

12. What grade did you receive in plane geometry? (Write A, B, C, D, or E; if you didn't take plane geometry, write X.) ___ 15

Problem: Tabulate the responses to questions on the class questionnaire.

Input: On I/O unit ___.

FORMAT for all records: I5

1st record: m (number of records following) (Format:F(5))

2nd through m+1 record: (punched cards that were turned in by students answering the questionnaire)

Output: Prepare a report tabulating the totals for each question and response. Use appropriate headings to identify results.

Laboratory Problem 47 - Grade Reports

Text Required: FORMAT

Problem: Write a program to process final student grades. For each student print a grade report.

Procedure: Grade point standing= $\sum c(i)*w(i)/\sum c(i)$

where c(i) is credits for the course and w(i) is the weight for the grade (4 for A, 3 for B, 2 for C, 1 for D, and 0 for E). If a grade is blank, the student is auditing the course; do not include credits for an audited course in the sum of credits. If the sum of credits for a student is zero, print zero for the grade point average.

Input: On I/O unit ___. For each student, up to ten records may exist. All of the records for any one student are together in the input stream. Each record indicates a course, credits and grade, and is written in the following form:

Cols.	
1- 8	course name (alphabetic)
10-25	student name (alphabetic)
26-27	credit hours (INTEGER)
28	grade (A, B, C, D, E, or blank)
30-38	social security number (INTEGER)

The end of all data is indicated by a trip record which contains a negative social security number.

Output: For each student print a report as follows:

	cols.	
First line	2-17	student name
	21-29	social security number
One line for each course	1- 8	course name
	12-13	credits
	17	grade
Last line	10-13	total credits for semester
	16-19	total credit hours
	25-28	semester grade point standing

Laboratory Problem 48 - Counting Students

Text Required: FORMAT

Problem: Search a data file for specific information. In this case, I/O unit ___ contains student records. The problem here is to find out how many full-time Freshmen, Sophomores, Juniors, Seniors, and Graduate students are listed.

Input: An undetermined number (fewer than 500) of student records are recorded. Each student record contains:

Cols.	
1- 5	Student number
6- 7	Home town code (disregard this)
8	Full-time, part-time code. 0 = part-time student and 1 = full-time student.
9-11	Overall grade point average.
12	Classification: 1 Freshman 2 Sophomore 3 Junior 4 Senior 5 Graduate

Procedure: Search the file, counting the number of full-time Freshmen, Sophomores, Juniors, Seniors, and Graduate students. You can disregard part-time students.

Output: Print in columns:

1-10	the number of full time Freshmen
11-20	the number of full time Sophs
21-30	the number of full time Juniors
31-40	the number of full time Seniors
41-50	the number of full time Graduate Students

Laboratory Problem 49 - Simplified Payroll

Text Required: FORMAT

Input: On I/O unit ___ there is one parameter record that indicates the number of employee records to be processed. It has 3 digits.

Employee Records - one for each employee (these records follow the parameter record).

Columns	Information in these columns
1- 6	Employee number (no decimal)
7- 9	Number of dependents (no decimal)
10-15	Number of hours this employee worked this week
16-20	Hourly pay for this worker (although no decimal is recorded in this field, cols 16-18 are to be considered to the left and cols. 19-20 to the right of the decimal)
21	Insurance code. A one denotes $2.22 to be deducted. A zero denotes no deduction.

Procedure: For each employee compute gross pay and net pay. Gross pay = hours worked times hourly pay. If the employee has worked more than 40 hours, he receives time and one-half for these excess hours.

Deductions:
- Federal Tax = (gross pay - (13* dependents))*.14
- FICA = gross pay * .052
- City Tax = gross pay * .0125
- Insurance = $2.22 or nothing

Output: For each employee print:

Printer Cols.	Information
1- 7	employee number
8-19	gross pay (pay before deductions)
20-30	net pay (pay after all deductions)

After all employee records have been processed, print:

1-20 (2 decimals)	average gross wages
21-40 (2 decimals)	average net wages

Notes: 1) Do not worry about rounding.
2) If Federal Tax turns out to be negative, set it equal to zero and proceed.

Laboratory Problem 50 - Alphanumeric Sorting

Text Required: Module 11

Problem: A deck of cards (200 or fewer) contains names and salaries of workers in a company. The president of the company wants two lists: the first a list of all employees in alphabetical order by last name, showing name and salary; the second a list of employees in order by salary (descending order), showing name and salary. Each card contains the employee's last name in columns 1-20, the first name in columns 21-40, and the salary (whole dollars only) in columns 50-55. The names are left-adjusted in their respective fields and the salary is right-adjusted in its field.

Laboratory Problem 51 - Inventory Application I

Text Required: FORMAT

Problem: The purpose of this program is to record inventory transactions. Your company maintains inventory for 40 types of gaskets. For simplicity we identify them as 1, 2, 3, ..., 40. Each day a computer run is made in which all orders and inventory receipts are processed.

Assume that this day your firm starts with 10,000 of each of the 40 types of gaskets. Orders and receipts are read from I/O unit ___ and inventory is "updated." Orders and receipts are interspersed in the input stream.

Input: Each record is 6 digits in length.

Columns	
1	record type, 0 (zero) means this is a customer order, 1 means gaskets received
2-3	indicates the type of gasket involved (1-40)
4-6	indicates the number of gaskets received or shipped

Procedure: As each record is read, either add to or subtract from the inventory of the appropriate gasket type. At the end of the run, for each of the 40 types of gaskets, print the gasket type and the number of gaskets left in inventory.

Output: (40 lines of output)

Columns	
1- 3	gasket type
10-20	number of gaskets on hand

Laboratory Problem 52 - Inventory Application II

Text Required: FORMAT

Problem: To program a system that will retain inventory records, write invoices and reorder merchandise. The XYZ Wholesale Company maintains an inventory of different types of gaskets (serial numbers 5, 8, 19, 21, 35, 66, 81, 82, 83, 98).

Input: I/O unit ___ contains ten status records. Each record contains:

Columns		
	1- 2	gasket serial number
	3- 7	inventory on hand at beginning of run (no decimal)
	8-11	retail price of this type of gasket (dollars and cents)
	12-16	reorder point (no decimals)
	17-21	reorder quantity (no decimals)

Following these records is an unknown number of customer orders. Each customer order contains:

6-10	number of gaskets ordered
11-12	type of gasket

Procedure: First, after creating the current status of the inventory of the firm, process customer orders. As each is read, the computer must decide whether the inventory is sufficient to ship the goods. If sufficent inventory is available, write an _invoice_ and reduce inventory--if not, write an invoice for the goods on hand and a _backorder_ for the remainder. If no inventory is on hand, write a backorder for the entire order.

Second, after all customer orders have been processed (and all invoices and backorders have been written), write one reorder line for each type of gasket whose inventory is <u>below</u> the reorder point.

Third, print the <u>current</u> status of each gasket.

Invoice:

columns	
1- 5	blank
6-11	company code
15-20	number of gaskets shipped
25-30	price per gasket
35-40	amount due in dollars and cents
50-52	type of gasket

Status Report:

columns	
3- 5	gasket type
7-12	gaskets on hand
14-19	# of gaskets backordered (excluding orders)
28-38	# of gaskets shipped
48-58	$ sales of gaskets shipped

Backorder:

columns	
1- 4	9999
5-14	blank
15-20	# of gaskets backordered
25-30	price per gasket
40-42	type of gasket

Reorder:

columns	
1- 4	8888
5	blank
6-11	# of gaskets
14-16	gasket type

Laboratory Problem 53 - Inventory Simulation

Text Required: Parts I, II and Lab Problem 17

Problem: Given 3 reorder-point, reorder-quantity combinations, determine the cost of each inventory policy using simulation.

Input: For each day's demand, generate a two-digit random number with a subprogram. Use the hundreds and thousands digits produced by the random number generator of Lab Problem 17.

Information: Assume the following:

a. Each reorder placed costs $50.
b. Each unit of inventory costs $.50 per day for storage (insurance, deterioration, etc.).
c. Each unit out of stock when it might have been sold creates ill will worth $1 per unit plus the $3 net income that would have resulted in its sale, or a total of $4 per unit.
d. There is a 3-day lag between the time merchandise is reordered and received.
e. Initial inventory is 100 units.
f. Lost sales are lost forever; they cannot be backordered.
g. Initially, no merchandise has been ordered for stock.

Policies: The three policies to be tested are:

Reorder-point	Reorder-quantity
18	20
10	50
05	80

Procedure: Start the simulation at day 1. Determine whether today's demand can be filled or partially filled from inventory on hand. Add costs of today's transactions to total cost; then determine whether inventory is above the reorder-point. If not, place an order (to be delivered three days hence). Repeat this procedure until 50 days' simulation is complete. Use the same 50 random numbers for each of the three simulation runs.

Output: Print, for each of the three inventory policies:

columns	item
1-11	reorder-point
13-23	reorder-quantity
25-35	cost

Laboratory Problem 54 - Markov Chain

Text Required: FORMAT

General:

Since businesses either thrive or die depending upon the soundness of decisions, there is a driving force to preview the future whenever possible. Often, through mathematical models, businessmen attempt a peek ahead in time. One factor of interest to many oligopolistic firms is brand share, that is, the percentage of market sales captured by the firm. These companies study their share of the market and the phenomenon known as "brand switching." As an approximation to reality, firms develop brand switching models that attempt to abstract from reality and describe brand share in future time periods. One such model is known as a Markov chain. It is an iterative matrix technique, simple in construction and although limited in predictive ability, it is believed useful enough by some firms to warrant their consideration.

The Markov chain consists of 3 arrays: a one-dimensional array (current share), another one-dimensional array (next period brand share) and a two-dimensional array (transition matrix). The current share array is simply the percentage share of the market currently held by each firm. Suppose that five firms in a market possess the following share of sales. The current array would appear:

firm 1	.20
firm 2	.15
firm 3	.10
firm 4	.30
firm 5	.25

The transition matrix contains one row and one column for each firm (in this case five rows and five columns). Each cell in the matrix contains a probability: the probability that a consumer will switch from brand "i" to brand "j" during one time period, where "i" is the ith row and "j" is the jth column. The transition matrix is determined after an extensive brand switching consumer survey.

One such transition matrix is:

PROBABILITY THAT A CONSUMER WILL SWITCH

TO BRAND j

		1	2	3	4	5
	1	.57	.03	.13	.16	.11
FROM	2	.15	.47	.15	.08	.15
BRAND i	3	.09	.06	.55	.15	.15
	4	.07	.01	.14	.64	.14
	5	.10	.05	.14	.19	.52

The entry in row 1, column 1 shows that there is a .57 chance that a consumer will not switch from brand 1 (no switch - he/she remains loyal) in one time period. Row 2, column 1 indicates that there is a .15 chance that a consumer will switch from brand 2 to brand 1 in one time period.

If we multiply the first cell in the current array times row 1 column 1 of the transition matrix (.20 x .57), we find that .114 of the consumers will remain loyal to brand 1 during one time period; and (.15 x .15)=.0225 of the market will have switched from brand 2 to brand 1 during one time period. If we multiply each cell in the current array times each cell in the first column of the transition matrix, the sum we get is the share of the market held by firm 1 after the first time period. We can do the same for each of the other firms. After the first period we find that the following is the new brand share array:

firm 1	.1915
firm 2	.0980
firm 3	.1805
firm 4	.2985
firm 5	.2315

If we again perform the necessary arithmetic using the above new current array and the transition matrix, we get the brand share for the third period. By continually repeating this procedure, we eventually find an equilibrium condition where a new iteration does not change any share value by as much as .0001

Problem: Write a program to compute the brand share of these five firms at equilibrium.

Input: I/O unit ___ contains 2 records. The first is the current share record (in order) which contains 5 two-digit numbers (without decimal points) in columns 1-10; columns 1-2 are firm 1 share, columns 3-4 are firm 2 share etc.; the second record is the transition matrix consisting of 25 two-digit numbers (in columns 1-50), representing the cells in order rowwise, that is, row 1, column 1; row 1, column 2; row 1, column 3; etc.

Output: Print the results as follows, including the alphabetic information:

```
EQUILIBRIUM REQUIRES XXXX PERIODS

  FIRM    SHARE
   1      .XXXX
   2      .XXXX
   3      .XXXX
   4      .XXXX
   5      .XXXX
```

Laboratory Problem 55 - Waiting Line Model

Text Required: Part II, Lab Problem 17

Problem: In some economic activities waiting lines (or queues) form because more demanders appear than can be served in one time interval. The solution to such a problem generally involves the determination of the optimum number of servers (that is, the number of servers that minimize cost or maximize profit).

Here we analyze a supermarket waiting line. We will determine the optimum number of checkout counters to install in the following manner: simulate 50 minutes of activity with one clerk (checkout counter), then simulate 50 minutes with two clerks, then three, etc., each time computing and printing the costs. As soon as the cost of N clerks is greater than the cost of N-1 clerks, discontinue the simulation. (In reality we would simulate many more minutes of activity, but because of computer cost limitations, we arbitrarily chose 50.)

Assumptions:

1. At most, one customer can arrive in any one minute.
2. Four minutes are required to check out one customer.
3. Each minute that a customer waits in line costs the store 80 cents in lost future purchases.
4. Each clerk receives 4 cents per minute salary.
5. There is a .3 probability that a customer arrives in line in any one minute. There is a .7 probability that no customer arrives in line in any one minute.
6. When a customer arrives in line, he/she remains in line until served.
7. Initially, 2 customers are waiting.

8. A customer will join the shortest line.

Procedure:

1. Generate 50 one-digit random numbers using the procedure of problem 17 as a subprogram.
2. Each simulated minute, look at the next random number. If it is a zero, one, or two, another customer enters a waiting line. If the random number is greater than two, no new customer enters a waiting line.

Output:

For each simulation run, print the number of clerks and the total cost.

part v

appendices

APPENDIX A

THE PUNCHED CARD

The punched card, Hollerith card, or IBM card, as it is variously known, is a paper device for storing information in a form which a machine can read. The card is 7 3/8" wide by 3 1/4" deep by 0.007" thick. Information is stored "in" the card by punching small rectangular holes in it. (The device which punches these holes is called a keypunch and has a keyboard which resembles a typewriter keyboard. The keypunch is discussed in Appendix B.)

The card is defined to have 80 vertical columns numbered 1 through 80 across the width of the card. The card is also defined to have 12 horizontal rows designated from top to bottom as 12, 11, 0, 1, 2, 3, 4, 5, 6, 7, 8, 9. The punching positions are defined to be the points at which the rows and columns intersect. Thus in each of the eighty columns there are twelve punching positions. By punching in one, two, or three of these twelve positions many different characters can be represented. If no punches are present in a column, the character stored there is called a blank. One punched card can, therefore, store eighty characters of information in any order. The coding for each of the possible characters which may be created using a standard keypunch machine is shown below. The keypunch also prints the punched characters at the top of the card so a person can easily read the characters punched.

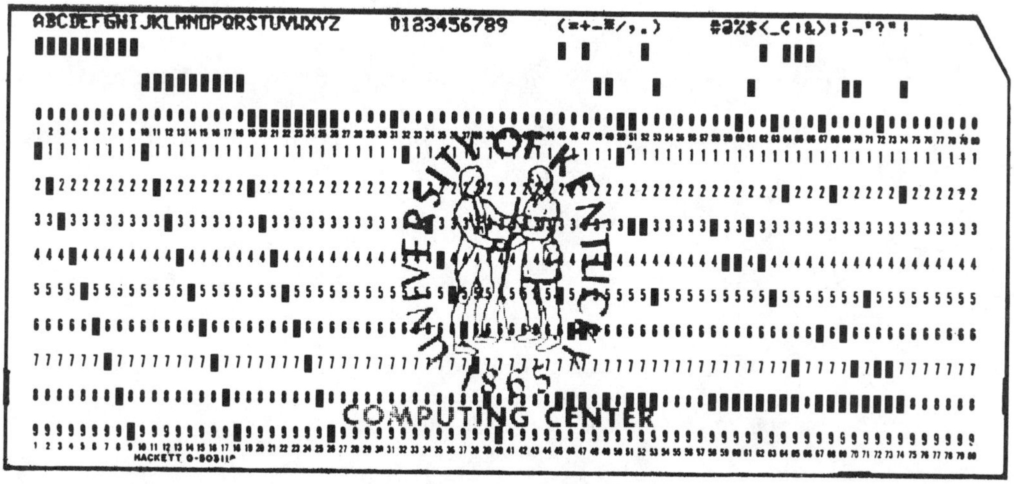

APPENDIX B

SIMPLIFIED KEYPUNCH INSTRUCTIONS

The numbers in parentheses which follow relate to the numbered components of the diagram of the IBM 029 keypunch on the next page.

a. Load the hopper (1) with cards. Any type card, regardless of color or corner cuts, will work.

b. Turn machine on if it is off. The switch (2) is located at right under the table.

c. Press down the right side of switch (3) so that the contacts are raised away from the drum (the contacts may be seen through the window (4)).

d. Turn all four center switches (5) up.

e. Push FEED button twice. A card is now ready to be punched. Use as a regular typewriter for lower order characters or letters. For upper order characters (i.e., numbers and special characters) hold down NUMERIC.

f. The numbered wheel (6) indicates the number of the <u>next</u> column to be punched.

g. When finished with the punching of a card press REL.

h. The next new card is now ready for punching.

i. If the keyboard locks (buttons have no effect), press the ERROR RESET.

j. When finished (or to clear the machine) flip the CLEAR switch (8).

k. It is possible, using the DUP key, to reproduce information in one card into another. Experiment with this feature to see how it works.

If you keypunch your own programs or data, there is a tendency to make use of some of those piles of "blank" cards which are inevitably left lying around keypunch machines. To do so is folly unless you check each card very carefully for punches. Someday, after you have saved $.42 worth of cards for the environment, you may blow a $30 computer run and waste half a day of your time because a card wasn't <u>quite</u> blank.

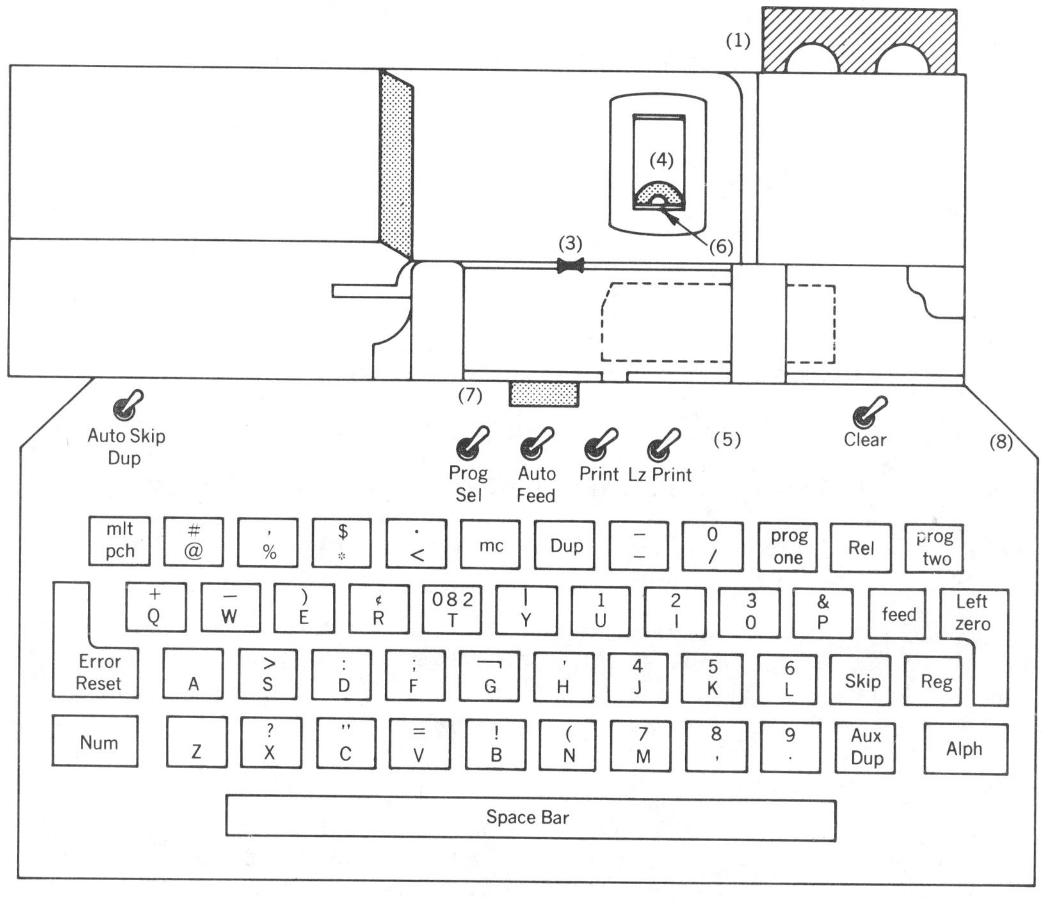

(2) not shown; switch under table on right hand side

APPENDIX C

$JOB CARD FORMAT AND OPTIONS

The $JOB card in a WATFOR or WATFIV job is the first card of the deck. It identifies the beginning of a new job. The contents are:

columns	1- 4	$JOB
columns	5-15	blank
columns	16-80	user identification and options

User Identification - An Example

Beginning in column 16 of the $JOB card, punch

CS220-PP-SSSNAME

where

CS220 is a course identification;

PP is a two-digit problem number (examples: 01 or 02 or 27);

SSS is a three digit student number (examples: 321 or 007);

NAME is user's last name followed by his first name but with no punctuation or blanks.

Notice that no commas or blanks may exist in the user identification field. Hyphens (minus signs) are used as shown above.

Optional WATFIV Features

Options, if any, follow the user identification field and consist of a keyword followed by an = sign followed by the option value or simply a keyword. Each option is separated from the information at its left by a comma. The last option is not followed by a comma. The options may be listed in any order. They must not contain any blanks. The options are:

1. LINES - This specifies the number of lines per page. If omitted, 61 is assumed.

2. PAGES - This specifies the number of pages of output allowed. If omitted, 100 is assumed.

3. TIME - This specifies the amount of time in seconds allowed for the job. If omitted, 30 is assumed.

4. KP - This specifies whether a Model 26 or a Model 29 keypunch was used to punch the source program. If omitted, Model 29 is assumed.

5. RUN - May be CHECK, NOCHECK, or FREE. CHECK specifies to check for undefined variables and halt execution when one is found. CHECK is assumed if the RUN option is omitted. NOCHECK specifies no checking for undefined variables. FREE instructs the computer to check for errors but not to stop the translation process when one is found; the execution of the program will be halted when a statement which was in error is actually executed.

6. LIST/NOLIST - This produces a source listing. NOLIST suppresses the listing. LIST is the default.

7. WARN/NOWARN - This allows all diagnostics to be printed. NOWARN suppresses all but fatal diagnostics. Default is WARN.

8. EXT/NOEXT - This allows a message to be printed when the programmer employs a feature of WATFIV that is an extension to the Fortran language. NOEXT suppresses these messages. EXT is the default value.

Examples of $JOB Cards

```
     cc
     1234           16
    ------------------------------------------------------------
a.  |$JOB           CS220-03-375SMITH
    |
b.  |$JOB           CS220-01-222JONESBILL,TIME=2,RUN=NOCHECK
    |
c.  |$JOB           CS220-27-123GREENFRANK,PAGES=3
    |
d.  |$JOB           CS220-11-943JANSENWILLIAM,KP=26
```

cc 5-15 are always blank

a. This card simply identifies the user as Smith, the problem as number 03, and his student number as 375. The assumptions of the job are: 61 lines of printed output per page, a maximum of 100 pages, thirty-second time limit, 29 keypunch and CHECKing during the run.

b. In addition to name, student problem number and student number information, this card specifies NOCHECK and a time limit of 2 seconds.

c. This card identifies the user, his problem number and student number as well as allowing 3 pages for the job. The other options default to their assumed values.

d. This card identifies the job as CS220 problem number 11, for William Jansen, student number 943, and specifies that the deck was punched on a 26 keypunch.

Your $JOB Card Format

Your instructor will describe the format of the $JOB card you will use; write that format below for reference.

```
columns--->   16       26       36       46       56
┌─────────────┬────────┬────────┬────────┬────────┬───
|$JOB         |        |        |        |        |
```

APPENDIX D

ALGORITHMS AND FLOWCHARTS

An algorithm is a procedure to solve a problem in a stepwise manner. It implies a sequence of operations or steps which will take place one after another in time.

A flowchart is a two-dimensional description of an algorithm which uses basic elements to describe both the operations of the algorithm and the order in which they take place. A flowchart is not a computer program but rather provides a convenient base from which a computer program (which is essentially a one-dimensional description of an algorithm) can be written. A flowchart, like a program, is an explicit set of instructions which describes a procedure for solving a problem.

Elements of Flowcharting

We shall now define a set of symbols which will provide a shorthand for describing an algorithm for solving problems which deal with numbers. A collection of these symbols will constitute the flowchart description of the algorithm or, more simply, a flowchart. The set of symbols constitute a flowchart language.

Terminal Block

A terminal block is used wherever the solution to a problem starts or stops. The block has either "enter" or "return" written in it. A particular flowchart has exactly one

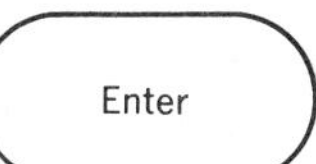

block and at least one

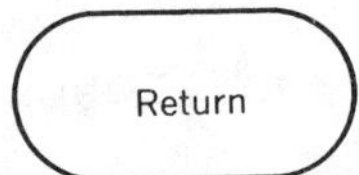

block.

Flow Arrow

The flow arrow indicates the sequence in which the steps described by the flowchart are to be executed. The shortest possible flowchart is

If a flow arrow changes directions several times, then several additional arrow heads should be used, e.g.,

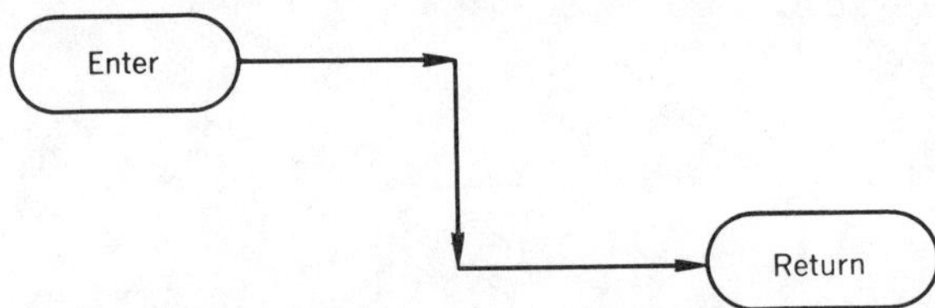

Variable

A variable is usually a letter of the English or Greek alphabet which stands for a number. A variable has much the same meaning in flowchart language as it has in algebra.

Expression

An expression in flowchart language is made up of previously defined variables (those that have had numbers assigned to them) and algebraic operators. <u>Any time a variable</u> appears in an expression it must have been previously defined to have a particular value. There are two basic ways of defining the value of a variable: the "becomes" symbol and the "read" verb.

<u>The "Becomes" Symbol</u>

The symbol "⟵" is used to stand for the word "becomes." The "⟵" symbol must always have a variable name on its left and an expression on its right. Any variable names used in the expression must have been previously defined. For example, suppose that T is to be the total of x, y, and z. To put it another way, T becomes x+y+z or, in our new notation, T⟵x+y+z. Anytime the "⟵" symbol is encountered it means to compute the value of the "<u>expression</u>" on the right of the symbol (e.g., x+y+z) and to assign the value of that result to the variable name (e.g., T) to the left of the arrow. This is the first of the two ways in which the value of a variable can be defined.

For example, consider

$$w \longleftarrow t + a * 6$$

In the expression above, t, a, and of course, 6 are quantities which have been previously defined to have values. The "becomes" symbol indicates that these quantities are to be combined, as indicated by the arithmetic operators, and the resulting number assigned to the variable w, which may or may not have been previously defined. If w had been previously defined, the original value would be replaced by the new one.

<u>Processing Block</u>

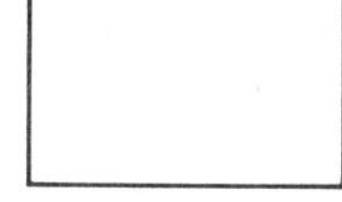

This symbol contains the computations used to solve the problem. The "becomes" symbol is usually used in conjunction with the processing block. A processing block must have at least one "in" flow arrow and exactly one "out" arrow. For example,

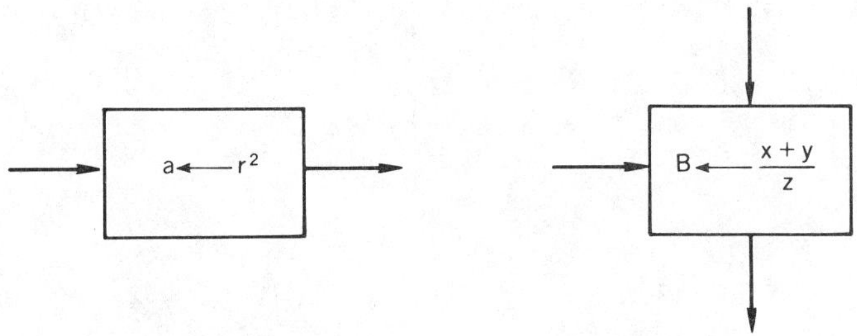

Input-Output Block

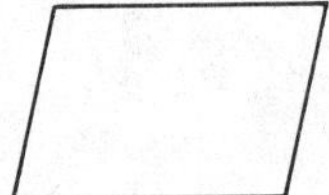

This symbol is used whenever information is read into or written out of the computer. For example,

implies an instruction which tells the machine to "read" a number and call it "x". After the execution of this block, x is defined to have the value read in. This is the second way in which a variable can be defined. The word "write" or "print" can also appear in the input-output block and it instructs the machine to move information out of the system. For example,

would cause the value of "s" to be written out by the machine. Of course, "s" must have been previously defined for the box to mean anything. An input-output block must have at least one "in" arrow and exactly one "out" arrow.

Decision Block

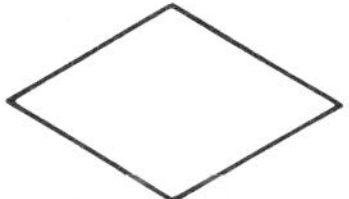

The decision block surrounds a question which can be answered "yes" or "no". The question is asked in terms of variables already defined in the flowchart. For example,

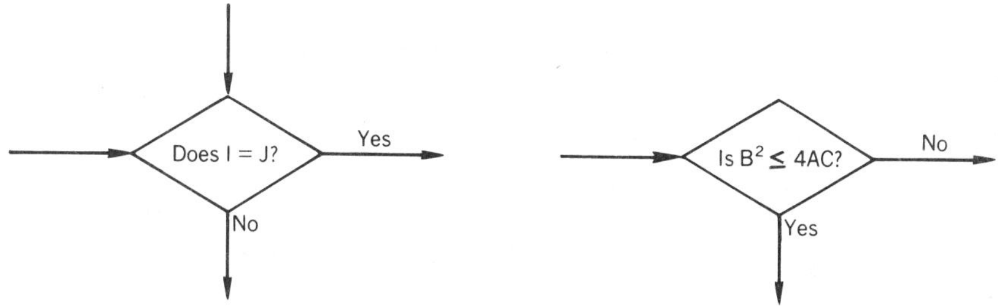

A decision block must have at least one "in" arrow and exactly two "out" arrows.

Looping Block

In this text a composite flowchart block is used to indicate looping through a set of blocks.

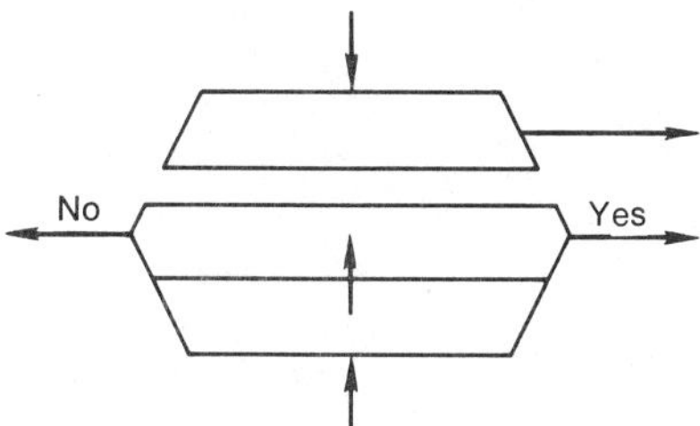

A detailed discussion of it appears in Part II in the section which covers the DO statement. This flowchart symbol is explicitly designed to represent the Fortran DO statement and, unlike the other symbols shown here, is not a standard flowchart symbol.

Connector

Sometimes having long flow arrows on a flowchart produces confusion, especially if these lines have to cross others. To solve this problem a connector block is used, as illustrated below.

This

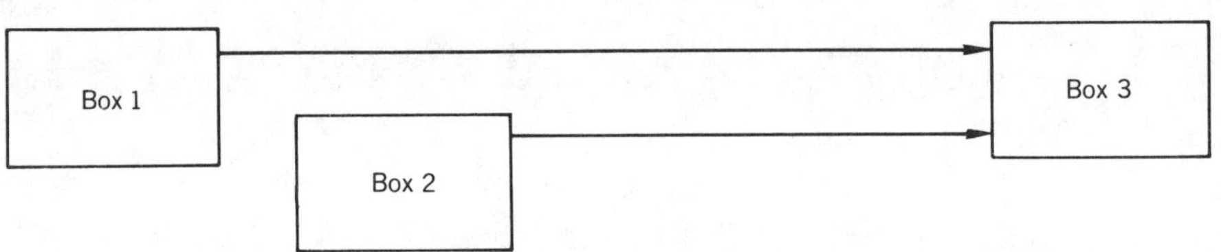

can be replaced by this

Off-page Connector

When a flowchart consists of more than one page, an off-page connector may be used to connect flowchart boxes on different pages, as shown below.

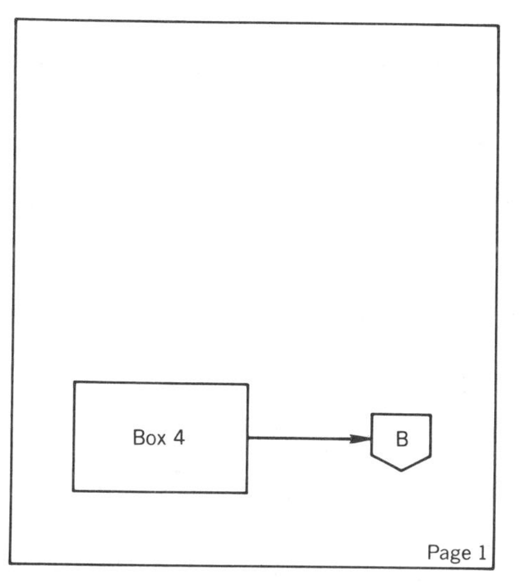

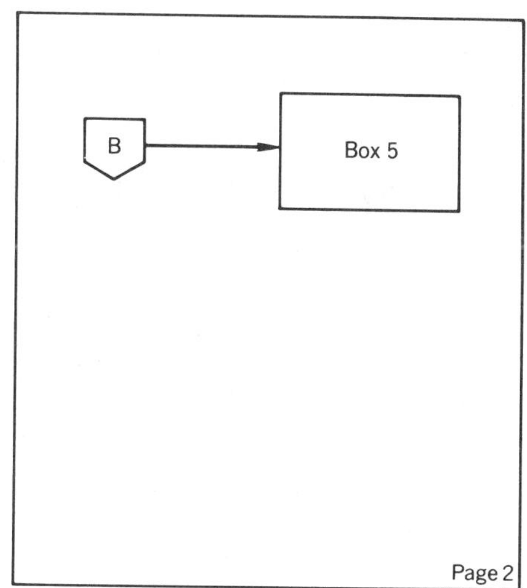

A Sample Flowchart - Summing a Series

Suppose we want to find the sum of the series

$$1 + x + x^2 + x^3 + \ldots$$

where x is a real number which is greater than zero but less than 1. Under these conditions it is clear that each term of the series will be smaller than the one before it. Suppose we will accept as a solution to our problem the sum of all those terms which are greater than one thousandth. We could describe the solution to this problem in several ways.

A Mathematical Description

Given

$$0 < x < 1$$

find

$$\Sigma x^n$$

such that each term >= .001 and n = 0,1,2,3,...

A Narrative Description

Obtain the value of x for which the series sum is desired. Check the value to see if it lies within the proper range, zero to one. If not, complain. Begin adding terms together, starting with 1, then x, then x^2 and continuing until a term with value less than one thousandth is found. Write the value of x and the sum computed.

A Stepwise Description

1. Obtain the value of x for which the series sum is desired.

2. If the value of x is less than or equal to zero, go to Step 10.

3. If the value of x is greater than or equal to one, go to Step 10.

4. Let a symbol "s" take on (stand for) the value one.

5. Let a symbol "t" take on the value of the symbol "x."

6. If the value of t is less than .001 then go to Step 12.

7. Let s take on a new value which is its old value plus the value of t.

8. Assign a new value to the symbol "t" which is its old value multiplied by x.

9. Go back to Step 6.

10. Write out only the value of x to indicate that it is not in the proper range.

11. Go ahead to Step 13.

12. Write out the value of x and the value of s which has been computed.

13. Consider the problem finished.

Note that the Stepwise Description of the problem is longer and more complicated than the Narrative one. While it may seem more complex, it is also more explicit. It is this move towards greater explicitness which will ultimately allow the student to use a computer to solve problems. The Stepwise Description depicts an algorithm for solving the problem, whereas the Narrative Description and the Mathematical Description do not.

The Stepwise Description is one which allows the solution description to "unfold in time" much as the performance of a piece of music would. In this sense it is a one-dimensional description of the solution of the problem.

In writing out a description of an algorithm, it is frequently useful to consider a two-dimensional description of the solution--a painting or a printed musical score, perhaps--which does not have to unfold in time but simply exists at a given moment with all of its parts visible.

One form of a two-dimensional description is the flow diagram or flowchart. Its advantages over the stepwise description include the arbitrary placement of the various steps on a sheet of paper and the freedom from having to number or name various steps. A flowchart description also permits easy addition or deletion of steps without affecting the order of other steps. This makes it useful during the preliminary planning of the algorithm.

A Flowchart Description

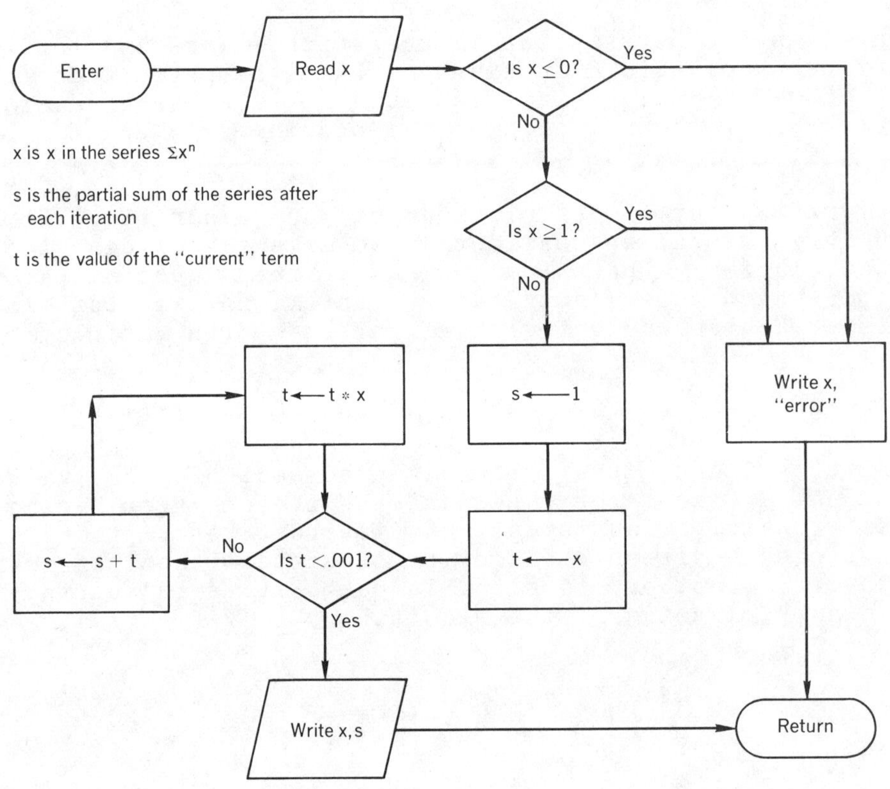

A Second Stepwise Description

For most programmers it seems easiest to conceive of a solution to a problem in terms of the Narrative or Mathematical Description, then draw a Flowchart Description, and finally devise a Stepwise Description which is the computer program for the solution to the problem. Here we show a Fortran program which sums the series.

```
      REAL X
      REAL S
      REAL T
      READ, X
      IF (X.LE.0.) GO TO 101
      IF (X.GE.1.) GO TO 102
      S=1.
      T=X
  103 CONTINUE
      IF (T.LT..001) GO TO 104
      S=S+T
      T=T*X
      GO TO 103
  101 CONTINUE
  102 CONTINUE
      PRINT, X
      GO TO 105
  104 CONTINUE
      PRINT, X, S
  105 CONTINUE
      RETURN
      END
```

APPENDIX E

SOME FUNDAMENTALS OF A COMPUTER SYSTEM

A digital computer system accepts a set of instructions (called a program) and executes these instructions quickly, faithfully, and precisely.

A computer system is composed of three basic types of components:

a. Main Storage (or memory),
b. Central Processing Unit (Control and Arithmetic Unit or CPU),
c. Input and Output Devices.

<u>Main Storage</u>

Main Storage is a set of storage locations, each of which possesses a unique address. Each storage location can hold information. The storage locations might be visualized as a set of post office boxes.

0	1	2
3	4	5
6	7	8
9	10	11

Two types of information are placed in the storage locations of a computer:

a. instructions
b. data

Instructions tell the computer what to do and the sequence in which the operations are to be carried out. The computer can understand various types of instructions such as:

a. arithmetic (add, subtract, multiply, divide)
b. input (read information into storage)
c. output (write information out of storage)
d. branch (take next instruction from specific storage location)
e. logic (is a value greater than another value, less than another value, or equal to another value?)

A programmer writes instructions in some computer language and these instructions are entered into computer storage. The computer then begins executing the instructions one after another until an instruction specifies a halt or branch to another instruction. As the instructions are executed, data are brought into storage by read instructions; they are stored in storage locations not occupied by instructions.

Data are any items of information other than the instructions to the computer.

As data are stored in storage, they are later accessible for computation, inspection, or output. The storage locations are general in that any location can be used for data or instructions. Once an instruction is placed in a specific location, that location is not then generally available to hold data. The converse is also true.

Some computers possess a small number of storage locations; others have a large number. The price of the computer is largely dependent upon the storage size rented or purchased.

Normally, all or a portion of computer storage is available to a "job" or program (set of instructions) while that program is in operation. When that program finishes, another program gains control of storage. The contents of storage are generally obliterated between jobs. So if the programmer wants some specific quantity in memory, he must arrange, through his programming, to put it there.

Central Processing Unit

The Central Processing Unit (CPU) contains control circuitry which interprets the instructions which are in storage and sends electrical impulses to the proper places in the computer system. Also contained in the CPU is the arithmetic unit which performs arithmetic operations.

Input and Output Devices

Input devices allow information which is stored on some external medium such as punched cards to be placed in computer storage. Output units allow information from computer storage to be duplicated on some external medium such as paper. Several input and output units are described below.

Card Reader - transforms information punched on tabulating cards into electronic signals and sends these signals over a cable into the storage of the computer. Performs input only.

Card Punch - transforms signals coming from storage over a cable into holes in punched cards. Normally performs output only.

Magnetic Tape Unit - reads information from or writes information onto magnetic tape. This unit is similar to a home tape recorder except that it records onto half-inch-wide tape instead of quarter-inch tape and it records characters and digits instead of sound. Performs either input or output.

Magnetic Disk Unit - records information onto or reads information from a magnetic disk, which is similar in geometry to a phonograph record. Its advantage over magnetic tape is that it can be read from or written on beginning anywhere on its disk surface rather than operating in a sequential mode. Performs either input or output.

Typewriter Terminal - A typewriter connected to a computer, frequently via telephone lines. Typing is performed in a conventional way except that data is sent into computer storage or from computer storage. Performs either input or output.

Optical Character Reader - Interprets print or type on a paper page and sends information over a cable into the storage of a computer. Performs input only.

Magnetic Character Reader - Interprets numbers printed with special magnetic ink (e.g., characters at the bottom of bank checks) and sends the information over a cable to the storage of a computer. Performs input only.

Optical Mark Reader - Interprets horizontal or vertical marks on a paper page (for example, test scoring sheets) and sends information over a cable into the storage of a computer. Performs input only.

Plotter - Interprets information from computer storage consisting of x-y coordinates and other control information and draws graphs, charts, or diagrams with a pen on paper. Performs output only.

Cathode Ray Display - Interprets information from the storage of a computer and displays letters, numbers, or other characters on the face of a TV-like Cathode Ray tube. With an attached keyboard, information can be typed and sent to computer storage. Performs either input or output.

A Diagram of a Computer System

The diagram below shows the most rudimentary kind of computer schematic. The solid arrows indicate the flow of information; the dashed arrows indicate that one device controls another.

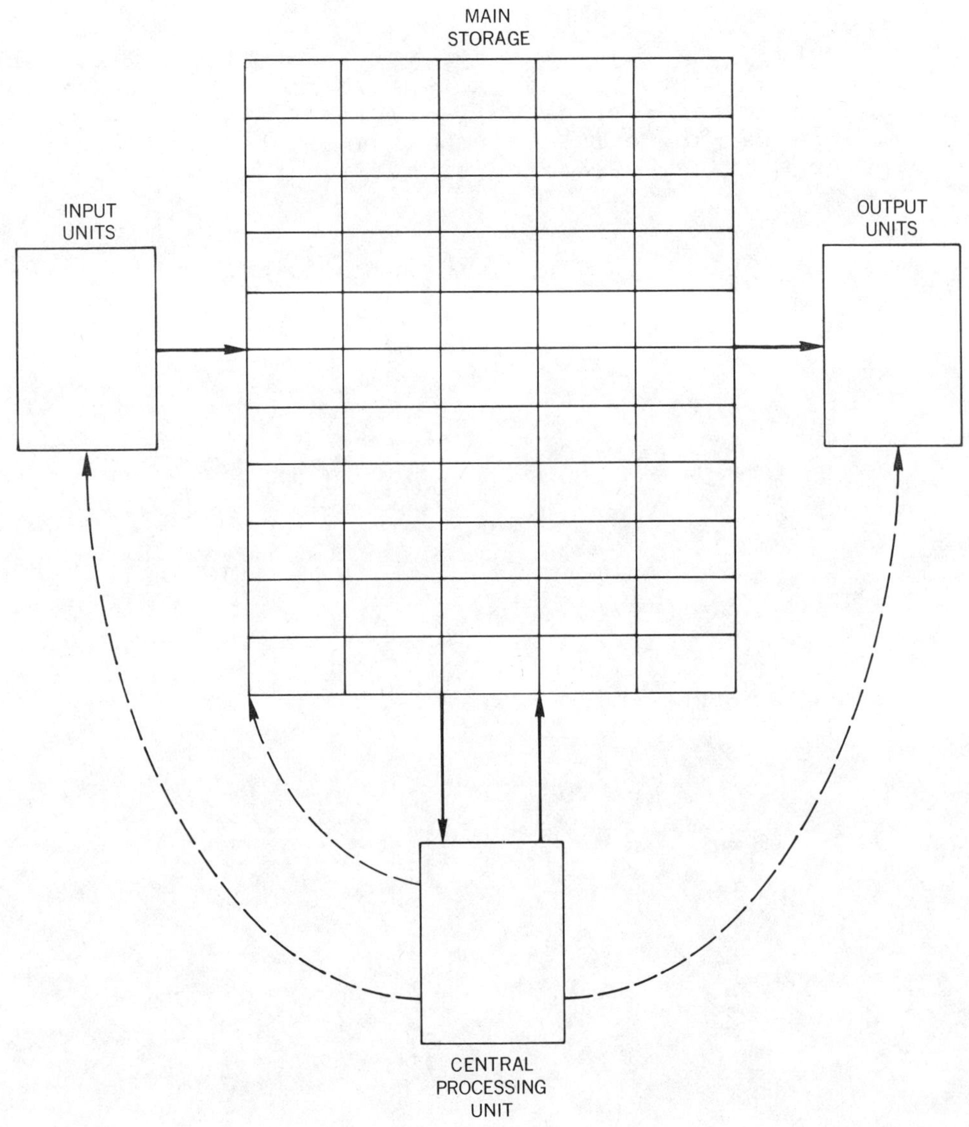

Binary Storage

A storage location in a computer is composed of electronic components which can store binary digits called bits. A bit can take on the values of either one or zero. A series of binary bits can then represent a number. To show this the decimal and binary equivalents for the numbers one through ten are represented below.

1	1
2	10
3	11
4	100
5	101
6	110
7	111
8	1000
9	1001
10	1010

Storage locations in the IBM System 360/370 computer can be viewed in several ways. Bits can be grouped to represent a number, a series of numbers, or alphabetic characters. When representing alphabetic characters, bits are logically divided into 8-bit segments which are called bytes. A byte can contain one alphabetic character. If one refers to a 32-bit location, it is customary to speak of it as a computer word. Therefore one word consists of four bytes, each of which consists of eight bits. A word can store an INTEGER or REAL number or up to 4 alphabetic characters.

The size of a computer's storage or memory is sometimes defined in terms of computer words and sometimes in terms of bytes of storage. Whichever term is used, in the IBM System 360/370 computer, a word is 32 bits and a byte is 8 bits or one-fourth of a computer word.

APPENDIX F

COMPILING AND COMPILERS

The Compiling Process

TSF or Fortran is not the "natural" or machine language (ml) of any computer. Every computer that understands Fortran must first translate it into its own language. Thus the Fortran program is transformed into a machine language program. The computer then solves the problem by following the steps in the machine language program.

When a computer follows a machine language program to solve a problem, the process occurs in the manner schematically illustrated below.

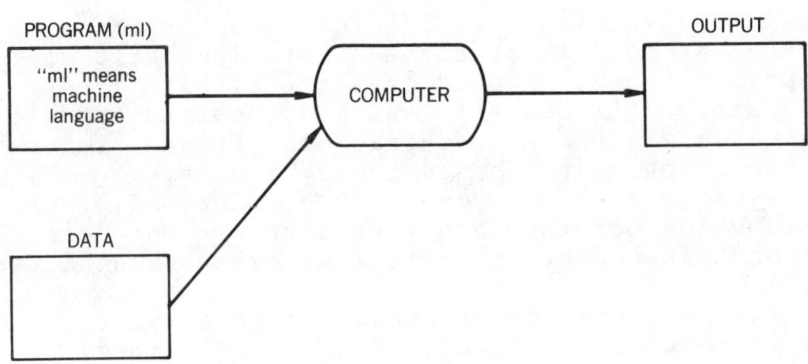

A program (written in the machine's own language) is put into the computer. Under control of this program the computer reads in data (or input). The computer manipulates these data and produces answers (or output).

In solving a problem in which the program is written in Fortran, this principle is applied twice. See the diagram and explanation below.

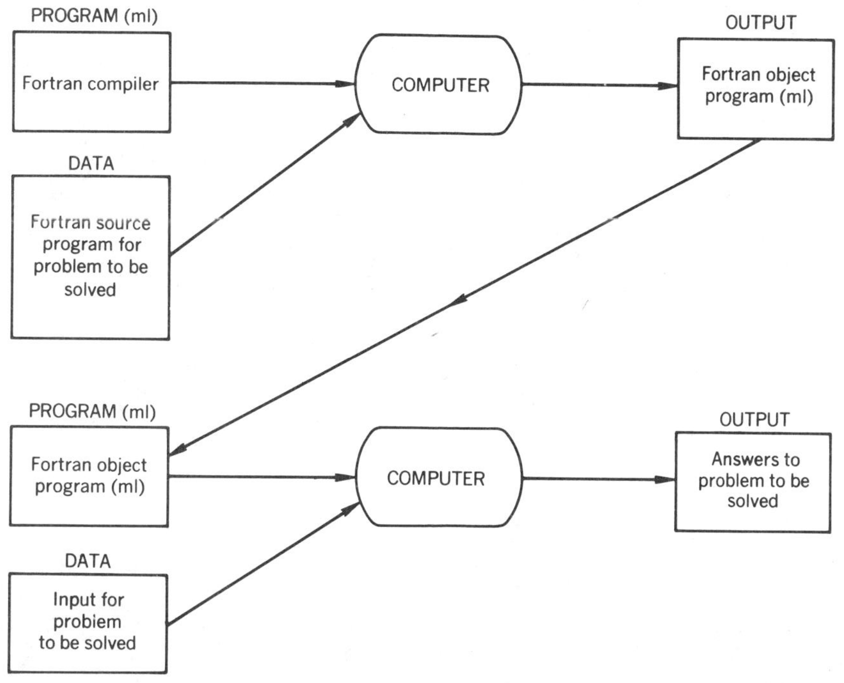

First a machine language program (called a Fortran compiler) is put into the machine. Under control of this program, data are read but the data are of an unusual sort: they are Fortran language statements, called a _source program_. The computer manipulates these data to produce "answers" which are also of an unusual sort. The output is the machine language equivalent to the Fortran program that was read in. Thus the Fortran source program is the input and a machine language program (called an _object program_) is the output. It is usually on cards or magnetic tape. Now to solve the original problem, the object program and the data for that problem are read in, manipulated, and answers are produced.

Load and Go Compilers

With many compilers it is possible to compile a Fortran source program and obtain an object program on cards (or in other machine readable form) so that it may be used immediately and/or be kept and used later. The advantage of using the object program (which is in machine language) is that there is no need to repeat the compiling process when one wants to reuse the program.

Some compilers such as WATFOR are called "load and go" compilers. These compilers do not produce an object program in a form that the programmer can reuse. The object program actually is stored in the memory of the machine as it is compiled; then when the compilation process is complete the machine language program is executed. This technique makes the "load and go" process very fast since the object program is not punched out nor read back in but rather resides in the memory all the time. On the other side of the coin, though, this technique limits the size of the Fortran program which can be run since both the compiling program and the object program must exist in the computer at the same time.

Some Available Fortran Compilers

Most computer manufacturers supply one or more Fortran compilers (translators) with their equipment. Most of these compilers use the American National Standards Institute (ANSI) specifications as the base of the language and then expand from there. The actual language specifications for a Fortran compiler for a particular computer usually embody language features and extensions which make it somewhat different from other Fortrans. In addition, computer hardware differences result in differences between Fortrans.

So even though the Fortran language is available for most computers, it usually involves significant conversion effort to transport a Fortran program from one computer to another. If the program is written using only the ANSI Fortran features, it will be more transportable from computer to computer. The more language extensions that are employed in a program, the more difficult it will be to transport it.

The ANSI specifications do not detail how a program should operate if data or statements are used improperly; so even the ANSI set of Fortran will act differently on different computers when errors occur.

Being unable to use computer programs on different computers is a national problem. Millions of dollars of investment in computer programs are sometimes wasted, either by installation of newer computers or by the inability of members of the computing community to use programs developed at other locations.

Various Fortran compilers exist for the same computers. For example, at this writing at least six different Fortran compilers operate on the IBM 360/370. The three most commonly used are Fortran G, Fortran H, and WATFIV. The characteristics of each are different. While WATFIV is extremely efficient in compiling and diagnosing a variety of possible problems, it is relatively slow in execution. For small, student-type jobs the execution phase is often small enough to be relatively unimportant. At the other extreme, the IBM Fortran H compiler requires a large amount of computer time to compile because it can generate a very efficient execution-time program. The IBM Fortran G compiler has characteristics between the Fortran H and WATFIV compilers: it compiles faster than H and slower than WATFIV, and the resulting program executes faster than WATFIV and slower (generally) than Fortran H. The programmer can therefore use the compiler that is appropriate for the job to be done. Many programmers test programs using WATFIV and later recompile using one of the others for actual production work.

When you want to develop a program, use a compiler that looks the program over very carefully, provides lots of error and warning messages, and, in general, doesn't pride itself on object time efficiency. Use of such a compiler will minimize your time in program development and possibly save you the embarrassment of a "bug" which slipped by. Once the program is believed to work correctly -- due to passing a set of test runs -- recompile to produce an object program with a compiler that brags about its object time efficiency. Do a set of test runs with this compiled program as well, even though you know the source program is the same as that you just checked out. Compiler writers are programmers too and, as you know only too damn well, programmers make mistakes.

Ten Statement Fortran Compilers

At least three compilers are available specifically for the TSF language. See the Preface to the Second Edition for details.

APPENDIX G

NUMBER SYSTEMS: AN OVERVIEW

Humans, at least in the western world, do arithmetic in the "base ten" (decimal) number system. Computers use the "base two" (binary) number system. But the student may have heard some computers referred to as "base eight" (octal) or "base sixteen" (hexadecimal). Why are there different number systems, what makes them different, what are the advantages of some over others? Before these questions are answered let us put forth a basic idea:

There is basic meaning in •••• or xxxx or ****, whether it is called 4, four, 100, &&, or ugh. It has a basic meaning to an intelligent being regardless of its name or even lack of name. You will probably find that your principal difficulty in studying number systems is divorcing yourself from the one you have used "forever": the decimal system.

Dissecting the Decimal System

We begin by taking the decimal system apart. Examine the decimal number 348.72 for example. It means

3 x 100 =	300.00
+ 4 x 10 =	40.00
+ 8 x 1 =	8.00
+ 7 x 1/10=	.70
+ 2 x 1/100 =	.02
	348.72

or put another way:

$3 \times 10^2 =$	300.00
$+ 4 \times 10^1 =$	40.00
$+ 8 \times 10^0 =$	8.00
$+ 7 \times 10^{-1} =$	.70
$+ 2 \times 10^{-2} =$	.02
	348.72

or still another way:

10^2	10^1	10^0	10^{-1}	10^{-2}
100	10	1	1/10	1/100
3	4	8	7	2

but this is really the starting point again.

The rule for determining the value of a base ten number is clear. For each digit in the number multiply that digit by ten raised a power dictated by the number of "positions" the digit is from the units position. Ten is the number raised to the power because there are ten characters in the system:

0
1
2
3
4
5
6
7
8
9

Each of these characters means something. For example 3 means ••• and 8 means ••••••••.

But when all of the characters have been used, say in a counting process, something must happen to mark the event. What happens is that the position immediately to the left of the column of characters already written is changed. For example,

0
1
2
3
4
5
6
7
8
9

10
11
12
13
14
.
.
.
19

20
21
.
.
.
.
97
98
99

100

Why did man select ten symbols instead of, say, 2 or 14? The number of "digits" on one's hands might provide a clue. The French have the vestiges of a system based on twenty (no shoes perhaps); some warlike tribes whose men always carried a weapon in one hand have a base five system. At any rate the link between a herder counting sheep on his fingers and then throwing a rock on a pile each time he ran out of fingers and our present number system doesn't seem too implausible.

Base Four

What do other number systems look like? Here is counting in base four.

Base Four	Base Ten
0	0
1	1
2	2
3	3
10	4
11	5
12	6
13	7
20	8
21	9
22	10
23	11
30	12
31	13
32	14
33	15
100	16

Note the repeated use of four symbols: 0, 1, 2, 3. Note that there is no single symbol "four" in a base four number system just as there is no single symbol "ten" in a base ten system.

A base four number such as 312 can be converted to base ten by simply using the same positional procedure shown earlier, and doing arithmetic in base ten:

4^2	4^1	4^0
16	4	1
3	1	2

$$\begin{array}{rcrcr} 3 & \times & 16 & = & 48 \\ 1 & \times & 4 & = & 4 \\ 2 & \times & 1 & = & \underline{2} \\ & & & & 54 \end{array}$$

The doubting student can continue the "correspondence counting" which compared base four and base ten if he/she is not convinced.

<u>Base One</u>?

What would a base one system be like? It would have only one symbol which could not be zero.

base ten	base one							
	1^7	1^6	1^5	1^4	1^3	1^2	1^1	1^0
0								
1								1
2							1	1
3						1	1	1
4					1	1	1	1
5				1	1	1	1	1
6			1	1	1	1	1	1
7		1	1	1	1	1	1	1

It could not represent zero except by "nothingness."

It would represent a number by the total number of times the symbol (in this case 1) was used, so its impracticality (and fundamentality) is obvious. It is a "degenerate" system and will not be described further.

Base Two

Is a base two system more useful? Yes!

base ten	base two				
	2^4	2^3	2^2	2^1	2^0
0					0
1					1
2				1	0
3				1	1
4			1	0	0
5			1	0	1
6			1	1	0
7			1	1	1
8		1	0	0	0
9		1	0	0	1
10		1	0	1	0
11		1	0	1	1
12		1	1	0	0
13		1	1	0	1
14		1	1	1	0
15		1	1	1	1
16	1	0	0	0	0
17	1	0	0	0	1

The system seems inefficient in that it takes five positions to represent the number seventeen when the decimal system requires only two positions. But efficiency is not always accomplished by more different symbols and fewer positions. If it were, perhaps man should consider a base eighty-five system, or a base four billion system. Or, better yet, a character for every possible number. The point here is that there are trade-offs between using fewer positions and more characters, and vice-versa. Man, it seems, has little difficulty working with ten symbols. Computers can most easily work with two characters or "states" such as on and off, yes and no, clockwise and counter-clockwise, or current flowing and current not flowing.

It turns out that, at present, it is more economical to have the computer manipulate a large number of bi-stable (two-state) devices than to use fewer devices which can have more than two states.

To illustrate the economics involved, one might consider a board with lightbulbs on it.

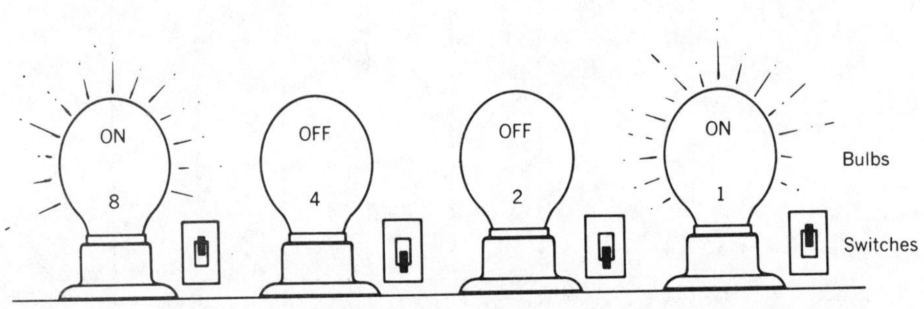

Here he can clearly represent any integer 0 to 15 just by turning switches. (The number 9 is shown.) If he is given two bulbs and told to do the same job by varying the intensity with which each bulb burns he has two immediate problems: more sophisticated equipment than switches is required to vary the light intensity and he must be able to recognize the varying intensities. He saves on light bulbs but is it worth it?

Binary Arithmetic Operations

The rules for arithmetic operations between binary numbers are simple--much more so than the rules for operations between decimal numbers. You may recall that you memorized addition and multiplication tables for base ten numbers. Memorizing the binary addition and multiplication tables is vastly easier. Probably a good thing, too, since our abilities for rote memorization seem to decline with age. Here's the add table:

	0	1
0	0	1
1	1	*0

The * beside the 0 in the "1 plus 1" position indicates a carry. 1 plus 1 is, of course, 10, the binary representation for the base ten quantity 2. As an example, consider

```
  10110    (which is 22 base ten)
+ 01101    (which is 13 base ten)
 100011    (which is 35 base ten)
```

It's ridiculously easy to do. If you want more practice, invent some arbitrary binary numbers and add them; check your results by converting everything to base ten.

The multiplication table is even easier.

	0	1
0	0	0
1	0	1

Take, for example, 101 times 011.

```
    101
    011
    101
   101
  000
  01111
```

It should be pretty clear why computers have such an easy time with base two. Multiplying is simply a matter of writing down the multiplicand in the appropriate position each time there is a 1 bit in the multiplier. We leave it to the student to develop the techniques for subtraction and division.

Two's Complement Notation

We haven't dealt with negative numbers yet. We could validly represent the binary equivalent of -26 (base ten) as -101010 (base two). But since an algebraic sign can have only two values, it seems reasonable to represent it as a binary quantity itself. Thus the left-most bit position of a binary number is designated as the sign bit. A "0" bit usually indicates that the binary number to its right is positive and a "1" bit indicates a negative number.

The IBM 360/370 uses a rather different system for representation of negative binary quantities. The system is called _two's complement notation_. The leftmost bit is still the sign bit but, if the number is negative, the bit configuration bears little resemblance to the corresponding positive number.

To form the two's complement of a positive binary number, do the following:

a. invert the number (that is, change all the ones to zeros and all the zeros to ones),
b. add one to the inverted number.

For example, to form the negative of 000010010 in two's complement notation, you would write 111101101 and add 1 to get 111101110. Even though the leftmost bit is the sign bit, it is treated along with the rest in this operation. We know now that 000010010 is plus 18(base ten) and 111101110 is minus 18(base ten). This scheme doesn't do much for one's intuitive grasp of negative binary numbers, but people don't deal with binary numbers very much anyway and the system works well for computers.

If we had a machine with a three bit word and the leftmost bit was donated for the sign, it could represent the following numbers:

```
3    011
2    010
1    001
0    000
```

-1	111
-2	110
-3	101
-4	100

A 1 in the leftmost position always indicates a negative number. The system has no "minus zero," which means that all negative numbers are smaller than all positive numbers. Just that fact alone avoids a very messy logical question which arises when the computer compares numbers. And, neatly enough, one can "two's complement" a negative number and get back its positive brother.

The absolute value of the smallest number which can be represented in two's complement notation is always one greater than the largest positive number.

Octal and Hexadecimal

If the binary system is so basic, what about octal and hexadecimal computers? Actually there is no machine which truly uses an octal or hexadecimal base. Scratch the surface of any present-day computer and you find a binary machine underneath. But binary converts easily to base four, eight, sixteen, and hence the use of these bases has advantages.

In general, a number of a system of base-n can be converted to its equivalent in a system of n-raised-to-the-power-m quite easily. (For example, base 2 to base 2^3.) One simply arranges the base-n number into sets of m digits beginning at the decimal point. These sets of m digits are then each individually converted from base-n to base-n-to-the-m. The resultant set of digits is the number in base-n-to-the-m. To convert a base-n-to-the-m number to a base-n number one simply applies the process in reverse.

For example, the binary number 100111110101 is the octal (base eight) number 4765. The doubting student can convert both to base ten to assure himself. Here is the simple conversion from binary to octal, obtained by simply grouping the binary digits in threes since $8=2^3$.

8^3	8^2	8^1	8^0	
1 0 0	1 1 1	1 1 0	1 0 1	binary
4	7	6	5	octal

What is the base ten value of 4765 (base eight)?

This sort of intermediate number system turns out to be useful to humans who go at least goggle-eyed if not smack out of their minds by looking at a number like

100111110101

Octal numbers look reasonable if one ignores the lack of 8's and 9's. In fact, they look so reasonable that they are sometimes taken for base ten - with unhappy results.

Hexadecimal (base sixteen) goes like this:

Base Ten	Base Sixteen
0	0
1	1
2	2
3	3
4	4
5	5
6	6
7	7
8	8
9	9
10	A
11	B
12	C
13	D
14	E
15	F
16	10
17	11
18	12
19	13
20	14

It is useful also as an intermediate base for computer-human conversation, since $16=2^4$.

For example, the binary number which was octal 4765 becomes hexadecimal 9F5 with the conversion as shown below.

16^2				16^1				16^0				
1	0	0	1	1	1	1	1	0	1	0	1	binary
9				F				5				hexadecimal

What is the base ten value of 9F5 (base sixteen)?

In all the number systems we have considered, if the first two symbols in a number system are 0 and 1, the base of the system itself is always written as

10

That is, ten in a base ten system is 10, two in a base two system is 10, sixteen in a base sixteen system is 10.

APPENDIX H

NUMERICAL CONSIDERATIONS IN COMPUTING

Floating-Point Storage Technique

INTEGER (fixed-point) numbers are represented simply as a set of binary digits in a computer word. For example, the number

43

or, as it might be written to show it as a base ten number,

43 (ten)

would be represented in a 32 bit machine as:

00000000000000000000000000101011 (two)

A number represented in this form can be quickly manipulated arithmetically by the computer. Unfortunately its maximum magnitude is quite limited. The largest value which can be represented in this form (donating a bit for the sign) is $2^{31}-1$ or 2,147,483,647, or somewhat more than 2 billion. But many things are larger than that: the number of atoms in a pin, diameter of the solar system in miles, the national debt, etc. Clearly, a general purpose computer needs to be able to handle numbers of greater range.

This is accomplished by dividing the computer word into two parts. One of these parts is used to store the significant digits (mantissa) of the number while the other stores a scale factor (base two exponent). For example, envision a ten bit computer word. In INTEGER form the largest number which could be stored is

+111111111(two) = +512(ten)

if one bit is donated for the algebraic sign.

But if the word is divided into two parts a much larger number can be represented. For example,

Now, if the decimal point is assumed to be at the extreme left-hand end of the mantissa, the largest number which can be stored is the number

$+.1111 \bullet 2^{1111}$ (represented in binary)
$= (1/2+1/4+1/8+1/16) \bullet 2^{15}$ (represented in base ten)
$= 15/16 \bullet 32{,}768$
or 30,720

Thus the range has been vastly increased by sacrificing some significance in the numbers which can be represented. (Recall that a 32 bit computer word was required to represent the quantity two billion. Thus, in the IBM 360/370, INTEGER numbers have a magnitude of $2^{31}-1$ or about 2×10^9, while REAL (floating-point) numbers range to more than 10^{75}. For a specific discussion of floating-point number representation for the IBM 360/370, see Module 12, Fortran Data Forms.

Usually more bits of the computer word are donated to the mantissa portion of the word than to the exponent.

The admittedly sketchy discussion of floating-point storage was presented to allow the student an understanding of the section which follows, which might be entitled: "Why computers don't always tell the truth."

Inaccuracy of Floating-Point Representation

It may alarm you to discover that a computer occasionally does not provide the correct answer even when no mistake has been made in the programming.

There are several sources of such errors. Some of these sources will be discussed below.

Representational Error

The computer would flunk the following test:

```
          REAL S, P
          INTEGER I
          S=0
          P=.1
          I=1
      987 CONTINUE
          S=S+P
          I=I+1
          IF (I.LE.100) GO TO 987
          PRINT, S
          RETURN
          END
```

The result will be something like

9.9999974

rather than 10. Why? Because .1 cannot be represented exactly in the binary number system as a finite number of digits although it can be in the decimal number system.

For the REAL number P the computer uses the form

(some binary mantissa)
times
(2 raised to some binary exponent)

where the binary mantissa is of the form

2^{-1} or 1/2	2^{-2} or 1/4	2^{-3} or 1/8	2^{-4} or 1/16	2^{-5} or 1/32
bit	bit	bit	bit	bit

Unfortunately, it is impossible to represent the number 1/10 by adding together a finite number of powers of two.

Asking a binary computer to solve this problem exactly is similar to asking a human to solve the problem

1/3+1/3+1/3

in the decimal number system.

The human must proceed:

```
.33333
.33333
.33333
------
.99999
```

and it is clear that since a finite number of digits is involved, the answer of "one" will not be found.

<u>Normalized Form</u>

General laws of mathematics sometimes fail to hold when the arithmetic is performed by computers. To illustrate, instead of using a floating-point representation of

(a binary mantissa (which is < 1 in absolute value))
times
(2 raised to a binary exponent)

a similar system of

(a base ten mantissa (which is < 1 in absolute value))
times
(10 raised to a base ten exponent)

will be used. The general effect is the same.

Assume that a computer can store three decimal digits for the mantissa and one decimal digit for the exponent. For example,

$$2.39=.239 \bullet 10^{1}=.2\ 3\ 9\ [1]$$

and

$$-.00531=-.531 \bullet 10^{-2}= -.5\ 3\ 1\ [-2]$$

where the quantity in brackets is the base ten exponent.

It can therefore represent numbers along the real number line in the range

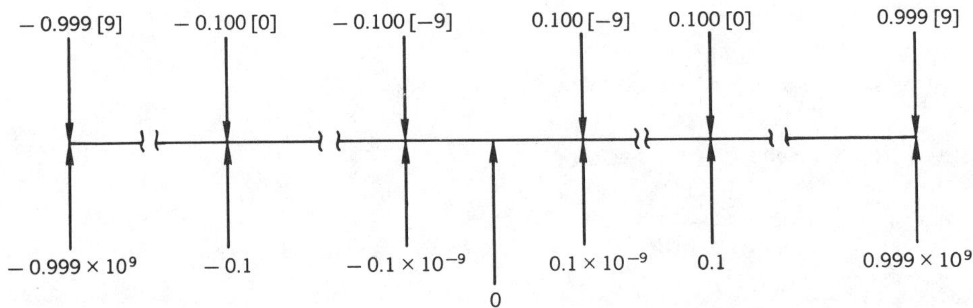

One additional rule for the storage of floating-point numbers is that the left-most digit of the mantissa may not be zero unless the entire number consists of zero digits. That is,

.0 3 8 [5]

is not a legal representation of $.038 \times 10^5$ but

.3 8 0 [4]

is. This latter form is called the normalized form of the number. Since only three significant digits can be stored, some calculations will be subject to truncation or roundoff error. Two examples are illustrated below.

The Cancellation Law

The cancellation law of mathematics says

a+e=a implies e=0

(i.e., if "a" and "e" are added together and the sum is equal to "a" this implies that "e" is zero).

This law does not hold for computers and consequently surprising results sometimes occur. The effect will be illustrated using the three-digit-mantissa computer.

Suppose a=222. and e=.333 and these numbers are stored as

a=.2 2 2 [3]

e=.3 3 3 [0]

Assume an <u>accumulator</u> (a separate location in memory where arithmetic operations are conducted) can hold numbers of any length.

To add "a" and "e" the number "a" is moved to the accumulator

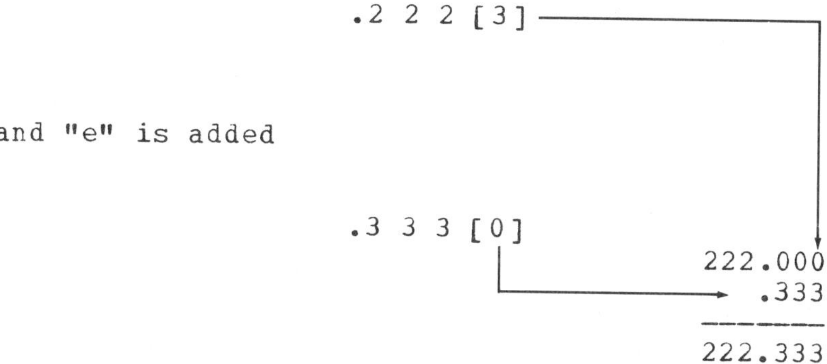

and "e" is added

giving the proper answer.

Now the answer is stored back into some other location in the machine, say location "b".

.2 2 2 [3] ⟵ 222.333

But in this "storing back" process only the most significant three digits are kept. Thus the effect is that the addition of a+e really failed to take place because "e" was small relative to a. The important point, however, is that e was not zero and yet a+e=a.

To illustrate this, write a program according to the following flow chart:

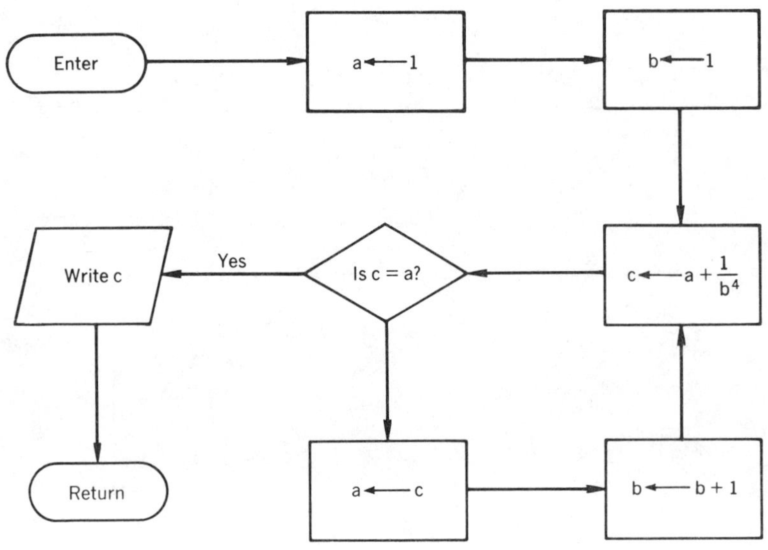

The fact that the computer is not "hung up" in an infinite loop and does indeed print c is proof of the proposition that

a+e equals a does not imply that e is zero

if a computer is doing the addition.

The Associative Law

Another law of mathematics which fails to hold for computers is the associative law for additon. The law is

$$(a+b)+c=a+(b+c)$$

or, in words, the order in which three quantities are added does not affect their sum. Computers, not having been properly educated, sometimes fail to comply. For example, assume a=421., b=11.7 and c=11.7.

Evaluating (a+b)+c first:

```
"a"      .4 2 1 [3] ———→ 421.00
"b"      .1 1 7 [2] ———→  11.70
                         ------
                         432.70
```

which is stored back in some location as

```
         .4 3 3 [3]
```

if rounding is assumed.

The second addition then takes place and produces

```
         .4 3 3 [3] ———→ 433.00
"c"      .1 1 7 [2] ———→  11.70
                         ------
                         444.70
```

which is stored back as

```
         .4 4 5 [3]
```

giving the result (a+b)+c.

Now evaluating a+(b+c) in a similar manner:

```
"b"      .1 1 7 [2] ———→  11.70
"c"      .1 1 7 [2] ———→  11.70
                         ------
                          23.40

         .2 3 4 [2]
                   ———→   23.40
"a"      .4 2 1 [3] ———→ 421.00
                         ------
                         444.40

         .4 4 4 [3]
```

which disagrees with the first result of .4 4 5 [3].

The results would also disagree with each other if truncation, instead of rounding, were assumed.

The preceding examples were presented chiefly to demonstrate that you should not expect exact results from a computer when you are using any form of floating point representation in any language.

For example, it would be inadvisable to write a program containing

```
REAL A
   •
   •
A=4.
   •
   •
IF (SQRT(A).EQ.2.)  GO TO 101
```

because the chances are quite good that SQRT(A) will come out as 2.0000004 or 1.999993 rather than 2.000000.

One should say something like

```
IF (ABS(SQRT(A)-2.).LT..00001) GO TO 101
```

instead.

> Moral
>
> "Do not do arithmetic on floating-point numbers and expect exact answers." Many involved and carefully written programs have been "bugged" because their authors did not know this principle.

APPENDIX I

STRUCTURED, MODULAR, AND SENSIBLE PROGRAMMING

In some senses a program, with a computer executing its instructions, can be considered as a "black box" into which data flow and out of which output and answers come. By calling the program a "black box" it is suggested that the user of such a program need not know how the program does what it does nor what algorithm it follows in order to be able to use it. The user needs only to know what inputs the program expects and what outputs it produces.

There are several difficulties with the idea expressed above. So many, in fact, that the entire process of computer programming is undergoing change. We illustrate these difficulties by first asking questions.

1) Does the program really work correctly in every instance? How can the correctness of the program be shown without an analysis of how it does what it does? Is showing that the program produces correct results in a set of "test cases" sufficient proof of its correctness?

2) If the program is found to contain an error, can it be fixed without unreasonable effort by the person who wrote it -- especially if he/she hasn't looked at it in some time?

3) Suppose the person who wrote the program is not available to make repairs. Can someone else do it?

4) Is there enough information written down about the program so that a person who doesn't know how it works can effectively use it?

5) Suppose that some large information-handling task needs to be done and we decide to do it by having several people participate in the writing of a large computer program. If programmers are people who simply produce "black boxes," can we be assured that the resulting composite program will work correctly?

6) Programs are usually written by people for other people (students for teachers, employees for employers, etc.).

Can the person bearing the general responsibility for the program's correctness examine the program and, with no more than a reasonable amount of effort, follow the program's logic? Can he/she determine the algorithm? Or, if he/she knows the algorithm, can he/she determine if it has been correctly implemented?

All these questions suggest that there is more to programming than simply producing a "working" program.

In the late 1960's serious proposals began to be advanced regarding the structure of programs, primarily to respond to the difficulties reflected by these questions. Some of the techniques used have come to be called, brilliantly enough, structured programming. In this text we have repeatedly made reference to good programming practice -- remember all those shaded boxes. Structured programming might be considered another extension of that idea.

Fractured Programming

The vast majority of programs which have been written since the electronic computer came of age are bad.[1] A bad program is usually bad in several ways:

1) It is incorrect. It does not solve the problem it was intended to solve.

2) It is poorly documented. Thus a person who has a problem similar to the one that the program purports to solve has difficulty using the program.

3) It is untrustworthy. It may be correct but no demonstration of its correctness is presented, so a person using it or relying on its results has no assurance that the answers it produces are right.

4) It is difficult to understand and therefore difficult to modify if the problem changes; further, it is difficult to fix if an error is discovered.

----

[1] With our value judgment "bad" we will tip our hats to the idea expressed in human relations circles that there are no bad people -- only people who sometimes do bad things. Maybe that's a good parallel, but programs don't have feelings, so we will call a program which does bad things, ever, a bad program.

Bad programs are the product of a process which we call <u>fractured programming</u>. It is fractured programming which has produced the image which society quite correctly has of the whole computing industry. If we were engineers our bridges would fall down more often than they would stay up. As a profession we programmers have paid tacit homage to the preposterous belief that a program was good if it obeyed the syntactic rules that the computer prescribed and produced the correct answer. For an industry that has moved as quickly as the automated information-handling industry has, we've been pretty slow to realize that this idea is absurd.

The results of this realization, however belated, have been many and varied. Some of the words associated with the desire to divorce ourselves from fractured programming are: structured programming, modular programming, good programming practice, top down development, bottom up testing, proving program correctness, GOTO-less programming, and others.

<u>Structured Programming: Canonical Forms</u>

Structured programming means different things to different people. But most who talk about structured programming can agree that a few basic ideas are always involved. We look at these ideas first and then proceed to other matters which some call structured programming and others call by other names such as modular programming or good programming practice.

The first core idea is that every algorithm can be expressed in terms of three basic (sometimes called <u>canonical</u>) composition rules. These rules are best illustrated in flowchart form.

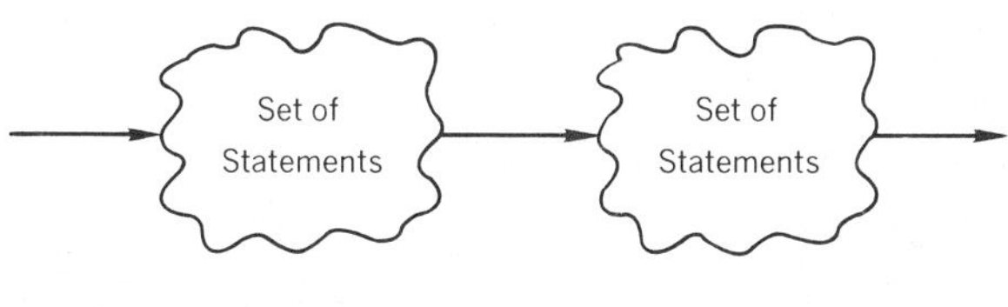

SEQUENCE - (then)

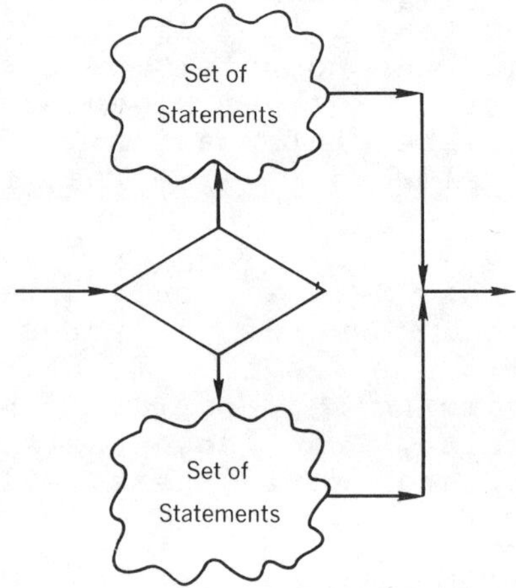

ALTERNATION - (ifthenelse)

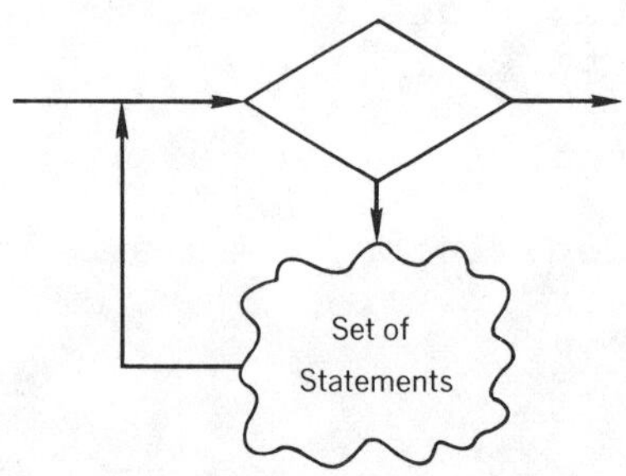

ITERATION - (dowhile)

Notice that each of the forms has but one entrance and one exit. Each of the "set of statements" could itself contain statements which depicted any or all of the three canonical forms, but no other forms. Thus one could have a loop within a loop or a loop following a decision. The canonical composition rules do not in any way exclude nesting. There exists, in fact, a mathematical proof that any algorithm which has but one entrance and one exit (we have previously called this a proper algorithm) can be expressed by using only these three structures.

The sequence structure is included primarily to indicate the basic progression by which algorithmic problem solving takes place. This was illustrated by Lab Problem 00. The alternation structure is based on the idea that a test is made during the execution of a program and the result dictates one of two paths which join and exit from the structure together. This was illustrated first by the Revised Flowchart for Lab Problem 2.

The third form, iteration, indicates that a test is made and, depending on the result of the test, an immediate exit from the structure is made or a set of statements is executed and then the condition is retested. Lab Problem 05 illustrated a form similar to this except that the test was made after the first pass through the statement block. The set of statements must at some time modify the condition being tested for or the loop will continue indefinitely.

North-South Programming

There is nothing particularly magic about the canonical forms. But the fact that all proper algorithms can be represented using only combinations of them suggests that programming might become more of a science than it is presently. It is hard to resist the feeling that some sort of common denominator for the order of program statements has been found. Future benefits may accrue if programs are written using the canonical forms; it is impossible to predict how far-reaching the results will be -- maybe fundamental changes in the ways programs are written, or computers writing programs themselves, or . . .

But there is an immediate advantage in using the canonical forms that is recognized by the "leading edge" of the programming community. That advantage is that programs become much more readable. This occurs partly because the reader knows that he/she needn't deal with more than the three forms. But it also occurs because use of the canonical forms reduces the degree to which the path of control of the program can jump around. For example, an IF statement which leads to two other IF statements, both of which in turn lead to two other IF statements, can send a person trying to read and understand the program into a situation which calls for 15 fingers and at least two heads. And you can almost give up at the outset on a problem such as: "I'm at statement number 13. How many ways could I have gotten here?"

What do the canonical forms offer? They make the logical order of the statements (the dynamic order, the order of execution) more like the physical order (the static order, the order of compilation).

This means that you can read a program from "north to south" when you are trying to understand what it does. There can be no wild transfers of control to distant parts of the program unless the canonical form (or structure) containing the branch extends that far and encompasses everything in between. And there can't be too many of these far-ranging structures, because, given any two structures, either they are consecutive or one contains the other -- they may not overlap.

The effect of this congruence, however rough, between physical order and logical order produces a simplifying effect similar to that which occurs when the base of the number system (say, base 10) is the same as the base of the measuring system (say, metric). While in a theoretical sense the answers may turn out the same whatever measuring system is used, in a practical sense the ease with which the process occurs is substantially increased.

Fortran and North-South Programming

Now that we've had the good news, here is the bad news, Fortran lovers. Many of the features of Fortran are just not compatible with the canonical forms of structured programming. There are some languages set up so that it is easy to program in the canonical forms and others that almost won't permit anything else. But Fortran doesn't fall in either category. If a programmer knew only TSF he/she could probably write structured programs without too much extra difficulty. But many of the features of Fortan, features which make it a powerful language, fly in the face of the canonical forms.

Consider first the ifthenelse form. Fortran offers the logical IF which permits a single statement to be executed if a certain condition is true but skips that statement otherwise. But the construction of the ifthenelse implies that there are <u>two</u> mutually exclusive <u>blocks</u> of statements, one or the other to be executed depending on a condition. To use the logical IF statement in the same way, you are forced into a construction such as:

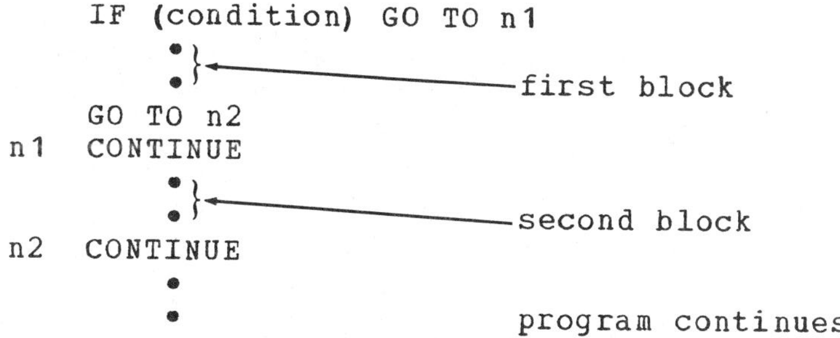

There are other languages, Programming Language One (PL/ONE), for example, which permit a construction completely without statement numbers or labels; this simplifies following the program logic. You could write statements such as:

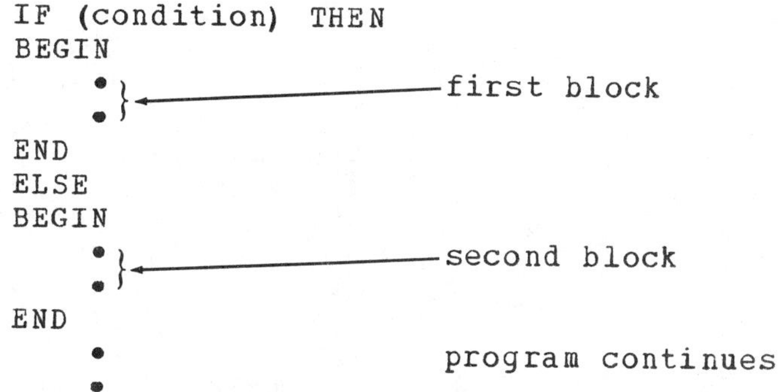

Turning to the dowhile form, we find that the Fortran DO statement is incompatible. The dowhile form specifies a test of some condition <u>prior</u> to entering a block of statements. Fortran does violence to this structure in two ways. First, most Fortran compilers enter the block of statements first and test afterwards; that can create all sorts of mischief. If you doubt that it works this way, try

```
      READ, N
      DO 101 I=1,N
      PRINT, I
  101 CONTINUE
```

with N=0 and watch it rip right through the loop the first time before it knows it wasn't supposed to.

Second, the only test that the Fortran DO permits is that of a loop counter, and an incrementing one at that. You might want to test for lots of other things -- whether the remainder term of a series was less than .003, for example.

Thus the Fortran DO is not a dowhile but is sort of a dountil, and not a very good one at that. To use Fortran to implement the dowhile canonical form you go back to the IF statement:

```
      n1  CONTINUE
          IF (not condition) GO TO n2
             •
             •
          GO TO n1
      n2  CONTINUE
```

If all this seems rather unwieldly, that's because it is. But if you use these structures, and only these, you'd discover that the programs you write would be much easier to read by a person who knew that your program contained only canonical forms. Perhaps the earliest serious suggestion that the structure of programs should conform to some standard was that unconditional transfer statements be banned. This came to be known as <u>GOTO-less</u> programming and its object was, again, to prevent the path of control through a program from hopping all over kingdom come. Clearly some other language than Fortran is needed for true GOTO-less programming. The GO TO statement is <u>the</u> way one transports himself about a Fortran program, canonical forms or no.

After the GOTO-less idea was hatched, however, it was pointed out that the <u>objects</u> of the GOTOs were probably as much at fault as the control-transferring statements themselves. In Fortran, then, we begin to look with suspicion on statement numbers. We have a couple of suggestions regarding a second best to GOTO-less programming which are easily implemented in Fortran and which aid modification and readability of programs greatly:

1) Never put a statement number on any executable statement except a CONTINUE statement. This facilitates program modification (and debugging, should you ever have to do it) and keeps you out of all sorts of trouble related to the ends of DO loops.

   Numbering only CONTINUE statements has an additional advantage when using Comments to explain what a section of the program is doing. If you want to branch to a set of statements, you can insert the Comment after the CONTINUE and before the statements which actually perform the manipulations. For example,

```
        GO TO 138
              •
              •
        GO TO 199
    138 CONTINUE
  C COMPUTES F(X) AND G(X) IF X IS NEGATIVE
        F=-3X**3+11*X
        G=....
```

You could, of course, put 138 on the statement F=... but then you don't have a place to put the Comment that includes it as completely in the section to which it applies.

2) Make each statement label in the program the object of one and only one transfer or DO statement. This makes it possible to know, with relative ease, where a transfer of control came from. It also tends to mark the "heavy traffic intersections" of the program, since several CONTINUEs will occur together there.

Both of these suggestions tend to increase the length of the program. Extra CONTINUE statements, however, add infinitesimally to the compiling time and nothing to the execution time. They are well worth it.

One word of warning: don't try to write programs in structured form from flowcharts that don't exclusively use the canonical forms. While it has been proven that any proper algorithm, and hence any program, can be written using only the canonical forms, doing the writing is something else again. To exemplify, redraw the following flowchart using only the canonical forms.

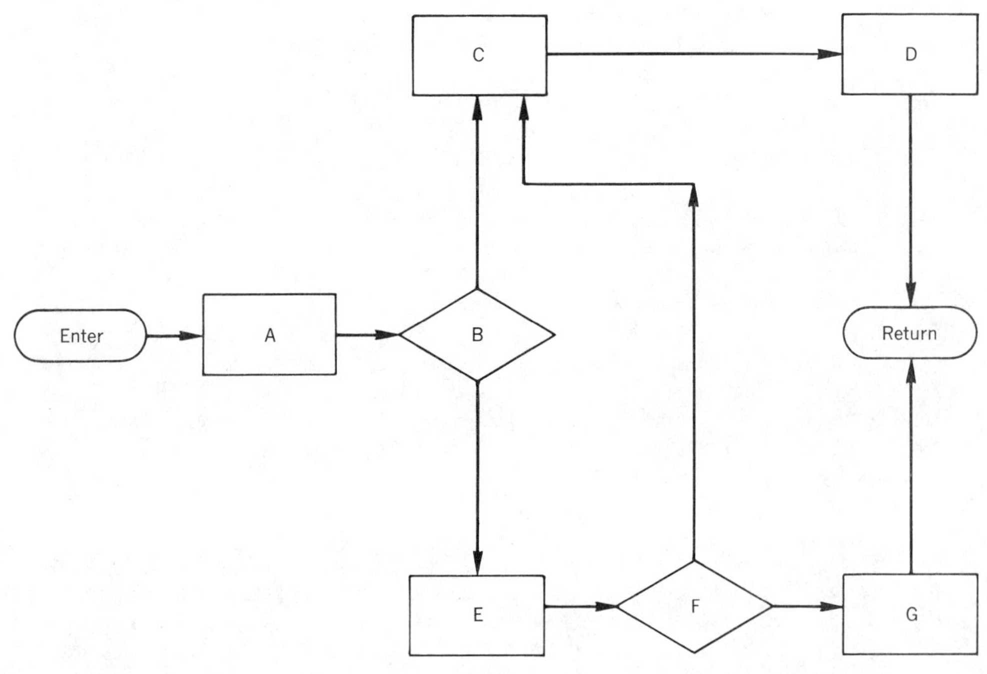

Designing Solutions vs. Solving Problems

By this time you well know what an algorithm is: a stepwise procedure used to solve a problem. If the problem is in terms of symbols then we can write instructions to a symbol manipulator (computer) to follow the algorithm and give us the answer. But while the solution of such a problem takes place in a stepwise fashion, it is not appropriate to plan the solution in a stepwise manner. Most planning, indeed most human conceptualization of complex matters, takes place in quite another way which we call <u>hierarchical</u>. We consider the overall schema or idea first. Then we consider parts of it. If we are careful we look at subparts of each part. At some point we fill in the details.

This isn't to say that you can never plan the solution to a problem in a stepwise fashion, but that such a process frequently leads to a technique of trial and error. If you have the alternative of an overall examination and plan, your chances of success are considerably increased.

When a program exists to solve a problem, there is not really a problem any more. Only time, inclination and resources are required for the solution. But the development of an algorithm or a computer program is a different matter. There is no ready-made stepwise approach for designing a stepwise approach to solve a problem.

Programmers, perhaps because of their associations with computers, frequently attempt to design solutions to problems using the computer's approach to solving problems, i.e., implementing algorithms. Perhaps the most concise way to convey this difference is a cartoon of some time ago depicting a man working at a desk with an electronic brain on the floor beside him. Signs over them read, respectively, THINK and COMPUTE.

Hierarchical Form

There is evidence to suggest that a person can keep in mind only three or four ideas at once. To avoid argument let us say that it is extremely unusual for a person to be able to deal with more than eight thoughts at a time; the more usual number for most of us would be half that. (Try, for example, to hold the names of all five Great Lakes in your mind at the same time.)

Careful consideration of this fact again suggests breaking a complex "thing" down into simpler elements which are related in some hierarchical fashion. An example which is familiar to most of us is the "outline" which gets produced in high school English classes. It has a title, some main ideas usually indicated with Roman numerals, some secondary ideas indicated with capital letters, etc.

The outline is indeed a helpful structure in constructing a piece of writing. It imposes structure in at least two ways: 1) it relates ideas in a hierarchical manner, and 2) it requires uniformity in the ways in which the members of the outline are expressed.

Consider the same principle applied to the construction of computer programs. First, corresponding to the title, we determine what the program is to be all about. Next we determine, on a gross level, what the principal parts of the program are to be. Then we look at each of these basic parts and reapply the principle, determining again the constituent parts. This approach lets us focus our attention on parts of the program, at different levels, with the assurance that all the parts will relate to each other when we finish.

Program Modules

Now that we have beaten you over the head with the preceding two sections regarding hierarchical problem solving, we come to an admonition: DO NOT WRITE ANY BUT THE SIMPLEST PROGRAMS IN A SINGLE, START TO FINISH, SET OF STATEMENTS.

It is difficult to quantify exactly what is meant by the simplest program. The question is similar to asking "What is the maximum number of words a sentence should contain?" A prevalent view is this: if the statements you use in a program or subprogram won't all fit on a single page of program listing, then the program or subprogram is probably attempting to do too much. Consider breaking it up into modules. Obviously, counter examples to this suggestion can be generated. But we feel it is still a good rule of thumb.

The technique by which programs can be partitioned or broken up into sensibly sized modules, each with its logical task to perform, is to use subprograms. Subprograms were originally developed to reduce the amount of computer memory required to solve a problem. (If you need the area of a triangle at three different points in a program, why put the code in three separate times or, alternatively, fuss with making the path of control such that it arrives at the appropriate code at the appropriate time?)

It is becoming apparent that the use of subprogram modules is as useful in the production of better programs as it is in saving memory. Subprogram modules should be used even if the code contained in them is executed only once! The slight additional time it takes to generate the necessary subprogram linkage is a small price to pay for isolating the essential logical elements of a program. (And the price can be reduced if the variables used by both the calling and called program are stored in COMMON rather than as arguments and parameters.)

Top-Down Design

It is not enough, however, to simply divide the program up into segments of code using subprograms. The modules must be related in a structure similar to an outline or a tree. Two words are critical in the development of larger programs: modular and hierarchical. The combination of these two concepts is being called top-down design or top-down programming. While we have used the principle of an outline or tree structure to motivate the idea of hierarchy of elements, the actual hierarchy of computer subprograms can be more complex. As the diagram below illustrates, one subprogram can serve one or more calling programs.[1]

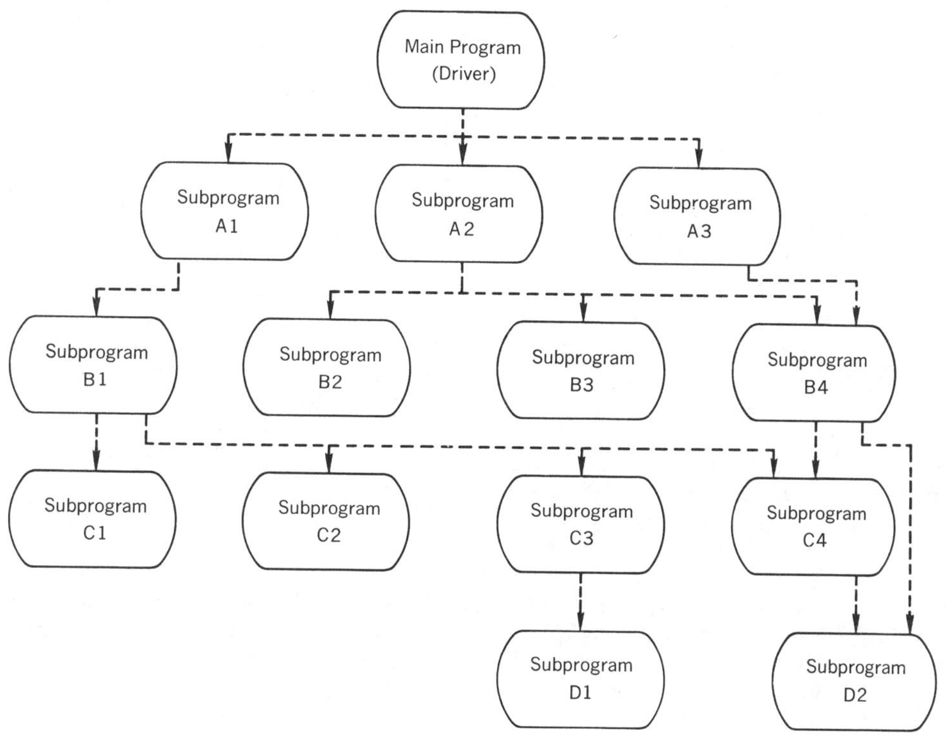

----

[1] In Fortran, a subprogram cannot call a subprogram which called it and a subprogram cannot call itself. In general a subprogram which is active, i.e., has been called and has not returned control to its calling program, may not be called again. In some other languages, reuse of active subprograms is allowed and is called recursion.

Simply looking at the figure in the preceding section does not tell us the order in which each of the elements is produced. The figure simply says that, in the end, all must be present and the linkages among them must agree. How it gets this way is a source of much discussion in the programming community at present. Many now advocate designing and building the most general modules first and testing them using bits of code, called stubs, to simulate the functions of the modules lower in the hierarchy. Others believe in development of the overall design from the top down but testing each of the sub-parts separately. This technique is called _bottom-up testing_, and is done by writing programs called drivers or exercisers, which call and test the modules under a variety of conditions.

Other Ideas for the Near Future

There is another school of thought which believes that the development of good large programs lies to a great extent in the management technique used to coordinate the programmers in their effort. The term _chief programmer team_ depicts such a technique. This technique, a discussion of which is beyond the scope of this book since it relates primarily to the production of programs by teams of people, is combining with other ideas to make the production of large computer programs a far more reliable process. Several years ago a very large computer program was developed by a well known manufacturer and released with several thousand distinct errors. Recently the same manufacturer was able to release another large program which had taken only a fraction as much time to write as the first and yet contained fewer than a dozen errors.

One distinguished member of the field maintains that a great deal of program writing difficulty is avoided if programmers simply have more confidence in the programs they write. His first rule is to avoid making any errors in syntax. There are only two reasons to make syntax errors: lack of knowledge and carelessness. Both can be eliminated by simple human effort.

Another technique which people in the field of programming are beginning to explore is that of _proving program correctness_. This relates to the idea that, since a program is simply a procedure by which symbols are manipulated, a program could be shown to be correct by a mathematical proof. This might seem pretty far fetched at the moment, but we suspect that such proofs will begin showing up in the future, perhaps with the computer itself aiding in the proof. Advances in proving program correctness depend very much on writing programs which use only canonical (or similar) forms.

One idea that has been advanced and somewhat accepted relates to program listing format. The idea is, when a loop occurs within another loop, indent the statements of the inner loop a few spaces. Thus, with several nested loops one sees automatically what level each loop is. The authors have looked at this idea, and some programs thusly written, and have decided to pass. A few strokes of the pen while looking over the listing will better outline the loops, in the manner shown in Part II. Program listings are not novels and should be read for understanding with a pen in hand anyway. Besides, outlining the loops is a good place to begin as you sit, peering darkly at the listing, wondering why the hell it didn't run _this_ time.

Program Testing

Proving program correctness is a different process from _showing program correctness_, which the business of testing is all about. Again, there is much debate about the role of design, algorithm, and program testing. We will say simply that testing is a necessary but not sufficient process for arriving at a belief that a program is correct. Put more pessimistically by one of the acknowledged authorities in the field: program testing can be used to show the presence of bugs but never their absence.

Actually this statement, while it may have the effect of ruining your afternoon, does not suggest that testing is not worth doing nor even that it is unimportant. Showing the presence of bugs is a worthwhile endeavor. A program can only have so many -- though that can be a lot -- and every one you find means there is one less. The more extensive and creative your testing is, the higher your probability of finding all of them. Secondly, while you can never be sure that there aren't any bugs in a program, if you've done careful testing you begin to develop this confidence that "by George, this thing might be OK." After all, no one guarantees that the sun will rise every day, but observation suggests...

Testing should be an integral part of programming; debugging should not. Write your programs carefully, test each part separately to the extent that you can. Consider any errors which show up as a serious attack on your quality as a programmer. Ask why they happened. On an overall basis probably more time is spent debugging programs than is spent writing them in the first place. That's an awful statistic. And the reason for it is that many programmers are careless. A prevalent attitude seems to be: some errors are inevitable -- why not go whole hog?

The most important thing about testing, bar none, is the will to do it. It really does take fortitude, not to mention time and thought, to try to find fault with something you have just created. If you are dedicated to really doing a good job of testing, half the battle is won.

Entire books could be written about testing. The procedures are different depending on the application and on the potential weak spots. What follows are thoughts which you might find appropriate. One is to let the machine do some of the testing for you. Build internal checks in the program, even if they might be removed later. Don't overlook the possibility that you can use the computer to generate test data for you.

It is important to develop several sets of test data. Start with a small set for which you know the answers. If your program handles that OK, go on to more stringent data. If the program seems to do well when it is being given good input, try data which will exercise some of the error-checking loops. Will it tell you what's wrong? Will it blissfully pretend that a zero by zero matrix is fine? Or that a 28 foot tall person is OK?

It seems surprising that a program can pass many artificial tests, no matter how punishing, and can fail with the real data that are supposedly correct, polished, and well behaved. Surprising, but it happens. Part of your test data should be real data for which you know the answers. Whether the data you use is real or artificial, you should calculate the answers ahead of time and then compare them with the computer's results. If you get the program output and then try to verify the results by hand, the chances are that you'll succeed -- even if the computer's answers are wrong.

One of the most innovative techniques for program testing, if you have the ego for it, is <u>game testing</u>. The procedure goes like this: you write the most idiot-proof code you can. Then give it to a person who has agreed to test it for you. He/she may not alter the code (unless you haven't sequence-numbered the cards, in which case it is his/her prerogative to drop the deck, leaving you to pick it up), but may subject it to the most punishing tests which can be devised. He/she attempts to break the program by giving it bad data, misreading the documentation, misinterpreting the results, etc. If your opponent is bright and dedicated to the project, and the process continues with you modifying the code each time he/she finds a bug or weak spot, ultimately you will have a sturdy section of code.

Finally, don't let anything the least bit peculiar slip by without an explanation. "Inconsequential" errors have a way of developing into full blown disasters at the most awkward times. There is really no such thing as a "small" error or a "little" bug in a program. A computer program is made up of a finite number of discrete symbols: either they are all there in the proper order or they are not. Program correctness is a binary property: it either exists or it doesn't.

Program Documentation

Computers, unfortunately, "generate" a lot of paper in a hurry. Among other things this means that programmers accumulate a lot of listings. The temptation is to heave them (that is, submit them for recycling) at the earliest possible opportunity. Our advice: DON'T. Keep preliminary runs, tests, debugging sorties, and the like until the project is finished, really complete. Many times being able to return to the listing of a version of the program which worked (before you added three bells and two whistles) can save your neck. Further, if you plan modifications to a working program, get a duplicate card copy of the program deck before you start rifling through the original.

When you undertake to write a program, begin a file folder or notebook for the project. Save every scrap of paper that pertains until the entire thing is done. The actions and thought processes that seem so clear today may fade into fog in a week unless you have some documentation, however informal, to remind you of them.

Programming becomes especially difficult for any but very small programs when the program specifications are not clearly defined prior to commencement of coding or program writing. These specifications should include not only a crisp description of the objectives of the program(s), but also careful logic descriptions and definitions of all variable names and their uses. Flowcharts can provide the logic descriptions; tabular listings showing the variable names, types, lengths, and usages are needed to prevent confusion in variable assignments. Record layouts, showing each input and output record, each field, its length and description and variable name, are needed. Duplicating this information in the form of Comment cards is usually desirable so that such information also remains with the Fortran program.

Additional documentation improves program use further. The author of the program and the date written should be shown as Comment cards at the beginning of the program. Each time program modifications are made, the author and date of the modifications should be shown as Comment cards.

All Fortran statements should be sequence-numbered and identified in card columns 73-80. One approach is to identify each modification in Comment cards near the beginning of the program as the 1st, 2nd, 3rd, etc. modification. Then use card columns 73 and 74 for the modification number (use 00 in the original program), columns 75 and 76 as the first two characters of the program name, and columns 77-80 as sequence number columns.

Other program documentation could include the author's views of how to modify the program(s) in the future to provide added facilities such as larger arrays or smaller memory requirements.

In addition, a users' guide is needed if persons other than the author are to use the program(s). The users' guide should restate the program objectives and should explain, to some degree, the methods and algorithms employed, program limitations, the meaning of messages which come from the program(s), resource requirements such as memory usage, disk or tape usage, running-time estimates, options within the program(s) and a deck set-up to run the program. In some cases, even further documentation is necessary.

The typical reaction to all of this is a very negative one. People who like to program often dislike documenting. It is often said that if people did all of this "extra" work, many fewer programs would be written and productivity would suffer.

This attitude has been responsible for disaster in the computing industry because, without proper documentation programs cannot be easily modified -- long time periods for modification result and large numbers of new errors are introduced.

The major point to consider here is that writing a program in the shortest possible time can never be a reasonable goal. The program must operate correctly to be useful and almost always it will be modified many times during its economic life.

Significant programs often require several man-months for the coding and testing phases alone. In some companies, because programmers neither like documentation nor are many of them good at it, special technical writers are employed to improve the entire process. However it is done, it is necessary.

Program Size

For some reason, many people beginning in the computer field seize upon the misguided idea that a primary goal of a good programmer is to write a program with as few Fortran statements as is possible. In fact, some people strike up contests where a prize or a bet rides upon minimizing the number of statements. Except for the academic exercise, there is little practical value in this.

The definition of an efficient program depends upon the circumstances of the institution involved. There is usually a natural trade-off between the amount of computer memory that a program occupies and the running time of the program. If a company uses a computer with a small memory, then perhaps program size should be minimized. But the number of program statements is not necessarily a good measure of storage requirements. Careful attention to data storage types and usage can often be more productive. Sometimes many more statements are required to allow a program to occupy less storage. One technique frequently used with some computer systems is that of overlay. This means that during program execution, portions of a program are brought into the computer memory, overlaying (erasing) other portions which are no longer needed.

Running time required is often the critical variable. Optimizing running time may require writing many Fortran statements in excess of the minimum. For example, converting data into INTEGER form prior to computation can reduce execution time but may require additional statements.

And the ability to maintain programs is a most important consideration. Most significant programs are modified often. The ability of computing people to respond to the needs of others may be the difference between success and failure, and writing programs with straightforward, simple logic, well commented and easily understood, may be the best response. This also usually requires writing more than the minimum number of Fortran statements.

So, no matter what variable of importance is the primary one for minimization, the number of statements in the program is rarely, by itself, important.

Elegance vs. Efficiency

There are unfortunately no good rules governing whether a particular shortcut should be taken. Clearly there are times when it is insane to follow the formal expression of a problem solution exactly. (For example, the computation of n! calls for multiplying by the value one. Who is going to write a program which does that?) On the other hand many programmers write horrendous sections of code which bear little or no resemblance to the formal process they are supposed to depict except that (hopefully) they provide equivalent answers.

Now that we've thrown out the two extremes we are left with a more difficult problem. What are the appropriate actions of a programmer who must compromise between elegance and efficiency? Basically the answer is simple. You document what you have done, starting with the formal description of your computation, and then you detail those techniques used to make the process more efficient.

Unless the explanation is terribly involved, a very good place to do this is right in the program listing itself. If there are reasons at times not to put such explanations in the listing, then the listing should certainly contain a complete reference to the document in which the explanation occurs.

APPENDIX J

DEBUGGING: IN GENERAL AND IN WATFOR-FIV

"An ounce of prevention is worth a pound of cure." This trite expression is nowhere truer than in the field of computer programming.

Debugging is a difficult thing to talk about because so much of what you do depends on what you did wrong in the first place. And trying to think about where you were least careful in the programming process frequently provides a clue regarding the source of the problem(s).

We could take the hard line and simply exhort you not to make any mistakes, but, having made one ourselves once, we understand that it can happen. So we follow here with some general thoughts about debugging and avoiding the need for it, as well as some features in WATFOR/FIV which aid in the process.

The "Throw It at the Machine" Syndrome

There is a tendency to write a computer program quickly, keypuch it quickly, and submit it to the machine quickly; the rationale is that "the computer can debug it for me." The computer can find syntactical errors in statements and find some coarse errors in logic such as transfers to non-existent statement numbers. But these are the errors which are easy to catch anyway. What the computer cannot do is find most errors in logic -- if you said X=A+B when you meant X=A-B or IF (D.EQ.E) rather than IF (D.NE.E).

There are two major ways to find logic errors. One is to run the program with data -- test data, hopefully -- and notice that the answers are wrong. But if you are in such a rush to get "on the air" with your program, the chances that you'll carefully check it with test data are small. A second approach is to step carefully through the algorithm. This should be done at both the flowchart stage and the program stage. For difficult sections of logic the "how would I follow this algorithm if I were an idiot?" approach works quite nicely. Define a schematic computer on paper and, with pencil in one hand and eraser in the other, go through the logic.

The person who simply sets up a program in a hurry and tosses it at the computer is wasting both machine time and his/her own. Much more time will be spent debugging such a program than would have been spent in doing it right the first time. Add to all this the amazing satisfaction you feel when a complicated program works the first time and you have several powerful arguments for careful desk checking of logic, syntax, data, and all keypunched material.

The "Data-Naiveness" Syndrome

A frequent source of difficulty in programming centers around the use of invalid or incorrect data. It is important for programmers to know the values of data especially during the debugging or testing phase of program development. The rule is simple: print out the input data and check it carefully. There is no substitute for knowing that the right values went in.

The "One-More-Bug" Syndrome

Most computer programmers are hard-working, clever people who have a great deal of self-confidence in their programming ability. It is difficult, early in their careers, for them to believe that they make many mistakes. Consequently, when a program does not operate properly, a common thought is that there is "a" bug. But in reality, there are probably several or many errors remaining. The result of this syndrome is to elicit behavior which consists of finding what appears to be "the" bug, rerunning the program, finding what appears to be "the" bug, rerunning ... It is a good bet that, if an error exists, more than one error exists. Believing that can result in a more thorough look at the program statements even after "the" bug has been located.

The "It-Cannot-Be-I" Syndrome

Prevalent in beginning programmers is the general belief that the machine must have made an error. Since programming logic can be complex and subtle, programming errors usually do not pop out of the page. Because the programmer has been so intensely involved in the logic of the program, a mistake can often be overlooked many times. Therefore, after poring over the logic dozens (or even hundreds) of times without seeing an error, the "natural" conclusion is that someone else (aha, the computer) has committed an error. A computer almost never produces an error because most computers are designed to make quite a fuss when a failure occurs. Frequently a person completely unfamiliar with the program under development can rather quickly spot errors which the programmer has passed over many times before. As noted earlier, an undefined variable can produce different symptoms on each run which can effectively reinforce the It-Cannot-Be-I Syndrome.

The "Now It's Finished for All Time" Myth

Most computer programs are similar to living organisms: they either change or die. When designing a computer program, the programmer can begin to imagine what types of changes may be reasonably desired in the future. With this in mind, the program can be designed to accommodate future change more easily. For example, instead of using the same constant in many different statements, a variable which is defined early in the program or read as data can be used. Then, if that value is to change, one program or data change will be required rather than a change to each of the many statements using that constant. An additional complication is that one or more statements using that constant could be overlooked when change is required.

A major source of programming error is changing program objectives or specifications during program development. When changes are needed after a program is partially written, programmers must either begin again or start patching and inserting new logic into existing logic. While the former approach may often be superior, it is seldom feasible. Therefore programs often become nightmares because program functions are changed without proper care. The use of flowcharts can minimize the adverse impact of change; the constant creation and revision of flowcharts force the programmer to define more carefully the initial program and set forth the precise changes when program modification is needed.

Centralizing input and output is also beneficial in coping with change and in reducing errors introduced by change. If all input and output is centralized somewhere within a program, then changes to input data types or numbers of variables can be more easily and effectively handled.

After six months without seeing a program, the programmer usually forgets about the logic and subtle aspects of a program. Comments imbedded into the program can help refresh a poor remembrance and an up-to-date flow chart can be especially useful here also.

Debugging Aids in WATFOR/FIV

Most major compilers have a specific set of debugging aids. What follows are some of those for the WATFOR and WATFIV compilers. If you are using another compiler, find out what helps are available.

In WATFOR/FIV the best and most frequently used debugging features are the extensive error messages. They give, usually, very good information about a wide variety of program bugs, during both compilation and execution. In particular, they tell you if you attempt to use a variable you haven't defined -- that's probably "Stupid Mistake Number 1" on the programmer's Hit Parade -- and if you attempt to use an illegal subscript. Many compilers simply let these devastating errors slip by with never a murmur, or with a curt "you blew it." The WATFOR/FIV error messages are safety devices -- good to have when you need, bad to develop a dependency on. Each time you get an error message you should think seriously about why it happened. Then make changes in the way you produce programs to reduce the probability that it will happen again. You might even start a log of "Boo-boo's I Have Made." A year of writing down your programming goofs would probably make quite a good programmer out of you.

Well, so much for the sermonizing; here are some other ways WATFOR/FIV can help debugging. These aids in debugging are not found in other Fortran compilers. You should be conservative about the use of these features, since once employed, they must be removed prior to transporting a program to another compiler. On the other hand, WATFIV is often used in the debugging stages of Fortran program development and later the program is converted for use with another compiler for production runs.

The (no kidding) Zigamorph (WATFIV Only)

Where a Fortran program is to employ some statements only for use with WATFIV, and these statements are to be deleted prior to re-compiling with another Fortran compiler, the use of the zigamorph can be productive. The zigamorph is a character which is a combination of 6 different keypunch characters and is not valid when using Fortran compilers other than WATFIV. But WATFIV stops scanning a Fortran statement when it encounters a zigamorph. Therefore, notations or reminders can be keypunched to the right of a zigamorph without affecting the validity of a WATFIV statement.

The zigamorph is a combination of the six punches & - 0 7 8 9 all punched into the same card column. A zigamorph can also be produced by multipunching the characters Z,P, H. (To punch several characters in a single column depress the multipunch key -- mult pch -- and hold it down while striking the characters.) For purposes of this text, a zigamorph will be represented by the character •. An example of the use of the zigamorph is:

```
PRINT, 'OK HERE' •DELETE THIS STATEMENT
```

Since the comment above is to the right of the zigamorph, it is not examined by the WATFIV compiler and only the statement to the left is used in the program, although the entire statement is printed on the source listing.

DUMPLIST Statement (WATFIV Only)

The DUMPLIST statement causes the names and values of specified variables to be printed if a program is terminated because of an error condition. The form is:

```
DUMPLIST /name/ list
```

where "list" is a list of variable names separated by commas. The word "name"is an identifier for the list of variables; it must be unique in the program and follow the normal conventions for naming variables. For example,

```
DUMPLIST/PROB1/N,X,Y
```

If the program or subprogram in which the above statement appeared were terminated because of an error condition, "PROB1" would be printed followed by the names and values of the variables shown in the list. If a subscripted variable name were included in the list, then all elements of that variable would be printed. If no values have yet been assigned, UUUU... is printed. When an error condition occurs, WATFIV generates output for all DUMPLIST lists appearing in the program or any subprograms which have been entered. The values printed are those which the variables contained when the program terminated.

Care should be exercised in using the DUMPLIST statements so that large amounts of needless outputs are not generated. It is wise to list only a few of the key variables. An example of usage follows:

```
      REAL A(4)
      DUMPLIST/MAIN/I,A
      DO 6 I=1,4
      READ, A(I)
 6    CONTINUE
      CALL SUB1 (A)
      RETURN
      END
      SUBROUTINE SUB1 (A)
      REAL A(4)
      DUMPLIST/SUB/X,Y
      X=A(2)*A(4)
      Y=A(1)/A(3)
      PRINT, X,Y
      RETURN
      END
```

In the above program, if an error occurs prior to the CALL (e.g., a data field being read is invalid), the contents of I and A will be printed. If an error occurs after the CALL (e.g., A(3) is equal to zero), the contents of X and Y will also be printed.

ON ERROR (WATFIV Only)

Another useful debugging tool is a statement of the form:

```
ON ERROR GO TO n
```

where n is a statement number in the program. This allows a program which has encountered an error to recover and take alternative, corrective, or other action. This feature can be activated only once in a program; however, any number of ON ERROR statements may appear in the source program. The last ON ERROR statement encountered before an error occurs is called the <u>active</u> statement and is the one which is executed. An example is:

```
ON ERROR GO TO 93
```

If some error occurs during the execution of the program in which the above statement is active, control will be transferred to statement number 93. For example:

```
      ON ERROR GO TO 93
      READ, VAL
        •
        •
        •
93    PRINT, 'BAD INPUT DATA'
```

If an error were encountered when reading a value into VAL, control would transfer to statement 93 and "BAD INPUT DATA" would be printed.

<u>Tracing (WATFIV Only)</u>

A feature exists to print the Instruction Sequence Number (ISN) of each statement in a set of statements each time any of those statements is executed. The ISN is the column of sequential numbers found at the extreme left of a program listing. Great care must be exercised in using this feature since vast amounts of output can result. Tracing is initiated by placing a $ISNON card (punched in columns 1-6) anywhere after an executable statement. Following that card, the ISN of <u>every</u> statement executed will be printed <u>each</u> <u>time</u> the statement is executed until a $ISNOFF is encountered. A $ISNOFF card suspends tracing. The program below:

```
    $JOB               SAM STUDENT
1             INTEGER I,S
2             S=0
    $ISNON
3             DO 1 I=1,3
4         1   S=S+I
    $ISNOFF
5             PRINT, 'FINISHED'
6             RETURN
7             END
    $ENTRY
```

would result in the following output:

```
***   ISN=  3  IN ROUTINE M/PROG ***
***   ISN=  4  IN ROUTINE M/PROG ***
***   ISN=  4  IN ROUTINE M/PROG ***
***   ISN=  4  IN ROUTINE M/PROG ***
FINISHED
```

M/PROG refers to the Main Program; if the $ISNON were in a subprogram, the subprogram name would be printed.

TRAPS (WATFIV Only)

TRAPS is a WATFIV subroutine which allows the programmer to control the activity of interrupts caused by errors in the program. Normally, WATFIV allows an unlimited number of fixed overflows but terminates execution of the program when any of the following occur: exponent overflows, exponent underflows, fixed divide interrupts, floating divide interrupts.

TRAPS allows the programmer to control the number of each of these conditions that will be tolerated before the program is terminated. The form of the CALL to TRAPS is:

```
CALL TRAPS (i,j,k,l,m)
```

where i, j, k, etc., are INTEGER variables or constants with the following meanings:

i = the number of fixed overflows tolerated,
j = the number of exponent overflows tolerated,
k = the number of exponent underflows tolerated,
l = the number of fixed divide interrupts tolerated,
m = the number of floating divide interrupts tolerated.

The default setting of these counters is:

i=infinity, j=1, k=1, l=1, m=1

TRAPS uses five counters that are set according to the CALL statement. The appropriate counter is decreased by one each time a particular interrupt occurs. When a counter goes to zero, the program is terminated. TRAPS may be CALLed any number of times. Each time a CALL is made, the counters are reset. To change the values of some counters but not others, specify a zero for those values which are not to be changed.

APPENDIX K

CONVERSATIONAL COMPUTING

In what can be termed batch processing or batch computing, a deck of cards is entered into the computer, processed, and the results obtained at a later time. Batch computing is the mode the student is probably most used to. Conversational computing, on the other hand, involves a person sitting at a computer terminal (usually a teletype, a typewriter-type terminal or a TV-like cathode-ray terminal). The terminal is connected, via telephone lines, usually, to a computer. In this conversational mode, the programmer can type a program, execute it, modify the program, re-execute it, etc. In addition, interactive programs are possible, where the program asks a question of the user. Based upon that answer the program proceeds. This dialogue can continue to allow an interaction between people and computers not easily possible with traditional batch processing. Further, users located at significant distances from a central computer can have access to a computer's capability via conversational computing at reasonably low costs.

CALL/OS Fortran

CALL/OS is a terminal-oriented, conversational programming system distributed by the IBM Company. Using CALL/OS, one can type a Fortran program and execute it immediately, correct errors, and rerun the program any number of times. CALL/OS contains a large subset of the Fortran language. The discussion which follows assumes that the terminal being used possesses both upper and lower-case letters, though terminals exist having only upper-case letters. The description that follows relates to an IBM 2741 terminal. After typing a line, you always press the RETURN key. If other types of terminals are used, then other keys might be used at the end of a line of input depending upon the terminal and the computer configuration.

To use CALL/OS Fortran you dial the phone number of the computer according to the procedures at your particular installation. After you dial up a computer it will request of you a certain amount of information such as account number, password, etc. Then type logon

The computer will respond by typing

ready

Then type:

enter fortran

to indicate that you want to use the Fortran processor. (Actually, CALL/OS can process two other computer languages also -- BASIC and PL/I -- and if you want to write programs in those languages, type the appropriate language name. Here, of course, we are concerned with Fortran only.)

At this point, begin typing Fortran statements, preceding each by a unique line number. The line number indicates the order in which the statements will later be executed. Usually the statements you type should be in lower case.

For example:

```
10   n=0

20   x=0
```

One or more blank spaces follow the line number. When a Fortran statement number is to be included, it follows the line number. For example:

```
35   7 format(i5)
```

Here the line number is 35 and the Fortran statement number is 7. Do not confuse statement numbers with line numbers; only statement numbers can be referred to by the program.

Although CALL/OS Fortran allows FORMAT-free input and output, it does not recognize

```
READ, A,B,C
```

or

```
PRINT, A,B,C
```

Instead, one writes

```
read(5,*) a,b,c
```

or

```
write(6,*)a,b,c
```

which perform the same functions. Unit 5 signifies input from the terminal and Unit 6 signifies output to the terminal. The '*' in place of a FORMAT statement number indicates that the data are to be read or written in free format form.

To provide FORMAT-free data, type numbers with blanks or commas separating them. To illustrate, suppose you type the following program:

```
10    2 read (5,*)x,y
20      b=sqrt(x)*y
30      write(6,*)b
40      go to 2
50      end
```

After the program has been entered, type

```
run
```

This is a CALL/OS command. Notice that commands begin with an alphabetic character whereas Fortran statements begin with a line number. Commands are executed immediately whereas Fortran statements are simply recorded for future use. When the

```
run
```

command is typed, the Fortran program is compiled (or translated) and execution begins if no machine-discoverable errors are found. With the above program, the computer will next type a question mark indicating that it has encountered a READ statement and wants data. At this point you can type

```
144,2
```

and the computer will type

```
24.
?
```

indicating that your answer is 24 and that, again, a READ statement has been encountered. The program will continue looping through these instructions until you press the ATTN key (on an IBM 2741) or the BREAK key (on a teletype-compatible terminal). At any time the ATTN key can be pressed to stop whatever the computer is doing and return control to the mode which allows you to type commands.

After a program has been input, corrections or changes are often necessary. To change or correct a statement, simply retype that statement using the original line number: the original statement is erased and replaced by the new one. Each time the

```
run
```

command is issued, the program is recompiled and re-executed. New statements can be inserted between existing statements by using a line number which is numerically between the statements involved. For example,

```
10      a=3
20      write(6,*)a
15      a=a+1
run
```

would result in the number 4 being output because the line numbers specify the order in which the statements will be executed.

To obtain a fresh, sequenced typeout of a program, issue the command

```
list
```

This will cause all of the statements to be typed. If a program is large and you only want to list part of it, say beginning at line number 125, then type

```
list 125
```

This will cause the typeout to begin at line number 125. The typeout will continue either until the end of the program is reached or until you press the ATTN key, whichever comes first.

Changes can be made to a particular statement by typing:

replace nn, 's1', 's2'

where nn is the line number, s1 is character string to be changed, and s2 is the character string to replace s1. Both s1 and s2 must be enclosed in single quotes.

Many other commands exist in CALL/OS. A few of them are shown below. The save command,

save name

where name is up to 8 characters in length, saves a source program which is then available for future use. After a program has been saved, it can be run by issuing the command:

run name

or it can be brought out of the library for modification by typing:

load name

or it can be erased by typing:

purge name

To terminate the terminal session, type

off

APPENDIX L

A VERY BRIEF CHRONOLOGY OF COMPUTING

There are two branches of the computer family: digital and analog. A digital computer obtains answers by manipulation of discrete quantities. These quantities might be beads on a stick (as in an abacus), magnetized spots on magnetic tape, electrical pulses, etc. Analog computers obtain answers by making some continuous physical analog of mathematical quantities. The physical quantity might be length (as in a slide rule), pressure, voltage, etc.

This appendix, indeed this book, deals only with digital or discrete computers as opposed to analog or continuous computers. But the dichotomy between discrete and continuous phenomena is so interesting on so many levels that we might take a moment to reflect on it. The Western world seems to be making a move toward the use of discrete systems and away from continuous ones. Some examples: 1) Programs have been written for digital computers to instruct them to simulate analog computers. 2) The pocket-sized digital electronic calculator, though several times more expensive, is replacing that genesis of analog computing devices, the trustworthy sliderule. 3) Digital clocks and watches seem to be shoving their analogue counterparts toward antiquity.

(An interesting liability to society created by the move to digital time pieces is illustrated by the recent observation of a seven year old. She could "tell time" just fine, but terms such as <u>clockwise</u> and <u>two-o'clock position</u> meant nothing to her. We may have to come up with some new concepts.)

Below in the briefest possible form we describe what seem to us to be the major events in the development of digital computing as it exists today.

<u>Year</u>	<u>Event or Machine</u>
circa 600 B.C.	Abacus comes into use - inventor unknown.

1642 A.D. Blaise Pascal of France builds the first adding machine.

1694 Gottfried Wilhelm Leibnitz completes "stepped reckoner" - an adding machine which "carries" automatically.

1786 J. H. Muller conceives idea of an automatic computer - never built.

1822 Charles Babbage of England builds a small model of a "mechanical difference engine" for computation of logarithm and similar tables; persuades British government to spend a million dollars in its development; engine not completed during his lifetime.

1830 Babbage conceives an "analytical engine" which has many characteristics of modern day computers even though it is mechanical and not electronic in design. This machine is never completed but involves brilliant parallels to modern computers.

1890 Herman Hollerith uses a forgotten Babbage idea and develops the punched card and a battery of equipment to process data stored on it: sorter, tabulator, etc. The U.S. Census Bureau, which discovers it isn't going to get the 1880 census published before 1890, sponsors the work. The Hollerith card, now also referred to as the punched card or IBM card, is the same size as the U.S. currency of that day.

1930 International Business Machines Corporation (IBM) markets its 600 series of calculating card punches which use relays as memory units - not computers except in the most rudimentary sense.

1938-1944 Various people and organizations invent, build, and experiment with electro-mechanical components and computers which take instructions from cards or magnetic tape and perform arithmetic operations.

Important, among others, are George R. Stibitz, Samuel B. Williams, and E. G. Andrews of Bell Telephone Laboratories who develop the "ballistic computer" and the Mark 22 Error Computer. The largest electro-mechanical computer ever to be built is the Harvard Mark I computer developed under the direction of Howard Aiken with the help of IBM.

1945 John von Neumann, working with J. P. Eckert and John Mauchly, proposes EDVAC (Electronic Discrete Variable Computer) which uses its memory to store both numbers and instructions for the operations it is to carry out. Thus the idea of the "stored program" is born.

1946 ENIAC (Electronic Numerical Integrator and Calculator) is completed by Mauchly and Eckert at the University of Pennsylvania; ENIAC is the first large scale electronic digital computer.

1947 The Association for Computing Machinery is founded.

A computer is built at Manchester University in England, using an electrostatic storage memory system called the Williams tube and a rotating magnetic drum for auxilary storage.

1948 The IBM CPC (Card Programmed Calculator) is developed by Northrup Corporation and IBM.

From 1949 on the history is largely related to the introduction of information processing systems by various groups and manufacturers. Some of the more important are listed below because of technical innovation, popularity, or because they represent a manufacturer's entry into the field. Adjectives describing a machine as large, fast, or popular apply to the state of the art at the time the machine was introduced.

1949 EDSAC (Electronic Delay Storage Automatic Calculator) - first computer to utilize the stored program concept - completed in Cambridge, England, under the direction of Maurice Wilkes.

BINAC (Eckert and Mauchly Computer Company) - sponsored by the Bureau of the Census.

1950 SEAC (Standard Eastern Automatic Computer) - first stored program computer operating in the U. S. - at the Bureau of Standards.

Whirlwind I, developed at MIT - uses a magnetic core memory also developed at MIT. Jay W. Forrester directs the project.

UNIVAC 1101 - ERA 1101; Eckert-Mauchly merge with Engineering Research Associates and the rotating magnetic drum 1101 is produced.

Digital plotting equipment makes its debut; later to be connected to computers, this equipment will make it possible to draw graphs and pictures - and a picture is worth more than 1024 words.

1951 SWAC (Standards Western Automatic Computer) - UCLA.

UNIVAC I (Universal Automatic Computer) - Eckert-Mauchly Computer Corporation - first installed at the Bureau of the Census. Features include a magnetic tape system whose operation is overlapped with arithmetic computation.

Whirlwind at MIT has attached to it a Cathode Ray Tube (CRT) as an output device. This innovation is to be added to a year later when a "light gun" or "light pen" is attached allowing the user to manipulate information on the TV-like screen and in the memory.

1952 MANIAC I - Los Alamos.

ORDVAC - University of Illinois.

EDVAC is finally finished at the University of Pennsylvania.

IAS COMPUTER - stored program computer using a cathode ray tube memory - (Institute for Advanced Studies, Princeton) - is completed by von Neumann.

ILLIAC (Illinois Automatic Computer) - University of Illinois.

1953 ORACLE (Oak Ridge Automatic Computer and Logical Engine) at the Atomic Energy Installation in Oak Ridge, Tennessee.

IBM 701 - Defense Calculator.

UNIVAC 1103 - powerful scientific computer with cathode ray storage and parallel arithmetic.

1954 JOHNIAC - named for John von Neumann - built at Rand Corporation.

DATATRON - Electro Data Corporation - machine features hardware index registers, hardware floating point, and a random access magnetic strip storage scheme.

IBM 650 - highly popular scientific machine with a high speed magnetic drum memory and auxiliary magnetic disk memory, RAMAC.

Late in 1954 Philco Corporation develops the surface barrier transistor; vacuum tubes will soon be on their way out as computer components. The change from tubes to transistors will mark the beginning of second generation computing equipment in about three years.

1955 NORC - giant IBM computer built for the U.S. Naval Weapons Laboratory.

BENDIX G-15 - popular small scale drum computer.

IBM 705 - first large scale computer to use a magnetic core memory.

1956 IBM 704 - popular, large, scientific machine. IBM and some of its customers write an algebraic compiler or formula translator called FORTRAN for the IBM 704. High level computing languages thus become part of the computing scene, opening up computer use to those in other fields.

BIZMAC - RCA's entry into the computing field.

LGP 30 - popular, small drum computer by Librascope Corporation.

E101 - Burroughs' first marketed computer.

1957 UNIVAC II produced by Remington-Rand; it has core memory.

TX-0 is produced by Lincoln Laboratories - it uses Philco's surface barrier transistor. The second generation of computing equipment has dawned.

DATAMATIC 1000 is produced by Honeywell and, indirectly, by Raytheon.

1958 IBM 709 is marketed - large scientific computer with tubes, core memory.

PHILCO 2000 - features include transistors, tape drives and data channels.

BURROUGHS 220 - last major vacuum tube computer.

UNIVAC solid state 80/90 - medium-sized second generation drum machine.

A general high level language, ALGOL-58, is introduced. Though never in as wide use in this country as Fortran it is more elegant and has a profound effect on the development of future high level languages.

1959 IBM 1620 - highly popular, small scientific machine of the second generation.

ATLAS design is completed at Manchester University in England; time-shared machine using a paging concept.

NCR 304 - earliest second generation business machine.

IBM 7090 - large, fast, highly popular scientific machine - a solid state IBM 709.

RCA 501 - business machine featuring the Common Business Oriented Language compiler (COBOL).

GE 210 - marks General Electric's entry into the computing field.

1960 CDC 1604 - first machine by Control Data Corporation - fast, solid state.

UNIVAC LARC - giant computer built by Remington-Rand for the Atomic Energy Commission.

IBM 7070 - popular, large business computer.

CDC 160 - popular business-oriented machine.

PDP 1 - first major machine by Digital Equipment Corporation.

IBM 1401 - highly popular, medium-sized business machine.

HONEYWELL 800 - features a multiprogramming system - business machine.

IBM develops a major remote terminal system for handling passenger reservation for American Airlines: SABRE.

1961 RCA 301 - popular small business machine.

IBM STRETCH (7030) - giant second generation machine built for the Atomic Energy Commission.

University of Waterloo produces an 11,000 statement-per-minute Fortran compiler called WATFOR. This development brings the cost of educating large groups of students in programming within reason.

1962 B-5000 - Burroughs' large scientific machine featuring hardware to accommodate the algorithmic language ALGOL.

Dartmouth College begins use of a teaching language they devised: BASIC.

1963 IBM 7040 - popular medium-sized scientific computer similar to the IBM 7090 in its instruction set.

CDC 3600 - large scientific machine - very fast.

The third generation of computing equipment begins to dawn at about this time. It is characterized by micro-components, monolithic integrated circuits, or sheer, blinding speed. Time-sharing also begins to come of age. Manufacturers begin to introduce compatible series of machines.

1964 HONEYWELL 200 - popular business machine using some of the instructions of the second generation IBM 1401.

CDC 6600 - the fastest computer available for several years to come - it contains one half million transistors - several satellite processors share and direct the central processor.

BURROUGHS B-5500 - a third-generation version of the B-5000.

GE 600 series is introduced - its circuitry is composed of micro-components.

General Electric announces a major time-sharing computer, the GE 645; it is ordered by MIT's time sharing PROJECT MAC (Machine Aided Cognition) and by Bell Labs.

IBM commits itself to the development of a New Programming Language called NPL; some farsighted soul will soon prevail and the name will be changed to Programming Language One or PL/1.

1965 UNIVAC 1108 II - a popular, large, fast, scientific machine of the third generation.

IBM 360 models 40 and 30 constitute the first two models of the 360 series - the several models, though different in design and speed, operate with essentially the same instruction set. Time-sharing is not included among the features of the original series. Features do include read only storage and "emulation." The series is intended to serve both scientific and business needs.

IBM markets the 1130 - a relatively small machine which is not compatible with the 360 series. It, along with its process control sister, the 1800, becomes very popular.

1966 IBM 360/67 - IBM's first major time-sharing product.

SDS Sigma 7 - third generation machine by Scientific Data Systems. A separately priced

COBOL compiler for the Sigma 7 is also announced by SDS. Now there is precedent for breaking the established hardware-software package up and the software industry begins to blossom.

PDP 9 - medium sized scientific computer featuring cathode ray graphic capability.

RCA Spectra 70 series is introduced. It uses monolithic integrated circuits and has an instruction set similar to the IBM 360 series.

1967 "Desk top" or "mini" computers begin to make their debut as large batch systems get further from the user and time sharing proves expensive.

Burroughs gets the contract for the processors of the ILLIAC IV.

Optical scanners begin to come on the market in force; some read marks, others read hand or machine written characters.

Computers which direct other machines (process control computers) become a large industry in their own right; more than 1000 are in operation.

Commercial Time Sharing firms begin to appear en masse. With a Teletype, password, and lots of money you can call up several computers.

1968 Wide interest develops in the area of Computer Aided Instruction (CAI). Special languages are developed.

Burroughs markets the B6500 series - most models have a new kind of memory: thin film instead of magnetic core.

NCR announces a self compatible line of computers: the Century series.

Goddard Space Flight Center puts the "supercomputer" IBM 360/91 into service. The IBM 360/85 is the fastest generally available IBM computer.

The possibilities of large data banks of information about individuals becomes a national concern; questions regarding invasion of privacy are asked increasingly by congress and the public.

1969 Control Data Corporation markets the CDC 7600.

IBM "unbundles" - the future holds divisions of hardware, software, service, etc. A more or less single industry has split up.

1970 Scientific Data Systems (SDS) and Xerox get together to form Xerox Data Systems (XDS).

IBM markets System 3 - a small, completely different line of computers - incompatible even down to a different punched computer card.

Honeywell buys General Electric's computer effort.

IBM announces System 370. Features include error correction circuitry, micro coding, and cpu identification hardware.

1971 IBM markets a very fast, large disk storage device - the 3330.

ILLIAC IV is completed at the University of Illinois; it is probably the fastest computer to date.

1972 A holographic - lasar related - memory with 10 trillion bit capacity is developed.

RCA withdraws from the computer business.

For those interested in details of the historical development of computers we recommend the following from which we drew heavily in preparing this chronology:

Saul Rosen's superb article, "Electronic Computers: A Historical Survey," in the ACM journal Computing Surveys, March 1969.

Mathematics and Computers by George R. Stibitz and Jules A. Larrivee, McGraw-Hill, 1957.

Both of these works and the references they contain will allow the interested student to look long and deeply into the past. As for the future, we invite you to join with us and watch. Or, perhaps, participate.

APPENDIX M

PROBLEM SOLVING WITH A COMPUTER--REPRISE

At the very first of this book we outlined ten steps which you might follow to have a computer solve a problem for you. We now present the same section again, with considerable embellishment. What follows is a very informal checklist of ideas, advice, reminders and what have you. Most of the items mentioned should remind you of matters we have dealt with in the text. All of the steps will not be appropriate for every program. And there will be items which we have omitted. We have left some blank space at the end of each of the ten steps so that you may write in your own items as you think of them or as you discover which ones are important to you. In some instances we assume that Fortran is the computer language which is being used; this tends to relate this section to the knowledge of the student. However, the ideas embodied are of a broader nature.

As with most attempts to divide up knowledge or ideas into little packages, there are overlaps among many of the steps which follow. Further, the process of developing a computer program entails a lot of feedback: you get to a certain point and discover you must change something in an earlier step. Be that as it may, if you try to use these steps, you may avoid some of the errors others have made -- and save yourself the pain of their discoveries.

I. Formulate the problem.

   A. Is the problem really one for a computer to solve?

      1. Is the problem large enough for the computer to be useful? Will the same basic problem be run often enough to make the cost required to instruct a computer to do it worthwhile?

      2. Is the problem too large to be solved? Do you have the facilities (time, assistance, etc.) for dealing with large quantities of data, putting them in machine-readable form, and insuring their accuracy? Is the number of operations required to do the problem so great

that even a computer may take years to solve the problem?

3. Is the problem a well defined one? Is it a problem which may be solved in a step by step manipulation of discrete symbols? If you had millions of years, pencils, and reams of paper could you do the problem yourself, or are there areas in the solution where the algorithmic approach is not appropriate?

B. Do you _really_ understand the problem?

1. Are you sure that the inputs you plan to use can be manipulated in such a way as to produce the outputs you want?

2. Are you sure that you are solving the right problem?

   a. If you are writing a program for someone else, do you understand completely what is to be done? Has he/she written it down for you? Do you understand what he/she really wants or what he/she _says_ he/she wants? Do you understand the context in which the problem is being solved and is the problem really appropriate in that context, or should you be dealing with a larger or different problem? After you've finished the problem, is he/she going to suggest additions which lead to patched-on and patched-up programs? How can you minimize such requests for modifications?

   b. If you are writing the program for yourself, have you asked the questions immediately above pretending that you, yourself, are the client?

   c. Are you trying to use the computer to solve more of a problem than you really need? Would it be better (more economical, cost-effective, etc.) to simply use the machine to solve a subset of your problem and deal with the rest of it by some other means?

   d. On the other hand, are you solving enough of the problem? Are there other parts you might consider including for processing by computer? Do you plan to do calculations by hand or by calculator after you get the computer results? Why?

e. Talk to someone about the problem. Can you accurately describe what is to be done?

f. Are you altering the problem to fit the computer? What concessions have you made to the computer?

C. Write a problem statement that describes what the problem is.

1. Don't restrict yourself to the computer portion of the matter, but include everything which lies between what you know now and what you want to know relating to the problem.

2. Now, consider that the computer is a symbol manipulator -- it takes in symbols you provide and produces symbols which, hopefully, increase knowledge. Think of your problem in that larger sense. The issue is what you have relative to what you want.

D. Start a folder or notebook on the project. Make the problem statement you just wrote the first item. As the problem statement changes, make additions or corrections. Plan to be surprised at how much the problem statement will change in the course of the project. Keep all the materials related to the project: your scrappy notes, all computer output, card decks. Think very carefully before throwing anything away.

II. Decide on a method for solving the problem.

A. Before you try to develop your own algorithm ask, "Has someone else solved the problem or one close to it?"

1. Have you looked in the program library or subroutine library of your computing center?

2. Have you checked with colleagues in the field to see if they have programs which might be used?

3. If you do find an already written program, will it run on the machine you plan to use? Is it in a language you understand in case you want to modify or check it? Are your data already in machine-readable form and, if so, is the data format going to create difficulties with a borrowed or otherwise-acquired program? What assurances do you have as to the correctness of the program?

4. If you can't find a complete program to solve your problem, are there subroutines available which you might use?

5. If you can't find, can't use, or don't want to use previously written programs to solve your problem, consider examining available algorithms. Search the literature in the field. Check the certified algorithms published by professional organizations such as the Association for Computing Machinery.

B. What computing resources do you have available? E.g., a fast machine, limited memory, interactive terminals, slow turn around? How do these factors influence your choice of an algorithm? Weigh the issues of computer time cost against programming time cost against program maintenance cost. What is the cost of running the computer you plan to use? For time, printed lines, etc.? Are there other machines available? Think about the balance between elegance and efficiency as it relates to the various costs.

C. Think of the input you have available. Think about the output you want to produce. How would you do the problem if you were going to do it by hand?

Can you think of other ways to solve the problem which take advantage of the things the computer does quickly and well which would suggest a different approach than you would use manually? Reread the problem statement.

D. Determine the approach you will use.

1. To help organize your thinking, write a general statement about what the program will do. But, write the statement as though the program already existed. This will give you confidence; also you can use the statement in the introduction to the documentation you write later.

2. Now break the overall job you have defined into a series of major tasks. Give some thought to what the most logical, natural segments of the problem are. Describe each of these major tasks together with a stepwise solution (algorithm) to the task. Now take each major task and subdivide it into subtasks. Continue the process of breaking complicated tasks into simpler ones until you have an algorithm composed of a hierarchical set of easily understood tasks and their associated algorithms. Each of these will become a procedure or subprogram in your program.

3. Consider each subtask as a simple but complete problem to be solved. It will have inputs and outputs. Concentrate on one subtask at a time, being confident that the subtasks will fit together to solve the overall job.

4. Decide on those values which will be constant in the method. Decide on those values least likely to change. Do you want to bring them in early? Many values in the algorithm, while "dimensionless" as far as the machine is concerned, denote real world quantities -- inches, people, etc. Are the units you are assuming for these values consistent with each other?

5. What output do you really want? Not considering the intermediate results for testing purposes, are you planning more output than you need? How

will the output be used? Will some of it be processed further? By hand or machine?

6. Now that you've decided on all the subtasks which form your algorithm, do you have a clear idea of the ways in which they are linked? Consider the relationships between the various modules and the data structures you will use to store the values the program is to work with.

E. Is your algorithm flexible enough to allow changes if the problem statement should change somewhat -- as it probably will? Where have you restricted yourself unduly?

III. Draw flowcharts depicting the algorithm decided upon.

A. Draw a master flowchart showing how the modules of the algorithm relate. Realize that a major reason for flowcharting is to aid your thought processes. Document the things you do and things you decide. Documentation helps as you go along. It helps later too.

B. Draw a flowchart of each module. Use standard flowchart symbols.

1. Include a separate sheet or section defining the use of every variable in the flowchart. Add it to the documentation.

2. Have you decided to use only the canonical forms of structured programming? If not, you must be doubly careful to follow up every branch the program makes. Try to keep the branches "localized."

3. Is the module you are flowcharting getting too complex, running off the page? Can you break it into subparts, each of which becomes a module itself?

4. Have you set up some standardized way of handling errors caused by bad data (or bad logic, for that matter)? Consider using a subprogram or preprocessing program that does nothing but service or detect errors. Also, consider a subprogram to perform the initialization of variables.

C. Look over the flowcharts you have developed. Ask yourself some questions:

1. Can you make your most complicated expressions simpler by computing them in steps? Print out these intermediate steps for checking.

2. Have you written efficient procedures? Remember, every operation takes time and/or memory space. Examine the highly iterative parts of your program -- the ones that eat up all the time. Concoct ways to avoid using subscripted variables in these areas. Avoid

doing processes within loops that could be done outside.

3. Examine the implications of your flowcharts in terms of memory of the machine. Don't use an array when one isn't needed. For instance, it is easy to think of an average in terms of an array: the sum of Xi divided by n. Don't get carried away! Use arrays when you need them; otherwise, save the time and memory space.

4. Assume your flowchart were followed faithfully by a machine which left answers and garbage strewn around the memory. Is your "housekeeping" such that the flowchart could be re-executed? Did you take care to initialize every appropriate variable before using it the first time?

5. Think about a person who comes after you to fix the program -- can he easily see what you've done? Or does your approach exmploy "neat" tricks to save a few microseconds or bytes and thus use logic that is hard for a human to follow?

D. Do a desk check. Trace the algorithm through with a very simple set of data. It's amazing what you can find that way.

IV. Write the computer instructions.

A. Decide on a computer language to use. The ones you know are doubtless the heavy favorites, but you might look around -- there are hundreds of languages. Are you doing simulation, list processing, text analysis? Is there a better language for your application? You might have to reflowchart the algorithm or change algorithms. It might be worth it.

B. As you begin coding, have a copy of the language specifications with you. Also obtain a manual of the particular compiler you will use and a "Programmer's Guide" for the machine if one is available. And, of course, this book should never leave your side -- keep it for confidence and good cheer if nothing else.

C. Doing proper Type Declaration of variable names is half the battle, since this is the area about which the flowchart says the least.

1. Be careful to select variable names that are unique and meaningful. Mind your spelling. Avoid trite names, keywords, built-in functions and subroutine names, etc. Keep a list of all the names you use and what each means. Equate the names to the flowchart counterparts.

2. Do you use the Type statement or other "static" methods to initialize values of variables? Don't -- if the program changes the variable later. Use variables for the more "complicated" constants such as pi or e. Set them early in the program. Look at each one intently, three times. Consider computing such constants. (e.g., pi is ATAN(1.)*4. and e is EXP(1.); they are easy to remember, deduce, check and/or convert to double precision.)

3. How do you handle subprogram calls? If you use common storage be very careful about alignment. Decide which variables are going to be in the argument-parameter category and which are going to be in common. Write the category down with the other attributes of the variable such as flowchart name, meaning, type, length, etc.

4. Do you ever call a subroutine using a constant as an argument? Aren't you scared?

5. Is the precision of the variables sufficient to do the job? Is the machine going to be able to store all you need it to? Consider alternate length possibilities -- byte, halfword, and double word storage. Ask yourself, in general, about the type you've selected for each variable. Also, can you safely reuse some memory space for another variable or array?

D. What differences are there between flowchart language and the computer language you've chosen which are going to give you problems? Fractions vs. integers? Mixed types? Input/output problems? Conventions in computing expressions?

E. Include comments to indicate what the general function of each module is. Include comments to document any differences between the formal process of the algorithm and the program. Include comments to describe differences between the flowchart and the program necessitated by the computer language syntax. Maybe include comments on the use of each variable or a reference to where the variable description can be found. Do not include comments to describe the obvious: e.g., COMPUTE Y AS X SQUARED followed by Y=X**2.

F. Will the program be writing out information just to read it in again later? Consider the format (or lack of same) you might use for such data and the devices on which you might store it.

G. Allow yourself the luxury of putting in intermediate output statements for testing purposes even if they aren't in the flowchart. Mark them well so you can remove them later or put them on a "switch" so you can deactivate them. Plan to print identifying information with each computer run: program name, date, time, data identification, etc.

H. You are printing out (echoing) all input, aren't you? If not, how do you know what problem the answer sheet will refer to? How do you know the input went in correctly?

I. Do you make the computer check for obvious errors? Input data out of range? Zero divisions? Subscripts too large or too small? Input data set not exhausted? Do you have a good system for identifying errors -- a simple subprogram perhaps?

J. Avoid non-standard instructions. Follow conventions. Assume somebody who is not so good at programming as you are will have to read and modify your code.

K. If memory space is a problem, find out about <u>program overlays</u>.

L. Do a desk check. Trace the program with simple data. Find the bugs now.

V. Assemble the data the computer is to use in solving the problem.

A. Put together some packages of test data first.

1. What input do you have access to for which you know the answers? Are there certain combinations of input values for which answers are known or which produce trends in sets of answers? Are there some simple analytical checks or results against each other? Are there data which should produce some known intermediate answers even if you don't know the final answers? Do the test data you've selected exercise at least the principal paths of your program if not all paths? See that each path will do the right thing with the right data and won't try to fake it with the wrong data.

2. Plan to test in at least two different sets of runs. In the first, see if the machine will give you the right answers under the most favorable conditions. Next try to break the program. Test its digestion by purposely giving it incorrect parameters.

3. Ask the meanest person you know to develop some test data for you. Make a contest out of the testing phase -- your program against his data.

B. Assemble the actual data.

1. Do you trust your sources? What bothers you most about the data? Investigate it. Are the data in the format you want them in? If not, what errors might occur in transforming them?

2. Now that you've looked more closely at the data, are there things in the program which might be worth changing? Are there some obvious limits to the values which the program could check for? Are there attributes of some of the data which would improve processing, e.g., no fractional values, so that you can use INTEGERS?

3. Do you mark the end of each set of data in the way the program expects it? Could the method

you use for marking the end ever be confused with an actual datum?

4. What are the differences between your test data and the real McCoy? Amount is an obvious one that can cause trouble. Are there other differences?

VI. Keypunch the program, data, and control cards.

A. This is one of the few places you may have to let the process get out of your control. Are you going to let someone else keypunch for you? One compromise is to keypunch the program yourself while someone else punches the data. It is hard to say which is more critical: errors in program punching or in data punching. Errors in programs are more devastating but also more likely to be caught.

B. Have legible copy to punch from. Be very precise about what you want. Consider using standardized coding forms for the program and data. The only thing in the world more literal minded than a computer is a keypunch operator. And he/she should be. Differentiate carefully between I and 1, between letter O and zero, between (and C, between 2, 7, and Z, and between 5 and S.

C. Are you going to punch the program yourself? Take advantage of the event to examine each statement carefully. Picture in your mind what each statement does, in the context of your program, before you punch it. When you are satisfied it is right, concentrate on punching it correctly. Use a card to mark your place on the coding sheet to avoid skipping or repeating sections of code. Use only cards you are <u>sure</u> are fresh. Find out how to use a <u>drum card</u> on a keypunch to reduce the likelihood of misplaced columns.

D. If you entrust your program or data to someone else to be punched, ask that it be machine verified. If it can't be, obtain a printed listing of all data for a visual check. Let one person read aloud while another scans the listing. Count lines and spaces. Look for extra cards left in the deck. Apply any easy cross checks you can think of.

E. Regardless of the method of preparation, put identification numbers and card codes on all cards. Your program should check these during input as well. Find a box that is the right size for your program if more than 200 cards are involved. If you opt for an unboxed deck, use several rubber bands -- not one that strangles (and mangles) the cards.

F. Data center clerks, machine operators, and even computer card readers have been known to permute or truncate card decks. Consider writing a small program to put your input on disk or tape. Make the necessary sequence checks. There is less likelihood of getting records out of order if they are on disk or tape!

G. Obtain a listing of all cards and store it away in your folder. What problems will you have if a listing is lost, original data sheets disappear, a card deck is dropped? Make provisions for these possibilities with back-ups.

VII. Submit the machine-readable form of the program and the test data to the computer.

A. Examine the compilers you might use for your testing runs. Choose one which does a lot of error checking. Hang object time efficiency -- you shouln't be using enough data to really be concerned with it initially.

B. Is it possible to test some or all modules separately? If you must test the entire package, consider printing out an indicator in each module when it is active. Also, are you printing out intermediate values as control goes from module to module so you can track down the locations of any errors?

C. Carefully follow the procedures for submitting programs specified by your computing center. If you are to run the computer yourself and must learn how, do so using a program that is known to work rather than the one you just wrote.

D. Do you have money in your computing account? Have you used the current password? Have you used the job control language properly for the compiler, I/O devices, and options you want? Have you examined the options which are available to help you decide if everything is working properly? Cross reference listings? Attribute list? List of machine coding? Have you given the machine operator the written information he/she needs to run the job?

VIII. Look at the results. Debug program or data if necessary.

A. Was your job cancelled by the system because it took too long? Because it asked for a tape or disk you hadn't told the operator you were going to use?

B. Did the program fail to compile? Did you make any syntax errors? (If so, go back to square one.) Why? Careless? Don't know the language? Didn't desk check? Consult the error message; fix the immediate problem. Don't resubmit the program yet! Go over the entire program with a fine-tooth comb without the aid of the machine. If you let a syntax error slip by, you doubtless have logic errors as well.

C. Did the program fail in execution? How far did it get? Did it print out some of the intermediate results you were careful to include as part of the output? Which module did it fail in? Did that module get the correct data to work with? What techniques for debugging are offered by your computing center or by the compiler you are using to help you find a really difficult bug? Can you add special program statements to help you isolate the problem? If you go over it 20 times and can't see the problem, ask someone else. Don't tell her/him what the program is supposed to do. Let her/him tell you what it will do. Plan to be surprised if he/she looks at it for 30 seconds and points right at the problem.

D. Are the answers there? If so, don't assume they are right. Compare them with the test data answers you worked out ahead of time. Do they match? If not, where is the <u>first</u> hint of trouble? (Errors are like shopping carts in a grocery store parking lot. They appear to breed and multiply.)

E. Even if everything seems perfect, sit down in a quiet place with the listing and a pencil. Write down each important idea you have about the results before the next thought blows it away.

IX. Document the program.

A. This step is out of place; but there is really no place to put it because documenting should be going on all during development. Documentation is really a process as much as a product.

B. Consider including the following items in the documentation:

1. The context within which the program resides. A person with no understanding of computers or the problem itself ought to be able to understand the context setting paragraph.

2. The problem statement.

3. Descriptions of the methods used, with references.

4. The overall logical structure of the modules and the function of each.

5. Operating instructions, machine requirements, memory requirements, language(s) used, input forms, etc.

6. Programmer name, address, organization, date of writing, testing, release. Dates of modifications and their nature.

7. Illustrated test run input and output.

8. Examples of running time requirements -- test data, other runs.

9. A disclaimer, saying that, although you've done your best, you aren't responsible for any mischief caused by errors in the program.

10. A program name -- some darling acronym you come up with when you are tired of thinking seriously about the whole business.

11. The program listing.

12. Line drawings to explain concepts for which English doesn't seem appropriate.

C. Just as the program is subject to modifications, the documentation is also. Consider using a text processing program to allow machine readable storage of the documentation.

X. Use or release the program.

A. Remove the statements you inserted for testing. Be careful. Rerun the program with test data and check the results. Get a fresh card copy of the source program for a back-up copy. If your deck is not sequence numbered to suit you, reproduce it with a sequence number adding program. Save a listing of all cards.

B. Consider getting an object deck with an execution time-efficient compiler. Rerun your test data with the newly compiled version. Match against prior test runs. Any discrepancies are as serious as a cat in a sandbox. Find the difficulty.

C. How sophisticated will the program's user be? Are you assuming knowledge that he/she might not have? Find a person willing to test run the program for you. Give her/him the program, documentation, and some data. Watch her/him struggle with it but don't help. (You won't be around when a person 1500 miles away tries to use the program.) Why does he/she have problems? What changes are suggested?

D. Now that you've been through all these steps, does it seem more reasonable that a carefully written, tested, and working program costs about $20 *per statement*?

APPENDIX N

A KEY TO COURSE ORGANIZATION

Perhaps the best way to plan your course is by looking carefully at the main headings in the table of contents while keeping in mind the sort of course you wish to teach. We'll hold our finger on the place while you do that.

Now you've noticed that the text is divided into five parts.

Part I describes a sparse subset of the Fortran IV language called Ten Statement Fortran (TSF). The ten statements covered there allow the student to do virtually any problem of a numeric nature which is amenable to solution in Fortran. Part I discusses constants, variable declaration, input, computation, output, decision-making, and subscripting. When PART I is begun it should be taught quickly and serially from beginning to end. During this period each student should work the several simple Lab Problems included in Part I. Because of later references, Problems (00 through 04), (05 or 06), 07, (08, 09 or 10), and 11 should be required. Each illustrates one or more vital concepts.

Part II expands some of the statements of PART I, then addresses itself principally to three topics: DO loops, FORMAT, and subprograms. It has PART I as a prerequisite.

Part III is a set of selected Modules concerned mainly with the Fortran language. Here we take up operations with logical, non-numeric and complex quantities, additional I/O features and storage methods, more control statements, equivalence, WATFOR/FIV compiler features, variable typing in general, and internal methods of storage used by Fortran in IBM 360/370. Also included are three reference modules on Fortran: physical statement order, built-in subprograms, and a summary of the language. Parts I and II are prerequisites to all Modules. In addition, some Modules have as prerequisites other Modules or Appendices. Such prerequisites are stated at the beginning of each Module. If prerequisite designators appear in parentheses, it indicates that the Module refers to the material but does not depend on it.

Part IV consists of all the Lab Problems which are not imbedded in Part I. Problems 12 through 25 should be of general interest; problems 26 through 41 will interest more those students in math and science; problems 42 through 55 will be of more interest to those in business and economics. On each Lab Problem there is a statement regarding what sections are prerequisite. The "footer" at the bottom of each lab problem indicates the general area of interest it serves.

Part V is a collection of appendices. There is debate in the computer science community about the applicability and timing of presentation in a beginning course of many of the topics covered by the appendices. The authors' solution to this question is simply to present this material as independently as possible. This allows each teacher to decide when to present such subjects as flowcharting, cards and keypunching, computer concepts, history of computing, structured programming, compilers, debugging, conversational computing, job control options, number systems, and numerical characteristics.

In addition, the appendices contain answers to exercises and WATFOR/FIV error messages. There is also a procedure describing how this text may be used if the WATFOR/FIV compiler is not available.

Teaching the Ten Statement Subset

Part I is a description of a subset of Fortran IV. Not only is the subset limited to ten statements but these statements are limited as well. It has been the authors' experience that it is wise to point out these limitations to instructors initially rather than having them pointed out by the students: "But, sir, it says here..." The authors feel that the limitations, though they are somewhat constrictive to the experienced programmer, serve a useful purpose in getting the student to the program-writing stage quickly.

Below is a discussion of each of the ten statements; restrictions to these statements are mentioned.

Statements in Ten Statement Fortran

Type Declaration Statements

(1) REAL variable
(2) INTEGER variable

Variable names in TSF are composed only of letters.

That Type Declaration statements are included in a minimal subset of FORTRAN may seem surprising. They are there because:

(a) They lend a definiteness to the nature of the variables the student is working with.

(b) They put into the hands of the program writer the responsibility for declaring the variables he is using, and thereby increase his awareness of the necessity for their proper use.

(c) They allow the natural extension of the language from scalar variables to subscripted variables without the addition of a statement to the language.

The choice, then, is really teaching either:

REAL and INTEGER typing
or
default typing and DIMENSIONing.

Since DIMENSIONing is not really necessary in FORTRAN IV, and explicit typing is extendable to COMPLEX, LOGICAL and extended precision variables, our choice was to teach the former of the two.

Input Statement

(3) READ, variable

This basic input statement, exemplified by the FORMAT-free READ in the WATFOR/FIV compiler for the IBM 360/370, can be explained to the student in a few words; it involves but one variable, one card, and one event. (Note: If the WATFOR/FIV compiler is not available see Appendix O for the TSF modification.)

Arithmetic Assignment Statement

(4) variable=expression

This statement provides for the basic manipulation of numeric data. All operations are defined. Change of variable type across the equality sign is permitted, as is mixed mode.

Conditional Transfer Statement

(5) IF(expression reop expression) GO TO stno

The conditional transfer statement provides the decision-making element. The logical IF statement with the GO TO trailer is chosen because of its ease of use and obvious consequences. No statement other than the GO TO is used as an IF trailer in TSF.

Unconditional Transfer Statement

(6) GO TO stno

Object of Transfer

(7) stno CONTINUE

The CONTINUE statement is the only numbered statement in TSF. There cannot arise, then, questions as to which statements can be numbered and which ones not; thus, attendant problems of explaining executable vs. non-executable statements at the early stages are avoided.

Output Statement

(8) PRINT, variable

End of Processing Statement

(9) RETURN

This statement provides a logical finish for the path through the algorithm. It provides a correspondence with the "return" in the flow diagram. Further, its meaning is more precise and causes less confusion than does the STOP statement which usually becomes entangled with the END statement in the student's mind.

Program Delimiter

(10) END

Sample Syllabus for a Semester Course

Chronological Order	Text
1	Introduction, Problem Solving with a Computer of Part I
2	Appendix A - The Punched Card
3	Appendix B - Simplified Keypunch Instructions
4	Appendix C - $JOB Card - specific format for student use.
5	Appendix D - Algorithms and Flowcharts
6	Part I up to Subscripted Variables including Lab Problems 00 through 04 and either Lab Problem 05 or 06.
7	Instructors' choice of Lab Problems 12, 26, 27, 28, 42, 43.
8	Remainder of Part I including Lab Problems 07, 11 and at least one of 08, 09 and 10.
9	Instructor's choice of Lab Problems 13, 17, 23, 37, 40, 44, 45.

The next five items could constitute lecture material while the students are working on the Lab Problems. Please don't expose the students to further Fortran laguage details at this point. They should solve several problems using only the Ten Statements, and their progress in developing their problem-solving ability should be carefully evaluated. It is all too easy for students to get absorbed in learning language details and never develop the ability to analyze a problem and program a solution to it.

10	Appendix E - Some Fundamentals of a Computer System
11	Appendix F - Compiling and Compilers
12	Appendix G - Number Systems: An Overview
13	Appendix H - Numerical Considerations in Computing
14	Appendix J - Debugging: In General and in WATFOR/FIV
15	Lab Problem 21
16	Part II through DO loops
17	Instructor's choice of Lab Problems 14 and 29
18	Part II through FORMATted Input/Output
19	Instructor's choice of Lab Problems 15, 18, 19, 20, 30, 31, 35, 46, 47, 48, 49, 51, 52, 54
20	Part II through Subprograms
21	Instructors's choice of Lab Problems 16, 32, 33, 34, 36, 38, 41, 55
22	Module 3: More Topics in FORMAT
23	Instructor's choice of Modules 1, 2, 4, 5, 6, 7, 8, 9, 10, 11, 12; Appendices C, K, L; remaining Lab Problems
24	Appendix I - Structured, Modular, and Sensible Programming
25	Appendix M - Problem Solving with a Computer - Reprise

Sample Syllabus for a Non-Credit Short Course

Chronological Order	Text
1	Appendix A - The Punched Card
2	Appendix B - Simplified Keypunch Instructions
3	Part I with Lab Problems 00, 02, 03, 04, (05 or 06), (08, 09, or 10)
4	Part II with selected Lab Problems
5	Module 3 - More Topics in FORMAT
6	Other topics depending on time and interests

APPENDIX O

TEN STATEMENT FORTRAN WITHOUT WATFOR/FIV

The only major difficulty one encounters in using this text when the WATFOR/FIV compiler (or any other FORMAT-free input-output compiler) is not available, occurs with the READ and PRINT statements. This appendix will allow the use of TEN STATEMENT FORTRAN under these conditions by dictating slight modifications to the programs the student writes.

1. Whenever the text deals with the statement

   ```
   READ, variable or list
   ```

   the student should substitute

   ```
   READ (5,99999) variable or list
   ```

2. Whenever the text discusses the statement

   ```
   PRINT, variable or list
   ```

   the student should substitute

   ```
   WRITE(6,99999) variable or list
   ```

3. Every program the student writes should contain a statement as follows:

   ```
   99999 FORMAT(5G15.8)
   ```

   The number 99999 is punched in columns 1-5 of the program statement card and the word FORMAT starts in card column 7.

4. The student may not use the statement number 99999 on any other statement (such as CONTINUE) in his program.

5. If only one datum appears on an input card, it must appear in card columns 1 through 15 and it must be placed in that field so that the extreme right-hand digit or character of the number falls in column 15. If two numbers occur on a card, the first must be as described above and the second must be punched in

columns 16 through 30; the number must similarly be "right-justified" in card column 30. If a third number is to be input it must be right-justified in column 45. Fourth and fifth numbers must be right-justified in columns 60 and 75 respectively. No more than five numbers may be punched on an input card. In summary, datum x is right-justified in field y as shown below.

datum x	field (columns) y
1	1-15
2	16-30
3	31-45
4	46-60
5	61-75

APPENDIX P

ANSWERS TO QUESTIONS AND EXERCISES

Page 24 CAT=-777.2 DOG=0.00098

Page 27

1. a. 0.00033 b. -0.128 c. 0.833800

2. a. 0.1338100E 02 b. -0.7888000E 01
   c. 0.3130000E-02 d. 0.9100000E-03

3. PRINT, AXE
   PRINT, RAKE
   PRINT, HOE

4. a. -0.5000000E 01 b. 0.1256000E 03
   c. 0.3200000E 05

Page 41

1. a. 6. f. 0.2
   b. 6. g. 105
   c. 15. h. 332
   d. -21.5 i. 25.
   e. 0. j. 5139

Page 42 Yes.

With a polynomial of order n, you would save $(n^2-n)/2$ multiplications.

2. All are valid.

Page 43

3. a. invalid; ABCDEFG has too many characters.
   b. invalid; two operators can't appear together.
   c. valid
   d. valid
   e. valid
   f. invalid; x cannot be used as an operator.
   g. valid

4\. a. 2 d. -7 g. 4
   b. 2 e. 2 h. 1
   c. 0 f. 6 i. 1

Page 44 If QUESTN is odd, then QUESTN/2*2 will equal QUESTN-1.

No.

Page 45 AZ would equal 8.0.

Page 57 1. a. false b. false c. false d. true

2\. a. invalid b. invalid c. invalid

3\. They are valid but useless; all three statements are equivalent to B=B+1

Page 58 4. A=8, B=8, C=10

5\. A=11, B=10

Page 61 You might test for HEIGHT being equal WIDTH/2.

Page 90 1. V=15

2\. Q=2

3\. S=10

Page 91 4. S=3000

5\. I continues to be 1 and the loop never ends.

6. S=0

Page 103 X(3)=X(LAMB)+X(NAT)+LAMB+NAT would produce
0.0+45.0+2+4
or 51.0 in X(3).

Page 109 The index is tested before the READ to see if a READ operation is necessary.

Disadvantage: you need one extra statement: the GO TO.

Advantage: if M is (mistakenly) < 1, the program will (properly) skip the READ statement.

Page 111 TEST(4) is being referred to.

1. 0.1450000E 02

2. 0.3850000E 01

Page 113 No, we cannot refer to Q as an array in an IF statement.

No, it is not necessary for SCORE to be subscripted.

Yes, a scalar variable SCORE could do the job.

Easily.

Page 116
```
1  1
2  0
3  2
4  1
```

A variable must be defined (given a value) before it may be used on the right hand side of an = sign in an arithmetic assignment statement.

1. a. valid
   b. invalid; the array XX consists only of locations XX(1) through XX(100)
   c. invalid; XX(0) does not exist
   d. invalid; XX needs a subscript
   e. valid
   f. invalid; XX(5) has not been defined

Page 117 2. a. no value; A not previously defined
   b. 39
   c. 30.5
   d. 35.
   e. no value; Y(8) does not exist
   f. 70.
   g. 27.

Page 129 It would work if the scores for each student were arranged in row-wise order in an array.

Page 130 1. a. RAT cannot be used as both a singly and a doubly subscripted variable.
   b. o.k.
   c. invalid variable name; too many characters
   d. POT(0) doesn't exist.
   e. o.k.
   f. RRRRRR cannot be used as both a scalar variable name and a subscripted variable name.
   g. X cannot be used both as a subscripted variable and a non-subscripted one.

2. a. 10.0 c. 6.0
   b. 2.2 d. 1.0

Page 140 a. & sign d. 7 characters
   b. decimal point e. / sign
   c. begins with number f. special characters

a. INTEGER   d. REAL   g. INTEGER
b. INTEGER   e. INTEGER   h. INTEGER
c. REAL   f. REAL   i. REAL

Page 144 1. a. no printing
b. would print 3
c. would print 1

2. a. no parentheses
b. LG
c. o.k.
d. (A-B) is a number, not a logical expression with truth value
e. o.k.; a 0.5 would make the statement clearer
f. trailer to IF statement cannot be another IF
g. o.k.
h. missing left parentnesis after IF
i. first 7 invalid

Page 151 1. a. 24

Page 152 b. 5   c. 55   d. 17

2. a. K is undefined outside the loop.
b. The initial value of index NN is less than 1.
c. The index K cannot be changed within the loop.
d. s must be ≥ 1; e must be ≥ b.

Page 167 1. a. o.k.; DO 6 K22 is a variable name.
b. DO 93 I=1,100,5
c. DO 666 N=1,NO666
d. DO 123 K=1,201,1
e. o.k.
f. DO 123 ICOUNT=1,10
g. DO 923 INDEX=I,J

2. 97 lines would be printed; they would be

```
1
1 1
1 2
1 3
1 4
5
1 1 1
1 1 2
1 2 1
1 2 2
1 3 1
1 3 2
1 4 1
1 4 2
1 5 1
1 5 2
2
2 1
2 2
2 3
2 4
5
2 1 1
  •
  •
96
```

Page 168 3. 13

4.

```
   INTEGER I
   REAL MOTHER (3000)
         •
         •
   DO 1 I=1,3000
   MOTHER(I)=43.8
 1 CONTINUE
```

5.

```
   REAL X(400),TOTAL
   INTEGER I
         •
         •
   TOTAL=0.
   DO 1 I=1,400
   TOTAL=TOTAL+X(I)
 1 CONTINUE
```

6. INTEGER I,J

```
      INTEGER I,J
         •
         •
      DO 1 I=1,4
      DO 2 J=1,30
      XXX(I,J)=0.
    2 CONTINUE
    1 CONTINUE
```

7. a. 25.   b. 25

Page 169 8. An infinite loop would occur, since 2,147,483,647 is the maximum value of an INTEGER; K could never exceed this value and hence the loop could never terminate.

Page 174 Read a record containing at least three values from the tape on tape unit 4. The format of the record is specified by FORMAT statement 333. Store the three values in Q, R, and S in that order.

Read NAT, T(2), and T(3) from unit 2 according to FORMAT statement 7.

Page 175 Write the values of W, X, Y, and Z as one record according to FORMAT statement 5. The numbers will be written on the magnetic tape mounted on unit 2.

Page 181

	C	B	A
a.	98	765.	4.3
b.	62	289.	8.7
c.	-7	.25	3.
d.	98	76.	1.2
e.	44	444.	4.4
f.	0	0.	0.
g.	error (run terminated); alphabetic characters in I field		
h.	25	-.3	-.2
i.	6	228.	9.8
j.	error (run terminated); decimal in I field		

Page 184	A	B
a.	87.6	54
b.	987.	3
c.	65.	43
d.	.7	3
e.	.9	6543
f.	87.6	54

Page 188	A	B
a.	ABCD	EFbb
b.	ABCb	Dbbb
c.	Abbb	BCDE
d.	ABbb	CDbb
e.	ABCD	EFG*
f.	CDEF	Gbbb
g.	error; the characters DE cannot be read with I2	

Page 196

```
$JOB            NAME
      REAL A,B,C,AVG
      READ(5,501) A,B,C
  501 FORMAT(F4.1,F3.0,F4.2)
      AVG=(A+B+C)/3.
      WRITE(6,601) AVG
  601 FORMAT(' ',F10.3)
      RETURN
      END
$ENTRY
```

```
$JOB            NAME
      REAL TOTAGE, AVGAGE
      INTEGER N1,N2,N3,N4,N5,AGE
      TOTAGE=0.
      DO 101 I=1,20
      READ(4,401)N1,N2,N3,N4,N5,AGE
  401 FORMAT(5A4,I2)
      WRITE(6,601)N1,N2,N3,N4,N5,AGE
  601 FORMAT(' ',5A4,I5)
      TOTAGE=TOTAGE+AGE
  101 CONTINUE
      AVGAGE=TOTAGE/20.
      WRITE(6,602) AVGAGE
  602 FORMAT('0','AVERAGE',12X,F4.1)
      RETURN
      END
$ENTRY
```

Page 202 The format 15F8.2 is exhausted each time the inner DO is completed, triggering a new record at the same time.

1. WRITE(6,306)(Q(I),I=1,99,2)

   which would print one or more lines depending on the FORMAT statement, or,

```
    DO 101 I=1,99,2
    WRITE(6,307) Q(I)
101 CONTINUE
```

   which would print 50 lines regardless of the FORMAT statement.

2. a. no parentheses around implied DO
   b. nothing
   c. AM used both as a subscripted variable and as a non-subscripted variable
   d. no right parenthesis at end
   e. leftmost parenthesis missing
   f. last two right parentheses must be omitted
   g. nothing

3. a. 1 b. 2 c. 3

4. a. 10 b. 10 c. 10

Page 226 MPY is not declared as REAL in the calling program.

The statement E=MPY(D,A) does not contain enough arguments.

H is used as an array name in R=G*H(I) but is not so declared in either the main program or subprogram.

Page 231 (See next page.)

Page 231 The boxes contain the final values after execution of the program and subprogram.

MAIN PROGRAM

Fortran Version	"Machine Language" Version
A=5.0	Duplicate contents of 600 in 602
B=10.0	Duplicate contents of 601 in 603
.	.
.	.
.	.
CALL SUB(A,B)	Execute SUB using 602 and 603
.	.
.	.
S=B	Duplicate contents of 603 in 604

600	601	602(A)	603(B)	604(S)
5.0	10.0	125.0	6250.	6250.

SUBROUTINE SUB

SUBROUTINE SUB(T,W)	
.	
.	
.	
S=2.5	Duplicate contents of 844 in 846
Q=50.	Duplicate contents of 845 in 847
.	.
.	.
.	.
T=Q*S	Multiply contents of 846 by contents of 847 and store result in (602)
.	.
.	.
W=Q*T	Multiply contents of 847 by contents of (602) and store result in (603)

844	845	846(S)	847(Q)
2.5	50.	2.5	50.0

a .TRUE. because
..TRUE.

.TRUE. 11. .FALSE.

.TRUE. 12. .TRUE.

.TRUE. 13. .TRUE.

.TRUE. 14. .TRUE.

.TRUE. 15. .TRUE.

cal quantity but it is being
the logical operator .OR.

an separate only LOGICAL

an separate only LOGICAL

LOGICAL; M is INTEGER.

12. Invalid: .OR. can separate only LOGICAL quantities.

13. .TRUE.

14. Invalid: .AND. can separate only LOGICAL

quantities.

15. .TRUE.
16. Invalid: .NOT. must precede a LOGICAL quantity.
17. Invalid: .NOT. must precede a LOGICAL quantity and .GT. must separate arithmetic quantities.
18. Invalid: .OR. is a LOGICAL operator; it must separate LOGICAL quantities.
19. .FALSE.
20. .FALSE.

Page 254 The following output is produced:

```
3    5  BOTH
4    9  NEITHER
4   10  NEITHER
7 T   20 F
```

139 complex numbers are declared; (1+1+1+1+35+100) each takes up 2 words: 2x139=278

Page 279 Statement a3 will be executed next.

If the statement following an arithmetic IF were not numbered it could never be executed.

C (value 3.0) will be printed.

Page 280 The next value is read into C.

Page 295

1. ABE: INTEGER, Type Declaration Statement (TDS)

2. UNIT: LOGICAL, IMPLICIT Statement (IS)

3. BIG: REAL, default

4. ABLE: REAL, TDS

5. ALAS: INTEGER, IS

6. ALACK: COMPLEX, TDS

7. AUTO: INTEGER, IS

8. BOY: INTEGER, TDS

9. SOUTH(2,2,2): LOGICAL, IS

10. CLEO: INTEGER, IS

11. JAM: INTEGER, default

12. QUEST: COMPLEX, IS

13. QUOTE: COMPLEX, TDS

14. ADCAT: LOGICAL, TDS

Page 318 The smallest number is -32,768.

The largest is 32,767.

The binary value 111111111111111.

Page 354 It will print $(n+1)^2$ lines.

The printed digits, when taken together, form the first n^2 numbers of that system, if the counting starts with zero.

Page 363 See Appendix H: Numerical Considerations in Computing (The Cancellation Law).

Page 450 Hardly!

Page 454 2549

Page 455 2549 also, obviously

APPENDIX Q

WATFOR AND WATFIV ERROR MESSAGES

This listing shows both WATFOR and WATFIV error messages and error codes, since they do not always indicate the same meaning. In the error code columns at the left, the WATFOR codes are shown in the first column and the WATFIV codes in the second column.

WATFOR	WATFIV	MESSAGE

Assembly Language Subprograms

WATFOR	WATFIV	MESSAGE
	AL-0	Missing END card on assembly language deck
	AL-1	Entry-point or CSECT name in an object deck was previously defined. First definition used

ASSIGN Statements and Variables

WATFOR	WATFIV	MESSAGE
AS-2		Attempt to redefine an assigned variable in an arithmetic statement
AS-3		Assigned variable used in an arithmetic expression
AS-4		Assigned variable cannot be half-word INTEGER
AS-5		Attempt to redefine an assign variable in an input list

BLOCK DATA Statement

WATFOR	WATFIV	MESSAGE
BD-0	BD-0	Executable statements are illegal in BLOCK DATA subprogram
BD-1	BD-1	Improper BLOCK DATA statement

Card Format and Contents

WATFOR	WATFIV	MESSAGE
CC-0	CC-0	Columns 1-5 of continuation card not blank. Probable cause - statement punched to left of column 7
CC-1	CC-1	Limit of 20 continuation cards exceeded

WAT FOR	WAT FIV	MESSAGE
CC-2	CC-2	Invalid character in Fortran statement; "$" inserted in source listing
CC-3	CC-3	First card of a program is a continuation card. Probable cause - statement punched to left of column 7
CC-4	CC-4	Statement too long to compile (scan-stack overflow)
CC-5	CC-5	Blank card encountered
CC-6	CC-6	Keypunch used differs from keypunch specified on $JOB card
CC-7	CC-7	First character of statement not alphabetic
CC-8	CC-8	Invalid character(s) concatenated with Fortran keyword
CC-9	CC-9	Invalid characters in col. 1-5. Statement number ignored. Probable cause - statement punched to left of column 7

COMMON

WAT FOR	WAT FIV	MESSAGE
CM-0	CM-0	Variable previously placed in COMMON
CM-1		Name in COMMON list previously used as other than variable
	CM-1	Other compilers may not allow COMMONed variables to be initialized in other than a BLOCK DATA subprogram
CM-2		Subprogram appears in COMMON statement
CM-3		Initializing of COMMON should be done in a BLOCK DATA subprogram
CM-4	CM-2	Illegal use of COMMON block or NAMELIST name

Fortran Type Constants

WAT FOR	WAT FIV	MESSAGE
CN-0	CN-0	Mixed REAL*4, REAL*8 in COMPLEX constant
CN-1	CN-1	INTEGER constant greater than 2,147,483,647 ($2^{31}-1$)
CN-3	CN-2	Exponent of REAL constant greater than 99
CN-4	CN-3	REAL constant has more than 16 digits, truncated to 16
CN-5	CN-4	Invalid Hexadecimal constant
CN-6	CN-5	Illegal use of decimal point
CN-8	CN-6	Constant with E-type exponent has more than 7 digits, assume D-type

WAT FOR	WAT FIV	MESSAGE
CN-9	CN-7	Statement number greater than 99999.
	CN-8	An exponent overflow or underflow occurred while converting a constant in a source statement

Compiler Errors

WAT FOR	WAT FIV	MESSAGE
CP-0		Detected in PHASE RELOCK
CP-1		Detected in PHASE LINKR
CP-2		Duplicate pseudo statement numbers
CP-4		Detected in PHASE ARITH
CP-5		Compiler interrupt
	CP-0	Compiler Error - LANDR/ARITH
	CP-1	Compiler Error - Likely cause: More than 255 DO statements.
	CP-4	Interrupt at compile time; Return to system

CHARACTER Variable

WAT FOR	WAT FIV	MESSAGE
	CV-0	A CHARACTER variable is used with relational operator
	CV-1	Length of a CHARACTER value on right side of = sign exceeds that on left. Truncation will occur
	CV-2	UnFORMATted core-to-core I/O not implemented

DATA Statements

WAT FOR	WAT FIV	MESSAGE
DA-0	DA-0	Replication factor greater than 32767, assume 32767
DA-1		Non-constant in DATA statement
DA-2	DA-1	More variables than constants in DATA statement
DA-3	DA-2	Attempt to initialize a subprogram parameter in a DATA statement
DA-4	DA-3	Non-constant subscripts in a DATA statement invalid in /360 Fortran
DA-5		Extended DATA statement not in /360 Fortran
DA-6	DA-4	Non-agreement between type of variable and constant in DATA statement
DA-7	DA-5	More constants than variables in DATA statement

WAT FOR	WAT FIV	MESSAGE
DA-8	DA-6	Variable previously initialized. Latest value used. Check COMMON/EQUIVALENCEd variables
DA-9	DA-7	Initializing blank COMMON not allowed in /360 Fortran
DA-B	DA-8	Truncation of literal constant has occurred
DA-A		Invalid delimiter in constant list portion of DATA statement
	DA-9	Other compilers may not allow implied DO-loops in DATA statements

DEFINE FILE Statements

WAT FOR	WAT FIV	MESSAGE
	DF-0	The unit number is missing
	DF-1	Invalid FORMAT Type
	DF-2	The associated variable is not simple INTEGER
	DF-3	No of records or record size=0 or>32767

DIMENSION Statements

WAT FOR	WAT FIV	MESSAGE
DM-0	DM-0	No DIMENSIONs specified for a variable in a DIMENSION statement
DM-1		Optional length specification in DIMENSION statement is illegal
DM-3	DM-1	Attempt to re-DIMENSION a variable
DM-2		Initialization in DIMENSION statement is illegal
	DM-2	Call-by-location parameter may not be DIMENSIONed
	DM-3	The declared size of an array exceeds space provided by CALLing argument
DM-4		Attempt to DIMENSION an initialized variable

DO Loops

WAT FOR	WAT FIV	MESSAGE
DO-0	DO-0	Illegal statement used as object of DO
DO-1	DO-1	Illegal transfer into the range of a DO-loop
DO-2	DO-2	Object of a DO statement has already appeared
DO-3	DO-3	Improperly nested DO-loops
DO-4	DO-4	Attempt to redefine a DO-loop parameter within range of loop
DO-5	DO-5	Invalid DO-loop parameter

WAT FOR	WAT FIV	MESSAGE
DO-6		Too many nested DOs: max=20 in WATFOR, no limit in WATFIV
	DO-6	Illegal transfer to a statement which is inside the range of a DO-loop
DO-7	DO-7	DO-parameter is undefined or outside range
DO-8	DO-8	This DO loop will terminate after first time through
DO-9	DO-9	Attempt to redefine a DO-loop parameter in an input list
	DO-A	Other compilers may not allow this statement to end a DO-loop

EQUIVALENCE and/or COMMON

WAT FOR	WAT FIV	MESSAGE
EC-0	EC-0	Two EQUIVALENCEd variables appear in COMMON
EC-1	EC-1	COMMON BLOCK has a different length than a previous subprogram
EC-2	EC-2	COMMON and/or EQUIVALENCE causes invalid alignment. Execution slowed; remedy - put double word quantities first
EC-3	EC-3	EQUIVALENCE extends COMMON downwards
	EC-4	A subprogram parameter appears in a COMMON or EQUIVALENCE statement
EC-7		COMMON/EQUIVALENCE statement does not precede previous use of variables
EC-8		Variable used with non-constant subscript in COMMON/EQUIVALENCE list
EC-9	EC-5	A name subscripted in an EQUIVALENCE statement was not DIMENSIONed

END Statements

WAT FOR	WAT FIV	MESSAGE
EN-0	EN-0	No END statement in program--END statement generated
EN-1	EN-1	END statement used as STOP statement at execution
	EN-2	An END statement cannot have a statement number. Statement number ignored
	EN-3	END statement not preceded by a transfer
EN-2		Improper END statement
EN-3		First statement of subprogram is END statement

Equal Signs

WAT FOR	WAT FIV	MESSAGE
EQ-6	EQ-0	Illegal quantity on left of equal sign
EQ-8	EQ-1	Illegal use of equal sign
EQ-A	EQ-2	Multiple assignment statements not in /360 Fortran
	EQ-3	Multiple assignment is not implemented for CHARACTER variables

EQUIVALENCE Statements

WAT FOR	WAT FIV	MESSAGE
EV-0	EV-0	Attempt to EQUIVALENCE a variable to itself
EV-1		Attempt to EQUIVALENCE a subprogram parameter
EV-2		Less than 2 members in an EQUIVALENCE list
	EV-2	A multiple-subscripted, EQUIVALENCEd variable has been incorrectly re-EQUIVALENCEd. Remedy: DIMENSION the variable first
EV-3		Too many EQUIVALENCE lists (maximum=255)
EV-4		Previously equivalenced variable re-EQUIVALENCEd incorrectly

Powers and Exponentiation

WAT FOR	WAT FIV	MESSAGE
EX-0	EX-0	Illegal COMPLEX exponentiation
EX-2	EX-1	I**J where I=J=0
EX-3	EX-2	I**J where I=0, J.LT.0
EX-6	EX-3	0.0**Y where Y.LE.0.0
EX-7	EX-4	0.0**J where J=0
EX-8	EX-5	0.0**J where J<0
EX-9	EX-6	X**Y where X.LT.0.0.,Y.NE.0.0

ENTRY Statement

WAT FOR	WAT FIV	MESSAGE
EY-0	EY-0	Subprogram name in ENTRY statement previously defined
EY-1	EY-1	Previous definition of FUNCTION name in an entry is incorrect
EY-2	EY-2	Use of subprogram parameter inconsistant with previous entry point
EY-3		Variable was not previously used as a parameter - parameter assumed

WAT FOR	WAT FIV	MESSAGE
	EY-3	A parameter has appeared in an executable statement but it is not a subprogram parameter
EY-4	EY-4	ENTRY statement not permitted in main program
EY-5	EY-5	Entry point invalid inside a DO-loop
EY-6		Variable was not previously used as a parameter - Parameter assumed

FORMAT

WAT FOR	WAT FIV	MESSAGE
FM-0	FM-0	Invalid character in input data
FM-2	FM-1	No statement number on a FORMAT statement
FM-5	FM-2	FORMAT specification and data type do not match
	FM-4	FORMAT provides no conversion specification for a value in I/O list
	FM-5	An INTEGER in the input data is too large (maximum = 2,147,483,647 = $2^{31}-1$)
FM-6		Incorrect sequence of characters in input data
	FM-6	A REAL number in the input data is out of range (1.E-78 to 1.E+75)
FM-7		Non-terminating FORMAT
	FM-7	Unreferenced FORMAT statement

Functions and Subroutines

WAT FOR	WAT FIV	MESSAGE
FN-0		No arguments in a FUNCTION statement
	FN-1	A parameter appears more than once in a subprogram or statement FUNCTION definition
FN-3		Repeated argument in subprogram or statement FUNCTION definition
FN-4	FN-2	Subscripts on right hand side of statement function. Probable cause - variable to left of = not DIMENSIONed
FN-5	FN-3	Multiple returns are invalid in FUNCTION subprograms
FN-6	FN-4	Illegal length modifier in Type FUNCTION statement
FN-7	FN-5	Invalid argument in arithmetic or LOGICAL statement FUNCTION
FN-8	FN-6	Argument of subprogram is same as subprogram name

WAT FOR	WAT FIV	MESSAGE

FORMAT

WAT FOR	WAT FIV	MESSAGE
FT 0	FT 0	First character of variable FORMAT not a left parenthesis
FT-1	FT-1	Invalid character encountered in FORMAT
FT-2	FT-2	Invalid form following a specification
FT-3	FT-3	Invalid field or group count
FT-4	FT-4	A field or group count greater than 255
FT-5	FT-5	No closing parenthesis on variable FORMAT
FT-6	FT-6	No closing quote in Hollerith field
FT-7	FT-7	Invalid use of comma
FT-8	FT-8	Insufficient space to compile a FORMAT statement (scan-stack overflow)
FT-9	FT-9	Invalid use of P specification
FT-B	FT-A	Invalid use of period (.)
FT-C	FT-B	More than three levels of parentheses
FT-D	FT-C	Invalid character before a right parenthesis
FT-E	FT-D	Zero length Hollerith encountered
FT-F	FT-E	No closing right parenthesis
FT-A	FT-F	Character follows closing right parenthesis
	FT-G	Wrong quote used for keypunch specified
	FT-H	Length of literal or Hollerith exceeds 255

GO TO Statements

WAT FOR	WAT FIV	MESSAGE
GO-0		Statement transfers to itself or a non-executable statement
	GO-0	This statement could transfer to itself
GO-1		Invalid transfer to this statement
	GO-1	This statement transfers to a non-executable statement
GO-2		Index of computed "GO TO" is negative or undefined
	GO-2	Attempt to define assigned GO TO index in an arithmetic statement
GO-3		Error in variable of "GO TO" statement
	GO-3	Assigned GO TO index may be used only in assigned GO TO and ASSIGN statements
GO-4	GO-4	Index of assigned "GO TO" is undefined or not in range
	GO-5	Assigned GO TO may not be an INTEGER*2 variable

WAT FOR	WAT FIV	MESSAGE

Hollerith Constants

WAT FOR	WAT FIV	MESSAGE
HO-0	HO-0	Zero length specified for H-type Hollerith
HO-1	HO-1	Zero length quote-type Hollerith
HO-2	HO-2	No closing quote or next card not continuation card
HO-3		Hollerith constant should appear only in CALL statement
HO-4	HO-3	Unexpected Hollerith or statement number constant

IF Statement (Arithmetic and Logical)

WAT FOR	WAT FIV	MESSAGE
IF-0	IF-0	Statement invalid after a logical IF
IF-3	IF-1	Arithmetic or invalid expression in logical IF
IF-4	IF-2	LOGICAL, COMPLEX, or invalid expression in arithmetic IF

IMPLICIT Statement

WAT FOR	WAT FIV	MESSAGE
IM-0	IM-0	Invalid Type specified in an IMPLICIT statement
IM-1		Invalid length specified in an IMPLICIT or Type statement
IM-2		Illegal appearance of $ in a character range
	IM-2	Invalid optional length
IM-3	IM-3	Improper alphabetic sequence in character range
IM-4	IM-4	Specification must be single alphabetic character, 1st character used
IM-5	IM-5	IMPLICIT statement does not precede other specification statement
IM-6	IM-6	Attempt to establish the type of a character more than once
IM-7	IM-7	/360 Fortran allows one IMPLICIT statement per program
IM-8		Invalid element in IMPLICIT statement
IM-9		Invalid delimiter in IMPLICIT statement

WAT FOR	WAT FIV	MESSAGE

Input/Output

WAT FOR	WAT FIV	MESSAGE
IO-0		Missing comma in I/O list of I/O or DATA statement
IO-2	IO-0	Statement number in I/O statement not a FORMAT statement number
IO-3		Buffer overflow-line too long for device
IO-6	IO-1	Variable FORMAT not an array name
IO-8	IO-2	Invalid element in input list or data list
	IO-3	Other compliers may not allow expressions in I/O lists
	IO-4	Illegal use of END= or ERR= parameters
IO-D	IO-5	Missing or invalid unit in I/O statement
	IO-6	Invalid FORMAT
	IO-7	Only constants, simple INTEGER*4 variables, and CHARACTER variables are allowed as unit numbers
IO-9		Type of variable unit not INTEGER in I/O statement
IO-A		Half-word INTEGER variable used as unit in I/O statements
IO-B		Assigned INTEGER variable used as unit in I/O statements
IO-C		Invalid element in an output list
	IO-8	Attempt to perform I/O in a FUNCTION which is called in an output statement
	IO-9	UnFORMATted WRITE statement must have a list
IO-E		Missing or invalid FORMAT in READ/WRITE statement
IO-F		Invalid delimiter in specification part of I/O statement
IO-G		Missing statement number after END= or ERR=
IO-H		/360 Fortran doesn't allow END returns in WRITE statement
IO-J		Invalid delimiter in I/O list
IO-K		Invalid delimiter in STOP, PAUSE, DATA, or tape control statements

JOB Control Cards

WAT FOR	WAT FIV	MESSAGE
JB-1	JB-0	$JOB card encountered during compilation
JB-2	JB-1	Invalid option(s) specified on $JOB card
JB-3		Unexpected control card encountered during compilation

WAT FOR	WAT FIV	MESSAGE

Job Termination

KO-0		Job terminated in execution because of compile time error
	KO-0	Source error encountered while executing with RUN=FREE
KO-1		Fixed-point division by zero
	KO-1	Limit exceeded for fixed-point division by zero
KO-2		Floating-point division by zero
	KO-2	Limit exceeded for floating-point division by zero
KO-3	KO-3	Too many exponent overflows
KO-4	KO-4	Too many exponent underflows
KO-5	KO-5	Too many fixed-point overflows
KO-6	KO-6	Job time limit exceeded
KO-7	KO-7	Compiler error-interruption at execution time, return to system
KO-8		INTEGER in input data is too large (maximum is 2147483647)
	KO-8	Traceback error. Traceback terminated
	KO-9	Cannot open WATFIV.ERRTEXTS. Run terminated
	KO-A	I/O error on text file

Logical Operations

LG-2	LG-0	.NOT. used as a binary operator

Library Routines

LI-0	LI-0	Argument out of range DGAMMA or GAMMA. (1.382D-76.LT.X.LT.57.57)
LI-1	LI-1	Absolute value of argument > 174.673, SINH, COSH, DSINH, DCOSH
LI-2	LI-2	Sense light other than 0,1,2,3,4, for SLITE or 1,2,3,4 for SLITET
LI-3	LI-3	REAL portion of argument .GT. 174.673, CEXP or CDEXP
LI-4	LI-4	ABS(AIMAG(Z)).GT.174.673 for CSIN,CCOS,CDSIN or CDCOS of Z
LI-5	LI-5	ABS(REAL(Z)).GE.3.537E15 for CSIN,CCOS,CDSIN or CDCOS of Z
LI-6	LI-6	ABS(AIMAG(Z)).GE.3.53E157 for CEXP or CDEXP of Z

WAT FOR	WAT FIV	MESSAGE
LI-7	LI-7	Argument .GT.174.673, EXP or DEXP
LI-8	LI-8	Argument is zero, CLOG,CLOG10,CDLOG or CDLG10
LI-9	LI-9	Argument is negative or zero, ALOG,ALOG10,DLOG or DLOG10
LI-A	LI-A	ABS(X).GE.3.537E15 for SIN,COS,DSIN or DCOS of X
LI-B	LI-B	Absolute value of argument .GT.1, for ARSIN, ARCOS, DARSIN, or DARCOS
LI-C	LI-C	Argument is negative, SQRT or DSQRT
LI-D	LI-D	Both arguments of DATAN2 or ATAN2 are zero
LI-E	LI-E	Argument too close to a singularity, TAN, COTAN, DTAN or DCOTAN
LI-F	LI-F	Argument out of range--DLGAMA or ALGAMA. (0.0<X<4.29E73)
LI-G	LI-G	Absolute value of argument .GE. 3.537E15, TAN, COTAN, DTAN, DCOTAN
LI-H	LI-H	Fewer than two arguments for one of MINO, MINI, AMINO, etc.

Mixed Mode

WAT FOR	WAT FIV	MESSAGE
MD-2	MD-0	Relational operator has a LOGICAL operand
MD-3	MD-1	Relational operator has a COMPLEX operand
	MD-2	Mixed mode. LOGICAL or CHARACTER variables may not be used with arithmetic variables
	MD-3	Other compilers may not allow subscripts of type COMPLEX, LOGICAL, or CHARACTER
MD-4		Mixed mode: LOGICAL with arithmetic
MD-6		Warning: subscript is COMPLEX. REAL part used

Memory Overflow

WAT FOR	WAT FIV	MESSAGE
MO-0	MO-0	Symbol table overflows object code, source error checking continues
MO-1	MO-1	Insufficient memory to assign array storage. Job abandoned
MO-2	MO-2	Symbol table overflows compiler, job abandoned
MO-3	MO-3	Data area of subprogram too large--segment your subprogram further
MO-4	MO-4	GETMAIN cannot provide buffer for WATLIB

WAT FOR	WAT FIV	MESSAGE

NAMELIST Statements

WAT FOR	WAT FIV	MESSAGE
	NL-0	NAMELIST entry must be a variable, not a subprogram parameter
	NL-1	NAMELIST name previously defined
	NL-2	Variable name too long
	NL-3	Variable name not found in NAMELIST
	NL-4	Invalid syntax in NAMELIST input
	NL-6	Variable incorrectly subscripted
	NL-7	Subscript out of range

Parentheses

WAT FOR	WAT FIV	MESSAGE
PC-0	PC-0	Unmatched parenthesis
PC-1	PC-1	Invalid nesting of parentheses in I/O list

PAUSE, STOP Statements

WAT FOR	WAT FIV	MESSAGE
PS-0		STOP with operator message not allowed. Simple STOP assumed
	PS-0	Operator messages not allowed: simple STOP assumed for STOP, CONTINUE assumed for PAUSE
PS-1		PAUSE with operator message not allowed. Treated as CONTINUE

RETURN statement

WAT FOR	WAT FIV	MESSAGE
RE-0		First card of subprogram is a RETURN statement
RE-1	RE-1	RETURN I, where I is zero, negative or too large
RE-2	RE-2	Multiple RETURN not valid in FUNCTION subprogram
RE-3	RE-3	Variable in multiple RETURN is not a simple INTEGER variable
RE-4	RE-4	Multiple RETURN not valid in main program

WAT FOR	WAT FIV	MESSAGE

Arithmetic and LOGICAL Statement FUNCTIONs

WAT FOR	WAT FIV	MESSAGE
		Probable cause of SF errors - variable on left of = was not DIMENSIONed
SF-1	SF-1	Previously referenced statement number on statement FUNCTION
SF-2	SF-2	Statement FUNCTION is the object of a logical IF statement
SF-3	SF-3	Recursive statement FUNCTION, name appears on both sides of = sign
	SF-4	A statement FUNCTION definition appears after the first executable statement: DIMENSION variable or order statements correctly
SF-5	SF-5	Illegal use of a statement FUNCTION

Subprograms

WAT FOR	WAT FIV	MESSAGE
SR-0	SR-0	Missing subprogram
SR-5	SR-1	Subprogram redefines a constant, expression, DO-parameter, or assigned GO TO index
SR-2	SR-2	Subprogram assigned different Types in different program segments
SR-6	SR-3	Attempt to use subprogram recursively
SR-4	SR-4	Invalid type of argument in subprogram reference
SR-7	SR-5	Wrong number of arguments in subprogram reference
SR-8	SR-6	Subprogram name previously defined - first reference used
SR-9	SR-7	No main program
SR-A	SR-8	Illegal or blank subprogram name
	SR-9	Library program was not assigned the correct Type
	SR-A	Method for entering subprogram produces undefined value for call-by-location parameter

WAT FOR	WAT FIV	MESSAGE

Subscripts

WAT FOR	WAT FIV	MESSAGE
SS-0	SS-0	Zero subscript or DIMENSION not allowed
	SS-1	Array subscript exceeds DIMENSION
SS-2		Invalid variable or name used for DIMENSION
	SS-2	Invalid subscript form
SS-1	SS-3	Subscript out of range

Statements and Statement Numbers

WAT FOR	WAT FIV	MESSAGE
ST-0	ST-0	Missing statement number
ST-1	ST-1	Statement number greater than 99999
ST-3	ST-2	Multiple-defined statement number
ST-4		No statement number on statement following transfer statement
ST-5	ST-3	Undecodable statement
	ST-4	This statement should have a statement number
ST-7	ST-5	Statement number specified in a transfer is a non-executable statement
ST-8	ST-6	Statement number constant must be in a CALL statement
ST-9	ST-7	Statement specified in a transfer statement is a FORMAT statement
ST-A	ST-8	Missing FORMAT statement
	ST-9	Specification statement does not precede statement FUNCTION definitions or executable statements
	ST-A	Unreferenced statement follows a transfer

Subscripted Variables

WAT FOR	WAT FIV	MESSAGE
SV-0	SV-0	Wrong number of subscripts
SV-1	SV-1	Array name or subprogram name used incorrectly without list
SV-2	SV-2	More than seven DIMENSIONs not allowed
SV-3	SV-3	DIMENSION too large
SV-4	SV-4	Variable with variable DIMENSIONs is not a subprogram parameter
SV-5	SV-5	Variable DIMENSION neither a simple INTEGER variable nor a subprogram parameter

WAT FOR	WAT FIV	MESSAGE

Syntax Errors (Errors in the form or arrangement of the statement)

WAT FOR	WAT FIV	MESSAGE
SX-0	SX-0	Missing operator
	SX-1	Expecting operator
SX-1	SX-2	Syntax error-searching for symbol, none found
	SX-3	Expecting symbol or operator
SX-2	SX-4	Syntax error-searching for constant, none found
SX-3	SX-5	Syntax error-searching for symbol or constant, none found
SX-4	SX-6	Syntax error-searching for statement number, none found
SX-5	SX-7	Syntax error-searching for simple INTEGER variable, none found
	SX-8	Expecting simple INTEGER variable or constant
SX-C	SX-9	Illegal sequence of operators in expression
	SX-A	Expecting end-of-statement
SX-D		Missing operand or operator

TYPE Statements

WAT FOR	WAT FIV	MESSAGE
	TY-0	The variable has already been explicitly Typed
	TY-1	The length of the EQUIVALENCEd variable may not be changed. Remedy: interchange Type and EQUIVALENCE statements

I/O Operations

WAT FOR	WAT FIV	MESSAGE
UN-0	UN-0	Control card encountered on unit 5 during execution Probable cause - missing data or improper FORMAT statement
UN-1	UN-1	End of file encountered
UN-2	UN-2	I/O error
UN-3	UN-3	Data set referenced for which no DD card supplied
UN-4	UN-4	REWIND, ENDFILE, or BACKSPACE references unit 5, 6, or 7
UN-5	UN-5	Attempt to read on unit 5 after end of file encountered
UN-6	UN-6	Unit number is negative, zero, greater than 7, or undefined

WAT FOR	WAT FIV	MESSAGE
UN-7	UN-7	Too many pages
UN-8		Attempt to do sequential I/O on a direct access file
	UN-8	Missing DEFINE FILE statement or attempt to perform sequential I/O on a direct-access file (IBM code IHC231)
UN-9	UN-9	WRITE references unit 5 or READ references unit 6 or 7
	UN-A	Attempt to perform direct-access I/O on a sequential file (IBM code IHC235)
UN-B		Too many physical records in a logical record. Increase record length
	UN-B	Record size in DEFINE FILE statement is too large (maximum = 32768), or exceeds DD statement specification (IBM code IHC233 or IHC237)
UN-C		I/O error on WATLIB
	UN-C	For direct-access I/O. The relative record position is negative, zero, or too large (IBM code IHC232)
UN-D		RECFM other than V is specified for I/O without FORMAT control
UN-A	UN-D	Attempt to read more data than contained in logical record
	UN-E	FORMATted line exceeds buffer length
	UN-F	I/O error searching library directory
	UN-G	I/O error reading library
	UN-H	Attempt to define the object error file as a direct-access file (IBM code IHC234)
	UN-I	RECFM other than V(B) is specified for I/O without FORMAT control (IBM code IHC214)
	UN-J	Missing DD card for WATLIB. No library assumed
	UN-K	Attempt to READ or WRITE past the end of CHARACTER variable buffer
	UN-L	Attempt to READ from an uncreated direct access file (IHC236)

Undefined Variables

WAT FOR	WAT FIV	MESSAGE
UV-0	UV-0	Undefined variable - simple variable
UV-1		Undefined variable - EQUIVALENCEd, COMMONed, or dummy parameter
UV-2		Undefined variable - array member

WAT FOR	WAT FIV	MESSAGE
UV-3		Undefined variable - array name which was used as a dummy parameter
	UV-3	Subscript is undefined
UV-4		Undefined variable - subprogram name used as dummy parameter
	UV-4	Subprogram is undefined
UV-5		Undefined variable - argument of the library subprogram named
	UV-5	Argument is undefined
UV-6		Variable FORMAT contains undefined character(s)
	UV-6	Undecodable characters in variable FORMAT

Variable Names

WAT FOR	WAT FIV	MESSAGE
VA-0		Attempt to redefine Type of a variable name
VA-1		Subroutine name or COMMON block name used incorrectly
VA-2	VA-0	Variable name longer than six characters. Truncated to six
VA-3		Attempt to redefine the mode of a variable name
VA-D	VA-1	Illegal DO-parameter, assigned or initialized variable in specification
VA-6	VA-2	Illegal use of a subroutine name
	VA-3	Illegal use of a variable name
VA-4		Attempt to redefine the type of a variable name
VA-8	VA-4	Attempt to use a previously defined name as FUNCTION or a
VA-A	VA-5	Attempt to use a previously defined name as a subroutine name
	VA-6	Attempt to use a previously defined name as a subprogram array
VA-B	VA-7	Name used as a COMMON block, previously used as a subprogram name
	VA-8	Attempt to use a FUNCTION name as a variable
VA-9		Attempt to use a previously defined name as a statement FUNCTION
	VA-9	Attempt to use a previously defined name as a variable
	VA-A	Illegal use of a previously defined name
VA-C		Name used for a subprogram previously used as a COMMON black name
VA-E		Attempt to DIMENSION a call-by-name parameter

WAT FOR	WAT FIV	MESSAGE

External Statement

XT-0		Invalid element in EXTERNAL list
	XT-0	A variable has already appeared in an EXTERNAL statement
XT-1		Invalid delimiter in EXTERNAL statement
XT-2		Subprogram previously EXTERNALled

INDEX